Liverpool Studies in European Regional Cultures 6

Networking Europe

Essays on Regionalism and Social Democracy

LIVERPOOL STUDIES IN EUROPEAN REGIONAL CULTURES
Series Editors: Ullrich Kockel and Máiréad Nic Craith

The series presents original research on the regional dimension of Europe, with special emphasis on regional culture, heritage and identity in the context of socio-economic development, offering an interdisciplinary and comparative perspective on the diversity and similarity of regional cultures

OTHER TITLES AVAILABLE IN THIS SERIES

Culture, Tourism and Development: The Case of Ireland
ed. Ullrich Kockel, Volume 1, 1994, ISBN 0–85323–369–1

Landscape, Heritage and Identity: Case Studies in Irish Ethnography
ed. Ullrich Kockel, Volume 2, 1995, ISBN 0–85323–500–7

Borderline Cases: The Ethnic Frontiers of European Integration
Ullrich Kockel, Volume 3, 1999, ISBN 0–85323–520–1

Watching One's Tongue: Issues in Language Planning
ed. Máiréad Nic Craith, Volume 4, 1996, ISBN 0–85323–611–9

Watching One's Tongue: Aspects of Romance and Celtic Languages
ed. Máiréad Nic Craith, Volume 5, 1996, ISBN 0–85323–621–6

The Irish Border: History, Culture, Politics
ed. Malcolm Anderson and Eberhard Bort, Volume 7, 1999,
ISBN 0–85323–510–4

NETWORKING EUROPE
Essays on Regionalism and Social Democracy

---

edited by Eberhard Bort
and Neil Evans

*Published on behalf of the
Culture and Economy Research Unit
at the Institute of Irish Studies,
University of Liverpool*

Liverpool University Press
2000

First published 2000 by
Liverpool University Press
4 Cambridge Street
Liverpool, L69 7ZU

British Library Cataloguing-in-Publication Data
A British Library CIP Record is available

ISBN 0–85323–941–X

Printed and bound in the European Union by
Redwood Books, Trowbridge, Wiltshire

Contents

II

III

IV

V

Preface

Eberhard Bort and Neil Evans

Freudenstadt is a picturesque spa town in the north of the Black Forest, near the former border between Baden and Württemberg in the south of Germany. Here, uncannily resembling Thomas Mann's 'Magic Mountain', the Social Democratic Party's Friedrich-Ebert-Foundation runs the Fritz-Erler-Academy, a conference centre cum hotel.

When, in 1990, the then Prime Minister of Baden-Württemberg, Lothar Späth, and the then Secretary of State for Wales, Peter Walker, signed an accord of inter-regional partnership, linking the Principality to the 'four motors' – the technologically-advanced European regions/federal states of Baden-Württemberg, Rhone-Alpe, Lombardy and Catalonia – the moment had come to take a closer look at the rationale and practice of inter-regional and cross-border relationships and models of co-operation. The Department of British and Irish Studies – i.e. that one-man academic think-tank Professor Christopher Harvie – at the University of Tübingen, slightly more than an hour's drive away from Freudenstadt, and the Erler-Academy decided to organise a joint symposium on inter-regional partnerships in Europe and their perspective. Chris Harvie, Eberhard Bort, and Alfred and Gotlind Braun of the Academy, took the initiative and invited academics, politicians, journalists and students to attend 'Freudenstadt I' in January 1991.

From this first exploration of the realities behind the catch-phrase of a 'Europe of the Regions', a *route directe* led both to the establishment of a Welsh Studies Centre at Tübingen University and to the Freudenstadt conferences developing into a fixture of the Fritz-Erler-Academy's annual calendar.

The 1992 conference highlighted working-class experience in the regions, from the fundamental transformation of the south

Eberhard Bort and Neil Evans (eds), ***Networking Europe,***
Liverpool University Press 2000, 1-4.

Wales industrial landscape to the 'conservative working-class' of Baden-Württemberg, touching on questions of identity and heritage as well as European policies – like the Social Chapter and the Single Market – and their impact on and in the regions. The following year focused on women's work and life and addressed the question of whether a regional Europe was something for women to embrace and look forward to.

Freudenstadt IV, in 1994, took its cue from the wave of racism and xenophobia which dominated the headlines in unified Germany, and the rise of Haider in Austria and Le Pen in France. Contributions ranged from the integration of refugees in post-war Germany, through comparisons with race-related disturbances in Wales to the fate of the first wave of *Gastarbeiter* in Germany as they are growing old in their adopted land.

'Networking Europe' became the agenda of the 1995 conference, the first of three symposia which tried to assess the role and potential of regionalism in Europe in the 1990s. 'Government and the Regions' in 1996 looked at the interaction between supranational, national, regional and sub-regional structures of government, with perspectives from places as diverse as Northern Ireland and the greater Stuttgart region, set up as an assembly above local councils, but below the Land parliament, in order to address infrastructure problems in that region of about 2.5 million people.

The 1997, 1998 and 1999 gatherings at Freudenstadt tried to assess regional developments and options, with a 1998 emphasis on job creation and the regions, after a series of elections — Britain, Ireland, France — concentrating on the proposed Assembly for Wales and the Scottish Parliament, and the potential for change in the run-up to the German general election of September 1998. Also discussed was the role of higher education in developing regional and inter-regional structures. Freudenstadt VII and VIII, as part of a proposed research project under the auspices of the Welsh Studies Centre, also dealt with comparing sustainable cultural tourism, looking at the Irish experience, with its plethora of successful summer schools, and Welsh and Scottish ways of marketing identity, with a view of drawing lessons for Baden-Württemberg.

There is a paradox involved in regionalisation. On the one hand, it is by now entrenched through the Maastricht Treaty and the establishment of the Committee of the Regions and other regional structures in Europe; yet there is, on the other hand, the need of the nation states to fulfil the Maastricht criteria, which makes them the predominant public players on the European political stage in the latter part of the 1990s.

'After the elections' being also 'before the elections' was addressed in view of the German elections of 1998, and with reference to that other paradox: prospects for European Monetary Union (EMU) and further integration, and the proposed expansion of the European Union.

The regional idea and movement, often seen as a 'natural' reaction and complementary process to the emerging supranational structures in Europe, have progressed, nearly regardless of political fashions and slogans like 'Europe of the Regions'. The necessity for border regions to co-operate in order to overcome their peripheral status in their respective national contexts has led to the establishment of the Association of Cross-Border Regions; a plethora of official Euroregions, supported by Brussels through the INTERREG programmes, have spread from the western European heartlands of the Rhine to the Franco-Spanish border and, after the fall of the Wall and the Iron Curtain, to the present eastern frontier of the European Union. Inter-regional partnerships have indicated that exchange and transfer is possible between core regions like Baden-Württemberg and more peripheral regions like Wales.

The comparative approach of the Freudenstadt symposia has been extremely fruitful. Lively debates and a high standard of discourse in a friendly and relaxed environment have been the hallmarks of the Freudenstadt meetings. Future conferences are destined to widen the scope, taking in southern and eastern European perspectives as well as remaining a critical companion to the Wales–Baden-Württemberg inter-regional axis.

After nearly a decade, we thought the time had come to collect a representative sample of papers given at Freudenstadt. We hope that the diversity reflected in the contributions to this volume will give an indication of the ground that has been covered at these gatherings in the Black Forest. In their diversity and their different times of composition, the contributions reflect developments over the past decade. Therefore, we have not, generally speaking, attempted to streamline or update them, trusting that they can stand on their own as they are.

Our thanks are due to Alfred and Gotlind Braun for the hospitality they have extended to the conferences since 1991, and for their trust and support for such an international venture. Without the financial backing by the Friedrich-Ebert-Foundation neither the conferences nor, consequently, this volume would have been possible. Chris Harvie, who initiated the Freudenstadt experience, is to be thanked for his unflinching enthusiasm and input into the symposia. The British Council has, over the years, been a valuable supporter of the Welsh Studies Centre at Tübingen University, and the Council will certainly play its role when this is transformed, as currently envisaged, into a full-scale British and Irish Studies Centre.

Thanks also to Ulli Kockel at the Institute of Irish Studies in Liverpool and all who read the proofs and made valuable suggestions in view of improving the text of this volume.

And finally, we would like to express our gratitude to Liverpool University Press for publishing this selection of the 'Freudenstadt Papers'.

Introduction[1]

Networking Europe: Understanding the Union from Below

Eberhard Bort and Neil Evans

I

Something strange is happening in Europe. It has been going on for two generations and it flies in the face of the longer-term history of the continent. The attempt to create a union of European states on the western portion of the continent – and the possibility of extending it into central and eastern Europe – is not a process for which the European past offers many precedents. Those it does offer are not good: Charlemagne, Napoleon and Hitler are still, at least in the latter two cases, names with which to frighten children. In the forty years since the EEC was created, there have been numerous attempts to disguise the novelty of the process of integration by searching for the deep roots of the European idea and many assertions of the historic unity of the continent. The results have been disappointing. Europe has been shown to have little geographical coherence: it is not even a continent, strictly speaking. Its name is taken from an obscure Greek myth with little real connection with the territory and was not commonly used before the eighteenth century. Even then only the educated classes developed a cosmopolitanism based on Europe, and this was quickly challenged by the nationalism which flourished in the next century.[2] The idea of European unity has recently and rightly been called a myth, a rewriting of European history to

Eberhard Bort and Neil Evans, *Networking Europe*,
Liverpool University Press 2000, 5-28.

stress a common destiny and culture, which overlays a real process of the creation of a new economic entity: [3]

> The myth of Europe is a bright narrative of values like freedom, democracy, welfare, solidarity, modern technology, and, above all, high culture. The myth attempts to recreate a 'Golden Age', while repressing the dark side of European history.[4]

What has been happening since 1945 is better understood as a reaction against the European past of fratricidal warfare, arising at the point when those conflicts ceased to be a stimulus to growth, expansion and civility, becoming instead a disastrous civil war in which Europe's dominance in the world was sacrificed. Contemporary European history is one in which the past offers few clues and only limited direction indicators. It may be that the closest parallels come from the development of the Holy Roman Empire, once so despised by nationalists but now rehabilitated as a model structure which combined a sense of German identity with the independence of its member states.[5] This structure was smashed by Napoleon, with far-reaching consequences for Europe's subsequent development, by enhancing the role of Prussia at the expense of the (Austrian) Empire.[6]

Paradoxically, there may be more clues from American history. It is now more than two hundred years since the 13 very different and proudly independent American colonies found enough common ground to unite against Britain. In order to do so they created a confederal structure which in many ways parallels that of contemporary Europe. This rather shambling edifice would prove to be too vulnerable to the imperial powers left with a presence in north America – Britain, France and Spain. Washington thought he detected 'one head turning into thirteen'. This threat, along with the fear of domestic insurrection, led to the creation of a federal structure.[7] In general terms, one could be mistaken for describing the Cold War era as the period which gave rise to the project of European unity. Certainly, at least one political scientist has recently seen the 'Philadelphian system' of government created in the 1780s as being a closer parallel to what a united Europe might look like than its traditional 'Westphalian system' of autonomous, sovereign states monopolising violence in particular, well-defined territories.[8] The United States even embraced an idea of enlargement which brought in very different societies in the west and quickly gave them political rights while uniting them all under a single currency and a central bank. In economic terms it was the state governments which created the infrastructure for economic development, much as regions are now frequently seen as the bearers of the hopes of economic regeneration in contemporary Europe. This framework allowed the United States to emerge as a superpower, and eventually – though with much hesitation – to become the arbiter of the world's conflicts. In this context, the hesitations over a European foreign policy and the differences of viewpoint over the former Yugoslavia slip into perspective.

Of course, we are not arguing that the United States provides a kind of blueprint for European development, but merely trying to emphasise the unprecedented nature of the European project and the need to develop new ways of understanding it. In America, the conflict between states' rights and federalism, between irreconcilable social systems and over the policy framework required for economic development manifested itself in a war which was proportionately bloodier than was the First World War. Only Europhobes of the deepest hue prophesy that closer European union will result in warfare. Other perspectives might be offered by a growing body of work on the development of federalism and not least by the excavation of its important role in the history of Britain, especially looked at from its widest imperial perspective.[9]

If the dynamics of European integration are unclear, so is the nature of the European entity which is being created. Is it a state? It shares some functions with the state but not other crucial ones such as military capacity. Any attempt to capture its nature has to draw on those different metaphors for the state, all of which illuminate aspects of the blend which constitutes the Union.[10] Perry Anderson has come closest to presenting a theory which covers this. It has two dimensions; firstly, a view of the trajectory of the development of the European state which derives, by comparison, from theories of state-building within Europe. However, the European Union differs from all the patterns of development he outlines because it has a deliberate design but it is neither emulative or total. The object – incremental development towards a democratic supranational federation – is distant. The second component is a view of the institutional workings and structure of the European state. Anderson may be left to speak for himself on this:

> The institutional upshot of European integration is thus a customs union with a quasi-executive of supranational cast, without any machinery to enforce its decisions; a quasi-legislature of inter-governmental ministerial sessions, shielded from any national oversight, operating as a kind of upper chamber; a quasi supreme court which acts as if it were the guardian of a constitution which does not exist; and a pseudo-legislative lower chamber in the form of a largely impotent parliament that is nevertheless the only elective body; theoretically accountable to the peoples of Europe. All of this superimposed on a dozen or so nation-states, determining their own fiscal, social, military and foreign policies. Up to the end of the Eighties the sum of these arrangements, born under the sign of the interim and the makeshift, had nevertheless acquired a respectable aura of inertia.[11]

This sums up the situation of up to a decade ago. Since then the changes have been profound but their direction is just as difficult to predict. One well-informed attempt offers a variety of options which the interested crystal ball gazer may choose from. They range from a European Federal Union via a Confederal Europe and a Euro-Atlantic alliance to a Continental Union.[12]

II

Faced with this situation at the cusp of the massive changes of the late 1980s and early 1990s, it was perhaps inevitable that a multinational group of scholars and political activists should adopt a more pragmatic and essentially non-historical approach to understanding Europe. General theories offered no real guides to events and the situation was so fluid that they would quickly date. We took a more empirical position and started from our own regions and looked out and generalised from them, compared them, thought about typologies. We tried to link these with general ideas which were part of the political culture of the left at the time. Some of the results are gathered together in the papers which follow. The approach might be considered to be an attempt to build up a view of Europe's regions from below – rather than starting with European-wide theories we started with regions we knew and looked outwards from them.[13] This meant that it was impossible to get a fully comprehensive view of Europe's regions and the way in which they related to the European Union as a whole. But a cohesive view of the relationship of regions to wider structures is rare enough even at a national level.[14]

Yet perhaps there was less loss in this than might be evident at first sight. Regions are the products of mobilisation and action as much as of economic trends and of historical memory. Some areas will be more coherent and focused than others.[15] They are expressions of regionalism – the active promotion of particular concerns – which chimes well with a new conception of regions themselves as being dynamic, rather than static. Rather than being defined by natural features, as was once the staple of geographical writing, they are increasingly seen as complex overlays of one historical period on another, as linked series of activities within particular spaces, and located within a wider and changing economic and social framework.[16] This helps explain why the impact of regions on the European polity has been uneven. Not all fractions of the continent have established their offices in Brussels – one recent count ended at 54 such offices. Relatedly, regional policy has been a convenience for the Community, a means of building political coalitions for policies of redistribution which is more widely acceptable than would be policies based on transfers between countries or classes. In order to achieve such coalitions, policies have had to offer something for more-or-less everyone, so the mobilised regions are far from being merely those which are particularly deprived. There is room for spoons of varying lengths and widths in the honey pot.[17] Indeed, in recent years it is prosperous regions as well as 'problem' ones, or areas with indigenous minority cultures which have learned to mobilise political resources.

On Thomas Mann's *Zauberberg*, a representative group of Europe's intellectuals gathered as a literary device to exemplify the tensions in Europe on the brink of the First World War. The setting in a sanatorium was a metaphor for the sickness of the society over which they kept a watchful eye. Our gatherings were on a less exalted height and consciously in the aftermath of the ending of the 'short twentieth century' which had been inaugurated by the Great War.[18] The prospects could be scary – Mafia in the former Soviet Union, the environmental crisis and the possibility of Macworld – a planet in which brains weakened by dubious beef would be manipulated by even more dubious media tycoons, and protesters silenced by libel actions. But more usually there was optimism. The Single Market project had produced a popular mood in favour of European integration and this time it seemed to be combined with the possibility that what would be created would be not the Carolingian Europe envisaged in the 1950s but a real 'Europe of the Regions'. Such a project seemed to have moved out of the political realms sometimes dismissed as utopian.[19] Appropriately the Fritz-Erler-Academy, as run by Alfred and Gotlind Braun, was anything but a sanatorium; a place of rest and reflection, of course, but below it seemed to be a Europe with a renewed energy, and one not intent upon tearing itself apart.

With few guides from history, the discussions focused on the present – despite the fact that a good proportion of delegates were always historians. Occasionally we strayed back into the past but rarely further back than 1945. In the course of the proceedings, Maestro Harvie whipped a short history of European regionalism out of the hat, and proposed a new approach to the whole history of Europe which would be appropriate to our times. It was often met with rather uncomprehending reviews, at least in metropolitan journals, though it made perfect sense to mountaineers like us.[20] The backbone of Freudenstadt was not history but considerations of the present state of Europe, and of our particular regions. Discussion ranged widely but most of the delegates always came from two zones – Germany, the intellectual and political centre of European integration, and the 'Celtic' fringes of the British Isles – an axis reflected in the origins of the two editors of this volume. This proved to be a fruitful mix of perspectives, rather confounding a recent commentator who finds Germany and Britain to be at opposite intellectual and political poles in Europe.[21] From this mix there were both parallels and sharp differences and these are the circumstances in which fruitful comparison – and by extension, wider theorisation – can take place. It was more in line with an earlier time when Goethe and Scott had admired and influenced each other, despite the fact that they never enjoyed our advantage of a personal meeting.[22]

III

This volume opens with a group of essays which take a wide perspective on the new Europe and its regions. Alfred Geisel takes his cues from Germany and the regional structure it built up after the war – though one which was, in general terms at least, in line with its historic federalism. This regionalism subsequently became a feature of most other European countries. The challenge he perceives is from the centralism of the EU; regional coalitions are a safeguard against this, particularly in view of the lack of a constitutional guarantee for the regions and the democratic deficit which exists at this level. Neal Ascherson follows this up with his emphasis on the region as the appropriate level in which the market can be regulated. He also broaches the issues of centralised Britain and Ireland (Geisel's vision does not quite reach to the western periphery of Europe) and looks towards the east and the enlargement of the EU. Phil Cooke and Kevin Morgan look at the links between Baden-Württemburg and Wales, combining this with a comparison of the internal structures of the two regions, in terms of government and links between firms. John Williams, in his elegant and ironic essay, is concerned with the vicissitudes of the European idea over the past decade and contrasts the success of the single market in harnessing popular enthusiasm behind the project with the failure of Maastricht and a single currency to effect the same trick. In the former case, the economic dimension was limited while the political pay-off was high; in the latter, the reverse has been the case. This approach also seems to entail the threat of pushing the idea of a Europe of the Regions to the backstage.

John Osmond looks out from his native Wales to examine the way in which devolution for Wales and Scotland has influenced regionalism in England. He finds that in 1992, under pressure from businesses, the Tory government established regional offices in the English regions in the way in which the Macmillan government did in Wales in the early 1960s, and suggests that the underpinning for regional government has been created by this. His comparison with Italy shows that successful regional creation needs to be matched by a sense of civic responsibility and consciousness – factors sadly lacking in southern Italy. His account of the Italian experience is derived from that of Robert Putnam, which has been criticised for its exaggerated north-south contrast, but its fundamental conclusion that civic traditions are vital – even if they cannot be located on either side of this divide – has not been challenged.[23] Tom Nairn completes the large-scale European jigsaw which is presented in the book's first section by locating some tricky and often forgotten little pieces – the European microstates – in the picture. Some might see these as the ultimate 'bourgeois regions' – in which greed for wealth displaces any wider concern for the whole. His challenging essay eschews this perspective in its celebration of diversity.

Jane Aaron begins a new section of the book by using literary sources to examine the experience of women in a deindustrialising Wales. She links women's politics with their industrial experience – or rather with its limited nature in a Welsh economy which historically was dominated by heavy industry. This means that feminism has been perceived as an alien and middle-class creed and the major contemporary political experiences for women in Wales have been their supportive role in the year-long miners' strike of 1984-85, along with their role in the Greenham Common demonstrations and peace camp. Muriel Casals shows that women's industrial experiences can be very different in other parts of Europe. The textile industries of Catalonia have provided jobs defined as women's – though with gender segregation. Women worked in spinning while men dominated weaving. Interestingly, this is the opposite sexual division of labour from the one which obtained in the Lancashire textile industry, revealing once again the contingent and arbitrary nature of such gender stereotyping. Beate Weber demonstrates, from her experience as mayor of Heidelberg, just what can be achieved – with the necessary political will and resources – by a sympathetic municipal administration to improve women's daily lot. Gotlind Braun's study of older women's plight in German society reminds us how necessary continuing political action is, while her comparative references show that the problems are not confined to Germany but also exist in France and Britain. Patricia Conlan displays the problems faced by women in a context very different from those of Wales, Catalonia and Germany, all of which are industrial societies. In non-industrialised Ireland emigration has been a central experience for women and at an even higher rate for women than for men. Irish society has – much like Aaron's industrial south Wales – idealised the role of women as matriarchs ruling the household with an iron hand. At the turn of the century it was common for Irish women's gravestones to record the passing of 'the best of all Home Rulers'.[24]

Patricia Conlan's essay bridges the gap between the group of essays concerned specifically with the experience of women and heads us to another central issue in contemporary European society: the consequences of migration. Mathias Beer looks at the issue from the opposite end of the telescope from Conlan by focusing on Germany as one of the key areas of reception of migrants in post-war Europe. His detailed study of west Germany's integration of refugees after the Second World War, and the subsequent phases of *Gastarbeiter* migration, comes to the conclusion that Germany's self image has not caught up with this development which has changed the nineteenth- and early twentieth-century experience when France was the epicentre of European in-migration and Germany essentially a country of emigration. Friederike Hohloch follows this up by examining the complexity of the impact of that process on post-war German society and the identity of the migrants. Concepts of migrant identities are fluid and alter at different stages of the life-cycle, while there is a constant distortion produced by the overarching myth of a return to the homeland. The relationship of ethnic cultures to German society is always problematic. Neil Evans completes this section by taking a broad view of Europe's racism. His starting point is the belief, common to many European nations, that their own experience and culture are particularly welcoming and tolerant. This is hardly borne out by an examination of the actual record of minorities in Europe and the reception given to them by their host communities. Yet he resists the idea that we should simply file this past under the heading of undifferentiated racism. Rather, he suggests ways in which more sensitive comparisons of national experiences might be made by focusing on Britain and Germany, and points towards a need for regional rather than national comparisons, which might highlight more effectively the social and economic determinants of ethnic conflict and the traditions of violence which are perhaps more accurately seen as regional rather than national.

Horst Glück's paper marks a shift in direction to considerations of indigenous political and linguistic cultures in Europe. Baden-Württemberg poses a problem for many analyses of voting behaviour, as the weakness of the SPD is much greater than would be predicted from class and religious indicators. He offers explanations which are historical and spatial – the late industrialisation of the region and the resultant domination of commuting farmer-workers in its social structure. Hence we have a political culture which can only be explained as the result of the uneven development of regions within both Germany and Europe. The contrast with industrial south Wales – and to some extent Wales in general – which arises in subsequent essays could hardly be sharper. There, a relatively early industrial revolution (compared with Baden-Württemberg) which generated largely one-class industrial villages which magnified solidarity has resulted in a remarkable over-representation of Labour in Welsh politics – far more votes than would be predicted by class factors alone. The explanation of this is that in Wales Labour has, from this social base, tapped into ethnic and cultural distinctiveness and consequently won seats in other parts of Wales in which the community underpinning of its south Wales valleys heartlands is missing.

Frank Conlan takes us into another zone of minority culture with his account of the Irish *Gaeltacht*. Political independence has allowed the creation of a life-support system for a language which was endangered long before Irish independence from Britain was achieved. Indeed he traces the origins of this policy back to the later days of British rule, with the late nineteenth-century concern for 'congested districts'. Robin Reeves addresses the issue of the working class and its politics, though his Wales is essentially driven by the Welsh language and its associated culture. Dai Smith takes a contrasting approach, refusing to condemn the commercialism and Americanisation of Welsh popular culture. Implicitly, this challenges the state support which has sustained both Irish and Welsh as minority languages and cultures. Heritage poses in a different form issues of commercialism, and Smith rejects the knee-jerk hostility to it which is so common on the left. Commercialism is for him a guarantee of popularity. Perhaps this is an easier position to sustain in a region where the predominant language is the same as the language of commerce than it would be in other parts of Europe. David McCrone, in a related essay, argues that the heritage exploitation of Scotland chimes with its national identity in many ways and fosters it. State subsidy – not in this case for a minority culture but to sustain one which is exploited commercially – is crucial to this and underpins it. Brian Jones takes a wider view of heritage and foresees a process emerging by which Europeans share their distinctive regional cultures and in the process construct a common European heritage. This heritage – or, in a wider sense, cultural – tourism will need to be environmentally sustainable, 'green' tourism. The failure of the German winter to produce sufficient snow for the skiers at the second Freudenstadt conference brought this issue firmly home to all the participants – and the concern has helped generate an intra-European research project.

As the end of the 1990s approached, the political landscape of Europe began to change steadily. The long dominance of the right began to crumble with the dramatic British and French election results of 1997 – and the victory for the SPD in Germany in September 1998. This change of scene inspired John Osmond to cautious optimism about the prospects for the 1997 referendum on an elected assembly in Wales. In his second contribution to this volume, he delineates the sharp contrasts in position between 1979 – when four out of five Welsh voters rejected the proposals of a discredited and terminally ill Labour government in the context of massive strikes in the public sector. The prospect in 1997 seemed different: a new Labour government with the dew of a spring morning on it rather than the stale smoke and beer dregs of late night corporatism. The overarching context of Europe and the association of devolution with economic prosperity, he predicted, would make a difference this time. In the upshot he was correct in both cases – both for his optimism and his caution. The cliff-hanging result was one of the most dramatic and nailbiting political experiences of the post-war era. The narrowest of 'Yes' victories by 0.6 per cent of the voters was nonetheless a massive swing towards regional government, if compared with 1979. This was a much greater transformation than in Scotland, though (in the words of 'No' campaigner Dr Tim Williams) 'not a nation struggling to be free'. It has been suggested that with better handling by the Labour Party the vote could have been a more emphatic endorsement of the proposals. Immediate comment stressed the east-west divides which were shown up in Wales by the brightly coloured maps which dominated the reporting on our TV screens. At least this made a change from the more usual stress on north-south divides which was confuted by the dependence of the 'Yes' vote on both the largely anglicised south Wales valleys and the increasingly beleaguered language heartlands of Carmarthen, Ceredigion and Gwynedd. More measured analysis is already modifying this picture. It is false to think of homogeneous blocks of 'Yes' and 'No' votes as produced by instant TV graphics; the margins between the votes were not so great in any area for regional homogeneity to be a viable analysis, while there were clearly very uneven distributions of for and against votes within the often large constituencies.[25] 'Yes' voters have been shown to be younger than 'No' voters and to be Welsh-born rather than English-born. Plaid Cymru supporters voted overwhelmingly for the proposals while Labour failed to mobilise its vote as effectively – but still almost 60 per cent of Labour supporters who voted were positive. The overwhelming majority of 'No' voters among Liberal Democrat supporters serves to confirm the Welsh party's position as a remnant of an older radicalism (a closet for shy Tories) rather than the carrier of a genuine radicalism in the present.[26]

Clearly, what the Welsh devolution campaign and the result of the referendum showed is the weakness of the political culture of Wales, particularly when much of the population does not read the Welsh press and almost a third do not receive broadcasting which pertains to Wales.[27] Such seemed to be the case in Scotland which voted for both a parliament and tax-varying powers in proportions which almost matched those of the Welsh vote against in 1979. Paula Surridge, Lindsay Paterson, Alice Brown and David McCrone offer a detailed analysis of the Scottish election and referendum results. They show conclusively that the Scottish desire for a parliament was (in contrast with Wales) not driven by identity or ethnicity, but rather by issues of social and economic welfare. The resounding 'yes' to the question of tax-varying powers was seen as the tool to achieve greater benefits in those areas. While it was to be expected that those who felt to be Scots would be in favour of devolution, it might come as a surprise that those who felt either British or even English were not significantly less in favour of a Scottish parliament! The authors also point out that the Conservatives lost, perhaps less surprisingly, because of their intransigent stance on the constitution. In a complementary essay, Ken Morgan presents a similar analysis, but from a broader British and European perspective. His invocation of de Tocqueville's view of Britain – that local politics was one of the things which preserved it from revolution in the late eighteenth and early nineteenth centuries – is a timely reminder of an analysis which has largely been forgotten in favour of his countryman Halevy's stress on the role of Methodism in this respect. It is also a reminder of a time when Britain was seen to be a beacon by which to navigate the political development of the continent – a position which is rare now. Morgan confirms this by arguing vigorously against the isolationism towards Europe which has afflicted Britain for a long period and was reinforced by the Second World War. The war is over, he tells us firmly. Britain now has need of lessons from the continent. As a former Vice-Chancellor of the University of Wales, he also discusses the role of universities in providing intellectual leadership for their regions and the ways in which this might contribute to a sense of Europe.

As the millennium approaches, the prospects of a regional Europe still look good, even if some of the euphoria of the early 1990s may have been eroded, or superseded by the intergovernmental process of preparing for the single currency. What is striking is the fact that the pressures for regional government and mobilisation have been continent-wide, and have even influenced countries like Italy where historical traditions have not favoured regional mobilisation. Now, regional government seems to offer one route out of the morass of its post-war politics.[28]

The end of the decade sees the prospect of a continent complete with regional levels of government; Britain is firmly on that road with the outcome of the Scottish and Welsh referenda in September 1997, and another term of office for Labour should lead to regional government in England too. Even Ireland, hitherto stubbornly resistant to the trend, seems to succumb, as the rules on regional aid change. Two regions have been created in order to retain the levels of subsidies which have underpinned the success of the 'Celtic Tiger' in the past decade.[29]

At the same time, as Eberhard Bort argues, the Good Friday Agreement of 1998 offers, despite the set-backs encountered since, the best prospect in Northern Ireland's three decades of the 'Troubles' of a return to regional government there, as well as a Council of the Isles which enhances the role of the Welsh and Scottish governments. Clearly, this agreement is very much a part of the new politics: its interlocking of both regional and national governments is a solution unthinkable thirty years ago.[30]

Not too far from Freudenstadt, two developments are worth mentioning – and have been topics of discussion at Freudenstadt symposia. To the south-west, the cross-border region encompassing Alsace, Baden and the north-east of Switzerland, one of the pioneer regions of cross-border co-operation and interaction,[31] has recently introduced a cross-border 'parliament', the Upper Rhine Council, with 73 elected representatives.[32] New incentives and further dynamic developments in the promotion of cross-border regionalism, based on the Karlsruhe agreement on cross-border co-operation of 23 January 1996[33] (which allows for the transfer of executive functions to cross-border bodies), are expected from this assembly. To the north-east, the greater Stuttgart region – 179 towns and villages – introduced a new elected assembly, which is still in the process of defining its role between the *Land* parliament and local councils. Its remit, as Helmut Doka, one if the assembly's elected members, explains in his contribution, mainly concerns infrastructure, transport and spatial planning in this densely-populated area of about 2.5 million people. Founded in 1994, a debate is currently raging about the competences of this directly elected regional body, hampered by the fact that the promoters of a greater role for the assembly – to be found primarily among the SPD and the Greens – are currently on the opposition benches in Stuttgart, whereas the conservative CDU backs its local administrative strongholds, mayors and district managers: the very forces who seem to try their utmost to deny the new structure sufficient competences.[34]

Nonetheless, both factors, the emergence and development of cross-border regionalism[35] and new forms of sub-state regionalism, highlight the salience of regional policies and initiatives.

Finally, we come to Chris Harvie, the creator of the Freudenstadt conferences, who appropriately has the last word in this interim summing up of their conclusions. He sweeps across the world, though with a focus on Scotland in Europe and the twin context of the 'rapids of revolution' from 1989 onwards and the technological changes – computers, mass air travel, wider access to phones and cars (along with the contraceptive pill) which have transformed the world since the 1960s. He manages to offer both a vision of a better future and a warning of the hell of Macworld. Calvinism will out!

As a reminder that Freudenstadt has not not just been a forum of theorising about regionalism, but also a focus for celebrating regional cultures, we have included in this volume a few poems by Tyneside 'Jingling Geordie' poet Keith Armstrong. Keith has, over the years, enlivened the cultural exchange between Tübingen and County Durham, another inter-regional network,[36] bringing with him – and to our gatherings in Freudenstadt – distinguished artists and singers like Marie Little, Jack Routledge or Jez Lowe.

IV

Regional structures, it seems, offer enhanced prospects of economic development in the future. They seem particularly adapted to the modern manufacturing base of 'flexible specialisation'. The uneven regional distribution of resources and growth, of course, underpinned Europe's economic development in the past. Regions were important players in Europe's industrial revolution and, in some respect, they were no respecters of national boundaries: the Ruhr formed links with Sweden and French Lorraine, and south Wales with northern Spain. There is a quite significant body of historical writing on the economic dimensions of such regions in the past, though this does not often connect very closely with current regional issues.[37] Yet in the nineteenth century national economic policy regimes were more significant factors in political economy than they are now. The current political economy points to an enhanced role for regions. This seems to be dependent upon size. States are too large, with political centres too far away from the areas of development, to make economic decisions which are properly informed about interconnections on the ground. They are also too small in the sense that industries and services need markets which are wider than those provided by the restricted territory of a nation state.[38] Nation states were once sealed economic units; the European Union has made such a conception outmoded: the coming single currency will add to this. Regions are by definition parts of larger entities. While, clearly, they are partly defined against other regional entities – Lancashire is not Yorkshire or Derbyshire, for instance[39] – they are also more porous than nation states for which national boundaries have always been central defining features.[40] This means that as governmental agencies, economic and social entities and foci of loyalties, they can have a crucial role in the difficult task of building a United Europe which does not simply become uniform but maintains the diversity which has been central to European history. Perhaps the major conclusion of all the theorising about the general European experience would be that diversity has been one of its defining features to a much greater extent than in other civilisations. The lack of any central control has allowed those with novel ideas to find a sponsor somewhere – unlike, say, the Chinese Empire whose centralisation stifled innovation from the late middle ages onwards.[41] Strong regional governments and identities offer the prospect of taking what was essential in the past into a future which is necessarily more integrated at a continental level.

The advantages of regional structures are civic as well as economic. The old republican idea of *vertu* has always depended on fairly small and knowable political communities for its success. This is reinforced by the nature of regional cultures. By definition these are diverse. In this volume we see various elements of this: indigenous minorities within established states, working-class cultures and ethnic minority cultures. Each region will have a different blend of these elements – and may lack some of them – but it is this mixture which gives it its specific identity rather than any homogeneous and essentialist idea of culture. Some of us witnessed a concrete example of the syncretism produced by the population shifts of the modern world by observing a wedding ceremony in the church at Freudenstadt. The couple were bikers and they left the church via an arch of broomsticks held by people dressed in the local 'traditional' costume. They were also saluted by bikers 'revving up', and they drove away accompanied by cars which sounded their horns in yet another salute. Some believe that this last salute was introduced into Germany by Turks, though it is now fully assimilated into German custom. A full understanding of contemporary Europe would involve an analysis of the varying blend of elements which this ceremony encapsulates, across the whole space of the continent.

The area where the civic potential of the region is least clear is in relation to gender. Feminism is a creed which is western – and aspires to be universal – in scope. Sexual discrimination has been, and is, European-wide, with regional variations only in form and intensity. Industrial south Wales has had weak traditions of women's work; Catalonia much stronger ones. Regions with strong traditions of heavy industry often have overly masculine images and identities. There have been similar variations in traditions of political action: stronger in Lancashire than in south Wales. But no European region offers a model of sexual equality to be copied by others. Might they offer more at a symbolic level? Europe derives its name from Greek myth and is feminine as are many of the symbolic representations of nations.[42] However, this is less a statement of equality than a reflection of the ready availability of women as symbols of abstract ideals which occurred precisely because they lacked real political rights. Marianne was the symbol of the French Republic from the Revolution onwards, but no woman in France voted before 1944. It has been suggested that oppressed nations have feminine symbols and imperialist ones masculine ones: Kathleen Ni Houlihan contrasts with John Bull. But a little thought proves this to be a false antithesis. Britain is also represented by Britannia and France, as we have seen, by Marianne. Germania also seems impeccably female. Cases do arise where real women have come to symbolise particular regions: the Brontë sisters Yorkshire, Gracie Fields Lancashire and Catherine Cookson Tyneside. The work of feminist writers in identifying places in which heroines lived might be the basis for constructing regional patterns of identity in which women can assume a proper place. But there seems little if anything in the region as such which is conducive to ideas of sexual equality. Indeed, in so far as regions fit in with a civic republican tradition, they carry the burden that the public man of that tradition was allowed to participate in disinterested civic work because of his freedom from domestic labour.[43] However, the very fluidity of regional identities and the fact that they are not as overlain with multiple stories of masculinity as is the nation-state might offer the possibility that they will be a suitable arena in which to display images of equality in the future.

V

Coming briefly back to our American comparison, the potential of regions for civic identity seems to be an advantage denied to the contemporary United States. The crisis of civic culture in America is widely assumed to be pervasive.[44] Americans are turning to Europe for models and inspiration, a reversal of their stance in the 1960s when the United States was held to offer the model of the 'civic culture'.[45] There seems to be little conception that it might be amenable to a regional solution. The states which constitute the union might seem to be an ideal basis for regional approaches. They have a certain economic viability. Massachusetts, for instance, has been the location of a much vaunted economic 'miracle', though close analysis proves this to be more the result of low-paid service jobs than of the more visible high tech occupations which are usually stressed.[46] This 'miracle' is often linked with Michael Dukakis's terms of office as Governor. A recent analysis of the problems facing democracy in America has singled him out as expressing a central one of them. In the 1988 Presidential election he tried to reduce the issues to management, to the extent that he proclaimed: 'This election isn't about ideology. It's about competence.'[47] This same study has defined America as a 'procedural republic', obsessed with fair procedures at the expense of fair outcomes. When it seeks a solution to this it looks at the local level rather than to regions.[48] American regions would seem to be rather too large to carry much emotional charge. The term 'sections', which Frederick Jackson Turner preferred, seems to sum up better the functional and non-emotive nature of the large areas involved. The point has been well made in a different context:

> Political community depends on the narratives by which people make sense of their condition and interpret the common life they share; ... human beings are storytelling beings...[49]

Only the old Confederacy – or the West – have narratives in this sense, and they seem not to inform a regional politics in America. States are an alternative to this and are, of course, political entities which also have clear identities attached to them – symbolised by the nickname which each state carries into the outside world. In some respects they suffer from the fact that they lack a clear geographical and historical basis – at least west of the Appalachians – though this is compensated for by the importance of their political decision making. But perhaps their political tradition is too much on the right to be useful as a real expression of civic identity. 'States' rights' is a cry too much tainted with the defence of slavery, and segregation, for it to have much appeal, at least on the left.[50]

This book does not close the door on regions and Europe. It makes its contribution to a view of the future of the Union which stresses its need for more democracy – even a democratic myth[51] – and for a conception of Europe which stresses its diversity. 'There is no historically homogeneous Europe,' Eric Hobsbawm reminds us, 'and those who look for it are on the wrong track.'[52] One recent view of what Europe is will perhaps command general if not universal assent from the contributors:

> There is not one culture which defines being European. Being European means precisely having more than one culture and mediating between cultures, being *intercultural*. Therefore being European cannot simply be defined in terms of a single legal nationality or even a constitution guaranteeing equal rights to all citizens and all cultural groups, important though that is.[53]

There are many more who need to stream through and leave their mark on the consciousness. Even quite sympathetic observers see substantial obstacles in the way of the achievement of a 'Europe of the Regions.'[54] The discussions will continue, both at Freudenstadt and more widely across the continent. Perhaps the atmosphere is sometimes a little rarefied at such altitudes. But what kind of a Europe would we construct without a measure of idealism and the impetus given by a vision?

Notes

1 Our thanks to David Sullivan for his helpful comments on a draft of this introduction.

2 For a survey, with key references in its notes, see Neil Evans, 'Beyond Nationalism? The Construction of Ideas of Europe', in David Sullivan (ed.), *Nation and Community,* Coleg Harlech Occasional Paper, 1994.

3 Sonya Puntscher Riekmann, 'The Myth of European Unity', in Geoffrey Hoskin and George Schöpflin (eds), *Myths and Nationhood*, London: Hurst and Co, 1997, pp.60-71.

4 *Ibid.*, p. 65.

5 Joachim Whalley, 'Talking about Germany, 1750-1815: The Birth of a Nation?', *Publications of the English Goethe Society*, Vol. LXVI, Papers read 1996 (Leeds, 1997). See also John Breuilly, 'Sovereignty, Citizenship and Nationality: Reflections on the Case of Germany', in Malcolm Anderson and Eberhard Bort (eds), *The Frontiers of Europe,* London: Pinter, 1998, pp.36-67.

6 Tim Blanning, 'Napoleon and German Identity', in *History Today,* Vol. 48 , No. 4, April 1998, pp.37-43.

7 A convenient general analysis of America in this era is Edward Countryman, *The American Revolution* (1985), Harmondsworth: Penguin, 1986.

8 Daniel H Deudney, 'The Philadelphian System: Sovereignty, Arms Control, and Balance of Power in the American States-Union, circa 1787-1861', in *International Organization*, Vol. 49 , No. 2, Spring 1995, pp.191-228.

9 See, for example, Murray Forsyth, *Unions of States: The Theory and Practice of Confederation,* Leicester: Leicester University Press, 1981; Michael Burgess, *The British Tradition of Federalism,* Leicester: Leicester University Press, 1995; John Kendle, *Federal Britain: A History*, London: Routledge, 1997.

10 James A Caporaso, 'The European Union and Forms of State: Westphalian, Regulatory or Post Modern?', in *Journal of Common Market Studies*, Vol.34, No.1, March 1996, pp.29-52.

11 Perry Anderson, 'Under the Sign of the Interim', in *London Review of Books*, 4 January 1996, p. 6. Reprinted in Peter Gowan and Perry Anderson (eds), *The Question of Europe*, London: Verso, 1997, pp.51-71.

12 Jacques Attali, 'A Continental Architecture', in Gowan and Anderson, *The Question of Europe*, pp.345-56.

13 For advocacy of this approach, in a British context, see Neil Evans, 'British History Past, Present - and Future?', in *Past and Present*, No.119, May 1988, pp.194-203.

14 For an exception see Frank B Tipton Jr, *Regional Variations in the Economic Development of Germany in the Nineteenth Century*, Middletown, Conn: Wesleyan University Press, 1976.

15 For a working out of this argument within north Wales, where the lack of nodality in mid-Wales as compared with the industrial regions of north-west and north-east Wales is stressed, see Neil Evans, 'Regional Dynamics: North Wales, 1750-1914', in Edward Royle (ed.), *Issues of Regional Identity: Essays in Honour of John Marshall*, Manchester: Manchester University Press, 1998, pp.201-25.

16 Michael Bradshaw, *Regions and Regionalism in the United States*, London: Macmillan, 1988.

17 Liesbet Hooghe and Michael Keating, 'The Politics of European Union Regional Policy', in *Journal of European Public Policy*, Vol. 1, No. 3, 1994, pp.367-99; Michael Keating, 'Europeanism and Regionalism', in Barry Jones and M Keating (eds), *The European Union and the Regions*, Oxford: Oxford University Press, 1995, pp.1-22.

18 Eric Hobsbawm, *The Age of Extremes: The Short Twentieth Century, 1914-1991*, London: Michael Joseph, 1994.

19 Susana Borras-Alomar, Thomas Christiansen and Andres Rodrigues-Pose, 'Towards a "Europe of the Regions"? Visions and Reality from a Critical Perspective', in *Regional Policy and Politics*, Vol. 4, No. 2, Summer 1994, pp.1-27.

20 Christopher Harvie, *The Rise of Regional Europe*, London: Routledge, 1994; for a sympathetic review of it see Neil Evans, 'Think Continentally, Research Regionally: Reflections on the Rise of Regional Europe', in *Journal of Regional and Local Studies*, Summer 1994, pp.1-9.

21 Mitsuko Uchida, 'Chalk and Cheese', in *Prospect*, February 1998, pp.24-28.

22 Angus Calder, 'Scott and Goethe: Romanticism and Classicism', in his *Revolving Culture: Notes from the Scottish Republic*, London: I. B. Tauris, 1994, pp.84-94.

23 Jude Bloomfield, 'The "Civic" in Europe', in *Contemporary European History*, Vol.4, No.2, July,1995. pp.225-32, esp. p.229. There is a very useful sampling of recent interpretations of southern Italy in Robert Lumley and Jonathan Morris (eds), *The New History of the Italian South: The Mezzogiorno Revisited*, Exeter: University of Exeter Press, 1997.

24 Joanna Bourke, '"The Best of All Home Rulers": The Economic Power of Women in Ireland, 1880-1914', in *Irish Economic and Social History*, Vol. 18, 1991.

25 Paul O'Leary, 'Of Devolution, Maps and Divided Mentalities: Constructing a New National Icon', in *Planet*, No. 127, February-March 1998, pp.7-12.

26 *Western Mail*, 6 April 1998.

27 Laura McAllister, 'The Welsh Devolution Referendum: Definitely, Maybe?', in *Parliamentary Affairs*, Vol. 51 , No. 2, April 1998, pp.149-65.

28 Adrian Lyttleton, 'Shifting Identities: Nation, Region and City', and David Hine, 'Federalism, Regionalism and the Unitary State: Contemporary Regional Pressures in Historical Perspective', in Carl Levy (ed.), *Italian Regionalism: History, Identity and Politics*, Oxford: Berg, 1996, pp.33-52 and 104-24, respectively.

29 Joseph Lee, remarks at Freudenstadt, June 1997; see also Eberhard Bort, 'Teilung des Tigers: Heftige Debatte um Regionalisierungspläne der Dubliner Regierung', *irland journal*, Vol.IX/X, No.4/1, 1998/99, pp.70-72.

30 For the development of these new politics see Paul Arthur, 'Anglo-Irish Relations in the New Dispensation: Towards a Post-Nationalist Framework?', in Malcolm Anderson and Eberhard Bort (eds), *The Irish Border: History, Politics, Culture*, Liverpool: Liverpool University Press, 1998, pp.41-55; see also Richard Kearney, *Postnationalist Ireland: Politics, Culture, Philosophy*, London: Routledge, 1996; and John Hume, *Personal Views: Politics, Peace and Reconciliation in Ireland*, Enfield: Roberts Rinehart, 1996.

31 See the late Hans Briner, 'Das Europa der Regionen - die Perspektive des 21. Jahrhunderts', in Malcolm Anderson and Eberhard Bort (eds), *Boundaries and Identities: The Eastern Frontier of the European Union*, Edinburgh: International Social Sciences Institute, 1996, pp.39-46.

32 See 'Oberrheinrat will Politik vereinfachen', in *Heilbronner Stimme*, 24 April 1998. It cannot really be called a parliament, as only half the Baden-Württemberg members are MPs, the other half are mayors and elected *Landräte*, with no specific mandate to represent the region; the Swiss representatives come closest to the paliamentary tag, as they are delegates from the Kanton parliaments.

33 See Horst Heberlein, 'Das Karlsruher Übereinkommen mit Frankreich, Luxemburg und der Schweiz über die grenzüberschreitende Zusammenarbeit', in *Bayerische Verwaltungsblätter*, 24 (December 1997), pp.737-44.

34 See Thomas Borgmann, 'Eine Niederlage für die Region?', in *Stuttgarter Zeitung*, 3 April 1998; and Alfred Wiedemann, 'Region auf der Kippe', in *Schwäbisches Tagblatt*, 21 April 1998.

35 See Eberhard Bort, 'Crossing the EU Frontier: Eastern Enlargement of the EU, Cross-Border Regionalism and State Sovereignty', in *Interregiones*, 6, 1997, pp.20-31. See also Udo Bullmann (ed.), *Die Politik der dritten Ebene: Regionen im Europa der Union*, Baden-Baden: Nomos, 1994; and Silvia Raich, *Grenzüberschreitende Zusammenarbeit in einem 'Europa der Regionen'*, Baden-Baden: Nomos, 1995.

36 The exchange visits of poets under the umbrella of the twinning between Tübingen and County Durham led to the bilingual publication of *Poets' Voices/Dichterstimmen* (1991), jointly published by Durham County Council and Tübingen's *Kulturamt*, containing work by Cynthia Fuller, Keith Armstrong, Michael Standen, Carolyn Murphey Melchers and Gerhard Oberlin.

37 Pat Hudson (ed.), *Regions and Industries: A Perspective on the Industrial Revolution in Britain*, Cambridge: Cambridge University Press, 1989; Royle, *Issues of Regional Identity*; Rainer Schultze (ed.), *Industrie Regionen im Umbuch / Industrial Regions in Transformation*, Essen: Klartext, 1993; *Regional Implantation of the Labour Movement in Britain and the Netherlands*, Special Issue, *Tijdschrift voor Sociale Geschedenis*, 18 Jaargang No. 2/3, July 1992.

38 Clive Trebilcock, 'The Industrialization of Europe, 1750-1914', in T C W Blanning (ed.), *The Oxford Illustrated History of Modern Europe*, Oxford: Oxford University Press, 1996, pp.52-53.

39 For useful comments along this train of thought see John K Walton, *Lancashire: A Social History, 1558-1939*, Manchester: Manchester University Press, 1988.

40 Malcolm Anderson, *Frontiers: Territory and State Formation in the Modern World*, Cambridge: Polity, 1996.

41 Jared Diamond, 'Diversity is Strength', in *Prospect*, July 1997, pp.26-29.

42 Maurice Aghulon, *Marianne into Battle: Republican Imagery and Symbolism in France, 1789-1880*, Cambridge: Cambridge University Press, 1987; *La France: Images of Woman and Ideas of Nation, 1789-1989*, London: South Bank Centre, 1989.

43 Bloomfield, 'The "Civic" in Europe', p. 223.

44 Robert D Putnam, 'Tuning in, Tuning Out: The Strange Disappearance of Social Capital in America', in *Political Science Review*, Vol.28, No. 4, 1995, pp.664-83.

45 Adrian Favell, 'A Politics that is Shared, Bounded and Rooted? Rediscovering Civic Cultures in Western Europe', in *Theory and Society*, Vol.27, 1998, pp.209-36.

46 Julie Graham and Robert J S Ross, 'From Manufacturing-Based Industrial Policy to Service-Based Employment Policy? Industrial Interests, Class Politics and the "Massachusetts Miracle"', in *International Journal of Urban and Regional Research*, Vol.13, No.1, 1989, pp.121-36.

47 Cited in Michael J Sandel, *Democracy's Discontent: America in Search of a Public Philosophy*, Cambridge, Mass.: Harvard University Press, 1996, p.313..

48 See Sandel's 'Conclusion' in his *Democracy's Discontent*, pp.317-51.

49 *Ibid.*, pp. 350-51.

50 Bradshaw, *Regions and Regionalism in the United States*.

51 Riekmann, 'Myth of European Unity', pp.70-71.

52 Eric Hobsbawm, 'The Curious History of Europe', in E Hobsbawm, *On History*, London: Weidenfeld and Nicolson, 1997, pp.217-27; p.226.

53 Bloomfield, 'The "Civic" in Europe', p.240.

54 Keating, 'Europeanism and Regionalism', pp.1-22.

Five Poems

Keith Armstrong

My Father Worked On Ships

My father worked on ships.
They spelked his hands,
dusted his eyes, his face, his lungs.

Those eyes that watered by the Tyne
stared out to sea
to see the world
in a tear of water, at the drop
of an old cloth cap.

For thirty weary winters
he grafted
through the snow and the wild winds
of loose change.

He was proud of those ships he built,
he was proud of the men he built with,
his dreams sailed with them:
the hull was his skull,
the cargo his brains.

His hopes rose and sunk
in the shipwrecked streets
of Wallsend
and I look at him now
this father of mine who worked on ships
and I feel proud
of his skeletal frame, this coastline
that moulded me
and my own sweet dreams.

Eberhard Bort and Neil Evans (eds), ***Networking Europe,***
Liverpool University Press 2000, 29-35.

He sits in his retiring chair,
dozing into the night.
There are storms in his head
and I wish him more love yet.
Sail with me,
breathe in me,
breathe that rough sea air old man,
and cough it up.

Rage, rage
against the dying
of this broken-backed town,
the spirit
of its broken-backed
ships.

Try To Understand Me

Try to understand me;
where I come from, where I'm going;
I'm drifting and I need you
to save my hopes from ruin.

You'll need to know what splits me,
my need for roots and dreams;
it's not the earth that hurts me,
it's the tyrants and their schemes.

My father sailed the world before me
to Rio and to Spain;
his father taught him shells and ships
and how to smile in pain.

Mother stayed at home and nursed:
came from a quiet place;
she ran the river and the green;
grew strong, with a gentle face.

I split my tongue in the early days,
shook off asthma as I grew,
fell into school and struggled out,
just clutching what I knew.

I was bred for something 'better',
for an office on 5th floor,
away from sea-spray and stray sheep,
with my name upon the door.
My mother and my father
scraped and saved for me,
bruised each other in the process,
gave up smoking and the sea.

Try to understand me,
why I've come back to earth;
it's because I need to know myself
and the landscape of my birth.

Success Road

On Success Road
you can strike it rich,
on a fruit machine,
at the flick of a switch.

On Success Road,
you can look for a job,
in an empty factory,
with the rest of the mob.

On Success Road,
there's a pall of gloom,
appalling prospects,
and a hint of doom.

On Success Road,
you're free to vote,
with no chances,
and no overcoat.

On Success Road
you can demonstrate,
minded by police,
and in a Right State.

On Success Road,
there's a horde of failure,
chilling statistics,
and pop-star mania.

On Success Road,
you're born to debt,
on the crumbling pavements,
and in the wet.

On Success Road,
you'll never succeed,
you're on a loser,
and you just can't speed.

On Success Road,
there is no choice,
but shout 'Revolution!'
and you'll lose your voice.

The Jingling Geordie

Watch me go leaping in my youth
down Dog Leap Stairs,
down fire-scapes.
The Jingling Geordie
born in a Brewery,
drinking the money
I dug out of the ground.

Cloth-cap in hand I go
marching in the jangling morning
to London gates.
Jingling Geordie
living in a hop-haze,
cadging from the Coppers
I went to the school with.

Older I get in my cage,
singling out a girl half my years
to hitch with.
Oh yes! I am the Jingling Geordie,
the one who pisses on himself,
wrenching out the telephone
his Father placed on the hook.

Listen to my canny old folk-songs;
they lilt and tilt into the dank alley,
into the howls of strays.
Oops! the Jingling Geordie
goes out on his town,
rocking and rolling a night away,
stacking it with a weary rest.

See my ghost in the discotheque,
in the dusty lights,
in the baccy rows.
Jingling Geordie,
dancing gambler,
betting he'll slip
back to the year when the Lads won the Cup.

Well I walk my kids to the Better Life,
reckoning up the rude words dripping
like gravy off my Granda's chin.
Whee! goes the Jingling Geordie:
figment of the gutter brain,
fool of the stumbling system,
emptying my veins into a rich man's palace.

Geordie Boy Bound

Lifting a glass:
lipping the rim that defined the narrowness
of your boyhood,
the night before Belfast
you drank yourself dry
to soak up the uniform fear inside.

Never ever had a chance.

Never even been
across your City to the East before;
spent out your meagre force
on games in the feudal West
before the khaki money bound you
South before Belfast.

Never had a chance.

Never touched the anger
of a real gun;
shot with your lips
or with a kick
against the slumped walls
of an empty street.

Never had a chance.

Never marched
except to school;
trailed your slackened shoes
through the litter and the mingy fog
to a cold assembly line.

Never ever had a chance.

Never really knew
pure hate;
sprayed your revenge from a modest can
or scratched a protest on a flash car body:
the kind you'd dreamt of on a screen.

Never had a chance.

Never had the sense
to really love;
mouthed a dull lust across the Bar
at naked calendars of dated women
or sank your teeth in a pillow.

Never had a chance.

Lifting a gun;
limping along a street like your own,
last night in Belfast
you died, dead scared
to hide this riddled ignorance in blood.

Never ever had a chance;
never, bloody well, had a chance.

I

The Future of Europe: Federalism – Regionalism – Centralism?

Alfred Geisel

Questions of regionalism raise an important question about the creation of states: not just about their internal structure but also as constructive elements in constituting any future European Community. I want to divide my own contribution into three sections: first, to define – and illustrate – the principles of constitutional construction; second, to outline contemporary developments in Europe; and finally to try to present some of the constitutional elements of a future 'European house'.

The German Experience

It seems straightforward to explain the phenomenon of 'federalism' by taking the Parliament of Baden-Württemberg, its tasks and its activities, as an example. According to our 'Basic Law' the Federal Republic of Germany is a democratic federation as well as a social market. The Länder which constitute it have their own status as states. Individual Länder, including Baden-Württemberg, have drafted their own constitutions which define the relationship between parliament and government, in ways which can vary from Land to Land. The 'Basic Law' merely provides the fundamentals of a democratic state. Although the federation can issue skeleton regulations to secure necessary uniformity (this also applies to environment and nature protection) further arrangements are left to the Länder.

Eberhard Bort and Neil Evans (eds), *Networking Europe*, Liverpool University Press 2000, 39-46.

From their status as states, the Länder parliaments have their own legislative authority. This partly competes with that of the federation, but has elements which are reserved to the Länder. Thus the parliaments of the Länder direct the composition of their bureaucracies and local authorities. The election of mayor and the councillors and the internal organisation of Land and communal authorities (for instance the county offices of the Land, and the constitutions of towns) may differ considerably from Land to Land. This authority also covers most of the building and police legislation, but the main jurisdiction of the Länder centres upon questions of socialisation, culture and education. Legislation which concerns state schools, private schools, museums or building preservation is directly enacted by the Land parliaments. They are also concerned with most university legislation and radio and television – as with Baden-Württemberg's communications law, which dealt with new information technology and regulated the licensing of private radio stations.

These examples show how important this jurisdiction is. Of course, the majority of the laws are passed by the federal parliament, but the Länder also participate in this legislation via the Bundesrat, or Federal Council, which is composed of representatives of the Land governments, not their parliaments. The Länder can thus substantially influence federal legislation.

Finally, it is very important to a healthy federalism that the Länder have sufficient financial autonomy. It is true that the Länder in the Federal Republic of Germany have relatively little fiscal authority (indeed, citizens would find it hard to see reasons for large differentials in tax burdens) but the Länder are entitled to a considerable amount of tax money (about 35 per cent of the total tax income) and as a result they have considerable political and organisational elbow-room.

European Devolution

At the beginning of the process of European unification, the German kind of federal organisation, with the division of competences between the federation and its member states, was entirely unique. Today, at least Belgium and Austria within the EU have comparable structures. Nevertheless it is obvious that over the last two decades regionalism, and even the promise of a true federalism, has been making headway all over Europe. Let me point out to you some examples of such regional structures; these admittedly have a smaller degree of sovereignty and autonomous competence but they have begun, especially within the areas of culture and education, to cut the ground from under the feet of conventional centralised structures.

This path has, for instance, been taken step by step in Italy, through the creation of fifteen regions in 1970. It is true that Italian regionalism is still characterised by a narrow range of legislative powers, although it is more marked in those regions – Val d'Aosta, South Tyrol – which have an exceptional statute. State control of the regions in Italy is still considerable, but, as we have seen since the early 1990s, regional feeling, especially in the north, could under certain circumstances destroy the Italian state.

In Belgium the process of regionalisation within a state which had so far been centralised began in the late 1960s. Step by step the three regions of Flanders, Wallonia and Brussels were created by 1980, through measures which passed to these regions important competences as well as financial resources. In today's Belgium, federative elements have almost reached a German level.

In Spain, regionalisation set in after the downfall of the centralised Franco dictatorship and the new constitution of 1978. Here, too, regions with a considerable range of legislative authority have been created step by step, with Catalonia and Euzkadi leading the way. Within the fields of culture and environmental preservation, for instance, this legislative authority is now so distinct that some constitutional lawyers would like to regard Spanish autonomy as a form of (uneven) federalism.

Finally, after 1981, France under President Mitterand helped twenty-two regions come into being. These, admittedly, have a planning function without legislative competence, and have the peculiar feature that the Regional Council's democratic representatives constitute its executive. Nevertheless this reform has been called a silent revolution, as France with its Jacobin centralism had been regarded as a classic example of the European unitary state since the days of Napoleon.

These developments – from my point of view encouraging ones – illustrate the fact that in each of the European countries the advantages of federalism and regionalism have become more and more evident. In my opinion, these advantages arise primarily from the fact that both principles seem cognate with the preservation and cultivation of the historical, cultural and linguistic peculiarities, as well as the social variety, of the states and communities of Europe. These principles ensure a vertical division of power in the state organisation, and thereby serve as a means of restricting power. At the same time they provide for an increase in liberty and participation by the citizens. When carried out at a lower level, state decisions are closer to the citizens. Competition between the Länder and the regions continually gives a fresh impetus to economic and cultural development, thereby promoting the vivacity of Europe.

Brussels Centralism

However, these favourable developments are adversely affected by the politics of the EU and its present organisation. At community level, the Brussels bureaucracy is an example of a highly centralistic institution. There are no important EC subordinate authorities within the European states; unlike Germany, with the Constitutional Court in Karlsruhe, the Bundesanstalt für Arbeit (Labour Office) in Nürnberg and the Bundesbank in Frankfurt. All administration and decisions of the commission are made at Brussels. For example, it is centrally determined whether, and to what extent, Sicily or Ireland should be granted economic aid. Brussels can even dictate to the individual member countries the extent to which they can assist backward regions within their own borders and by their own means. As a result, the pursuit of independent structural and regional politics in the Federal Republic of Germany, for instance (where by any standards there are underdeveloped areas, with unemployment rates up to 15 per cent) has become almost impossible.

This centralism can have some odd results. A decree passed by the Commission in February 1990 says that within the sphere of the Community, apples whose diameter measures less than 55 millimetres must not be sold but in future will have to be destroyed.

This centralism, which is hardly checked by parliamentary means, is particularly dangerous in the area of cultural and educational politics. The German Länder are right to complain that, through real or assumed privileges granted by the Single European Act, the EU is extending its influence into cultural spheres which, according to our constitution, are genuine affairs of the Länder. The number of EU instructions and resolutions which deal in detail with questions of education and training is steadily growing. I also want to point out an EU Council of Ministers instruction on radio services, passed solely in reference to its competence for economic activities. The Council did not, or would not, realise that this also touched upon general questions of cultural politics. The federal Bavarian Free State has brought an action in the European Court against this instruction. On this basis will be decided whether the Community should take cognisance of the internal constitutional structures of its member states.

The centralism emanating from Brussels has, of course, also triggered countervailing reactions and developments. A new level is in the process of formation, which we conceive as the 'Europe of Regions'. This refers to the increasing co-operation which has brought regions closer to one another, across the borders and also over the heads of national governments. By such cooperation, regions can supplement, and often develop, new initiatives within state co-operation, for instance, in technology, research co-operation and youth exchanges. The partnership between Baden-Württemberg and such regions as the Rhône-Alps, Catalonia, Lombardy and Wales is an example of this regional cooperation, in the areas of economic, educational and technology policy. Finally, an Assembly of European Regions is one step further towards the 'Europe of Regions'. An initiative of the former French Prime Minister Edgar Fauré, this assembly enables the regions of all the EU states, and of various states in the Council of Europe, to co-operate.

A Regional Chamber

Lastly, what should, or could, a future Europe look like? Since the principles of federalism and regionalism offer many advantages, and the first signs in this direction are encouraging, it is consistent that regions should be granted the institutional and legal possibilities of cooperative organisation within a growing Europe. However, this calls for an alteration of Community treaties and the extension of the European Community law in a federal direction. As a political realist I know that this path will be a stony one. A fundamentally new constitution for Europe, like the European Parliament's Spinelli draft of 1984, seems at present unlikely. But it seems necessary to develop further the Single European Act, carefully but consistently, and further to expand the federal and regional elements.

It is most important to me that the principle of subsidiarity becomes a basic element in the structuring of the Community and in the organisation of its legislative and executive functions. It is true that, as far as environmental politics are concerned, the principle of subsidiarity has already entered the EEC treaties through the Single European Act. This principle must become universally influential in all the spheres of EU politics. Thus the Community may only engage in new tasks, if their fulfilment on a European level is absolutely necessary, while questions which can be handled closer to the citizens and effectively within the member states or in the regions, should also be settled there. Since even Jacques Delors, former President of the EC Commission, has now declared himself for the principle of subsidiarity, I hope that this will not remain lip-service but be part of the planned reform of the treaties.

It is not sufficient to stipulate the principle of subsidiarity by treaty only. In practice this principle can only become fully effective if there is a clearly defined division of competence between the European Community, its member states, countries and regions. Although 'European' powers in spheres like environment and energy will be necessary, the nations, or countries and regions, must stand their rightful ground within the European concert.

In my opinion, any federal structure of the European Community requires an additional regional organ on the Community level. In all countries with a federal structure the member states participate in federal legislation and administration via a distinct organ (in the USA the senate; in Switzerland the Diet; in the Federal Republic of Germany the Bundesrat or Federal Council). If the regions wish to have a share in the European decision-making process which requires their competences, rights or interests, they must have access to a European organ which introduces such concerns immediately into the policy process. In the form of the Council of Ministers, the member states of the EU already dispose of one such organ at EC level, whereas the countries and regions had no institutional representation. The 'Council of the Regional and Local Territorial Authorities', which was set up in Brussels by an act of the EU Commission, was only an advisory and informative body. But it was not founded on treaty; it had no formal right to be heard nor any right of initiative or veto. Such an advisory board offered no effective protection of the interests of the regions at EU level. The Committee of the Regions set up at Maastricht, which can give an opinion on Commission legislation, is an improvement, but it could be further developed into a contractually-safeguarded regional board possessing such powers specified above.

This demand may sound utopian; yet to me it seems necessary to preserve the regional variety within a future Europe. If the European Parliament, by means of its 'Charter of Regionalisation' in 1988, made the creation of constitutional regions also part of its programme for those states which still have centralistic constitutions, the adequate legal and institutional instruments must be provided. Therefore in a reformed European Community there must be room for the representation of regional interests.

I enter this claim both as an ardent federalist and as a strong parliamentarian. It will not be sufficient to promote the federal element in the European Community without also making the European Parliament the central organ of decisions. The present distance between the Community's organs and its citizens mainly derives from the circumstance that the European Parliament does not have the functions of a real parliament. This democratic deficiency must be reduced. Only a strong European Parliament, along with its necessary federal elements, will be able to counteract the power of centralistic forces. Only a real parliament will attract the attention of the media. Without these, EU-level decisions will never become understandable and transparent to the citizens.

A Europe of the Markets or A Europe of the Peoples?[1]

Neal Ascherson

Since 1989, the whole of Europe – not just the West, or the lands where Thatcherism or Reaganite economics ruled – has entered an age of markets. Indeed, this change began in the East, in the lands of the old Soviet empire, well before the revolutions which overthrew Communist regimes. The most vivid example is – or was, because it is already (in 1992) beginning to pass away – the re-emergence of almost mediaeval trading patterns in the regions of Europe between the Baltic and the Black Sea. Through the middle and late 1980s, great markets appeared, served by long land trade routes which in turn were traversed by something close to caravans of merchants. The most unexpected thing about these markets, perhaps, was that they were developed and dominated by the Poles, a people whose traditional culture had seemed quite inimical to the lowly and materialistic claims of mere trade. But it was Polish merchants, acting as unlicensed individuals who often used bribery and pressure to bring their bundles of goods across frontiers, who set up the enormous network of open-air markets which reached from Vilnius in the East to its western terminus at the Potsdamer Platz in what was still West Berlin, from Warsaw across Romania to Istanbul and then – in a complicated cross-traffic involving carpets and dollars – across the Black Sea to Odessa and back to Poland by train.

This absolutely authentic emergence of the market ought to remind us of some basic truths about what markets really are and need. First of all, free markets are not literally free. The more free they are, the more police they need to stamp out gangsterism and protection rackets, to restrain the sort of competition that ends with bloodshed and to maintain something like a consistent standard of probity in weights,

Eberhard Bort and Neil Evans (eds), *Networking Europe*, Liverpool University Press 2000, 47-52.

measures and financial dealings. The freer they are, in short, the more markets require regulation in order to survive. In the Polish case, this regulation was provided by fairly ad hoc groups of godfathers (the great Russian mafias, native or Caucasian, had not yet moved onto this stage), who commanded armed thugs to be called in if necessary. At the centre of each big trade centre was the inner group of those who set the daily black-market exchange rates of various currencies against the Dollar and the D-Mark.

This episode raises a larger question: what sort of long-term political authority best suits the needs of a free market economy? It is too easy to repeat: plural democracy. Democracy at what level? David Marquand has suggested that economic integration leads to political integration, and that a united European supragovernment is the corollary of the Single European Act and whatever lies beyond it. But this is not the whole truth. If the paradox of the free market is that it requires state authority to function properly, and sometimes quite interventionist state authority, then we are not necessarily talking about the nation-state. It seems to me probable that regional government is the level best adapted to the free entrepreneur in the 1990s, best not only for the small to medium business but often for the multinational corporation as well. We are looking into a European future in which supranational and subnational government will matter to economic development, but in which the nation-state instance – once with a monopoly of economic authority – will matter less and less.

Since 1989, the regionalisation process in the European Community has moved forward very rapidly. Let us agree that a Euroregion must be defined by an administrative/governmental structure of some kind, and not just by distinctions of culture. That disposes of problems about what is a 'natural' region. There will be, as there already are in Germany, regions which have their origins in ancient kingdoms, and others which were invented a few years ago for the convenience of foreign occupying armies (Nordrhein-Westfalen). There will be huge regions and tiny city-states, rich regions and impoverished ones. The real challenge posed by this process – which is, incidentally, a 'natural' one initiated by no conscious decision although encouraged and recognised by the EU governments and the

Commission – is that of member states with no regional tradition, whose history is one of rigid centralisation. Here, given that even France has moved into the creation of regional governments, Britain and Ireland are the great offenders.

Now, having said that free markets require policemen and governments, it has to be admitted that this truth is not universally recognised. Eastern Europe is at present applying undiluted Thatcherism to itself, in the name of economic reform. Those new governments are using free-market doctrine with a literalness and consequence which in fact was never dreamed of in the United States or Britain, where *laissez-faire* of that intensity – beyond the abundant but deceptive rhetoric – would have led to rioting on the streets and the fall of both Great Communicator and Iron Lady.

This untreated and dogmatic marketism presents three dangers. The first is that the new democracy itself will succumb in Poland, Hungary or Czechoslovakia. People will grow fed up with the unemployment, privation and insecurity of 'reform' and reach for something more authoritarian – probably right-wing protectionist nationalism, rather than neo-Stalinism. The second danger is that the programme of regionalism, away from the nation-state, will come to a halt, although in fact this may be the political structure which best supports a 'mixed' economy combining free capitalism and public regulation – or even a social-democratic type of economy in which there is a large element of redistribution.

A third danger is this: that the post-Communist nations of Eastern Europe will revert to the condition of virtual colonies. This was the logic of the German *Mitteleuropa* vision, before and during the First World War: an industrialised western heartland (adding Lorraine and the Saar to Germany, of course) which exploited a de-industrialised hinterland of Balkan and Eastern states as a captive supply of cheap labour, raw materials and food. Rebellion against this destiny, above all in its Nazi form, created much of what was genuine in that curious amalgam of nationalism and Stalinism which dominated the East European left after 1945. Could *Mitteleuropa* happen again now, as rustbelt industries collapse from the Elbe to the Dnieper leaving only rich earth and unemployed millions?

I am fairly confident that most of these dangers can be avoided. This is because the main influence on the new democracies is neither American nor British, but German – the doctrines of the social market economy and of redistribution between rich and poor regions. The crude imperialism of Wilhelmine Germany is over; instead, German business requires the industrial skills of Czech or Polish workers, as well as their low wages. There is not going to be any Marshall Plan for the 1990s; such direct injection of gigantic sums of capital is unthinkable today, even though Eastern Europe has already, since 1989, lost more of its capital stock than Germany did in the Second World War. But, as a much less satisfying substitute, there is going to be large-scale western investment in East-Central Europe: takeovers and expansions as well as asset-stripping closures.

Germany, again, has given an example of how a regional structure can be used for redistribution of wealth to equalise living standards. But it is important not to be blind about who is doing what here. It is tempting, and in the long term legitimate, to talk about the leakage of authority from the nation-state, upwards to supranational authority and downwards to regions. Meanwhile, though, and in practical terms, it is precisely the nation-state that is performing the redistributive function for Germany's component regions. Bonn actually does it. The nation-state, not only in Germany, may be at present the best or even the only guarantor that an effort will be made to achieve a single standard of welfare provision across the whole territory composed by the regions.

And how might this look at a European level? On the one hand, there is the danger that the new Europe will feel that it no longer needs the peripheral regions (given that a substantial part of the rationale for subsidising them was really political and derived from Cold War priorities). The new European Community, absorbing the less poverty-stricken post-Communist states, would then move slowly away from the old Brussels goals of equalisation through redistribution, transforming itself into a two-stage, two-class entity of winners and losers – core and periphery with a vengeance. But the other possibility is that Brussels will in fact become more effective at managing it than national governments have been. The EC's track record so far with fund allocation has been encouraging – better, by far, than that of some member states.

The British anomaly seemed likely to remain and to go on obtruding. The resistance of British governments since 1979 to any real form of regional devolution of power has been discouraging, and has had the effect of widening the gap between British and European political cultures at a moment when it should be closing. But it is worth speculating on the constitutional future here. If Britain 'broke up'[2] – with Scotland moving into 'independence in Europe', as proposed by the Scottish National Party – this might free Charter 88's genteel and belated bourgeois revolutionary England to begin its own transit towards more 'European' political structures. The Austrians, after all, did not want Austria-Hungary to break up, and yet when it did they achieved a clear identity and a chance of progressive modernisation which they could not reach under the Habsburgs – even though it was soon to be snatched away from them again and restored only after 1945.

What, finally, is the relationship between regionalism and nationalism? It is a close one. The regionalism we are looking at, with its strong 'social' component, is obviously intimately related to the sort of modernising, forward-looking nationalism which demands to 'join the world' rather than to get off the world in order to rejoin the past. It will not be surprising if some small nations – Slovenia or Scotland, for example – go for the full formality of sovereign state independence simply because it is the only way to achieve what is in fact not much more than 'Euroregion' status within the Community. And the 'who-whom' question about regionalism, once posed, suggests that it is much the same groups who stand to benefit most from moderate nationalism and regional autonomy: the economically-active middle class, seeking to assert itself through new technologies, and the intellectuals. Those who made the opposition groups which led to the 1989 revolutions are beginning to lose political power in East-Central Europe – but they may prove to be the real beneficiaries of the new political and economic landscapes which emerge in a united Europe in the twenty-first century.

Notes

1 In working these notes into a coherent text, I am very grateful to the discussants at Freudenstadt, whose comments in the subsequent debate I have incorporated here. Acknowledgements especially to Neil Evans, Michael Keating, Christopher Harvie, Eberhard Bort, Dai Smith and Logie Barrow.

2 See Tom Nairn, *The Break-Up of Britain*, London: Verso, 1977.

The Wales–Baden-Württemberg Accord

Phil Cooke and Kevin Morgan

Introduction

In March 1990 the Secretary of State for Wales, Peter Walker, and the Minister President of Baden-Württemberg, Lothar Späth, signed an accord linking these two Euroregions in an economic and cultural collaboration agreement. Although this surprised many in Wales, the spadework had been put in, since the early 1980s, mainly by Wyn Roberts, the Harrow-educated, German speaking, Welsh Office minister. Because of his responsibilities for economic affairs, especially inward investment, he had visited the Land on numerous occasions, not least in trying to encourage Robert Bosch, the German electronics firm, to locate in Wales. In the process, tentative discussions about wider partnerships occurred.

It is worth noting the Späth strategy of regional co-operation in Europe. In the 1980s, Baden-Württemberg was one of the most aggressive sponsors of regional alliances in Europe: by 1990, agreements had been concluded with Rhône-Alpes, Lombardy, Catalonia and Wales, covering such things as technological collaboration, research and development links and economic and cultural exchange in general.[1]

The Späth strategy was predicated on the view that in a borderless European market there was a need for inter-regional partnership for exchanging information about market opportunities and for new kinds of technological alliance at the regional level. In this view regional governments are able to act much more flexibly than their national counterparts and, being closer to the developmental problems in their locales, this is an additional reason why the regional dimension might assume a

Eberhard Bort and Neil Evans (eds), *Networking Europe*, Liverpool University Press 2000, 53-66.

much greater role in the 1990s. This was also the time when national governments in the Community were losing some of their regulatory autonomy to supranational authorities in Brussels.[2]

Joining the 'Four Motors': Wales at the Starting Line

The Welsh involvement in the ambitious inter-regional alliance initiated by the Späth administration occurred as a result of both 'push' and 'pull' factors.

Push Factors

The Späth administration sought a leading growth-region from Britain to join the pact but, casting its gaze at the obvious choices, the south-aast of England or East Anglia, it could, to quote a Welsh Development Agency (WDA) manager, 'find no one to talk to'. That is, English regions have no regional state apparatus, whereas Wales did. The Welsh Office, with a cabinet-ranking Secretary of State, and the Welsh Development Agency are significant ports of entry for the kind of agreement Späth was seeking.

The prestigious Robert Bosch company, headquartered in Stuttgart, had recently announced it was to make a £110 million investment in opening a new alternator plant near Cardiff. The plant, which would employ 570 initially, building to 1,200 by 1995, occupied less than 20 per cent of its total site. The likelihood of future expansion and, more importantly, inward investment by German firms in the Bosch supplier network, alerted the Land government of Baden-Württemberg to the importance of Wales to future inter-regional governmental and industrial links.

Pull Factors

The other reasons for the partnership between Wales and Baden-Württemberg were the positive economic indicators and the changing economic structure in Wales.

Recognition developed that Wales was becoming one of the more dynamic reconverting regional economies. At the end of 1989, the Secretary of State for Wales had announced that Welsh unemployment was, at 6.9 per cent, lower than that of West Germany at 7.5 per cent. Moreover, unemployment had halved between 1986, when it was 14 per cent, and the end of 1989, the most rapid short-term decline in Britain. Hence, Wales was seen as something of a 'boom region' by the Baden-Württemberg government, while the latter was seen as the sort of engineering-rich manufacturing region from which major benefits could accrue.

Wales had the kind of cultural, political and, increasingly, industrial identity which is familiar to regionalised political economies in Germany and, to varying degrees, elsewhere in the EU. The German networked economy is based on the existence of government and industry links at regional and local level, and these are the conduits through which technical expertise is diffused throughout the system. Though that system lacks a parliament in Wales, the regionalised governmental apparatus exists and this has been used to great effect by both the Baden-Württemberg government and Bosch: in fact the latter used this apparatus to set up its training system in record time.

In other words, Wales offered much potential as an important alternative source for labour (at 50 per cent of German costs) with good access to the UK as a growing engineering market for Baden-Württemberg firms. The latter offered opportunities for firms in the Welsh engineering industry to improve access to European markets and raise skill, technology and value-added profiles.

The Question of Welsh Industrial Performance

Unlike Baden-Württemberg, Lombardy, Catalonia and Rhône-Alpes, Wales is far from being a regional 'motor' of its national economy. Each of the former regions is among the top three contributors to GNP in their respective nation-states, while Wales is ninth. Furthermore, even the UK's richest standard region, the South-East, would, were it in the former West Germany, be bottom of that particular GDP per capita league table. Wales had both a lot to learn and to earn.

Training and Skills

Like the rest of Britain, Wales had a training system which, until very recently, could be called antediluvian. In numerical terms, the statistics looked comparable on a per capita basis as between Wales and Baden-Württemberg.

In 1989 the latter had a little over 270,000 trainees in the dual system of vocational education, part based in the factory or office, part in vocational schools. With a population of 9.25 million, that was a vocational training rate of 2.9 per cent. In 1988, Wales had 14,900 under various forms of the Adult Training Strategy, 23,600 under the Community Programme, 10,900 in Voluntary Projects, 24,000 on the Youth Training Scheme with 8,100 employees in receipt of Local Training Grants to Employers. These figures exclude those on purely private training schemes. The Welsh total for 1988 was 81,500. Therefore, with a population of 2.75 million that was equal to a training rate of 2.9 per cent, exactly the same as that in Baden-Württemberg.

The key difference, of course, was the respective quality of the training being offered. Few, if any, of those being trained in the Welsh schemes were in receipt of the kind of theoretical training available in Germany. Few would have received training directly to upgrade skills in large- or small-scale industry and crafts, as was the case for 86 per cent of the Baden-Württemberg trainees. As it was put to the authors by a middle-manager from the Training Agency in Wales attending a day school on training needs for the future:

> ... we've spent the last ten years managing schemes to keep kids off the unemployment registers. How are we

> expected to suddenly start turning out technicians and craftsmen for the engineering industry?

In other words, there was perhaps no greater area of need for training than amongst the trainers themselves.

Of even greater concern in the British case was the uncertainty surrounding the new vehicles for training service delivery, the Training and Enterprise Councils. Not only was the Training Agency untutored in training for enterprise generally, but it was unclear how the costs of the training necessary to meet the requirements of a modern, advanced economy were to be met. Unlike the German system, where firms pay a compulsory levy which contributes substantially to the training budget, British firms are opposed to such compulsion. As a result, the Thatcher government reduced even the relatively limited areas in which a levy system operated, namely the Industry Training Boards, replacing them with voluntary agencies.

Changing Skills Profile

Hence, it is not surprising that the Confederation of British Industry (CBI)/Training Agency Skills Shortage Survey for 1988 showed 47 per cent of British and 28 per cent of Welsh firms surveyed reported unsatisfied skills needs. The survey also showed that the occupation most often in short supply was professional engineers followed by machinists, computer technicians and fitters. So there were clear and long-standing weaknesses in the training delivery system. Despite this, evidence shows that significant changes had been taking place in the occupational structure of engineering employment in both Britain and, more strikingly, Wales. Available statistics showed three important things. First, professional engineers were easily the fastest-growing occupational group throughout the 1980s in Britain and Wales. The Welsh rate of growth was more than five times that of the British rate. Second, the rate of employment decline in the grades below professional engineer was less in the late than it was in the early 1980s. In Wales, many of these grades, having declined less than the British rate in the 1978-83 period, were actually growing in the 1983-89 period (e.g. technicians, administrators, supervisors and operators). But thirdly, and this is even more pronounced for electronics engineering, a real difference emerged on a British scale between employment growth in the upper-skill echelons and decline in the lower. However, whereas in Britain any group from clerical grade downwards was likely to be in decline, in Wales during the 1983-89 period such grades were more likely to have been expanding in number of employees.

One final point that needs to be made about the differential rates of growth for professional engineers and technicians as between Britain and Wales is that Wales started from a lower base. For example, in 1978 less than one per cent of Welsh employees in engineering were in these two categories whereas in Britain nearly two per cent were. By 1989, the differential was three per cent to five per cent. In electronics, the differential moved from under one per cent in Wales compared with five per cent in Britain in 1978 to five per cent in Wales and thirteen per cent in Britain by 1989. Thus, the lower incidence of perceived skills shortages in Wales compared to Britain was explained by the lower historical level of demand.

Technology Transfer

Technology transfer is densely diffused in Baden-Württemberg through the Steinbeis consultancies, Max Planck Institutes and the Fraunhofer Association. Wales, by comparison, is, again, less developed. This is not to say that the importance of establishing technology transfer agencies and mechanisms has not been recognised. However, the problem has been to set up a technology transfer delivery service which works. The key facilitator in the short history of technology transfer in Wales has been the Welsh Development Agency. With the exception of inward investing manufacturers, private consultancies, the university colleges and other higher education institutions (easily the major technology transfer resources, receiving in 1990 over £15 million per annum on industry-funded research), the WDA is the main focus for technology transfer, a role it has taken seriously only since 1984.

The Innovation Experience and the WDA

WINtech was established in 1984, charged with the task of linking industry with scientific research centres. It was centralised, publicly-funded, prone to political interference and, though staffed with some technologists and engineers, the efforts of these were undoubtedly spread too thinly. All of this stood in sharp contrast to the decentralised Baden-Württemberg system of technology transfer through consultancy. The problem of WINtech 'having fingers in too many pies' was recognised as a major weakness by the new management installed in 1987 by Peter Walker, the incoming Secretary of State for Wales. WINtech was dismantled, part of it going to the newly-established Welsh Development International (Strategic Initiatives Division), another part went to a new Technology Advice and University Liaison Office, while a third part became Welsh Development Technology Marketing. WINtech's funding was absorbed into the WDA's Technology Growth Fund, a venture capital initiative. WINtech used also to manage the Department of Trade and Industry schemes such as the Regional Technology Centres, later managed from the Technology Advice and University Liaison Office.

In the early 1990s much of this apparatus was absorbed into a new Corporate Development Group with responsibility for 'Source Wales' and other supplier development programmes. In the WDA 'meltdown' of 1994 consequent upon the Public Accounts Committee's critique of WDA procedures, a new Technology Transfer division was established in Principality House, much of the work of which involves administering European Union innovation programmes such as STRIDE, Regional Innovation Strategies and 'Information Society'.

An indication of the problems faced in seeking to implant a centralised, public-sector technology-transfer agency into industry is shown historically by WINtech's experience with the electronics industry in Wales. The latter is characterised by a mix of foreign direct investors and indigenous small and medium-sized enterprises (SMEs), few of which have significant dealings with one another. WINtech's Manufacturing Technology Centre was set up to bring firms in specific sectors together with specialist consultancies on a part-subsidised, part fee-paying basis in order to inform companies about new products. However, insufficiently large firms showed an interest, and resources were insufficient to enable indigenous SMEs to take advantage of new, but conceivably risky, ideas. So the Manufacturing Technology Centre was also a casualty of the unwinding of WINtech. The modem approach of encouraging firms to self-manage through technology and supplier clubs and consortia is more successful and highly valued. It could be said that, by 1995, some useful learning from Baden-Württemberg had already taken place.

Technology Transfer and Two-Tier Europe

Amongst the earliest inter-regional programmes adopted by WDA was 'Eurolink', putting together initially twenty Welsh firms with firms in Baden-Württemberg, of which many ended up concluding commercial contracts. Subsequent projects included forging further links between Welsh and German firms through the technology centres (e.g. the WDA Centres of Excellence and the Steinbeis Foundation – Baden-Württemberg's small firm innovation facility) and funding them through EU programmes such as SPRINT or BRITE. It was also intended that there would be regular two-way exchanges of WDA Technology Transfer and Steinbeis staff. Such exchanges would be focused on working with groups of five or more companies in a particular industry. By 1995, the numbers of Welsh firms benefiting from Eurolink had reached 112 in all the 'four motor' countries as well as regions.[3]

The importance of moving towards higher value-added output through supporting technology transfer into and out of innovative indigenous companies was only part of the necessary process of upgrading levels of know-how and innovative capacity in Wales more generally. There remains a real prospect of a two-tier Europe after 1992.[4] With high value-added, high-wage, knowledge-intensive production in the south Germany–south-East France–Switzerland–north Italy aggregation, low-skill, low value-added, low-wage flexi-production was likely to be spread to the Atlantic and Mediterranean areas (with Eastern Europe an even cheaper, low value-added locational option). In the late 1980s, Sony and Sharp, two early Japanese investors in production plants in Wales, decided to locate their R&D operations for Europe in Stuttgart (Baden-Württemberg) and Oxford respectively, citing the better techno-logical competences of the local company populations and labour markets as prime reasons. Wales, and other less favoured regions, could ill-afford not to be able to attract such economic activity. Training and technology transfer were two key, yet poorly-developed, mechanisms for avoiding the developmental blockages and regional disparities associated with the prospect of a two-tier Europe.

Networking and Inter-Firm Linkages

In the early 1990s large firms began sub-contracting much of their production out to smaller firms, who in turn were encouraged to network amongst themselves to learn good practice. Firms exchange information as they develop and re-design the product or process they have contracted to buy or supply. In this way technology transfer is 'embedded'[5] in the system in a much more thoroughgoing way. The German (and especially Baden-Württemberg) system encapsulated this model reasonably well. By comparison, this kind of industrial culture, prevalent in the old industrial districts of nineteenth-century Britain, had been substantially weakened by, amongst other things, Britain's history of capital concentration, the development of the self-sufficient 'modem corporation' and the relative decline of inter-firm collaboration in favour of a maker-based model of cut-throat competition as described by Best.[6]

However, policy changed. Regional assistance decreased and became geographically less extensive in the 1990s. Unemployment declined rapidly in Wales at the end of the 1980s, not least because of a large influx of foreign direct investment. Moreover, the kind of investment then arriving was more inclined to seek regional and local milieux which could offer more than simply cheap labour. Flexibilisation philosophies have meant that there is, in theory at least, a greater propensity for foreign direct investors to seek local suppliers. Finally, there has been a significant rise in the number of SMEs in Wales, aided in part by the efforts of the WDA and local economic development initiatives taken by county and district councils.

Concluding Remarks: Can the 'Four Motors' Moderate Europe's 'Two Tiers'?

The great spectre of the post-1992 Single European Market is that levels of economic welfare between regions will become even more starkly polarised than they are at present. Despite problems of overheating in the economically advanced regions, economic power will continue to accumulate there even as investments are made in cheaper labour and property market areas. One option for the less-favoured European regions is to take on the 'safety-valve' role many have played in the past, accepting inward investment as a means of mopping up unemployment. That option is both an obvious sign of political and economic weakness and a less than reliable future prospect as some of Europe's even less favoured regions to the east become affiliates of the European Community. Another option is for less favoured regions to seek actively to come to terms with the new industrial order to which the more effective economic units of Europe subscribe.

The regionalised form of networking, developed to a high level of sophistication in Baden-Württemberg, linking-in Wales, through the 'four motors' initiative, is beginning to have a supranational effect. We have written about the ways in which, from a low base, Wales in partnership with Baden-Württemberg, is seeking advantage from such arrangements.

The three key elements of a regional strategy warrant clear identification. The first of these is the element of *learning-by-interaction.* Here, at the firm level, innovation is induced in the process of inter-firm transaction, as distinct from before or after it. Second is the generalisation of *networking* as a mode of information exchange, whereby collaboration is seen as an efficient means of enhancing efficiency while tempering the inefficiencies of more cut-throat forms of competition. And thirdly, providing a matrix within which such transactions operate, are *public-private forms of interaction* which seek to ensure appropriate conditions for successful innovation to occur. The difficulties and the long lead-times necessary for the establishment of a networked system should not be overlooked. However, there are signs that the training and technology transfer nettles are being grasped and the first steps up the learning-curve have been embarked upon in Wales.

Of key interest is the question of whether development and innovation approaches and systems developed elsewhere can be transferred. Three points are worthy of reconsideration here. The first is that where political will exists, as clearly is the case in Wales, local recipient agencies such as the Welsh Office, the Welsh Development Agency and the University can themselves learn by interaction. The case of the policy-shift within the WDA, moving from a centralised service delivery system to the more decentralised Technology Transfer model, which was influenced by the Steinbeis approach, is a case in point. Difficulties clearly abound, but the basic policy-vehicles do at least exist, can be adjusted and are susceptible to their own processes of development through exchange and learning. A second and very important point about transferability is that where this is initiated by a live player (such as Bosch in the Welsh case) something closely approximating the parent-model stands that much more chance of being transplanted. The speed with which local technical colleges have been able to meet Bosch training requirements in Wales is testimony to that. Moreover, the role of such colleges in spreading that learning experience to other firms in the locality should not be overlooked; indeed this is already beginning to happen. Time alone will tell whether or not the Bosch training culture takes root. For the moment it seems sensible not to foreclose the possibility.

The final point concerning the question of transferability of foreign experiences devolves into what we shall refer to as the 3-Cs: credibility, co-ordination, and continuity. *Credibility* refers principally to the institutions in the recipient environment. First of all there has to be 'someone to talk to', as the history of the Baden-Württemberg link shows. That is, there has to be a credible official institutional milieu with which outside agencies can deal. Over time, however, the credibility of the regional institutions (e.g. the WDA) will stand or fall on the calibre of their expertise (i.e. technical skills, knowledge of local industrial problems, etc.), a point that is becoming clearer to the more advanced local and regional authorities in Europe.[7]

Part of this credibility is linked to the second 'C', namely *co-ordination*. The channels by which higher-level initiatives reach practical reality have to be clear. With supranational, national, regional and local level initiatives abounding, there has to be a clearing house, if not a 'one-stop shop', to which responses can be referred. Here it is worth recalling a point which the CBI made in its appraisal of government innovation policy, namely, that much of the initiative was vitiated by the fact that small and medium-sized firms, supposedly the main clients, encountered enormous difficulties in finding 'a way through the labyrinth of schemes'. 'Business Connect' in Wales should contribute to this, though its belated launch and meagre funding give grounds for some anxiety in this regard.

The last 'C' concerns *continuity*. One of the problems often associated with policy milieux is that political change produces sharp discontinuities. This is the negative side of the WDA experience described above. The Steinbeis Foundation, with its quasiindependent status, is better able to adjust to changes in economic and political environments, and this continuity has considerably assisted the technology transfer process in Baden-Württemberg. For Wales, this condition of discontinuity is exacerbated by the tendency for massive policy-shifts to follow governmental changes, or even to be a feature of a single administration. Without these 3-Cs the best intentions are likely to be ineffectual.

Finally, we turn to the question posed in the heading to these concluding remarks. Can the 'four motors' moderate the spectre of a two-tier Europe? There are continuing fears, especially with respect to R&D, innovation and technological change that the Single Market after 1992 will hasten the concentration of knowledge-intensive activity towards the geographical cores of the Community. One response to this problem – evidenced in the tendency for R&D laboratories to be located in knowledge-intensive rather than less favoured regions – is for the EU to simply reallocate structural funds to counter such effects. However, it is more important for the EU's total resource allocation process to be examined from a regional perspective, and for co-ordination and continuity of that allocation process to be undertaken in regionally sensitive ways. Otherwise the EU's credibility as a moderator of social and regional equality will inevitably suffer. There are some signs that the Structural Funds are beginning to be used in ways that seek to enhance the innovation potential of less-favoured European Union regions.[8]

The 'four motors' link between the favoured regions is a significant departure for all those concerned about the prospect of a two tier Europe. But the linkage between favoured and less-favoured regions points to an important possible alternative way for a 'Europe of the Regions' to develop. Unless the potential for interactive learning by regions is developed on a much larger scale than has been attempted hitherto, we shall have to resign ourselves to a two tier Europe. If we do so in a committed way, however, the rhetoric of a 'Europe of the Regions' may be transformed into a material reality.

Notes

1 See Christopher Harvie, *The Rise of Regional Europe*, London: Routledge, 1994.

2 See Phil Cooke, T Christiansen and G Schienstock, 'Regional Economic Policy and a Europe of the Regions', in P Heywood, M Rhodes and V Wright (eds), *Developments in West European Politics*, Basingstoke: Macmillan, 1997.

3 A Harding, R Evans, M Parkinson and P Garside, *Regionalisation, Regional Competitiveness and the Case for Regional Government in the UK* (Report to Joseph Rowntree Foundation), Liverpool: John Moores University/European Institute for Urban Affairs, 1995.

4 D Leborgne and A Lipietz, 'How to Avoid a Two Tier Europe', paper given at the Symposium on Regulation, Innovation, Spatial Development, Cardiff, September 1989.

5 M Granovetter, 'Economic Action and Social Structure: The Problem of Embeddedness', in *American Journal of Sociology*, 91, pp.481-510.

6 See M Best, *The New Competition*, Cambridge: Polity Press, 1990.

7 K Dyson (ed.), *Local Authorities and New Technologies: The European Dimension*, London: Croom Helm, 1988.

8 Cooke *et al.*, *art. cit.*

The Forward March of Europe Halted?

John Williams

The structure of this paper is something like a drama in three acts. The first act covers the 1992 programme, arguing particularly that a relatively innocuous economic scheme effected a considerable political change. The second act indicates the intention of the Commission to use the revived project of European Monetary Union to achieve a further substantial leap towards European Political Union, and suggests why this use of the tactic which had been employed over the 1992 programme could not easily be replicated. The third act briefly advocates a more explicit separation of the economic and the political strands and proposes a possible way forward. At each stage some specific attention is given to the concerns of the regions.

The conceit of the analogy of 'a drama in three acts' is certainly not meant to suggest that the present paper lays claim to any correspondence with the classical unities of balance and fulfilment. On the contrary the three parts of the paper are given very different weights – at least in terms of space. The greater attention given to the 1992 programme, now largely historical, is justified by the extent to which an understanding of the conditions of its spectacular success is essential to more recent developments, and also because of the light it casts on the way the development of a European economic policy had influenced the nature and balance between both the member states and the various regions up to *c.* 1990. If this upsets the classical unity of balance, the failure to provide an obvious 'ending' equally offends notions of completeness and equilibrium. But this, it is pleaded, is inherent in the ongoing nature of the object of developing European unity; it is not implicit in the character of the analysis as some unkindly imply when they suggest that laying all economists end to end would reach no conclusion.

Eberhard Bort and Neil Evans (eds), ***Networking Europe,***
Liverpool University Press 2000, 67-80.

Act I

For a decade-and-a-half after the establishment of the European Economic Community (EEC) by the 1957 Treaty of Rome, the original six member states seemed to enjoy a dynamic economic growth. This was a source of both envy and attraction for some other European countries, perhaps especially Britain which, along with Denmark and Ireland, was formally admitted into the EEC in January 1973. That this roughly coincided with the slowing down of the earlier dynamism of the EEC was much less a consequence of the enlargement of the Community than it was the result of the two severe oil shocks, and of the early 1970s breakdown of the Bretton Woods international monetary settlement which had contributed to an extraordinary quarter century of international trade expansion. Whatever the reason, the impetus towards greater European integration faltered: it was to reverse this decade-long trend that the programme for the single economic market was explicitly devised and launched in 1985.

In this fundamental aim of reviving and promoting the 'idea' of Europe, the programme was a brilliant success. Already by the late 1980s the energies and enthusiasms of the member states were directed towards the common object of putting in place the mechanisms necessary to ensure that the single market would be realised, on schedule, by the end of 1992. This contrasted sharply with the early 1980s bickering over the relative size of budget contributions. It is necessary to ask, therefore, why the 1985 initiative was so successful, necessary both to understand what happened then and also to appreciate why the apparently similar 1990s initiative towards a single European currency has not followed a similarly triumphant path. One largely fortuitous aspect was timing. Not only did the mid-1980s see the almost unchallenged acceptance of the ideas of liberal economics, but they also witnessed a world-wide upturn in economic activity: new initiatives flourish better in an atmosphere of economic buoyancy. But putting that aside, and without taking any claim to completeness, it could be said that several particular features of the 1992 programme were especially relevant to its success.

Most important was the nature of the initiative itself. At the centre of the programme was the removal of non-tariff barriers (NTBs). What are these? They include things like border controls and checks; differences in national technical regulations and standards; and the natural preference of the various national governments, when doing their own substantial buying, to take their custom to their own national producers. The European Commission spared no effort to convey the impression that all this involved changes of enormous significance. There were sixteen huge commissioned consultants' reports and a best-selling popular cheer-leader,[1] all designed to prove that the removal of the NTBs was a major economic break-through.

It was, indeed, of some economic importance but its real significance was psychological and political. There is now fairly general acceptance of the demonstration that the direct economic benefits of removing the NTBs were relatively minor,[2] and that much of the evidence gathered for the Commission itself confirms this. The dysfunction arose because the impression being conveyed was that the 1985 initiative would create free trade in Europe. But free trade within the EC did not depend on the 1992 programme. It already existed in 1985: tariff barriers between the members of the Community had effectively been removed nearly two decades before the être1986 Single European Act. Paradoxically, the real strength of the programme was its (relative) economic weakness. In the general atmosphere of acceptance of liberal economics, there was little opposition from the member states.

What was significant was implementation. The very particular and specific nature of the various non-tariff barriers meant that their removal required particular and specific rules and regulations. Already by 1991, some two hundred directives had been issued. To make a reality of the single economic market, so evangelically endorsed by Mrs Thatcher, it was essential that the Commission should draft and negotiate with national ministers a stream of directives. It can plausibly be argued that it was at this period and in connection with this impeccably right-wing project that the 'interference' from Brussels received its greatest momentum and legitimisation.

It is suggested, therefore, that the undoubted success of the 1992 programme derived from its essential nature. It was an economic programme: yet the direct economic benefits were small and the claimed indirect benefits were highly uncertain. But although presented as an economic text, there was a powerful political subtext. The essential object had very properly been to release the European idea from a decade of stagnation: the promotion of European unity was, in any event, the *raison d'être* of the Commission. It was brilliantly presented: in accepting the Single Economic Act of 1985, even Mrs Thatcher had been effortlessly enticed by her greed for the economic free-market cheese into the political mouse-trap.

In so far as this explains the 1992 success, it can also help to explain more recent set-backs on the road to European integration. First, however, it is necessary to add to this background by indicating some of the major characteristics of the European economy as it had emerged by the late 1980s, and to point to some of the tensions involved. What pattern of trade and industry had by *c.*1990 emerged in Europe after nearly two decades of free trade? The question is interesting in itself, and also as an empirical test for a basic theoretical tenet that, over time, within a free trade area very large differences in income and prosperity would be ironed out.

In the trends of trade and production in manufacturing – which accounted for four-fifths of European visible trade and where manufacturing output represented a large part (30 to 45 per cent) of total national income in the major countries – one central fact stood out.[3] By the late 1980s the EC contained just one world class economic power: this was emphasised by the simple fact that in 1989 West Germany ran a larger surplus on trade than did Japan. Some 35 per cent of all EC exports to the rest of the world emanated from West Germany which, at the same time, accounted for two-fifths of all EC manufacturing output. This last point is underlined by the even more dramatic nature of the pattern of manufacturing trade between the individual member states: West Germany ran a surplus with each of the other countries and the size of the surplus was tending to rise over time. The massive size of West Germany's surplus with the rest of the EC – it amounted to 34 billion ECUs in 1987 – was a significant factor in locating EC output: the basic result was that the pattern of EC trade over the two decades before *c.*1990 tended to concentrate output and employment at the centre. The experience did not seem to bear out the theoretical presumption that any imbalance would automatically tend to correct itself.

Although the stark nature of the imbalance was almost entirely unrecognised at the time, there was a more diffused unease. In particular even many of those on the European left who were enthusiastic about the ideal of European unity were anxious about the strong stress being given to liberal market approaches. In generally unspecific ways there was worry, sometimes alarm, about the feared unfavourable effects on social and distributional aspects. The Commission's response was to offer the reassurance that the EC Regional and Social Funds existed to counter such tendencies. But when subjected to close analysis the Commission's assurances carry little credibility either empirically or in the robustness of their instruments for correction. A brief indication of the scale of the problem as it emerged by the second half of the 1980s is given by the fact that per capita income in the EC's wealthiest regions (Groningen in Holland, and Hamburg in Germany) was four or five times as great as in the poorest (Thrakis in Greece and Extremadura in Spain).[4] The discrepancies were, moreover, tending to increase and were being accentuated by the re-emergence of mass unemployment.

Against this background the existing instruments for EC regional policy quite simply looked inadequate: there was a clear disjuncture between their power and the scale of the problem. The total EC budget was at the time just over one per cent of the EC's gross domestic product and 60 per cent of that was earmarked for the Common Agricultural Policy (CAP) – and most of the CAP funds still went to the richer countries of northern Europe. The modesty of the amounts remaining for the Regional and Social Funds was then compounded by the infrastructure projects (mainly in the de-veloping countries of the south) and youth training (mainly in the older, decaying industrial area). These had the virtue from the point of view of the Commission, with its attachment to liberal economics, of being schemes which could be said to improve the working of the market (removing inefficiencies): they did not seriously challenge the operation of the markets. For youth training to be effective, for example, the right skills have to be taught and there must then be skilled jobs waiting for them in their native countries: otherwise there will be frustration or a flow of bodies along the improved infrastructures leading towards the centre. Serious correction required significant redistribution from the centre.

It is here that the background pattern of trade and industry which has been outlined meets the views on regional inequalities. The regional problem was seen almost entirely in terms of failure at the periphery; it was an interpretation which made invisible the increasing dominance of the centre and the persistent pattern of inter-EC trade. These were not seen and, as the next section will show, continued not to be seen as problems and thus there was no need for them to be recognised and confronted.

Act II

By 1989, the Commission had launched the next leap forward in the form of the Delors plan for monetary union. Act II thus started before Act I, the 1992 programme, had been fully played out. This was neither accidental nor careless: indeed, 1992 could be said to have caused 1989. In 1985, when Delors and the Commission were desperately looking for a way to 'get Europe moving again', a push for monetary union had been considered but explicitly ruled out: it would be 'hopelessly divisive', something for the far future. It was the extraordinary momentum built up by the single economic plan which allowed the monetary union project to be taken out of the closet and dusted down.

The intention was, moreover, to use more or less exactly the same general strategy which had worked so well for the 1992 project:

- There was to be a specific timetable (to preempt endless discussion) to enable the whole scheme (just like the 1985 proposals) to be put in place in seven years from acceptance in principle;

- The method was to use an essentially economic programme to push towards greater political integration;
- The economic proposals were based on an explicit acceptance of neo-classical liberal economics.

All this had worked brilliantly for the single market project. Why has it not done the same for monetary union? As a preface to any explanation a few brief non-technical comments on the economic basis of the proposals are necessary.

The basic point that emerges from both the initial Delors plan and its extensive elaboration in a special 1992 edition of the official journal *European Economy*, is that the dominance of liberal economics was even more marked than it had been in the single market proposals. Thus the sole declared aim of monetary policy was to be 'price stability'. Other possible policy objectives – the maintenance of employment or balanced growth – were simply not mentioned. Moreover the intention was to place this beyond political reach: price stability was to be written in to the constitution of the proposed new Central Bank, which was to be given total political independence.

That this represented something of a hardening of attitude can be seen by making a brief comparison with the Cecchini Report which had presented the justification for the single market programme. Cecchini had deemed it necessary to claim that the 1992 project would make possible a policy of co-ordinated European inflation (all member states agreeing to raise levels of economic activity at more or less the same time). Indeed, it was this which allowed the claim to be made that the programme would eventually lead to a significant net increase in jobs to offset the immediate, and more certain, job losses. The credibility of this claim could be, and was, questioned:[5] the issue here is simply that at that time it was deemed necessary to present the programme as a policy for maintaining employment. The plan for monetary union was set out and justified without the level of employment being identified as an object of policy. The stress is not on the possibility of co-ordinated expansion, but on the need of the Central Bank to impose discipline on national budgets.

Much the same shift in balance could be seen over regional policies. Cecchini had deemed it essential to address the issue of regional inequalities and then present the Community as playing a significant role in redressing these disparities – even if the inadequacy of the instruments for so doing was glossed over. The emphasis in the case for EMU is quite different. Any form of supra-national redistribution is viewed with suspicion, and could even be dangerous in weakening the incentives to productive activity in the poorer countries by creating a 'state-welfare dependency' (more or less the same argument used by Malthus at the beginning of the nineteenth century against any form of assistance to the poor). The fate of the weaker peripheral economies was seen to depend almost entirely on their own commitment to 'generalised modernisation' which would require 'a comprehensive and credible change of regime'.[6] Essentially, this meant that everything should be reduced to the test of the market.

One last background factor behind the initial burst for monetary union needs to be mentioned. There is no doubt that much of the model for the proposed forms was taken from West Germany which had clearly been the great European economic success. The Commission's interpretation — which was widely shared by analysts and other experts — attributed the success almost entirely to the German pursuit of sound money. It was then implied that what had been good for Germany would necessarily be good for all the rest. There is obviously substance in each of these contentions, but they do also require qualification and analysis.

To begin with it requires some forcing before Germany, with its large social welfare sector, can be made to fit comfortably into the free market stereotype. In addition, it is doubtful – even granting its high importance – whether monetary policy can be made to bear all the weight of explanation of German dominance. To do so is to abstract monetary policy from other distinctive national features of the German society and economy at this time, such as: the supportive relations between banks and industrial firms; a particular system of industrial relation; and a long tradition of education and vocational training. Perhaps more fundamentally it ignores the possibility that an equally active and direct cause of German success rested in its superior productive competence, particularly in engineering. This productive basis allowed a unique, but not necessarily conscious, division of responsibility between public authorities and private capital. The Federal government and the Bundesbank maintained a tight fiscal and monetary policy, and a competent manufacturing sector evaded the otherwise contractionist policies of that by selling into other EC markets running, as was demonstrated earlier, large trade surpluses with the other member states. The significance of this alternative interpretation is that it made it literally impossible for Germany to act as the model for all the member states. Even apart from the inability of most to have matched the German level of manufacturing competence, it was simply not possible for all EC countries to secure economic success by running surpluses on intra-EC trade: they cannot all have surpluses with each other.

This background can help to explain why the quest for EMU failed to repeat the apparently effortless success of the 1992 programme on which it was so directly modelled. Explanation is especially necessary since the logic of the (smoothly accepted) single market pointed directly towards the need for monetary union. It is true of course that the overall circumstances were less favourable: the economic buoyancy of the late 1980s gave way to halting activity and high unemployment throughout the Community. The events in eastern Europe also made this a period of political turmoil.

It might be thought or argued that a more direct cause would arise from a resistance to the more explicit embodiment of right-wing economic views in the proposals for monetary union. It would be comforting so to think. In fact there is no evidence on a wide-enough scale to support the view that the left in Europe was either sufficiently resurgent or obviously focused on challenging the deep-rooted economic liberalism of the Community.

The more likely explanation is much simpler, and can also be used to point a way forward to the generally desirable end of greater European integration. Each of these initiatives was using an economic policy to drive forward a political object. The difference was in the way and the extent to which the economic policy impinged upon the existing practices of the member states. The single market, as indicated earlier, had not been imposing on the member states the removal of their individual tariff regimes: that, if it had been necessary, would have represented a major shift. Instead, free trade already existed and the absence of tariffs on intra-EC trade was a condition of membership: it was what was meant by the earlier term Common Market, the ark of the EC covenant. Its acceptance was necessary for new states joining (as Denmark, Ireland and the United Kingdom did in January 1973), although prior negotiations could allow an agreed time-span for full compliance. The single market proposal more simply aimed at logically completing this process by removing various non-tariff barriers on intra-EC trade. It is not contended that this was problem-free or did not encounter any resistance: governments and other public bodies were not keen to conduct their own purchasing on the basis of EC-wide tendering. (And even when they had agreed, ingenuity and determination could always shield the shorn lamb from the wind: it would be interesting to know, for example, how many French police forces no longer buy their vehicles from the national champions). In other areas the need to lay down detailed specifications, which would have precipitated endless discussion and bickering, was avoided by two simple and sensible expedients: the principle of 'mutual recognition', and the notion of 'Essential Requirements'. In the case, for example, of technical standards for manufactured goods, the principle of mutual recognition provided that if, say, a washing machine was legally sold in any EC country, it was impossible to block its import into another EC country on the ground that it did not meet local technical requirements. Of course, each national government still had the obligation to its citizens to protect public health, safety and the environment: but again instead of directives laying down detailed specifications, there was a simple outline of the principal features which products had to have ('Essential Requirements'), and compliance with these 'European Standards' guaranteed access to all European markets. Similar expedients ('home country control' in financial services) for other areas need not be recited here. For the present argument it is enough to note that the removal of NTBs both chimed in well with the ethos of the time about extending competition and, if sometimes uncomfortable, did not seem life-threatening to national interests.

Monetary union was an economic policy horse of an entirely different colour. Its adoption involved, and was clearly seen to involve, reducing some of the central economic functions of the national governments. In contrast to 1985-86, therefore, the political cost was made rapidly and starkly visible. The Delors Plan was launched in 1989 on the crest of the enthusiasm for the single market and was generally endorsed in principle in the summer of 1990. But at the Inter-Government Conference at Rome in December of the same year the Commission's hopes for a smooth implementation began to fall apart. Jaques Delors was moved publicly to proclaim that all the governments were reneging on their commitment to time-tabled progress and none of them were sound on EMU: '... ask the German, the Spaniard, the Dutchmen, the Frenchmen what they think [of EMU] in the bottom of their hearts,' he declared bitterly. A year later, at Maastricht in December 1991, the Treaty did include some steps which were explicitly directed towards political union. These steps were, however, mostly round the edges of the problems. Roughly stated they concerned: the introduction of community citizenship: moves towards a common foreign policy over some unanimously agreed subjects; the implementation of a common security policy (framed by the Western European Union and to conform with NATO obligations); and greater co-operation over legal matters involving, for example, visas, immigration and rights of asylum. The only one directed towards the Community's own constitutional arrangements provided for some limited strengthening of the powers of the European Parliament.

Act III

The problem here is that the dramatic resolution (if there is to be one) has not been reached – indeed, could be said still to be a long way off. The purpose of this brief tailpiece is thus mostly to comment on the scene-shifting that has taken place. Most dramatic was the collapse of the settlements in eastern Europe leading to the re-unification of Germany. Even apart from this, as indicated by the end of the last section, an action replay of

1985-92 has been shown not to be possible: using an accepted economic means as a stalking horse to obtain a political end which was little specified. It is not that the desire for further European integration has dried up: it is rather that EMU has laid bare the accompanying national political costs. One consequence is that what many had earlier seen as a preferred way forward - a Europe of the Regions - has, along with a central concern about regional inequalities, been pushed back stage.

What should be the response to these shifts? The one proposed here is frankly polemical. It argues that the move towards further European political integration needs to be openly pursued. The Delors plan for monetary union, and its further elaboration in the special issue of *European Economy,* set out in some detail the form of union being proposed and the instruments through which it was to be effected. Although it was always obvious that there were also political connotations, the nature and status of the Commission's political project was completely unclear. Indeed, the stages and objectives of political integration have never been defined in a specific and programmatic document equivalent to the report on EMU.

One can see the force behind such evasion. A fully-articulated document would need to confront such indelicate matters as: the kind of relationship (what variety of federalism?) between the national governments and the centre; the need to justify or modify the anomaly of a non-elected (and practically non-accountable) Commission being the only body which can propose legislation; and the parallel oddity of the Council of Ministers (with its network of committees manned by officials and junior ministers) acting in secret as the executive body of the European Union. The essential position remains as one in which the Commission proposes, Ministers dispose – and the parliament trails a fair way behind despite some recent halting steps to reduce the democratic deficit.

Even so condensed a statement is enough to make clear that these matters are not going to be resolved quickly or smoothly. But a more direct statement of intentions, or even possibilities, would open the way for discussion over the nature of the political checks and balances and the extent (if any) to which political agents can (or should) exercise control over the institutions and policies. The significance can be illustrated from the two areas which were at the centre of the previous sections. It would be widely conceded that monetary union is a logical requirement of a comprehensive single market. There are, however, other forms it could take besides the one actually proposed of total political independence and the single objective of price stability. The former, as Kohl demonstrated over the imposition of his terms for German monetary re-unification, goes even beyond the power granted to the Bundesbank; the latter requires a faith beyond all experience that all other desirable economic goals – high employment, growth, equitable distribution – will automatically follow. All this has a direct connection to the other issue of regional inequalities. The particular proposals for EMU would block any direct interventions to redress these. Redistribution from richer to poorer countries was to be constrained, and ensured by keeping Community income low. The burden of adjustment (meaning contraction and unemployment) is then pushed on to the weaker peripheral countries which are to be disciplined through tight monetary control.

The present argument, which runs counter to much of this, rests on two fundamental assumptions which need to be clearly stated. Both are deemed to be prerequisites for a closer European integration which is to be stable. Firstly, that what is needed is greater democratic involvement and control; and secondly that regional disparities should not be excessive. The first is essential to secure wide political acceptance; the second to avoid a threatening source of division. Implementation would require a drastic change of direction. It would probably also demand postponement of enlargement: negotiation of apolitical settlement between the existing fifteen member states will be complication enough.

A large part of the first two sections was prepared some years ago for an earlier Freudenstadt conference. If the adjustments made here have been limited that is not because the initial piece was carved in stone: wholesale revision would have inappropriately shifted the balance towards the (then) unknown and remote territory of the later 1990s. But neither would it have been appropriate to present the piece as an exercise in historical archaeology, an old bone recovered from an ancient graveyard. The basic findings and conclusions are – it is obviously a matter for subjective judgement – still thought to have relevance. In particular that the shift to the pursuit of EMU made it impossible to hide an inevitably contested political purpose behind a relatively uncontroversial economic shield. It is a situation that would have been unavoidable whatever the form taken by EMU, but the particularly rigid form proposed presented the implications for the political control of the member states in especially stark terms. Moreover, it still seems pertinent to point out that closer European integration, if it is to be stable, is likely to be threatened by regional inequalities which are excessive (greater, for example, than in the United States). Clear-cut lines of division within the European Union are dangerous. This is true not only of the disparities discussed in the first two sectors but also of the recent chatter about a two-track path to EMU which might disguise the immediate differences between members at the cost of erecting long-term barriers. It thus still seems appropriate to tackle more explicitly the political problems of greater integration; and the hiatus over monetary union – the slow recognition by the EU's witch-doctors that Maastricht has long been dead – presents the opportunity for such a shift. It won't happen, but there should at least be more realisation of the dangers inherent in the Commission's preferred course.

Notes

1 See P Cecchini, ,*1992:The European Challenge: The Benefits of a Single Market*, Aldershot: Ashgate, and Wildwood House, 1988.

2 See T Cutler, K Williams and J Williams, *1992:The Struggle for Europe*, Oxford: Berg, 1989.

3 The evidence for this section is based on the Tables in Chapter 1 of Cutler *et al.*

4 See T Padoa-Schiopp, *Efficiency, Stability and Equity: The European Community*, Oxford: Oxford University Press, 1987.

5 Cutler *et al.*, pp. 70-74..

6 *European Economy* , No. 44 , 1990, 'One Market. One Money', p.277.

Unitary Britain and Regional Europe

John Osmond

The Nation State

Britain and Europe are two arenas that compete for attention when assessing Wales' place in the world. Increasingly, however, a third, world-wide dimension has to be taken into account. In the 1990s the global economy is undermining the British nation-state as much as Wales and Scotland or the European Union. By the global economy is meant the dominance of multi-national companies together with the ever-growing, world-wide nexus of communication and currency movements. Together, they are fatally undermining nation-state powers and sovereignty. One response is a movement throughout the world to continental patterns of governance. In our own case this last is represented by the evolving institutions of the European Union. At the same time parallel regional structures, below the nation-state, are emerging as well. Together, the continental and regional levels of governance have some hope of subjecting global economic and cultural forces to democratic discipline.

It is the nation-state, of course, that from this perspective remains the problem. Part of the confusion that results from this analysis, however, is the issue of nationalism. There are, in fact, two kinds of nationalism involved – big nation-state nationalism, and small-nation nationalism of the kind found in Wales and Scotland. In the 1990s the latter is no longer confined to the nationalist parties in these countries. Increasingly it is to be found within wings of the other progressive parties as well: Labour, the Liberal Democrats, and even some elements of the Green parties. In Wales it is represented by a small-nation nationalist grouping that emerged inside the Welsh Labour

Eberhard Bort and Neil Evans (eds), *Networking Europe*, Liverpool University Press 2000, 81-99.

Party in the mid-1990s. Aligning itself with a similar pressure group that appeared on the Scottish scene in the mid-1980s, it calls itself Welsh Labour Action and is campaigning for an Assembly 'with real power'.[1]

Distinctions within the unitary British state between small- and big-nation nationalism (perhaps characterised by a lower-case *n* and an upper-case *N)* are important. Raymond Williams constantly emphasised it, for instance in an interview in 1984:

> There are two kinds of nationalism. There is that nationalism which reinforces the idea of the traditional nation-state. This nationalism has been given added impetus under the Thatcher governments as we saw at the time of the Falklands/Malvinas episode. But this kind of nationalism is also shared by the Labour Party, as was so vividly revealed by their support for the British intervention in the South Atlantic. The other kind of nationalism is that which questions the whole basis of the unitary British state. I think that the first kind of nationalism is reactionary and the second is progressive. This argument starts from the analysis that existing nation-states of the size of Britain are both too small and too large for useful politics.[2]

Taking this analysis forward, what does being a small 'n' Welsh nationalist mean in the mid-1990s? Reiterating the view of Saunders Lewis, in his 1926 lecture *The Principles of Nationalism,* it is to say that Wales does not wish for an independent sovereign state on the nineteenth-century pattern. Instead, it seeks a place for a relatively autonomous country within the framework of a European Union of the Regions. Both the nation-state and regionalist positions outlined here face dilemmas. Those who seek to promote the nation-state confront Raymond Williams' analysis, a reactionary *cul de sac* down which the Europhobic English nationalists within the Conservative Party are travelling. Equally, however, the regionalist approach contains many problems.

A starting point in tackling these questions is to examine some of the arguments that were deployed during the 1970s when devolution politics were last an important question for

British politics. The Labour Government of that decade not only wrestled with Wales and Scotland, but with the regions of England as well, though as something of an afterthought. Concern with England was prompted by Tam Dalyell's 'West Lothian Question'[3] and the growing mutterings of a revolt from Labour MPs in the north of England.

By way of a response the Government produced, in December 1976, a document seeking to discover, as it put it, 'ways people in England would like to see our institutions develop'.[4] The press hand-out that accompanied it said 1,000 bodies across England were being consulted. We never heard the outcome of that investigation. Indeed, the document *Devolution: The English Dimension* was quickly forgotten at the time and has not been resurrected since.

Reading it today there is a sense of perspectives having changed a great deal in a relatively short period. The document made no specific proposals but rehearsed some of the arguments in favour, and against, regional government in England. The case for change was seen to be:

- Lightening the burden on central government.
- Bringing government close to the people.
- Rendering the work of nominated bodies – that is, the Quangos – subject to local democratic control.
- Providing a layer of government to deal with matters – such as planning, infrastructure, water and health – at an intermediate level between central and local government.

Arguments against change were:

- Constitutional implications, in particular the powers of ministers to maintain national policies, and the role of Parliament.
- Financial implications.
- The problem of drawing boundaries.
- Effects on other institutions, especially the possibility of drawing functions away from local government when it had only just been reorganised.

The constitutional implications were seen as the most serious, though it is interesting to observe that no mention is made of the 'West Lothian Question' and the potential for English regional devolution to address this. More generally, the whole tenor of the devolution proposals in the 1970s as revealed here – for Scotland and Wales as much as for England – emphasised the economic primacy of Whitehall. Devolution was seen as involving essentially social policy matters. Economic policy – including regional policy, development grants, and public investment – were to remain firmly with central government. The paper emphasises several times the economic unity of the United Kingdom which, it said, had many important aspects including:

> ... not only external economic relations, the management of demand in the United Kingdom as a whole and the framework of trade, but also the task of devising national policies to benefit particular parts of the United Kingdom and of distributing resources among them according to relative need.

The conclusion was unambiguous: 'The Government will retain direct control over economic management and over regional policy and commercial policy.'

Change in the 1980s

The 1979 general election, which was precipitated by the devolution referenda in Scotland and Wales, marked a watershed. The incoming Conservative government was highly centralist. It launched a sustained attack on local government including rate capping, imposition of the poll-tax, and the abolition of the Greater London Council and the other English metropolitan authorities. Notions of regionalism were also given short shrift. The Regional Economic Planning Councils, established in the mid-1960s, were abolished in 1981.

At the same time the 1980s saw the beginnings of an intellectual transformation in Labour thinking towards economic planning and the central state. In 1982 a Labour Working Group, headed by John Prescott, then spokesman on regional affairs and devolution, published a radical paper in light of previous thinking, *Alternative Regional Strategy*. This argued against Whitehall centralism and made the case for economic regeneration from the bottom up, by building new economic and financial institutions in the regions of England as well as in Wales and Scotland, and making them democratically accountable.[5]

Such thinking was further developed through the 1980s, with the European dimension adding significantly to the argument. In 1988, for instance, Sheffield MP Richard Caborne, then Labour's Parliamentary spokesman for the regions, published a paper entitled *Regional Renaissance: Meeting the Challenge in Europe*. This contained the following statement:

> In the past regional initiatives have concentrated on attracting inward investment. Whilst this is to be encouraged, experience has shown that the low skill, branch plant economy associated with this type of investment is the first victim of recession. A successful policy must therefore combine the instruments of regional policy with policies that focus on strengthening the indigenous economy in all the regions...
>
> Equally important, a new regional policy must shift the focus of decision-making to the regions. Not only is this in the interests of greater democracy and accountability, it is also the means of establishing a better balance in the economy and the basis for more sustained growth throughout the country.

While such fresh thinking – heavily influenced by the European regional dimension – was beginning to emerge on the Left during the 1980s, something similar was happening, if not on the mainstream political Right, then certainly in the realm of business and trade. During the 1980s mechanisms for allocating the European Regional Development Fund and subsequently Structural Fund moneys through the 'programme approach' resulted in pressure from the European Union on what had previously been considered domestic concerns. So, for instance, the Commission began to insist on the production of detailed regional programmes, based on 'partnerships' between the various public and private agencies involved in economic development.

The launching of the Single European Market, the European Economic Area and further enlargement of the Union heightened awareness of the opportunities and competitive threats of a trading bloc of some 380 million people. Business leaders in Britain became increasingly concerned about the weakness of the business support infrastructure in the English regions, compared with similar areas in continental Europe.

A landmark study on the economic development lessons that needed to be absorbed was published in 1992 by the organisation Business in the Community together with Coopers and Lybrand. 'We believe within the UK there is a lack of recognition of the increasing threat that the full extent of inter-regional European competition represents,' the study declared.[6] It examined four contrasting European regions – Catalonia, Limburg in the Netherlands, Lombardy and Hamburg – and noted that each contained powerful economic development bodies at a scale and with sufficient autonomy to achieve 'critical mass'. As a result they can:

- Raise and apply resources from within their region.
- Take decisions.
- Implement a European/international strategy at a scale which enables the region to compete effectively against other locations.

This idea of 'critical mass' was a keynote conclusion, and provides a useful additional identity marker in the continuing debate over what should constitute a definition or description of a region in the European context:

> 'Critical mass' is likely to differ from area to area, for example our study areas ranged from 1 to 8/9 million people, but the key factors are that economic development covers a geographic area for which there exists a

shared identity, with the result that common development needs and objectives can be established; that all relevant public and private organisations in the area can be and are involved in formulating and implementing strategy; that economies of scale in research, marketing and administration are facilitated; that liaison with UK government and with the EC is effective; and that a sufficient level of skills and resources is available to offer a broad range of high quality support services.

The Integrated Regional Offices

It was against the background of pressure such as this that the Conservative Party manifesto at the 1992 general election made a commitment to the introduction of integrated regional offices. In April 1994 the Departments of Trade and Industry, Employment, Environment and Transport were combined into ten new regional offices – for London, the South-East, the South-West, East Anglia, the East Midlands, the West Midlands, Yorkshire and Humberside, the North-West, the North-East, and Merseyside. The result is that an embryonic government administration for the regions in England has been put in place.

The new offices are each responsible for administering a single geographical area. They are responsible for administering or advising on £6 billion of public spending. They also administer the newly integrated programme for inner-city regeneration, the Single Regeneration Budget, combining twenty separate programmes, worth initially £1.4 billion. For the first time 2,800 staff from four different ministries in the regions are all accountable to one Senior Regional Director. The combined running costs add up to £90 million.[7]

This process is precisely what occurred in Wales under the Macmillan government in 1962-63 and was the direct precursor of the establishment of the Welsh Office in 1964. The precedent is clear, though initially at least the new English regional offices and their directors smack of the old French prefectorial system.

Their operation soon attracted the attention of MPs in these terms. Peter Kilfoyle, Labour MP for Liverpool Walton, complained to the Public Accounts Committee:

> I cannot even discover how the structure works, who gives the final nod. The system seems to be running secretively, with grants of up to £3.8 million awarded without any elected representative considering the application. The regional director seems the most powerful influence in the process. He has extra powers which lead me to think of him as a viceroy appointed by a faraway power, with little or no regard for local opinion or democratic rights. Is this network of civil servants and Quangocrats giving value for money or is their function more political in nature?[8]

Quite apart from this structure, other government departments and quangos, including the NHS, have a strong presence at the regional level in England. English quangos now spend an estimated £50 billion a year, with much of the spending – around £30 billion from higher and further education, urban regeneration and housing – transferred from local government. The then Prime Minister, John Major, revealed that in the South-West alone there were 43 different regional outposts of central government employing 26,000 people.[9]

Although the new integrated regional offices are tightly controlled by the civil service, their creation did not occur without opposition and a Whitehall rearguard action. There was a hard-fought Cabinet debate despite the Manifesto commitment, with John Major holding out against the change, which was supported by Michael Heseltine, President of the Board of Trade, and Kenneth Clarke, the Chancellor of the Exchequer. Heseltine and Clarke, reflecting Conservative business pressure, made the case on grounds of efficiency. Major, it seems, was worried about the political implications of institutionalising the English regions on such firm economic foundations.

Major was right. His view was confirmed, if in a backhanded way, by Howard Davies, speaking in February 1995 when he was still Director-General of the CBI (shortly before becoming Deputy Governor of the Bank of England):

> There is a growing consensus that a regional focus for decision-making across the public sector needs to be created, and one with business input ... Regional businesses have definitely welcomed having a single point of call for government in their region. But curiously rather than appease the enthusiasm for regional autonomy, and make them think the government really does care about the world beyond the M25, the Integrated Regional Offices seem to have had the opposite effect. It's woken them up to what they have been missing. This is perhaps not surprising. History suggests that reform is a slippery slope. The most dangerous time for a centralised regime is when it begins to unbend.[10]

The British Debate over English Regionalism

An indication that the 'centralised regime' was beginning to 'unbend', if not crack, came from John Major himself, at the end of 1994. His New Year message, in which he highlighted Labour's devolution programme in such hysterical terms – 'teenage madness' and 'one of the most dangerous propositions ever put to the British nation' – had the virtue of at least foregrounding the debate. It made clear that in future the so-called integrity of the United Kingdom – the position of Scotland and Wales, but also the regions in England – would be projected as the other side of the coin of European integration as a key battleground between Conservatives and Labour.

It also threw Labour on the defensive and forced it, for the first time in the 1990s, to do some serious thinking about its policies for the English regions. The devil, as it is said, is in the detail. There are signs that in examining the detail Labour is making substantial progress compared with its position in the 1970s. The party's first instinct, however, was to backtrack, revealing the cautious, essentially conservative character of the Blair approach. Nothing – no policy, commitment or principle – should be allowed to get in the way of winning the next election.

Press reports in the wake of Major's attack indicated that Blair was to scale down the commitment to powerful regional government throughout England. They would not be set up unless there was clear demand. Instead, the party would democratise the quangos and hospital trusts set up by the Tories, by bringing together an indirectly elected group of councillors for each of the English regions. An exception would be London, which was the only capital city in Europe without an elected strategic authority.

This position was given the title *Devolution on Demand* by the Institute for Public Policy Research (IPPR), the left-leaning think-tank, in a paper published in May 1995. This formed the intellectual framework for the Labour policy consultation paper *A Choice for England* published the following month. The IPPR paper struck a sceptical note, suggesting that the English regions were 'essentially artificial constructs': 'The lack of a strong regional identity in England undermines the usefulness of comparisons with our European neighbours.'[11]

However, Tindale, a Londoner, undermined this assertion with a strong, indeed passionate, identification with the London 'region': '... it is impossible to deny that in London there is a clear and insistent demand to be allowed our government back.'

Similar attachments can be found in the south-west, certainly Cornwall; Wessex, Essex, and certainly, too, in the various regions in the north of England, especially the north-east where there is a fully-fledged Campaign for a Northern Assembly. Regional sensibility within England is actually exceedingly strong, with a range of markers from contrasting landscapes and economies, to an astonishing range of regional accents and literary traditions.

What needs explaining is not the lack of existence of English regional identities, but why their political dimension and representation is so weak. The answer is to be found in the long record of a powerful centralised state system – bound up with the Monarchy and Parliament – starting with the Norman Conquest, a history that only now is beginning to unravel. In turn this is linked to the English tendency to think first of their position in the class structure when considering who they are, rather than their locality or community. Yet the English are as much bound up with overbearing central state structures, though in different ways, as are the Scots or the Welsh. As Raymond Williams once put it:

> It can be said that the Welsh people have been oppressed by the English for some seven centuries. Yet it can then also be said that the English people have been oppressed by the English state for even longer.[12]

Stephen Tindale reveals an underlying agenda when he unconsciously refers back to that 1976 consultation paper *Devolution: The English Dimension* and its worries about the economic integrity of the British unitary state. Tindale's version is described in a section headed 'The Social Democratic Dilemma':

> The Left's dilemma over devolution stems from the fact that its new enthusiasm for the politics of identity and locality conflicts in important respects with its historic commitment to equality. Social democracy needs to maximise the sense of community between everyone living in a state.
>
> Devolution could undermine political support for fiscal transfers, by making redistribution more visible. The Northern League in Italy supports greater regional autonomy precisely in order to preserve more of its wealth from Rome and the South. Fears about fiscal transfers were exploited by the anti-devolutionists in the 1970s. They may yet prove accurate with regard to Scotland and Wales.[13]

An answer to Tindale's 'social democratic dilemma' is actually to be found in Italy and an important study of Italian regional government, *Making Democracy Work,* published by the American political scientist Robert Putnam in 1993. Twenty potentially powerful regional governments were established in Italy in 1970 as part of a constitutional settlement that had been promised since the end of the Second World War. As institutions they were virtually identical in form, though the social, economic, political and cultural contexts in which they were implanted differed dramatically. They ranged from the pre-industrial societies of Sicily and other regions of the south, to the post-industrial societies of Emilia Romagna, Lombardy and the others of the north. Some were Catholic and feudal; other Communist and modern.

Their experiences over the past quarter of a century have varied greatly. Some have proved relative failures – inefficient, lethargic, corrupt. But others have been remarkably successful, promoting investment and economic development, pioneering environmental standards, creating innovative, job-training centres for the young and day-care programmes for the elderly.

In his study, which traces the history of the past twenty-five years, Putnam asks the essential question: what is the explanation for these differences? He discounts government organisation, which is more or less the same from region to region in Italy, though of course the way government is *implemented* varies widely. Ruled out, too, are party politics and ideology, relative social stability and political harmony, population movements, and even differing levels of affluence and prosperity.

Putnam concludes that the difference is due to what he calls *social capital,* by which he means social organisations such as co-operative networks, voluntary organisations and the depth of civic society generally. The regional democratic governments of northern Italy have on the whole worked because they were dealing with societies that valued solidarity, civic participation, and integrity. They were communities traditionally organised in a horizontal way with a highly developed degree of individual citizenship expressed through strong civic, usually voluntary, institutions.

On the other hand, regions like Calabria and Sicily were traditionally less 'civic' in character. That is to say, they were organised more vertically, with hierarchic social structures, classically divided into peasants and bosses, in which obligations were imposed rather than mutually shared – 'Things must change so they can stay the same ...', and so on. Putnam traces the differences back more than a millennium to when republics were established in places like Florence, Bologna and Genoa and developed traditions of civic engagement and successful government:

> For at least ten centuries, North and South have followed contrasting approaches to the dilemmas of collective action that afflict all societies. In the North norms of reciprocity and networks of civil engagement have been embodied in guilds, mutual aid societies, co-operatives, unions, and even soccer clubs and literary societies. These horizontal civic bonds have under girded levels of economic and institutional performance generally much higher than in the South, where social and political relations have been virtually structures. Although we are accustomed to thinking of the state and the market as alternative mechanisms for solving social problems this history suggests that both states and markets operate more efficiently in civic settings.[14]

The Economic Case Restated

By the same token, when Stephen Tindale poses a choice between economic regionalism and social democratic redistribution he is presenting us with a false dilemma. Redistribution and hand-outs – the old-style carrot-and-stick regional economic dispersal policies – are at best short-term responses to regional inequalities. More often than not they only serve to reinforce the underlying structural problems that persist in less-favoured regions. This is old-style regional economic thinking, more characteristic of the 1960s than the 1990s.

When it emerged, Labour's consultation paper was far more incisive than Stephen Tindale's analysis. It contained a trenchant critique of the 'actually existing' regional administration and quango state in England. It even called in aid the right-wing thinker Karl Popper's *Poverty of Historicism* to expose its inefficiency. Popper was an ardent opponent of 'democratic centralism' – arguing that it is always easy to centralise power, but far more difficult to centralise the information for the wise wielding of that power. Labour's document warned that the lack of a democratic regional structure meant that the English regions were losing out in Europe, quoting an Audit Commission report to this effect:

> Both the reform of the structural funds and the creation of networks are part of the EC's broader aim to expand its level of contact and policy dialogue with sub-central units of government in the community.[15]

Most importantly the Labour consultation document restates emphatically the economic case that the lack of a clear regional structure in England has made it more difficult to develop an effective regional economic policy, so pulling the emphasis away from Tindale's 'social democratic dilemma':

> England is handicapped by a serious regional imbalance. Political, financial and economic decision-making is concentrated in the City of London and Whitehall. This has profound implications for access to investment. In order to correct this imbalance Britain needs an economic strategy which is geared to the particular needs of its regions. This can only be developed by those regions themselves.[16]

The need for regional self-motivation and self-sufficiency has to be understood in a world-wide context. It is increasingly recognised that we are witnessing a global market place in which the pace of economic and technological change is accelerating. There are now vast flows of capital at an international level and increasing interdependence of production activities. The globalisation of economic relations has been fostered by revolutions in communication systems and information technology.

At the same time there has been a shift towards decentralised forms of organisation and management in both the public and private sectors. Power is dispersed more widely through organisations. Structures are becoming cellular rather than pyramid-like in their formation. Global forces and multinational companies are not impervious to spatial considerations.

There is now a growing human geography and economic literature charting the inter-connections between globalisation on the one hand, and localisation on the other.[17] Foreign direct investment by multi-national concerns is being seen as attracted to regions which have a co-ordinated drive to innovation in specialised areas, with clusters of linked activities and firms, and supply chain networks. In this way the most dynamic of the emerging regional economies are dovetailing naturally into the emerging global economy; the global and regional economies are proving to be two sides of the same coin. The best-placed regions will be those that, through political mobilisation, have developed technology-intensive clusters of related activities. These are the 'motor' regions we hear so much about, motor regions because they are in the vanguard of learning and innovation. This is the 'bourgeois regionalism' which for the foreseeable future is likely to provide the regionalist impulse with its main dynamic.

A Europe of Regions

During the last phase of the devolution debate in Britain in the 1970s regionalism was not perceived to be anything like as central as it is in the 1990s to economic development. Neither – from the English/ British perspective at any rate – was it seen as fitting so naturally into a Europe-wide framework.

In the 1990s, however, the regions have become a key part of the contemporary debate on the future of Europe. The nature of borders within the European Union is changing. On the one hand nation-state frontiers are breaking down, while on the other there are emerging new, sometimes much older, borders – porous certainly, but economically, culturally and politically of growing significance. The most sensitive of these new/old borders are the ones that butt against, and often actually straddle, those of the nation-states themselves. There are many examples, ranging from Catalonia, between France and Spain, to Lorraine and Saarland between France and Germany. Together they are creating new/old fault lines that are breaking up nineteenth-century nation-state Europe. In the words of the

Northern Ireland writer Edna Longley, these European border regions have the character of 'cultural corridors', essential communication routes in the emerging new Europe.

The new borders embrace regions of enormous diversity – in size, history and identity. Some of the new entities are familiar – old or previously existing states like Lithuania, Serbia and Scotland, or long-standing aspirants to nationhood like Wales, Brittany or the Basque Country. Some are completely new to what hitherto we have known as western Europe, like the eastern states of Belorussia and Moldovia. Others are simply administrative units like Upper and Lower Normandy – convenient divisions of an historic region decreed from the capital of a nation-state. Still others have elements of nationality and administrative rationale, like Andalusia, Alsace, Piedmont or Wallonia. Others again were conceived bureaucratically, yet appear to be rapidly acquiring a neo-national life of their own, like the Lyons-Grenoble (Rhônes-Alpes) conurbation in France, and Baden-Württemberg in Germany.

It is interesting, too, that in the endless debate about what constitutes a region, the mainstream European experience is that identity issues are paramount, rather than what might be considered more objective factors such as size or even geography. In England it seems to be assumed that a region must have a significant population running to millions. Hence the smallest of the ten regions defined by the new integrated regional offices is the North-East, with just over three million inhabitants, while the largest is the South-East (outside London) with nearly eight million people.

In continental Europe a different tradition prevails. In Italy seven regions (for example, Umbra) have a population of less than a million, while four (for example, Lombardy) have a population of five million. In Germany the city-state of Bremen has a population of 667,000, while North Rhine Westphalia has a population of nearly 17 million. In Spain La Rioja has a population of 263,000, while Catalonia has a population of just over six million.

However the components are defined, this mosaic is creating the idea of a 'Europe of the Regions', a structure fit for the twenty-first century rather than the nation-state Europe with its roots in the nineteenth. Accelerated European economic and political integration has resulted in the redrawing of the boundaries between market and state. The Single European Market has effectively undermined traditional nation-state regional policy and promoted the region to a more autonomous presence, not just in the European market but in the global market as well.

Within Europe, the region has been recognised institutionally with the establishment of the Committee of the Regions. This Committee is now pressing to be given equal status with the other European Union institutions, alongside the European Parliament, the Council of Ministers, the Commission, the Court of Justice, and the Court of Auditors. A paper drawn up for presentation to the 1996 Intergovernmental Conference (IGC) on revising the Maastricht Treaty, by the President of the Committee of the Regions, Catalonia's President Jordi Pujol, is also calling for a revision of the Treaty in the key area of subsidiarity. It wants a re-wording of the second paragraph of Article 3b of the Treaty of the Union to include specific reference to the role of the regions:

> The Community shall take action, in accordance with the principle of subsidiarity, only if and in so far as the objectives of the proposed action cannot be sufficiently achieved by the Member States, or by the Regions and local authorities endowed with powers under the domestic legislation of the Member State in question.[18]

The Europe of the Regions remains a fluid and unfocused notion, a direction of the will rather than a blueprint. No one map can capture its sense. Yet it is on the map in the 1990s in a concrete economic way that was only dimly perceived in the 1970s, certainly so far as England is concerned. And at least one aspect of the direction now seems unmistakable: a transcendence of the rigidities of big, upper-case Nation-State nationalism by the flexibilities of small, lower-case regionalism.

Notes

1 See the *Western Mail*, 3 July 1995 which, recording the Campaign's inaugural meeting, reports that it 'ditched its provisional title – CARP (Labour Campaign for an Assembly with Real Powers) – in order to fall into line with a Scottish campaign with similar aims, Scottish Labour Action'.

2 The interview was conducted by Philip Cooke and first published as 'Nationalisms and Popular Socialism' in *Radical Wales*, Vol.2 (Spring 1984), Cardiff: Plaid Cymru. It was reprinted as 'Decentralism and the Politics of Place', in Raymond Williams, *Resources of Hope*, London: Verso, 1989.

3 Named after the Labour MP Tam Dalyell's West Lothian constituency, this draws attention to the anomaly that in a devolved Wales and Scotland, Welsh and Scottish MPs at Westminster would continue to be able to vote on English matters concerning education, the health service and so on, whereas English MPs would not be able to vote on the same matters as they apply to Wales and Scotland. Yet, as the peoples of Wales and Scotland know only too well, MPs at Westminster are continually voting on matters that do not affect their own constituents' interests. In any event it would be surprising if a convention did not emerge that, whenever specifically English concerns were debated and voted upon, Welsh and Scottish MPs would refrain from participating. This would allow England to pursue divergent policies in such fields as education and the health service. Therein lies the problem for Labour centralists. However, to state the problem only demonstrates the reality that over-rigid symmetry in constitutional structures can be a negation rather than enhancement of genuine democracy.

4 *Devolution: The English Dimension - A Consultative Document*, London: HMSO, December 1976.

5 Labour Regional Policy Working Group, *Alternative Regional Strategy: A Framework for Discussion*, London: the Labour Party, September 1982.

6 Business in the Community and Coopers & Lybrand, *Lessons from Continental Europe: Promoting Partnership for Local Economic Development and Business Support in the UK*, London: Business in the Community, 1992.

7 David Hunt, then Secretary of State for Employment, speech to the Institute of Directors, February 1994.

8 *Independent on Sunday*, 5 February 1995.

9 *Hansard*, Vol 252, Col 275, 16 January 1995.

10 Howard Davies, speech to regional newspaper editors, London, 6 February 1995.

11 Stephen Tindale, *Devolution on Demand — Options for the English Regions and London*, London: IPPR, May 1995.

12 Raymond Williams, 'Wales and England,' in John Osmond (ed.), *The National Question Again —Welsh Political Identity in the 1980s*, Llandysul: Gomer, 1985, p.18.

13 Stephen Tindale, *op. cit.*, pp. 9-10.

14 Robert D Putnam, *Making Democracy Work — Civic Traditions in Modern Italy*, Princeton: Princeton University Press, 1993, p.181.

15 Audit Commission Report, *A Rough Guide to Europe*, London: HMSO, December 1991, p. 40.

16 *A Choice for England —A Consultation Paper on Labour's Plans for English Regional Government*, London: The Labour Party, July 1995.

17 See, for instance, the paper produced by Michael Storper of the Lewis Center for Regional Policy Studies, University of California, in September 1991, 'Technology Districts and International Trade – The Limits to Globalization in an Age of Flexible production'.

18 European Union Committee of the Regions, *Opinion on the Revision of the Treaty on European Union*, Brussels, 20 April 1995.

Interstitial Sovereignty, or Fleas and Elephants: Micro-sovereignty in the New World Order

Tom Nairn

Micro-nationalism

Between 1789 and 1989, tiny states were mainly a joke: 'relics', 'fossils' or (often) something more unsavoury, like tax-havens (Liechtenstein), unseemly foci of conspicuous consumption (Monaco), or vulgar pustules of duty-free commerce (Andorra). There seemed no place (or only a deplorable place) for such survivals in the age of nationalism.

During that age, nations were allowed to be small (Luxembourg, Iceland) but there were certain limits. The limits were set by what were regarded as the basic developmental tasks which nations (serious or 'real' nations) had to assume. Such tasks were resumed in the concept of 'viability'. Real independence demanded viability, which tended in practice to mean a certain minimum scale. Mini-states like the two mentioned were only just within the (oddly shrinkable) limits established by the common sense of the international order, but they could always be smuggled in: unimportant exceptions to every rule, etc.

Common sense is no longer what she was. The rules seem to be changing. In April 1993, the voters of Andorra (with a population of 54,500, mostly foreigners) voted themselves a new democratic constitution by a 75 per cent majority, and two months later the country was admitted as a full member of UNO. The old 'Co-Princes' (President Mitterand and the Bishop

Eberhard Bort and Neil Evans (eds), *Networking Europe*, Liverpool University Press 2000, 101-108.

of Urgell in Spain) found their sovereignty removed. They had been transformed overnight into figurehead monarchs whose sole remaining duty was to safeguard the new constitution (with the framing of which they had little to do, and which the Bishop had sternly opposed).

Odder still: Andorra is not 'in Europe', and probably never will be. By the new commercial accord which will regulate its relationship with the European Community, it is in effect a duty-free ship moored permanently in the middle of the Pyrenees. Within this minuscule Singapore none of the EU's tax, citizenship and social rules apply. Until 1993, the statelet had Home Rule, and got the best of both worlds from France and Spain. Now it has Independence, gets the best of all worlds from Community Europe as a whole, and is even admitted to the Council of Europe. Not bad for a despicable relic of feudal times.

Before the first Independence elections in December 1993, a caretaker government ran things under the premiership of Oscar Ribas Reig. His view of Andorra's Euro-future is worth citing here:

> We are in but not of Europe. Our identity would be submerged by joining Europe as it stands. Yet we remain European, and wholly dependent on Europe. This anomaly is resolvable only through a common approach to the EC by all the micro-states together. What it demands is a general understanding and regulation of our differences. My government intends to pursue this policy...

Microstates of the world, unite; you have nothing to lose but your privileges and your identities. What Ribas Reig looks forward to is a Europe of anomalies – a 'common house' in which all rooms will not necessarily be open to everyone, and the same rules – notably the same economic rules – need not apply to all. This is more or less the contrary of 'the European dream' stemming from the Treaty of Rome and culminating somewhat dismally in the Treaties of Maastricht and Amsterdam: free trade, common currency, the unhindered movement of both capital and people and then – on this supposedly solid economic foundation – a common citizenship and politico-cultural community.

Beyond Viability

The post-1989 world has been dominated by the disappearance of Communism and the second coming of nationalism in the East. Yet here is an example of newly emergent national independence in the West – one not so easily compatible with the received idea of the East falling apart while the West sagely unites. A tiny example, of course. All the miniature states together would still be in some ways insignificant. But it is not clear that the implications are so insignificant.

No one ever dreamt that Andorra, San Marino or Jersey could be 'viable'. But what if 'viability' itself no longer means anything? Since 1989 the economy has been effectively globalised for the first time. All economic and social modernisation must henceforth proceed in global, or globally-conditioned, terms. Maybe this was always true, but now it seems indisputably true: there are no other 'viable' alternatives. The retrospective tragicomedy of Socialism in One Country (or more precisely, One Empire) is the proof of this.

Judged by the old viability-theory, the implication seems to be that political independence is thenceforth meaningless. Divorced from genuinely separate and distinctive development, sovereignty can serve no purpose. Nationalist mobilisation now really is what Marxists used to say it was: a snare and diversion, concealing the mounting hegemony of Big (global) Business. If the big battalions have really triumphed, then the duty of the small must be to surrender and stop pestering humanity.

Tell that to the Andorrans! The new Minister of Culture there pointed out to me that an exactly contrary reading of the same post-1989 changes is possible – more or less the one which prevailed in Andorra in April 1993. It goes like this: because all peoples are now so inescapably bound into a single world of socio-economic development, political freedom will become more significant, and not less. Precisely because sovereignty is thus circumscribed, what remains of it is more vital than ever before. Far from surrendering to progress, therefore, smaller peoples and less advantaged regions must assert themselves more vigorously. Politics is their one key to survival. What matters is no longer 'viability' but democratically-affirmed constitutionality. That alone can provide the necessary minimum of power, leverage and dissent within a global economy ruled (inevitably) by large-scale transnational forces.

In the new order, therefore, scale itself may count for less. The small (Slovenia, Wales, Euzkadi, Estonia), the very small (Luxembourg, Wallonia, Ulster, Corsica) and the minuscule (Andorra, Isle of Man, Gibraltar) share common concerns within the new configuration. For all of them the 'one world' following 1989 could mean emancipation, rather than effacement. Since the economic question has been (in a deep or structural sense) resolved by market capitalism, the common politico-cultural question is how to negotiate a future inside that fate. Just how many people are involved in each negotiation, and over how large an area, may no longer be so important a question.

Closure to Openness

Autarchy was the limiting case of 'viability'. Micro-states may be the limiting cases of post-viability. During the Age of Nationalism closure – or partial closure – was a condition of development, and first-cycle nationalism was one aspect of that. Post-1989, with the economic problem settled in principle (though not of course in practice), such closure has become impossible to be conceived as a general model of modernisation. At the deepest, strategic level, societies have no option but to swim in the single ongoing tide of victorious market capitalism.

There is an interesting contrast between these limiting cases. Autarchy (like Free Trade) was a theoretical construction. No truly autarchic society ever existed. But tiny states exist all right, and a remarkable number have persisted through the 1789-1989 period. There are six in Western Europe.[1] Along with Switzerland, they are the most prosperous of European societies. Without falling into 'Small is Beautiful' sentimentality, one may wonder if (as so often assumed) they constitute a mere flea-circus.[2] Or could it be that the hour of the flea has come at last?

Consider the flea. Very small states are almost necessarily 'open societies'. In an extreme and obvious sense, their existence depends upon symbiosis. They can neither take anyone else over nor shut themselves off into a purified nationalist world of their own. But as such they can be seen as posing a new question. Are they marginal relics and oddities – or are they model (if extreme-case) entities? Where all (even the USA) have become relatively small, does the flea have anything to be particularly ashamed of? We ought to be studying them more seriously.

There is a longer-range historical reason for doing so. So far I have been considering only the age of big nationalism. Before 1789, of course, there were a large number of mini- and micro-states in Europe. Indeed the central ideological current of Enlightenment Europeanism flowed from distinctly flea-like origins in the Italian Renaissance and, before that, from an Antiquity composed of tiny statelets. That was the current then magnified and borne around the globe by new, bigger states like France and Britain. However, if the big battalions have now done their main developmental work, is it not legitimate to expect a return of the small?

Eastern Smallness

The familiar examples of miniature statehood are in the West. There are, however, three situations (or problems) in Central-Eastern Europe which on the face of it seem to call for some form of micro-sovereignty: Sarajevo, Trieste and Kaliningrad.

The wars in Bosnia have made Sarajevo the most famous of these cases. In his plea for a solution to the conflict there, George Soros argued that Sarajevo should be saved from Great-Serb assimilation and transformed into a 'beacon of the Open Society' in Eastern Europe.[3] Shortly after his talk, an agreement was reached to keep the city and its surrounding area under UNO's protection for a period of two years, while the final division of Bosnia was settled. What are the implications of the argument, and of this situation? While a United Nations protectorate may provide a temporary solution (and may last longer than two years), nobody thinks of it as permanent. But what could permanence consist in? It would have to be some form of statehood, presumably founded on a treaty and guaranteed by the international community of states. Such a state would also have to be supported by the Sarajevans: like Andorra, it would need a written constitution, a referendum, and all the normal democratic forms.

It is not clear at all whether these are realisable aims in practice, in this particular case. But what needs also to be considered is the background of principle and theory. On that plane, too, there are obstacles in the way. The existing assumptions of international relations may not prevent micro-state formation, but they certainly do not favour it. There is nothing surprising about that. The new international order is mainly a by-product of the 1789-1989 epoch, farther rigidified by half a century of Cold War. Nation-state self-determination is its backbone. The template it works with is basically an elephantine one, even although the Wilsonian doctrine of 1917 and later did allow smaller and smaller elephants to accede to respectability.

Elephantiasis also remains dominant in the field of theory. The theory of nationality politics quite naturally takes the nation (ethnos or culture, real or invented, eternal or fleeting) as its unit. Nationalism assumes an entity viable in national terms: a territory of a certain size, speaking a language, normally with peasants and folksongs, aiming to modernise in its own terms – and so on. Great advances have been made in understanding the dynamics of this process. It is no criticism of these to point out that they do not deal with the question of very small, non-ethnic or interstitial sovereignty. But the effect is that neither international relations nor its current theory have any ready formula or model to apply to such cases. They remain 'accidents', 'survivals', or 'anomalies' to be either reabsorbed into the standard norms or handled in a quite *ad hoc* fashion.

The most striking historical example of this is given by Trieste. A Habsburg 'New Town', planted at the top of the Adriatic in the nineteenth century, Trst/Trieste was meant to be the Empire's main seaport. It had (and still has) a mixed population of Slovenes, Italians, Croats, Greeks, Jews and Germans. Stranded by the break-up of Danubia in 1918, the city and its hinterland were seized by the Italians as part of the post-First World War settlement. During the Fascist period it was of course forcibly Italianised; then in 1944 equally forcibly cleaned up in the other direction during a brief occupation by Tito's army. The Allied Army of Occupation then ran the enclave for about ten years, until a treaty assigned it back to Italy in 1954.

In the perspective of this short paper, the most interesting feature of that period was the plan for a kind of *de facto* independence put forward by the Allied Administration. It could see no future for the place except as a free port, with an externally guaranteed local government. The aim – in truth the only aim which makes any sense there – was to try and re-utilise the city's location and means of communication as 'the seaport of *Mitteleuropa*', the 'gateway to the East' (and so on). Regrettably, this plan was foiled by Cold War priorities. The line had to be drawn, Trieste had to be in the West (which meant Italy), and that was that. Fifty years on, the line has gone, Slovenia has taken over from Yugoslavia, but Trieste remains on the extreme periphery of a disintegrating Italy, all its problems unresolved. It too could be a beacon. At the moment it remains a pretty feeble Italian glowworm.

The third case is the Kaliningrad exclave, where another historic city, Prussian Königsberg, has been isolated between Russia, Poland and the newly independent Lithuania. It is not even on the periphery of, but actually outside its former Motherland, contemplating a future which looks fairly hopeless and conflictual unless a self-rule formula can be found.

City-state Futures

For reasons indicated above, small or tiny states are likely to be inherently open, civil and often poly-ethnic too. The extent to which Sarajevo, Kaliningrad and Trieste evolve in that direction will be a prime example of the possibility and the general conditions for micro-sovereignty and interstitial sovereignty in the new order, particularly in Eastern Europe. Interstitial sovereignty seems appropriate as a term in discussing small sovereignty-situations which are lodged among or between others. Fleas tend naturally to find themselves thus lodged. Andorra's long history depended on playing off French against Spanish sovereignty; Gibraltar's new history will hinge on doing the same with Britain and Spain; all three eastern examples find themselves in similar dilemmas.[4]

Also, as far as policy influences are concerned, one would have thought there might be definite advantages in trying to effect change on such a relatively small scale, as compared to over half a continent.

Notes

1 'Andorra, Monaco, San Marino, Liechtenstein, Jersey and the Isle of Man. Gibraltar will probably soon make a seventh.

2 In the flea-stereotype their relationship to the elephant-world is usually dismissed as parasitism, exploitation or straightforward crime.

3 Broadcast on UK Channel 4 'Opinions' series, August 1993, text published in *The Times* and other places.

4 Perhaps the most striking recent case (but outside the range of this paper) was the Falkland/Malvinas conflict. Those who suggested at the time the sole way out was artificial statehood for the islanders were derided. Was it not obvious that independence for just 2,000 people on a few barren rocks would always be wholly unviable?

II

Women in a Wales Without Miners

Jane Aaron

In 1987, Gwyn A Williams electrified the delegates to the National Federation of Women's Institutes in Wales with an account of an apparent revolution in contemporary Welsh employment patterns. He concluded his address by telling them:

> I don't know whether it is still possible to talk of a working class in Wales. But if it is, then the working class of Wales is a working class of women. This is the most explosive social revolution to have occurred in Wales for 200 years. This is a fundamental transformation which has not yet registered on the public mind ... In Wales, this is a world turned upside down.[1]

He was referring to the manner in which the fall in male employment figures in Wales during the 1980s – the consequence of the speeded-up demise of Wales' traditional heavy industries – was accompanied by a sharp rise in female employment. According to statistical records, there are now, for the first time in recorded history, more women than men in paid work in Wales. But Teresa Rees, in a recent article, queries Professor Williams' apocalyptic rhetoric in the above passage, and argues that the recent changes in male and female employment patterns are not in fact as revolutionary as he suggested.[2] She points out that women have, of course, always worked in Wales, but that a great deal of their labours have not previously figured in the statistical registers of employment. Neither they themselves nor their societies rated their contribution as workers. We find plenty of examples of this syndrome within the pages of Wales' literary heritage. A novel set in the first decades of this century, for example, Caradog Prichard's classic *Un Nos Ola Leuad*, represents its boy narrator as

Eberhard Bort and Neil Evans (eds), *Networking Europe*, Liverpool University Press 2000, 111-27.

dependent for his livelihood on the meagre earnings of his single parent mother as a washerwoman.[3] Today's statisticians would register her as 'self-employed within the heavy service industries', but in the novel itself her identity as valiant family breadwinner is entirely subsumed under her other identity as mother: she is 'Mam', not 'a worker'. No glamour, and little recognition, has previously been attached to women's work and poor relief.

In terms of the type of work available to the majority of Welsh women today, and the social status attached to that work, little has in fact changed. Welsh women are still largely employed in untrained low-paid jobs, and 45 per cent of them are still only able to find part-time employment. Even though on average a woman only absents herself from the workforce for child-bearing purposes for seven out of her likely forty-odd years of employment, girls' career choices and the attitudes of their prospective employers are still governed by the notion of women as primarily mothers. Consequently, the expenditure of in-work training is deemed less profitable in their case; they are less likely than men to be appointed to jobs with a clear career path, and less likely to be promoted if they do manage to secure such a position. Gender segregation still operates within the workforce, with a concentration of women in the service industries and in low-paid office work. But two things have changed, fundamentally. Firstly women's paid work, however fragmentary, is now more likely to be entered on employment records and is therefore more quantifiable and more noticeable. Secondly, not only are male employment figures relatively low, but that icon of labour which featured so largely in Wales' representation of itself to the world – the coal miner – has virtually disappeared. With the notable exception of the worker-owned Tower Colliery at Hirwaun, the deep mines of south Wales have closed, and have left behind them a vacuum, not only in terms of employment prospects but also in the way in which the Welsh see themselves.

Commenting on the changes in male employment in a recent essay, Merfyn Jones emphasises their traumatic suddenness: in Wales during the 1980s 'a whole economic and industrial trajectory, established during the Industrial Revolution, was ...

dissolved in one decade'. This dissolution, he argues, had far-reaching consequences for the Welsh sense of identity:

> the abrupt creation of a Wales without miners devastated far more than the mining communities themselves. It also punctured a whole nexus of images and self-images of the Welsh ... Paid work in industrial Wales had been men's work, and the Welsh identity ... resonated with masculinity ... The considerable alteration in employment patterns discernible in Wales meant that ... a Welsh woman's identity had now to be allowed for, an identity deeply disruptive of traditional male assumptions.[4]

The advent of the new era is envisaged with some anxiety in this passage. Aspects of its phraseology – 'a Welsh women's identity had now to be allowed for,' for example – sound somewhat begrudging, and some fear is suggested by the notion that when this identity emerges it will necessarily be 'deeply disruptive'. The Welsh woman is apparently about to arise like some traumatic return of the repressed, and take vengeance upon the males who have rendered her invisible for so long. Now that the rock of the miner's image has been rolled away from its previous pre-eminence as identity figure-head, Welsh social historians and sociologists are anxiously training their analytic spotlights on the vast hole left exposed. What they – with some trepidation – are finding there, emerging at last from the murky depths into the light of public attention, is women, hard at work, as they ever were. But to be fair to the male historians, in some cases there is no suggestion of apprehension in their comments upon the new situation. For Gwyn A Williams, for example, it seems to have been more a matter of 'well, if we can no longer have our Welsh heroes, then let us by all means have our Welsh heroines. The miner is dead: long live the miner's wife.'

But if the miner's wife has suddenly acquired a status other than that of the stereotypical 'Mam', then what is she? Who is she? What are her characteristic passions and pursuits, her equivalents of the rugby, the male-voice choirs, the miners' libraries, the trade-union politics – all those features which added colour and definition to Welsh identity but which were so very definitely men-only concerns? Women in Wales bear a heavy responsibility at the moment. Not only are they now in many cases the economic as well as domestic mainstay of their families, but they are also being asked to construct for themselves, and make apparent to the world, social and cultural identities which will fill the gaping void in the Welsh self-image.

A number of factors, I would suggest, render it difficult for them to do so. Firstly, lack of time and lack of energy after the sheer exhaustion of a typical working day. The miner's leisure hours may have been few but at least they were his own. The woman worker, on the other hand, returns from her job to more domestic labour: her greater involvement in paid employment has not been accompanied in the United Kingdom by substantial changes in the provision of state or work-based child care, or by a significant redistribution of duties within the home. Jane Pilcher, in a recent essay, shows that though Welsh women are by now eager in theory to share household duties with male partners, most find it difficult to instigate egalitarian practice in reality. Unlike some of the mothers and virtually all the grandmothers she interviewed, the younger women Pilcher spoke to were happy to laugh away the old-fashioned notion that the performance of domestic chores was a necessary ingredient of feminine identity and an emasculating threat for males. Nevertheless, analyses of their reported domestic arrangements indicate that these women continue to bear the main responsibility for house-work. Pilcher concludes, 'Younger generations of Welsh women may no longer be investing their feminine identities in the domestic sphere to the same extent as older generations; nevertheless, they seem likely to continue to invest their time and effort, alongside participation in paid employment.'[5]

As for the problems presented by the lack of alternative child care, the Swansea performance poet Penny Windsor included in her first verse collection a poem which humorously, and yet with anger, conveys the plight of the working mother. In 'Latch-Key Kid', a modern Mam attends a job interview:

> 'But what will you do in the holidays?' the interviewer said
> What indeed?
> What was there to do with my sweet-natured, latch-key kid
> but deny her existence?

or rent or invent a granny or mother-in-law
or give up the idea of working at all?
'My first husband takes her to stay,' I lied,
as though the country was crowded with cast-off husbands
of mine
'we're on excellent terms.'
I smooth down the fold of my pinafore dress
and blink at my brand new past.
The man rumbles on, like far away thunder,
'and after school, half-term, what happens then?'

Ah, what happens then?

I flick through the years
playgroups and nurseries, childminders, neighbours and
friends,
the impossible places reached on lumbering, always-late
buses,
the hours that never quite matched with the hours at work,
the guilt,
the hum of exhaustion like telephone wires in the wind.

'My sister' I said, 'she takes her',
'She lives down the road,
and my aunt on occasion, next door but one,
but anyway, Gran's in the attic...'[6]

But though she proceeds apace with a flow of colourful fictions intended to reassure her prospective boss, she does not get the job.

Penny Windsor's poem points to a number of identifying traits in the situation of the contemporary Welsh working mother. Firstly, the extended family of unemployed older female relations, who could previously have been relied upon to provide child care assistance, has been much eroded, through the fragmentation of previously stable communities and because those older women are often now themselves in employment. In their absence, the unfortunate interviewee desperately has to invent them. Not only does she have to conjure up a fictional support system, but she also has to dissemble her own fatigue – 'the hum of exhaustion like telephone wires in the wind'. Neither she nor her prospective employer appear to consider the possibility that her child care problem might be in any way his responsibility, or the responsibility of the state; it is her own personal problem, which she must sort out if she is to compete satisfactorily in a job market overstocked with unemployed candidates. And given that she is looking for employment in a country in which the average female wage is only 65 per cent of average male earnings – a ratio which is amongst the lowest in the European Community – her chances of finding work which will allow her to pay for adequate private child care are slender. But to get the job which represents the only way out of the poverty trap for herself and her child, she has to make her situation as a working mother appear one she can easily, light-heartedly, cope with – nothing to it, nothing heroic about it. Under such circumstances it is difficult for women themselves, as well as their society, to get a clear view of their situation and to see the political dimensions of the personal dilemma.

A second feature of contemporary Welsh women's lives reflected in the poem has both negative and positive aspects, from the point of view of female liberation. The interviewee appears to be an unmarried mother: her 'first husband', like her sister and 'Gran', seems to have been invented – 'I blink at my brand new past,' she says. As such she can be considered representative of a population in which, in 1992, over half the live births occurred out of wedlock. These figures, like the employment records, represent a relatively sudden and dramatic change: just over a decade previously, in 1980, only one child out of eleven was born illegitimate in Wales.[7] The frequency of illegitimate births has eroded the moral stigma traditionally associated with both mother and child (but not father) in such cases. The woman in Penny Windsor's poem invents a spouse for practical reasons, rather than to defend herself against possible accusations of personal impropriety. She experiences guilt feelings because she's afraid that her work commitments mean that she does not have the time to be a good-enough mother, not because she is a single mother.

This does constitute a major change from past attitudes. In the nineteenth and early twentieth century unmarried mothers were the particular scourge of a Welsh chapel culture eager to establish itself, in English eyes, as formidably respectable if nonconformist. Scenes in which the erring 'fallen woman' was viciously expelled from chapel membership became a characteristic feature of the fiction of the period.[8] But, in 1993, the attacks of the then Secretary of State for Wales, John Redwood, on Welsh single mothers were generally greeted with anger. His attempts to reawaken, in the mothers themselves and in the populace at large, the old bitter idea of illegitimacy as a sign of disgrace and libidinous irresponsibility received very little support. They seemed, if anything, to backfire against him, and to increase his marked unpopularity as the mouthpiece of a hard right Conservatism intent upon reinforcing blatantly Victorian values, rather than to tarnish contemporary Wales' view of its women.

Before launching such a campaign, Redwood must presumably have assumed that the history of the retention of the Victorian double sexual standard into mid-twentieth-century life in Wales meant that his project would receive popular support: the fact that it very definitely did not is a marker of significant, and in this case liberating, social change. It was a change welcomed in many cultural contexts a decade before Redwood's ill-chosen stand. The poet John Tripp, for example, in an early 1980s poem, hailed with relief the arrival of the overtly sexually liberated 'New Welsh Woman':

> I see her often
> in places where the blinds
> are no longer drawn, where light
> comes flooding into rooms.
> ....
> She is a sex grenade
> hurled out of the dust
> of Victorian diaries, and the frightened lust
> of her long-dead sisters.
>
> 'I bet you think I'm shocking,' she says...
> 'On the contrary,' I reply;
> 'Where have you been hiding for centuries?'[9]

Nevertheless, for all this increased openness on the sexual front, the woman in Penny Windsor's poem is still forced to dissemble her private life in order to survive. Because the change in sexual morality has not gone hand in hand with political change – with, say, the establishment of state nurseries for all under-school-age children – the life of an unmarried mother in Wales today is often likely to be as hard, and as thwarted in terms of the possibilities of her fulfilling her potential, as the life of her great-grandmother. 64.7 per cent of single mothers in Wales were without paid work in 1991.[10] These women's enforced reliance upon the arbitrarily changing regulations and restrictions of the Department of Social Security can be as personally frustrating and demeaning as any Victorian woman's dependence upon a male domestic tyrant. And if the single mother does have a lucky break, manages to find a job, and enters upon the whirligig of making-do and patching up of work and child care described by Windsor, it is unlikely that the conditions of her employment will help her to see her plight in political rather than personal terms. The daily working circumstances in typical female jobs do not facilitate the mobilisation of a general outrage against the conditions forced upon the employees. Service industries, office work, small businesses, home work, or part-time factory work – none of these provide the kind of opportunities which went to form traditional working-class confrontational politics. Massed male workers in the old heavy industries may have been unintentionally supplied with working conditions which facilitated the dissemination of shared awareness of oppression and the bonding recognition of shared frustrations and concerns, but the home-worker, the isolated secretarial assistant, or the harassed part-time worker desperately dashing from work to home to look after her children, is not so fortuitously placed.

But, it may be asked, why has the post-1960s feminist movement not done more to provide women generally with a clear-cut perspective from which to conceive of the personal as the political, and to protest more vociferously than they now do against such conditions? Why has it not succeeded in overtly politicising Gwyn A Williams' new working class of women? The answer to this question no doubt lies partly in the middle-class image of contemporary feminism; in Wales, it has been suggested that it might also have to do with the perception of the movement as an alien Anglo-American phenomenon.[11] The particular slant of recent anti-feminist propaganda may also be in part to blame: during the 1980s, the backlash against feminism tarnished its image by means of campaigns which succeeded in associating the movement in the public mind with an exaggeratedly anti-male animosity. It is difficult for women living under conditions of heavy male unemployment, in which the situations of their fathers, brothers, husbands or lovers are at least as dire as their own, to adopt such politics without modification, whatever they may feel about the domestic behaviour of their male acquaintance. It is easy to see why Welsh women en masse, and particularly south Wales women, might feel more inclined to group together in defence of their men rather than to take up arms against them. The out-of-work male may well feel depressively envious of his female partner's increased job opportunities, pitiful as they are, and is more likely to be an object of her concern rather than of her hatred. An honourable sense of the impossibility of 'hitting a man when he's down' may well check a woman in the expression both of any new measure of self-assertiveness she may have gained from her employment and of her grievance at the double burden she now has to carry.

It is hardly surprising, therefore, that the phenomena which probably did most to politicise the women of Wales during the 1980s was not the feminist movement per se, but the 1984-85 miners' strike and the 1985-86 north Wales slate quarry workers' strike. Women's participation in the support groups which rallied to the strikers' aid constituted for many their first awakening to the possibilities of public political protest. Although few literary publications by women emerged out of these disputes, the quarry workers' support group published a bilingual volume to commemorate their struggle[12] and, in 1986, the Women's Press produced a text which effectively records the feelings and experiences of the many Welsh women who were mobilised during the strike years. Jill Miller's *You Can't Kill the Spirit: Women in a Welsh Mining Valley* is a collection of oral records of the miners' strike and its consequences. Its all-female contributors are univocal on the benefits which, paradoxically enough, the strike brought with it. Nita, for example, says:

> I didn't get educated until I joined the women's group ... there were incredible gains. One of them was making the men see us all in a different light, and gaining their respect, and we didn't need to burn our bras to do it. No one had given us a second look before, or taken any notice of us around serious matters ... I spoke at a rally in Reading ... It was unbelievable: this ordinary woman who liked to sit in the house knitting, was now going to speak in public.

The year of the strike is generally presented by the contributors as a year of awakening, an awakening into realisation of the role they were now called upon to play – after a lifetime of obscurity – in the public world of power struggles and political action. They had no guilty qualms about the huge gain in personal confidence many of them accrued from the experience, for they were fighting not primarily for themselves, but for their menfolk, and for the survival of their communities. Their strengthened sense of personal identity went hand in hand with a newfound pride in their community's identity, a pride which, for some of the women, was connected with a sharpened sense of Welshness. As Gwyneth expresses it:

> The [women's] group gave me a lot more confidence to express my feelings, thoughts and ideals. My ideas became much clearer, and as a result I was more determined that ever that we shouldn't and wouldn't give in to this government which was trying to destroy a community that took generations to build ... I'm proud to be a miner's wife, I'm proud to be part of that community. I'm proud to be Welsh too.[13]

Though the strike itself was, of course, defeated, in its aftermath the women's increased sense of community spirit and political consciousness was not readily dissipated. It found active expression in the many ventures for women's continuing development which were established, such as the Dove workshops in Banwen, the Valleys Initiative for the Employment of Women, and the South Glamorgan Women's Workshop. Co-operation is of the essence of these formations. Mike Jenkins, in a poem published in 1986, sees the women's co-operatives as the true continuum of the spirit of the Valleys, during a period otherwise marked by its betrayal. In the poem 'Print of the Valley', which is dedicated to the Bargoed Women's Co-operative, the speaker's desolation at seeing what used to be National Coal Board pits become privately-held museums is offset by his discovery, 'in another place', of:

> proud women stitching a green future
> over acres of waste.
> Rows of houses become chattering machines ...
> The print of the valley
> on every cloth.[14]

The greenness of the future the women are here depicted as working towards appears to constitute a reference to Welsh women's involvement in green politics, as well as community politics, and in particular, perhaps, to the Greenham Common movement. The 'Women for Life on Earth' march which led to the setting up of the first camp at Greenham was organised by women from south Wales, and started off from Cardiff. Many Welsh women lived at or visited the camp during the 1980s, and Greenham women reciprocated by allying themselves with the women's support groups during the strike years. References to the peace movement, and to green politics generally, are rife in both Welsh- and English-language women's poetry and prose. In 1985, a Welsh-language novel set in Greenham and narrated by one of the protesters won the Prose Medal at the National Eisteddfod, the Welsh equivalent of the Booker prize;[15] as for poetry, during the 1980s there was hardly a woman poet in Wales who did not have her Greenham poem, though the same could not have been said of her English equivalents.

But Welsh women's increased political awareness has not been channelled only into grassroots protest movements. For the first time in recorded history, more women than men voted Labour in Wales in the 1992 General Election, and a record number of 24 female candidates stood for election. Unemployment and the demise of international socialism may have had a demoralising effect on male voters, but women's increased participation in work, and maybe also some of Labour's recent policy changes (its drive to increase the number of women MPs, for example, and perhaps also its advocacy of at least some measure of devolution for Wales) seem to have strengthened Welsh women's affiliation with the socialist move-ment. It is as if the politicising experience of the miners' strike has awakened women to their role in that process which Raymond Williams described as characteristic of Welsh political life:

> that association between a specific understanding of community in terms of the extending obligations of neighbourhood, very much attached to a place, moving on through the sense of community under stress ... finding its collective institutions, and ... from that to a political movement which should be the establishment of higher relations of this kind.[16]

The sharpened sense of community, the formation of collective institutions to protect it, and then the strengthened allegiance to a political movement which is seen as having the community's interests at heart, are trends clearly perceivable in the recent political affiliations of contemporary Welsh women.

For all that, traditional Welsh communities can by no means be said to have offered women positive and liberated roles. Indeed, as two feminist critics, Gwyneth Roberts and Katie Gramich, have recently pointed out, Williams himself in his fictional works depicted women as paying a heavy price for their community loyalties.[17] Women may have been essential to the maintenance of the community, but they functioned to such an effect by their passive acceptance of secondary supporting roles. Yet, as the miners' strike women showed, it is not the community ethos in itself which holds women back, but the patriarchal attitudes entrenched within certain communities. The women's support group members experienced themselves as the overtly active upholders of the community rather than its passive, much-put-upon base.

At any rate, it can certainly be said that a sense of community is a characteristic feature of many contemporary Welsh texts by women; it is, for example, one of the distinguishing features in the work of a black woman writer from Cardiff, Leonora Brito, whose first collection of short stories has recently been published. In her tale 'Digging for Victory', a young black girl gains both an increased awareness of her community and a sense of that community as betrayed. The story is set in the early 1950s, and concerns a visit paid by Winston Churchill to the Cardiff Docklands. The warship in which he arrives manages to breech the dock walls, and the local people are called upon to help to dredge up the scrap iron left exposed by the training away of the canal waters. Churchill himself issues the call to arms:

> He was calling on all able-bodied persons to offer their services in what was shaping up to be a great task of reclamation ... 'This is a test of our national character ... Our resolve ... You should come prepared to toil, sweat' ... His voice continued to echo in the streets around us, right up as far as the green domed mosque in Sophia Street, where the words came out in Arabic.[18]

Though the heterogeneous nature of the community is thus concisely conveyed, all the inhabitants are required to show themselves true Brits and unite in the dredging effort. The narrator succumbs to Churchill's D-Day rhetoric, and at first is glad to have done so:

> As for me, I experienced a moment of happiness and contentment as I looked about me ... Here and there I saw coloured people, Docks people like myself, helping with the task in hand. It was just like the war-time, I thought, when Britain would have stood alone, if the Empire hadn't rushed to her aid. Jamaica was the first with the Spitfire fund! Our family would always remember that, and father had gloried in it.[19]

But her sister Teeny, who has already shown some spirit by refusing to seek office work in the whiter areas of Cardiff, preferring to take poorly-paid, heavy service jobs in the Docks, certainly does not glory in her sister's acquiescence:

> Teeny was unimpressed when I recounted my story to mother, late that night. 'The more fool you,' she chipped

> in. 'Fancy handing over all that scrap iron. I'd have kept it. You were entitled. It was a treasure trove.'
>
> 'But that's why Mr Churchill made his special appeal, Teeny,' I said. 'On behalf of the nation. All that stuff was needed. Urgently.'
>
> 'Needed for what?' she asked nastily. 'An iron curtain?'[20]

Here the racially varied communities of south Wales are shown as having been once again hoodwinked and stripped of their rightful property, their mineral assets, in the name of a British 'national character'. They gain nothing from the transaction but the expen-diture of their labour, and a hollow sense of bonding, induced by the entirely inappropriate summons as to war. Teeny's last reference to 'an iron curtain', in the context of the 1950s Cold War, implies that she perceives the Docks people as being bamboozled by call to arms against a Red enemy, which cuts directly against their own interests as a community exploited under capitalism.

The machinations of a nomad capitalist system, which, as Raymond Williams put it, 'exploits actual places and people and then (as it suits it) moves on,'[21] is also represented as an overwhelming threat to community life in another recent fictional work from south Wales, Christopher Meredith's *Shifts* (1988). In this novel, the deteriorating economic prospects of a blighted area are intricately interwoven with a study of shifting gender relations, in a manner which makes it a fitting text with which to conclude my essay. *Shifts,* a fictionalised representation of the closing down of the Ebbw Vale steel works in 1975, shows the steel workers, soon to lose their livelihood, as very much aware of the shifting patterns of male-female employment in the Valleys. In one scene, for example, two shift-workers consider their likely job prospects:

> 'They're opening a marshmallow factory on the industrial estate' Wayne said.
>
> 'It's the married blokes I do feel sorry for' Sully said.
>
> 'Fifty jobs' Wayne said. 'Don' feel sorry. They'll probably on'y take on women. Some of us will live off our wives.'[22]

The consequences for men and women of such a major change in the traditional gender role pattern are foreshadowed in this text by the portrayal of one of the steel-workers' unconventional marriage. Keith, the novel's chief protagonist, refuses to adopt the stereotypical macho role, even in the face of his wife Jude's affair with his friend and lodger Jack. He takes no retaliatory action, and his passivity eventually communicates itself to his wife not as indifference but as a free offering to her of the opportunity to evolve.

Hitherto, part of the attraction of her affair with Jack lay for Jude in the possibility it offered of escape from a decaying existence; she experiences her life, both within her marriage and within the valley community, as 'being trapped with a failing machine, and no morphine.' But by the close of the novel, when she finally rejects Jack's suggestion that she leave the area with him, Jude has come to see that what she most desires and needs to do is to develop her own sense of identity. Neither of the two men, she feels, have 'got anything to do with me' – that is, with her central self – but Keith's attitude allows her more space in which to develop. From this perspective, the dying Valley itself is transformed under her gaze:

> The map of clouds were softer, golder, the ridges hazier, admitting of more possibilities than before. Briefly ... she felt only the great space.[23]

Jude's relative detachment from both of her lovers is necessary in a world in which she will no longer be presented with the seductive opportunity of shaping her sense of identity around a dominant and central male figure. Like many another housewife of the early 1970s, Jude has hitherto been economically entirely dependent upon her husband, but at the close of the novel she looks forward to a future in which she, rather than the by now unemployed Keith, will be the family bread-winner. The text implies that the space opened up before her by the passing away of the macho male image is a space for new possibilities, not an empty vacuum. This space, not previously enjoyed by the Valleys woman, is of course to some extent a development forced upon her by circumstances rather than one which the woman herself has deliberately chosen, and yet it is one which potentially represents the dawn of more egalitarian possibilities for both men and women. But the opportunities it offers will only reap positive results in terms of heterosexual relations if Welsh men generally, like the central character of Meredith's novel, can trust women sufficiently to accept without rancour the prospective evolution of their independent identities.

Notes

1 Gwyn A Williams, quoted in Teresa Rees, 'Changing Patterns of Women's Work in Wales: Some Myths Explored', in *Contemporary Wales*, Vol.2, 1988, pp.126-27, from a *Western Mail* report of the W.I. meeting (24 April, 1987). For a detailed account of the shifting patterns in Welsh women's employment, see Gwyn A Williams, 'Women Workers in Wales, 1968-82', in *Welsh History Review*, Vol.11, 1982-83, pp.530-48.

2 Teresa Rees, *op. cit.*, pp.126-28.

3 Caradog Prichard, *Un Nos Ola Leuad*, Dinbych: Gwasg Gee, 1961; trans. Menna Gallie, *Full Moon*, London: Hodder and Stoughton, 1973, and Philip Mitchell, *One Moonlit Night*, Edinburgh: Canongate Books, 1995.

4 R Merfyn Jones, 'Beyond Identity? The Reconstruction of the Welsh', in *Journal of British Studies*, Vol.31, 1992, pp.347 and 349.

5 Jane Pilcher, 'Who Should Do the Dishes? Three Generations of Welsh Women Talking about Men and Housework', in Jane Aaron, Teresa Rees, Sandra Betts and Moira Vincentelli (eds), *Our Sisters' Land: The Changing Identities of Women in Wales*, Cardiff: University of Wales Press, 1994, p.45.

6 Penny Windsor, 'Latch-key Kid', in *Dangerous Women*, Dinas Powys: Honno Press, 1987, pp.37-38.

7 For a record of these figures, see John May (comp.), *Reference Wales*, Cardiff: University of Wales Press, 1994, pp.21-22.

8 See, for example, Eleazar Roberts, *Owen Rees: A Story of Welsh Life and Thought*, London: Elliot Stock, 1894, pp.302-15; or Richard Llewellyn, *How Green was my Valley*, London: Michael Joseph, 1939, pp.102-08.

9 John Tripp, 'Mrs Pankhurst's Granddaughter', in *Passing Through*, Bridgend: Poetry Wales Press, 1984, p.52.

10 See Sandra Betts, 'The Changing Family in Wales', in *Our Sisters' Land*, p.21.

11 See Ceridwen Lloyd-Morgan, 'From pre- to post-feminism?', in *Planet*, 99 , 1993, pp.22-25.

12 Quarry Workers Support Group, *Safwn gyda'n gilydd/We stand together*, Blaenau Ffestiniog, n.d.

13 Jill Miller, *You Can't Kill the Spirit: Women in a Welsh Mining Valley*, London: Women's Press, 1986, pp. 35,37,106,110.

14 Mike Jenkins, 'Print of the Valley (For the Bargoed Women's Co-operative)', in *Invisible Times*, Bridgend: Poetry Wales Press, 1986, p.22.

15 Meg Elis, *Cyn Daw'r Gaeaf* (Before Winter Comes), Talybont: Y Lolfa, 1985.

16 Raymond Williams, 'The Importance of Community', in *Resources of Hope*, London: Verso, 1989, p.113.

17 See Gwyneth Roberts, 'The Cost of Community: Women in Raymond Williams's Fiction', in *Our Sisters' Land*, pp.214-27; and Katie Gramich, 'The Fiction of Raymond Williams in the 1960s: Fragments of an Analysis', in *Welsh Writing in English: A Yearbook of Critical Essays*, i, 1995, pp.62-74.

18 Leonora Brito, 'Digging for Victory', in L Brito, *Dat's Love*, Bridgend: Seren Press, 1995, p.71.

19 *Ibid.*, p.73.

20 *Ibid.*, p.74.

21 Raymond Williams, 'Mining the Meaning: Key Words in the Miners' Strike', in *Resources of Hope*, London and New York: Verso, 1989, p.124.

22 Christopher Meredith, *Shifts*, Bridgend: Seren Books, 1988, p.182.

23 *Ibid.*, p.201.

Women and Work in Catalonia: Is Catalonia still a Working Society?

Muriel Casals

Introduction

My paper is related to the history of women's work in Catalonia and to the current situation of our labour market. I would like to offer some reflections using ideas taken from the history of economic thought.

To begin with, let us have a short look at the Catalan background. Catalonia is one of the oldest industrial regions in Europe, with all the strengths and all the weaknesses older industrialisation implies for an economy now, at the end of our century. Being an old industrial country shapes our culture. We enjoy industrial activity, which means the ability to create wealth, but suffer from the industrial crisis at a moment when it becomes increasingly difficult to find markets for industrial production. Competition with newly-industrialised countries opens up questions about our economic future. Will mature industrial countries insist on producing material goods or would they rather become service producers, entering into a post-industrial era? The answer is not a clear one.

Catalunya, la fàbrica d'Espanya

Richard Cobden, the British economist and entrepreneur who travelled to Catalonia in 1846, pointed out the main reason for successful industrialisation in a country without the key natural

Eberhard Bort and Neil Evans (eds), *Networking Europe*, Liverpool University Press 2000, 129-40.

resources of the time (mainly coal and iron). The reason he gave was that Catalan people acted 'collectively'.[1]

Truly, even though Catalonia did not have the basis for industrial development, our economic history shows an early industrial revolution. After some brilliant episodes in medieval history, there was a long period leading to the collapse of feudalism and the installation of a social system based on small-scale ownership. That meant a relatively shared income which favoured the diffusion of economic activity.

As normally to be expected (and when we say 'normal' we mean: according to the British pattern of Industrial Revolution), the first industry was textiles. But because of the lack of coal and iron, the second industrial wave did not follow accordingly: the metal industry (as would have been 'normal'), and textiles remained *the* industry for a much longer time. Little diversification of industrial activity and strong specialisation in textile production – which lasted until the second half of the twentieth century – are the characteristic features of the Catalan economy. One important consequence of textiles as the predominant industry has been the presence of female work. Women have been working in textiles – from the beginning, and everywhere.

The Catalan industry was open to external markets, be it Spain and its colonies or Europe. Inward-orientation would not have made possible the actual development. In 1856, when the first industrial statistics were made available in Spain, the figures showed the industrial strength of the Catalan economy. At that time, 11.2 per cent of the Spanish population produced 25.6 per cent of the industrial goods. In these statistics, all figures representing the Catalan part of any kind of industrial production within Spain are higher than the Catalan percentage of the population in toto, except for food which could hardly be called an industry at that time. Textiles being the main Catalan produce, the sector was particularly concentrated: Catalonia produced 66.3 per cent of the total Spanish production.[2]

Figures for industrial workers show that in 1863, within the Barcelona spinning industry, the proportion of men and women employed was almost half and half.[3] Spinning was the part of the textile process which also employed an important proportion of children's work: 27 per cent of the Barcelona population aged between 10 and 15 years were spinning workers.[4] Weaving, in contrast, employed mainly adult male workers.

This is to point out that working women have been the normal pattern within the Catalan tradition, both as factory workers, and working at home. Here it is relevant to mention that when working at home they have been doing it both for industry (the parts of the process that can be done outside the actual place of manufacturing) and for the reproduction of the labour force (i.e. the care of the family). This industrial work at home as a very common social and economic behaviour allows us to assert that female participation in industrial production was, and is today, more important than what we can see from statistical figures.

In Catalan economic and social history, we often find references to female work as complementary to male work. This way of thinking we can see in statements arguing that women's wages need not to be as high as those of male employees, as they are seen as an income which is supposed to complement family provision. Thinking of that kind is indicative of a situation where many women do not quit their jobs when they get married. A long tradition of women being part of the labour market is an inheritance (positive, I believe) coming from a long industrial tradition.

Catalonia was the main, almost the only, industrial region in Spain before the strong wave of industrialisation in the 1960s. In 1900, the Catalan population was 11.1 per cent, while the region's industrial production was 38.6 per cent of Spain's. The textile orientation of the Catalan industry was even then so strong that it represented 82 per cent of the total Spanish textile production.[5] This situation has been defined as 'Catalunya, la fàbrica de Espanya' – that is to say: Catalonia, Spain's factory. The catalogue of the exhibition organised under this title ten years ago is a good synopsis of Catalan industrial history.[6]

In 1960, at the beginning of the big economic transformation of Spain, Catalan production made up 24.5 per cent of the total Spanish industrial output, and the figure was 25.7 per cent in 1975, when economic recession was appearing in old industrial regions. As a rule, until 1983, roughly a quarter of Spanish industrial goods were being produced in Catalonia.[7]

The fact of being *the* industrial and the more economically-developed part of Spain has had adverse consequences for the Catalan economy. It has limited the traditional aperture towards external markets. Being part of a politically united country has meant that Catalan producers have claimed the right to the Spanish market's protection for Catalan manufactures. This protectionism from external competition allowed Catalan firms to sell to the Spanish market at higher prices, compared with international levels. This could be seen as good from a short-term perspective, but it is surely negative in the way it limits the search for lower production costs, mainly the incentive to introduce technological change.

One reason why the Catalan industry had difficulties in reacting to the opening of the markets when Spain became a member of the European Community in 1986 came from having, over a long period, enjoyed the opportunity to sell to a market which was forced to accept high prices. On the other hand, the Spanish market was a limited one (not a big population and low income), so the demand was always below the productive capacity.

A high level of industrialisation meant that Catalonia has been attractive for people from rural Spain. Strong Spanish immigration, lasting till 1980, is the main explanation for the Catalan 'demographic explosion'. From 1,966,382 inhabitants in 1900, Catalonia reached 5,958,208 in 1981 (which is more or less the current number); that means a growth of 303 per cent.[8]

Immigration was especially strong during the years 1916-30. During this period of Catalan economic expansion, an average of 35,000 people arrived every year.[9] Immigration became important again during the 1940s. Even though it was difficult to live in big cities, as consumer goods were hard to come by, Barcelona and other old industrial Catalan cities like Sabadell and Terrassa were chosen by immigrants as their destination. That actually happened contrary to government policy which wanted to avoid migration towards big cities. Police officers guarded the Barcelona railway stations, as well as those in Madrid, in order to force those arriving without sufficient means of living at their destination to return back to the places of their origin. Of course migrants learnt to cheat authorities, by jumping out of the train some kilometres before the station. Doing the last part of their journey on foot shows how strongly these people were willing to move to the cities.

They came looking for work in what they, full of hope, saw as a working society. This expression indicates the capacity to create jobs giving substance to Catalonia's socially integrated life. They came to mix with Catalan people, to become part of Catalan society. That was fairly true during the 1930s when Catalonia was able to integrate the newcomers, but became much more problematic during Franco's regime, as Catalan institutions were outlawed. That meant: no Catalan school system, no media, and no possibility to offer the immigrant population the opportunity of becoming citizens of the country they had come to live in.

Looking at the index used by demographers and defined as 'activity indicator' (the proportion of people working in relation to the total population between the ages of 15 and 65 years old), we see how true it is that Catalonia was a society were one could expect work.

These figures show that in 1930 and 1950 all adult males were working, surely even more than were legally permitted (the legal minimum working age was 14). This means that some boys under 15 and some men over 65 were employees. For women, the activity indicator is of course very much lower, but we should point out the fact that figures are those of women having a working contract. Far more women were surely at work, but they were not officially employed.

***Table 1** Activity indicator*

	1930	1950	1975	1981
Total	63.5	63.8	63.1	58.0
Men	104.5	102.3	92.9	84.2
Women	25.7	36.7	33.9	32.3

Source: A Cabré and I Pujades, 'La població: immigració i explosió demogràfica', in *Història Econòmica de la Catalunya Contemporànea,* Vol.5, Barcelona, 1989, pp.11-128; p.87.

The Situation Today

Catalan population figures have, for some years now, been stagnating at around six million people. 'Internal' immigration has stopped; the influx from northern African countries is the one which is expected to grow in the near future. European law about immigration is an important factor. At the present, Spanish authorities are restrictive as Spain is perceived as the natural southern gate for immigration to the European continent.

The most interesting fact regarding demographic developments in Catalonia has been, during the whole century, the very low birth rate. Only during the 1960s and 1970s did the fertility rate increase, and that was because of the different behaviour of people who had come from southern Spain.

As a consequence of immigration, Catalonia is a region with a very important presence of citizens born in other parts of Spain. They constituted 30.6 per cent of the population in 1994, the proportion of Catalan-born people being 67.3 per cent, and the natives of foreign countries contributing only two per cent.[10] These proportions were different (with an even stronger presence of people born in other parts of Spain) only a few years ago when the population growth resulted almost entirely from migration. And it is necessary to point out that an important part of those falling into the category of Catalan-born are first-generation Catalans.

There is no doubt: Catalonia is a melting-pot. To bear that in mind is important both for the ones who came to Catalonia and for the old Catalans. People coming from other Spanish regions are not always aware of the fact that they arrive in another country, that they have to learn another language, to live with a different set of cultural references. And Catalan people do not always know the best way to make the immigrants' integration easier. There are even voices saying that integration is not a necessity and that we could live in a dual society. Discussions regarding the school system have been controversial and interesting. Happily, the *Generalitat* (the Catalan regional government) adopted a universal system for public schools which avoids language segregation and assures all boys and girls to be able to speak, to read and to write both in Catalan and in Spanish by the time they have finished secondary school.

Table 2 *Catalan Population, 1994*

Total	Men	Women
6,001,000	2,931,500	3,069,500

Source: Institut d'Estadística de Catalunya, *Mercat de treball 1994*, Barcelona, 1995, p.55.

Table 3 *Natural growth, 1994*

Births	54,424
Deaths	52,194
Growth	2,230
Marriages	30,044

Source: Institut d'Estadística de Catalunya, *Moviment natural de la població, 1994*, Barcelona, 1996.

Is Catalonia still a Working Society?

If we wonder whether or not it is possible to find a job in Catalonia, the answer is not so clear nowadays as it was during the first half of this century. First of all, the age structure of the population has changed; there are more older people today (thanks to the very substantial increase in human life expectancy). The other big change has been the attitude of young people regarding education. A very large proportion of young people are delaying their entrance into the labour market and choose instead to spend more time within the education system.

A large number of people over 18 years of age are attending university. This is, of course, because they want a degree, but also because they do not find an interesting job – or even a job at all.

Here, the rate of activity (defined as the proportion of people active in the labour market) is no longer showing the situation we saw previously, when the number of workers was bigger than the number of people legally able to work. In 1994, the rate of activity was 52.3 per cent for the whole population; 65 per cent for male, and 40.6 per cent for female. These are, indeed, not very high rates for an industrial society.

***Table* 4** *Catalan population over 16 years old, 1994*

	Men	Women
Total	2,403,100	2,573,900
Active	1,560,500	1,044,600
Employed	1,290,300	762,500
Unemployed	270,300	282,200

Source: Institut d'Estadística de Catalunya, 1995, p.43.

***Table* 5** *Rate of activity, 1994*

Age	Total	Men	Women
All age groups	52.3	64.9	40.6
From 16 to 24 years	53.8	54.6	52.9
From 25 to 54 years	77.5	93.8	61.5
More than 55	16.6	26.7	8.6

Source: Institut d'Estadística de Catalunya, 1995, pp. 44-73.

If we look at more detailed figures, we find that 97 per cent of the male population between 35 and 39 years of age are active. For women, the figure is 70.3 per cent. These are high rates of activity. As the rate of activity for the young population is also high, we can assert that there is a demographic explanation to the overall low Catalan rate of activity: the large proportion of old people.

The situation becomes even more pessimistic-looking when we take a glance at the figures dealing with employment. The rate of employment (that is to say the proportion of employed people among the population of some age category) was, in 1994, 41.2 per cent for the whole population, 53.7 per cent for men, and 29.6 per cent for women.[11]

There are two counterbalancing forces at play in Catalan society: (1) the decision, or better the wish, to be active, that is to say, to be actively involved in the labour market; and (2) the needs of the economy, that is to say the demand for labour.

While (1) is strong, (2) is not. The question we should be able to answer is whether the Catalan economy is still wanting to be an industrial one. If the answer is yes, this would mean that we can expect to see people in employment. But if the answer is no, the need for work will be smaller and smaller. And, of course, female workers are the first to become redundant.

Let us have a look at the unemployment figures:

Table 6 *Unemployed population (percentage of active population), 1994*

	Total	Men	Women
Whole	21.2	17.3	27.0
From 16 to 24 years	40.9	38.7	43.5
From 25 to 54 years	17.6	13.2	24.1
More than 55 years	11.3	12.6	8.0

Source: Institut d´Estadística de Catalunya, 1995, p.225.

As these figures show, unemployment affects mainly young people and especially women. This is not surprising.

Maybe as a reaction, a positive one, to the inability of the economy to provide work, or better to give employment to every person wanting to be active, the latest figures show that, during the year 1995, 58 per cent of all new jobs were self-created.[12] This means that if someone wants to work, he or she should try to create his/her own enterprise.

Fifty per cent of all new entrepreneurs in 1995 were women, and their enterprises are mainly in the service sector. This type of entrepreneurship has permitted the activity rate of Catalan women to rise by one point, to 41.3 per cent, in 1995.[13]

What about Economic Theory?

The best-known economist who devoted special attention to the role of women in society is J Stuart Mill. For him, inequality in the work-place is at the root of the domestic subjection of women. In the same classical tradition, Friedrich Engels pointed out that working for a salary is the condition for women's liberation. Fifty years before Mill, W Thompson, another of Bentham's followers, had explained that, with the help of industrial technology, physical strength was no longer a necessary condition for reaching higher rates of productivity; thus, he argued, there were no technical reasons for lower female salaries, only social reasons.

That was the point made by Mill, who explained in a very modern way how the distribution of income is linked to social evolution; how productivity depends on education and training; and how equality in this field requires a set of social rules other than individualistic competition.

By way of criticising the predatory culture of the early (and not so early?) capitalism, I would like to go back to Thorsten Veblen. His critical writings are addressed to a society in which people lacking ferocity (sic) are seen as infirm and, being infirm, women are not appreciated as workers. Veblen believed that only a re-emergence of the instinct of workmanship over the predatory instinct could end the subjugation of women.

Conclusion

To conclude, let us go back to Catalonia. We have a long tradition of women in work, but not enough female workers turning up in the statistics of employed people to allow us to be defined as a country were work is shared by both men and women. The conditions under which the Catalan economy is developing currently do not favour the increasing desire of women to enter the labour market.

Too many signs seem to point out that we are going to buy almost every commodity abroad (cheap goods from the new industrial countries, sophisticated ones from the more mature ones) and are on our way to becoming a post-industrial region. The decline of old industries runs its course unhindered, and an illusion of modernity provided by a booming service sector may make us forget that the word 'service' suggests there must be something to serve. As this something has to be some kind of industry, I think that the future of work (female and male alike) must rely on the ability to find an industrial future. What kind of industries and which kind of work? That is another question. And it is not an easy one to answer.

Notes

1 E Lluch, 'La "gira triumfal" de Cobden per Espanya (1846)', in *Recerques*, No.21, Barcelona, 1988, pp.71-90.

2 J Nadal, 'La indústria fabril española en 1900: Una approximación', in J Nadal, A Carreras and C Sudrià (eds), *La economia española en el siglo XX: Una perspectiva histórica*, Barcelona, 1987, p.48.

3 J Maluquer and J Torras, *La formació d'una societat industrial*, Vol.1, *Història Econòmica de la Catalunya contemporànea*, Barcelona, 1994. p.157.

4 *Ibid.*, p.156.

5 J Nadal, *art. cit.*, p. 48.

6 See Ajuntament de Barcelona. *Catalunya, la fàbrica d'Espanya. Un segle d'industrialització catalana, 1833-1936*, Barcelona, 1985.

7 See Banco de Bilbao. *Renta Nacional de España y su distribución provincial, 1955-1975*, Bilbao,1978; and Banco de Bilbao. *Renta Nacional de España y su distribución provincial* (various years).

8 A Cabré and I Pujadas, 'La població: immigració i explosió demogràfica', in *Història Econòmica de la Catalunya Contemporànea*, Vol.5, Barcelona, 1989, pp.11-128; p.83.

9 *Ibid.*, p.42.

10 *Ibid.*, p.57.

11 Institut d'Estadística de Catalunya, 1995, p.113.

12 Instituto Nacional de Estadística, *Encuesta de Población Activa*, Madrid, 1995.

13 *Ibid.*

Towns Fit For Women, Towns Fit For People

Beate Weber

1865: Allgemeiner Deutscher Frauenverein: 'Accessibility of all educational opportunities for women, right of free choice of profession, participation of women in all interests of the state.'

1872: Teachers' Conference in Weimar: 'Women must be enabled to gain, in its general mode and interests, an education equivalent to the formation of the human spirit of the man, so that the German man will not be bored in his home and paralysed in his dedication to higher aspirations by the intellectual short-sightedness and narrowness of heart of his wife, but rather be supported in these by his wife's understanding of these interests and her warmth of feeling.'

1879: August Bebel in *Woman and Socialism*: 'The reservation that women understood nothing of public affairs, fits them no more than millions of men.'

Statistics

Presently, Heidelberg has *c.*145,000 citizens, of whom*c.*76,500 are women and *c.*68,500 are men. Of a total of 54,100 employed people 43.8 per cent are female and 56.2 per cent are male. By the end of 1992, 1,329 women and 1,785 men were unemployed.

Heidelberg has the first female lord mayor in Baden-Württemberg – directly elected by the people for a period of eight years as chair of the town council (with individual vote) and head of an administration of 3,200 civil servants.

Of the 40 members of the town council, 11 are women: four out of the SPD's eleven, three out of the GAL's eight, two out of the FDP's two, one out of the FWV's five, and one out of the CDU's twelve.[1]

Eberhard Bort and Neil Evans (eds), ***Networking Europe,*** **Liverpool University Press 2000, 141-53.**

Of the 36 town hall offices, eight are headed by women, ranging from the main office to legal advice, women's affairs, libraries, and the press office. Of 3,216 employees on the city's pay roll, 1,475 are women. As elsewhere, the figures for women are higher in the lower to medium ranges of income. But this is about to change with the imminent implementation of the *Frauenförderplan* (women's support scheme). There is already a high proportion of part-time jobs (511, out of which 459 are held by women); but job-sharing is also practised, particularly between women, with great success and considerable gains in personal freedom. The personnel and organisation office offers in-depth advice, and there is a special advisory point for women in the administration. An equal rights commissioner for women has organised meetings for female staff members.

Women's Policies before my Term of Office

Before 1990, women's policies had developed little impact on the decision-making processes in local administration. In 1986, a municipal advisory office for women was opened, under the organisational umbrella of the Central Office in the Department of the Lord Mayor. Budgetary means were made available, amounting to DM 4,800 (*c.*£1,600), as from 1987. At the beginning of 1990, the office was renamed 'Women's Office of the Municipality of Heidelberg' (Frauenbüro der Stadt Heidelberg), without change in concept or deepened institutional integration. Financial support for specific tasks concerning women was split between diverse budget positions, with the consequence that means were not called upon due to lack of information about their availability.

Initiatives, forwarded since 1983 mainly by the ASF (Arbeitsgemeinschaft Sozialdemokratischer Frauen, or Association of Social-Democratic Women), the women's organisation within the SPD, and proposals to install an 'executive post for the realisation of women's equality in local administration', situated in the Lord Mayor's office, were blocked by both the lord mayor and the town council's majority.

What I stood for in 1990

Heidelberg could, I argued, make conditions of life and work for women much more positive in manifold ways, as women are directly affected by many decisions in local administration. A turning-point in municipal policies was urgently needed: policies for women must be accepted as an intrinsic task for local democracy.

My aims were:

- An equality office, i.e. a commissioner for women's equality with sufficient competences as well as sufficient personnel and resources;
- A scheme designed to motivate women and further their interests;
- A town development concept which takes account of women's needs and seeks for new ways in transport, accommodation and environmental policies;
- Increased influence for women on local administration decision-making processes;
- All-day child-care facilities for children of all ages in all parts of the town;
- Institutional support for the Heidelberg 'Frauenhaus' (Women's Centre) and the local Anti-Rape Organisation;
- Permanent support for the women's night-taxi service.

The European Experience

The European Community has proved beneficial for women: EU guidelines concerning 'equal wages for equal work' and 'equal opportunities in education and training', 'equal access to social security', and many other way-paving decisions have brought about, at least legally speaking, equality for women in the European Union.

Yet we all know that we have a long way to go to reach full and practical equality, and that it will take a long time until many of our demands will be met with universal approval. The 'Benda-Report'[2] for the German Constitutional Court talks about practical equality to be achieved far beyond the millennium if the present pace of realisation continues.

What has Happened since I Came into Office?

After going through several town council readings, I succeeded in mid-July 1991 in establishing – as of 1 October 1991 – an independent 'Amt für Frauenfragen' (Office of Women's Affairs), directly linked to the lord mayor's office. This was an important step in making women's equality an intrinsic part of all local administration decisions. Women's policies were elevated to the same level as other resource policies in the town hall:

- The Women's Office has its own budget. The budget's development reflects the Office's growing significance. Over the past six years, we spent between DM 800,000 and 1.1 million (between £260,000 and 330,000) on women's policies (not including personnel or administrative costs).
- The Director is, simultaneously, women's commissioner and equal in status to other departmental directors.
- The position is directly linked to the office of the lord mayor.

The Office has the following competences:

- Submission of proposals within the framework of its remit.
- Duty to comment on all proposals concerning specific topics relevant for women.
- In all relevant issues the Office has to be involved, amounting to a right of veto inside the administrative structure.
- Participation in decisions concerning personnel (advertising of posts, assessing applications, participating in interviews).

The remit of the Office comes in three groups:

- Participation in the communal decision-making processes: securing equal opportunities; introducing specific proposals and initiatives into the proceedings of administration and town council; monitoring the administration's performance and its impact on women; tabling of recommendations and proposals aimed at improving the situation of women and at correcting existing disadvantages.
- Tasks aimed at the improvement of the situation of women within the administration: participation in collating a report on the situation of women working in the town administration; tabling of recommendations concerning women working in the town administration.
- Tasks connected with the Office's role as contact point for the citizens of Heidelberg: counselling and help for female citizens; regular public office hours; contacts to women's organisations, trades unions, economic organisations, institutions, etc.; participation in and organisation of events, conferences, etc.; research into specific women's themes; preparation for studies, interventions, reports and information material for town council and administration.

In co-operation with her reliable staff and through her enthusiastic and circumspect work, the new Director of the Women's Office has, since her instalment in April 1992, strengthened the confidence and trust of Heidelberg's women in their town hall administration and the performance of their lord mayor. Within the town administration, low-wage groups have been abolished and attractive new jobs have been created (for example, in the citizens' offices, with manifold remits and lots of creative space); unattractive jobs (mainly clerical) have also been, to a good degree, abolished.

The personnel and organisation office has become a contact point for employees seeking counselling before or after holidays, particularly in connection with child-birth and upbringing. A personnel plan has been passed aiming at a development where discrimination of women will be overcome; and an agreement for the protection of employees from sexual harassment has been signed. All possibilities for a better ranking of women in the typical areas of employment (child care, clerical work, etc.) are being exhausted. Using activities like personnel meetings for women, the permanent involvement of the women's office in the town's publications, as well as working groups and a conference about administration reform and its impact on women, internal consciousness of women's interests is constantly being raised.

In the Office's initial phase, two exhibitions drew particular attention:

- 'Against Their Will': a harrowing depiction of violence against children, particularly against girls, set up in the town hall, found great resonance;
- 'Stronger Than You Think': an exhibition targeting young girls from the age of twelve, introducing them to appropriate literature. This exhibition was set up in close co-operation with the city library, was illustrated by the renowned Heidelberg cartoonist Marie Marcks, and took off from Heidelberg on a well-attended tour of Germany.

Why Women Must Get Involved in Town Planning

Experiencing the 'city' is completely different for men and women; women's perspectives, though, have in the past not found entry into town planning. Above all, the changing conditions of life and work have consequences for day- and night-life, for the relationship between job, family, and leisure time, for the different age groups and their demands, which must all be brought within the realm of decision-making in municipal politics.

When I gave the Office of Town Planning the task of developing framework plans for each part of the town, this offered the welcome opportunity of taking into account the specific wishes, ideas and needs of women. We followed the recommendation of the Women's Office to install so-called 'Future Workshops for Women', which enabled the tabling of women's interest in an immediate and uncensored way, as well as providing framework and sound basis for contacts and social networks.

Reflecting a model drawn by the philosopher and political commentator Robert Jungk, those affected by policies were supposed to articulate themselves and to learn to activate their own creativity and engagement: to take the complaint 'out of the mouth' and 'into the hand'. Each of these Future Workshops is organised in three phases: critique, utopia, realisation. In 1992, two of these workshops were started, and in 1993 five more followed, in accordance with the progressing work of the town-planning office, and in co-operation with that office's work.

All questions concerning town planning – the relationship between accommodation and work, transport, structural policies, infrastructure, cultural services, effects of centralisation and decentralisation – are playing their part as do all aspects of social town-life as, for instance, whether changing age patterns are being proactively included in planning: with an increase of elderly people in town, the number of older women in need of financial and organisational support will grow.

How are changing family structures and a changing way of life acknowledged in a modern housing and environmental planning process? In this area, there are manifold possibilities for towns by, for example, making building societies construct flats within which kitchens and space for looking after infants are combined, within which every member of a family has his or her own room, avoiding nonsensical fixations (large, under-used bedrooms or living rooms at the cost of other rooms), offering common spaces apart from the lift or the laundry, etc.

Of growing importance is the question of rent levels. As female incomes are, on average, around 30 per cent below male incomes, possibilities for creating self-owned flats must be sought, particularly bearing in mind the increasing numbers of single women – especially older women – and single mothers, as they cannot, on their own, finance those kinds of rent.

In terms of the living environment, common facilities are of special importance, allowing for communication besides the shopping centres. Regrettably, the options for a town administration of influencing service infrastructure (doctors, pharmacies, shops) are extremely limited, as we have seen time and again. Where influence is possible is in structured spaces like children's playgrounds which, naturally, belong to the inhabited spaces of mothers or grandparents, but do not very often reflect that fact. Our playground concept, a co-production of our landscaping office with the child and youth office, aims at correcting that.

Communal transport links, often not geared towards school or job periods, between suburbs and the inner city, or even just to cemeteries where deceased partners lie, may prove an almost insurmountable obstacle if not included in the earliest phases of planning. Flexible services, using mini-buses to create links between otherwise scarcely accessible peripheral areas and the city centre, are being introduced as a remedy.

The newly-created decentralised citizens' bureaux (five so far) allow access to town-hall business in the suburbs, thus lowering distance and threshold-crossing inhibitions in dealings with the administration, and eliminate potential discrimination (nobody is seen going to the welfare office). Without adding significant organisational costs, women with children and the elderly find easier access to the town administration. Apart from that, it helps avoid car journeys into town and thus reduces traffic congestion.

Transport Questions are Potentially Explosive

As decisions have hitherto been made mostly by men aged between thirty and sixty, the fixation on the individual car is unsurprising, as in that age-group the availability of a car is extremely high among men in contrast to women. In Heidelberg, the figures are as shown in Tables 1 and 2.

Table 1 *Permanent access to a car in Heidelberg (per cent)*

Age	Men	Women
18 - 45 years of age	61	46
45 - 65 years of age	73	37
Over 65 years of age	55	14

Table 2 *Non-permanent access to a car in Heidelberg (per cent)*

Age	Men	Women
18 - 45 years of age	29	41
45 - 65 years of age	19	52
Over 65 years of age	39	83

Yet, only 10.4 per cent of males in Heidelberg between 45 and 65 years of age possess a public transport pass (women: 16.6 per cent); in the over-sixty-five age group, the figures are 19 per cent (men) and 25.3 per cent (women). These figures prove impressively the necessity for changes in transport and commuter planning.

Thanks to the engaged efforts of Heidelberg's 'Academy of the Elderly', a reduced-price seniors' pass (ticket 60 plus) has been introduced, which is already used by way over 10,000 senior citizens.

Childcare — An Investment in the Future

The necessity for towns to provide adequate services for child care is obvious. These must be flexible and adjusted to the needs of jobs and professions, of high quality, offered decentrally and by qualified personnel. Unfortunately, the municipalities are left nearly entirely to their own devices by the Land and the Federal Republic. With a tremendous financial effort, particularly in investment (buildings and equipment) and personnel, Heidelberg will, by the end of the 1990s, have reached, in the area of all-day child-care institutions, a coverage of over 97 per cent. We are already leaders in Baden-Württemberg, offering over 25 per cent of our child-care places in all-day care. This is irrevocable in the light of the job situation of parents in Germany.

Where legally possible, wage levels among child-carers have been improved, and responsibilities within the institutions more clearly structured, in order to achieve greater stability among the employees. Even after the abolition of the kindergarten guidelines by the Land, their substance is secured in Heidelberg by a town council decision.

Town planning demands more respect for the demands and needs of women. About 50 per cent of households in Heidelberg are one-person households; a large part of them are one-woman households. Residence-density has fallen to 1.9 (compared with 2.2 in 1970). There are no less than 97 women on the most urgent short list of the local housing office. 125 single mothers and 158 single women are looking for a subsidised home. How many women are looking for homes and are being sent away is difficult to estimate.

New, integrated models of living, but also different forms of financing must help to secure long-term homes for women. The situation of women in the eastern Länder is worse by far. That is why measures must be taken on the federal level, apart from the efforts by municipalities.

Culture and Education for Women?

Participation in education and training must be safeguarded for women, particularly those who missed chances through their commitment to raising a family. In some cases, education having been missed out completely, opportunities of retrieval must be offered. Adult education centres, as well as the Academy for the Elderly already mentioned, offer a broad spectrum of courses, in addition to the important services of the City Library and of other cultural institutions. More than 70 per cent of adult education customers are female, which points at the necessity for a comprehensive programme backed mainly by the city's budget.

To make these programmes truly accessible for women, regular publication of what is on offer is indispensable: information brochures like the 'Heidelberger Frauenfrühjahr' (Heidelberg Women's Spring) and 'Heidelberg für Frauen' (Heidelberg for Women) are doing just that.

Essential for the use of cultural services is that fears are overcome. That is the reason why Heidelberg funds the night taxi for women, a measure which, alas, passed the town council with the narrowest majority of one vote. After a trial run between autumn 1991 and spring 1992, a revised service has been permanently installed since July 1992, supported by the town with *c.*DM 300,000 (*c.*£100,000) annually. Including the revenue contributed by the customers, this adds up to DM 600,000 (£200,000) invested in a safe way home at night. The measure was devised in close co-operation with the municipal public transport authorities and also covers journeys between bus stops and home.

Fear in Town — A Political Task

Although this service protects a great number of women from intimidation and harassment, it can only partially solve problems of male violence against women. There is also a danger of seeing the problem as solved, along the lines of: 'Men have territorial claims to public space, women can at best get a transit visa.' To counter that tendency, a study entitled 'Security Sensitivity and Spaces of Fear of Women in Town: The Example of Heidelberg' visualises to what degree potential as well as actual threats influence women's everyday life. It demonstrates that this is not an individual fringe problem – as some might rashly assume – and that there is no panacea in town planning.

The empirical basis is a detailed poll among 572 women from Heidelberg, conducted in September and October 1992. The study is part of a concept called 'Women in Town Planning and Municipal Politics'. The problem of fear zones and infringement on the freedom of movement must be combated on two levels:

- A transformation of public spaces adequate for women's needs is necessary, with concrete improvements – proposals are being worked out by two female town-planners working on the project.

- The study must be seen as a building block in the ongoing task of publicising women's interests in the area of town planning.

The Heidelberg study is characterised by the breadth of its empirical data and by the joining of town planning proposals with participatory approaches. It is hoped that it will help other equal opportunities offices, women's commissioners and women's initiatives in their work.

Social Factors Massively Influence Town Life

Increasing readiness to use violence among adolescents must lead to determined offers of help and not – as proposed by many in view of the present, difficult financial situation – to scrapping of services. We must finance jobs, not unemployment. Thus, the town administration, in co-operation with the Department of Labour Exchange office, has installed 'Heidelberg Services', in order to give the long-term unemployed a sensible task which will, hopefully, lead them, step by step, back to normal employment. In this context, the present situation on the federal level of limiting investment into jobs is deeply worrying.

In problem areas of the town, where several disadvantaging factors cumulate, emphasis is laid on communal work, organised by the youth office – in conjunction with the welfare office and other interested parties, like the churches. Social aid and subsidies for youth work has increased over the last couple of years from DM 50 million to DM 70 million (£17 million to £23 million); youth aid trebled over the same period. These are alarming figures, but they must lead to reinforced engagement, not to withdrawal.

Fifty-three per cent of welfare recipients are women. Older women, in particular, need preventive aid, involving adequate forms of housing and flexible and mobile services, as demanded by the structural concept initiated by the town council. Short-term nursery places as subsidised by the town can only give limited help in emergency situations, mostly to give relief to women. Church and other charitable institutions and their social services are financially supported.

What the situation will look like when tens of thousands of women who still work for 'God's wages', i.e. on an honorary basis, take a bow and exit from social service, nobody dares imagine. The state is far from acknowledging this in any adequate form. The generation of women who are between 25 and 40 years of age today have higher professional qualifications and better incomes than their predecessors; they will not forego all this in old age and be roped into social services without remuneration. Should compulsory service also be abolished, the whole realm of social services will collapse, if we do not develop concepts in time and act on them. The municipalities will not be able to shoulder the financial effects of misdevelopments – as in the field of environmental policies – on their own and without supportive legislative frameworks.

There Remains a Lot to be Done, Working for Women's Equality

All these municipal initiatives will be insufficient without a sustained financial and legislative back-up from the other relevant political levels. Nonetheless, we can do a lot in our own town. In Heidelberg, we have taken a big step forward, and the coming years will, hopefully, see further improvements – in consciousness and in reality.

Notes

1 SPD = Social Democratic Party of Germany; GAL = Green-Alternative List; FDP = Liberal Party of Germany; FWU = Independent Voters' Union; CDU = Christian Democratic Union.

2 So called after the President of the German Constitutional Court in Karlsruhe, Ernst Benda.

Female, Old and Poor: German Unification and the Financial Situation of Older Women – A Short Survey in 15 Figures

Gotlind Braun

Introduction

Although I am, by education, not an expert in the field of social security, my work as a volunteer in a local branch of a large welfare organisation, as a town council member, as head of an association which offers sheltered housing to old people and, finally, on the board of a movement of senior members of the Social Democratic Party (SPD), has brought me into close contact with the problems of women, particularly the problems encountered by *older women*.

First of all, I will give five brief sketches outlining the lives of five women and their situation in old age. Following that, there will be a short survey considering the financial situation of women in old age. I will point out structures in the German system of social security which have a scandalous result: after a woman's typical life between employment, family work, and eventual re-entry into employment, many old women are fobbed off with inadequate pensions! And because these structures are not very likely to be changed, there is little hope that, in the future, old women will be better off than their mothers.

Eberhard Bort and Neil Evans (eds), *Networking Europe*, Liverpool University Press 2000, 155-73.

Five Women — Five Lives — Five Old-Age Incomes

- ***Helga R., born 1928, old-age pensioner since 1981***

Her schooling ends during the Second World War; an opportunity for vocational training does not present itself. From 1948 she helps in her parents' firm, seven days a week. In 1956, she marries a businessman, again taking responsibility not just for her household and the children's education, but also for their shop (during the day in the shop, accounting in the evening, besides being housewife and mother). The typical life of a so-called 'supporting family member'.

After being divorced from her husband, she is employed from 1969 to 1981. Due to ill health she becomes a pensioner aged 53, receiving a pension of DM 724 (*c.*£290) a month for her 12 years' insurance. Apart from that she receives support for accommodation (as a subsidy for her rent) and social aid. After having paid rent, electricity, water and telephone charges, DM 16 (*c.*£6.50) remain for daily living costs.

Helga R. tries to accommodate herself as a 'poor woman' by pursuing activities which do not cost – borrowing books in the local library, working in a senior citizens' group, playing cards with friends...

- ***Helene B,. born 1913, old-age pensioner since 1978***

She is born as the twelfth child of the family. After school, aged 14, she is employed, first in a butcher's shop in a small town, near where the family lives, later as 'family help' with a family in the city. In 1934, aged 21, she marries, and has two children (in 1936 and 1942). In 1946, her husband leaves the family. She gets by as a cleaning woman, cleaning a school – and having cleaning jobs with private households, albeit without insurance. As from 1964, she works as a telephonist in an office, until she retires, aged 65. She receives a monthly pension from social insurance of DM 635 (*c.*£254), and an additional pension from her time in public service of DM 355 (*c.*£142), which makes a total of DM 990 (*c.*£396).

Her sons are supporting her, paying part of the rent; sometimes she receives used clothing from friends; and she buys only bargain offers when it comes to food.

- ***Maria Sch., born 1920, old-age pensioner since 1980***

After her flight from the East she settles in Mecklenburg (GDR) and works there for 35 years, in the morning as a secretary in the town hall, in the afternoon as an agricultural labourer at the Co-operative (LPG). Until 1968 she looks after her parents, who have only a minimal pension, and thus live with her. All this is only possible because of her being able to sell vegetables, eggs and rabbits produced on her small private garden; this additional income also supports her when she receives, as from 1980, a GDR pension of 470 Marks. Since 1990, after unification, she receives 660 Marks (but by now her garden products are no longer sought after as before and mainly enrich her own table). She now earns some extra money by delivering newspapers.

- ***Margarete T., born 1922, old-age pensioner since 1982***

After her flight from Siebenbürgen (Romania) she, too, works in an LPG for 35 years – in the kitchen and in agricultural production; she also works as a cook at functions and festivals.

As an old-age pensioner she receives, since unification, DM 600; she still needs to cook at functions, and sometimes helps her niece in their restaurant.

- ***Ida K., born 1938, pensioner since 1996***

She was born as the youngest of four children on a farm in the Austrian Alps. After finishing school, she starts working close to home in a restaurant, but then moves on as a domestic servant to a family in southern Germany. Here, she marries and has two daughters (1971, 1973); from 1976, she works half the day in a rehab centre and also looks after her mother-in-law who lives with her in the same house. In 1995, she suffers grave injuries in a traffic accident and is no longer able to work; since 1996, she receives a pension of DM 860 which will be lowered at the age of 60 to about DM 800.

In contrast to the other women, Ida is not alone in her old age. Together with her husband's pension, they both can live comfortably.

The Pension Formula ('Rentenformel')

For all gainfully employed persons – except civil servants – this formula decides the level of pension they will receive in old age. The formula has been in effect since 1957, when the first substantial reform took place within the social-security system in Germany. (Another reform was carried through, effective from 1992, but the main principles of the formula have remained unchanged.

The *four factors* involved are being multiplied – and we see: if one factor is small, the outcome will also be considerably affected. This, as we will see, affects the pensions for women in an extraordinary way.

The formula meets the needs of (male) workers ideally, if they have been employed for 40 or 45 years, full-time, having earned at least an average wage or salary during their active years.

Figure 1 The four factors which determine the pension level

Individual factors		General factors
percentage of individual pension rating base (P)	X	General pension rating base (B)
ratio of individual gross-earnings to gross-earnings of all insured		average gross-earnings of all those employed in the year which precedes that in which pension will be paid for the first time

Pension Formula: (P x B) x (J x St) = yearly pension

number of years in insurance that are credited (J)	X	constituent* of increase per year credited (St)
- periods in which contributions have been paid ('Beitragszeiten') - periods that are credited, as if contributions had been paid (sickness, unemployment, army service) ('Ersatzzeiten', 'Ausfallzeiten')		* pensions at age 65: 1.5 % miners' pensions: 2 % pensions in cases of incapacity: 1 %

Standard Case of Pension Level

This pension level is defined as the percentage of net average earnings reached by a pensioner who fulfils the standard conditions, i.e. *c*.40 years of average earnings. The pillars in the figure show the development of net income of active people and the 'ideal' pension. At the bottom of the figure, the percentages are given. As we may see, the figures have always been closer to

60 per cent than to 70 per cent, the figure which had been the original goal. The striking difference between the figures for 1989 and 1990 is a result of German unification, taking into account the lower level of the five *Neue Länder* (new federal states of ex-German Democratic Republic).

Figure 2 Pension level

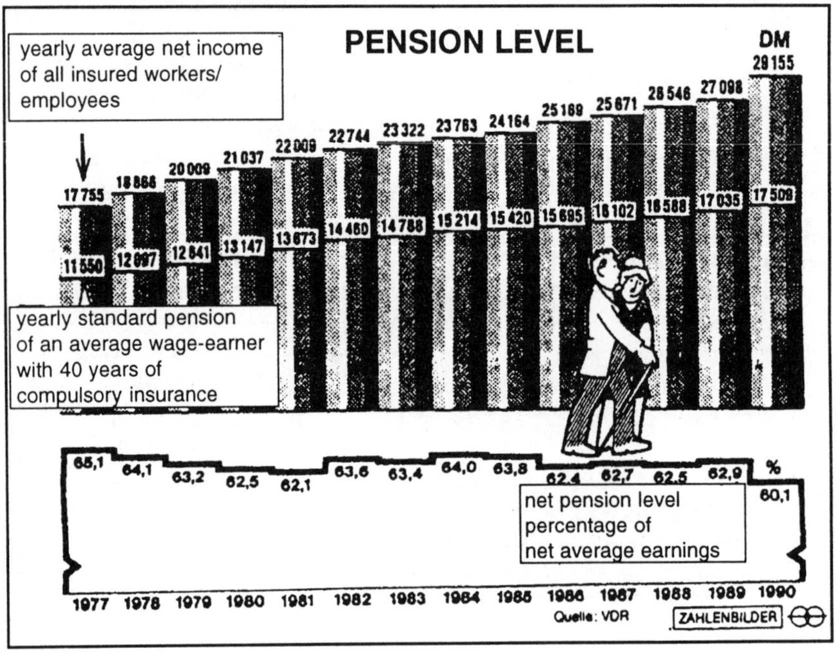

Ideal Case vs Facts

Figure 3 shows the development of the standard pension (continuous line) in the years from 1950 to 1983, in comparison with the average pension in the employees' insurance (dotted line) and the average pension in the workers' insurance (bottom line). The sharp increase in the middle of the 1950s is the effect of the pension reform in 1957: the 'dynamic pension' (index-linked pension). After 1977, even under the employees' scheme, only a lower level of average pensions is achieved because of the fact that more women with lower pensions are included (more women of this age group have been employed than before, but a substantial part of them did not have full-time jobs).

Concerning the workers' scheme, it must be noted that, although male high-earning industry workers (*Facharbeiter*) are included, the large proportion of women points to the fact that the average figure for pensions is way down below the standard pension level.

Figure 3 Standard pension level

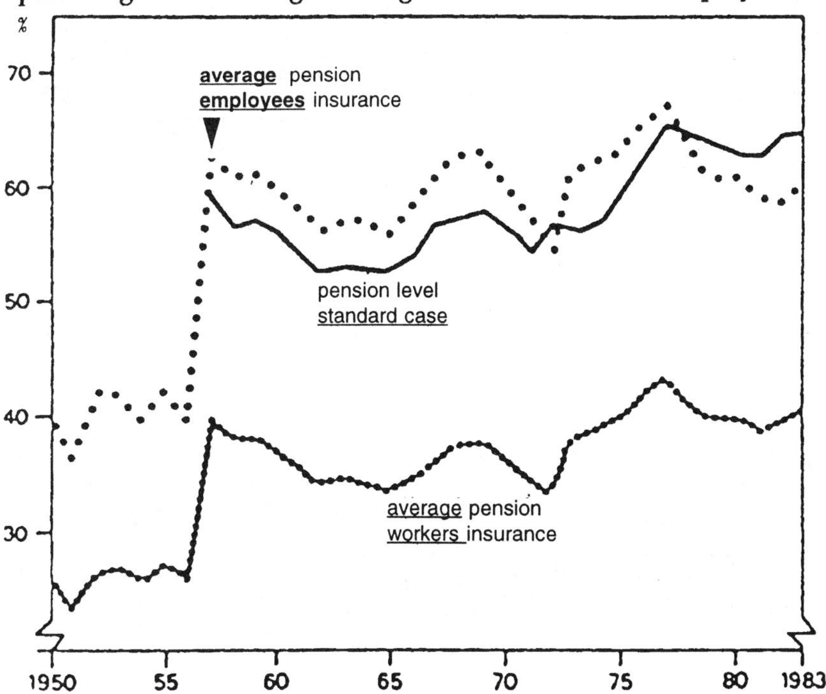

Wage Discrimination

In the past, women have earned considerably less than their male counterparts, as the figures concerning the development of earnings show for people who were born around 1910 and who went into retirement between 1970 and 1980. At best, women can reach 60 per cent of the average wage level.

Figure 4 *Wage Level in relation to average wages*

But this is not a thing of the past only. Even at present, discrimination against women results in wages or salaries for women which are 30 per cent below those of men. Even if women do the same work, they earn less.

Another way of looking at this is the fact that in the 1980s more men than women were placed in the higher wage groups or salary brackets (Fig.6).

Figure 5 A comparison of male and female weekly/monthly wages/salaries

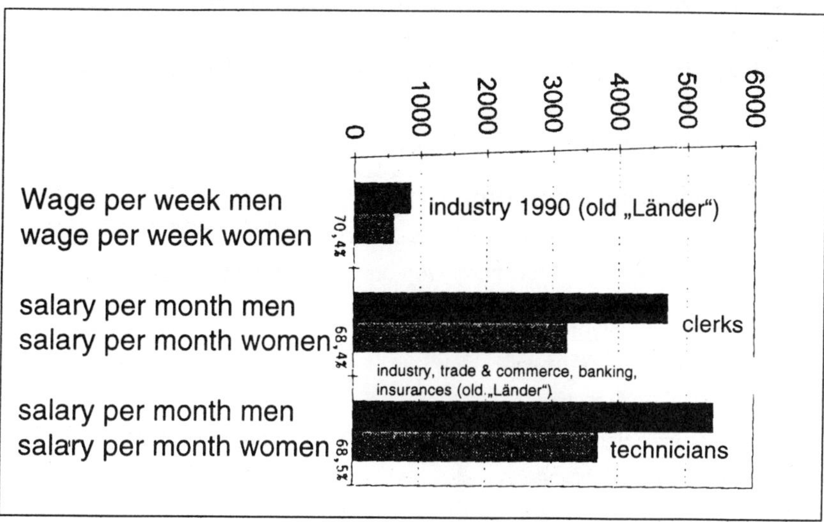

Figure 6 The male/female salary situation in the 1980s

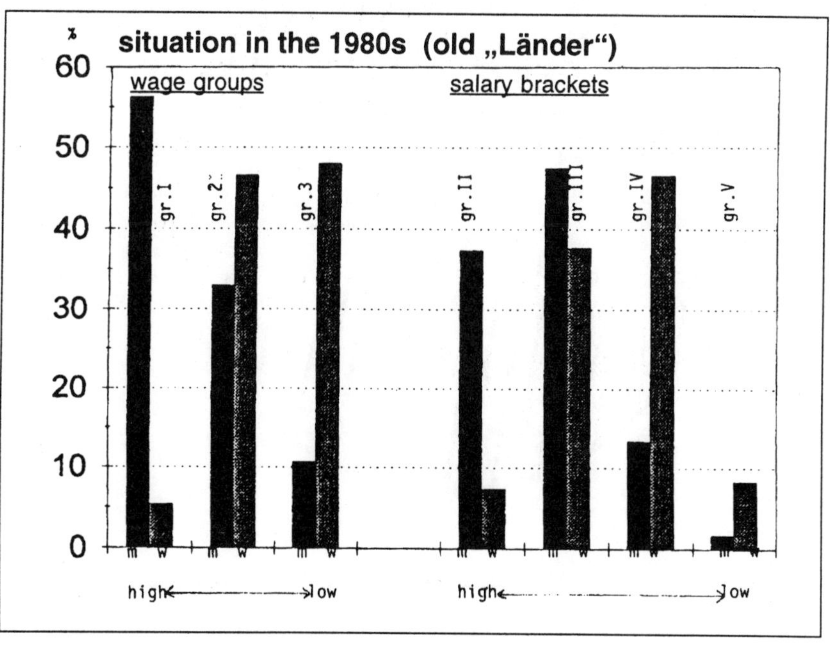

When, like in 1986 in the metal industry, low wages have been a point at issue during the collective bargaining process and the Trades Unions argued for considerable improvements for lower paid groups, the employers would argue that most workers in low-wage groups were only earning an additional part of a family income.

***Figure 7** Collective bargaining*

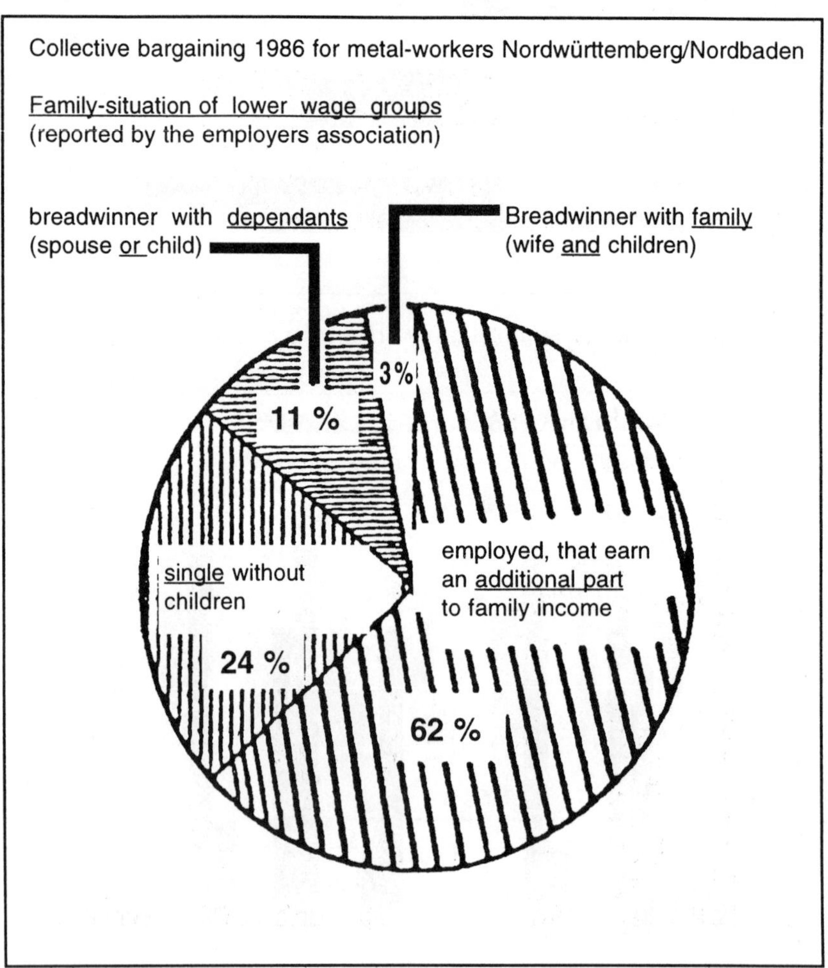

Discontinuous Working Life

The second factor in the pensions formula is time: how long has one been gainfully employed?

The largest group among women (22 per cent) achieve between 15 and 20 years of employment; the largest group among men (38 per cent) achieve more than 45 years in the workers' scheme. The ratio among salary-earners is not much better.

Figure 8 Number of years ... workers' scheme

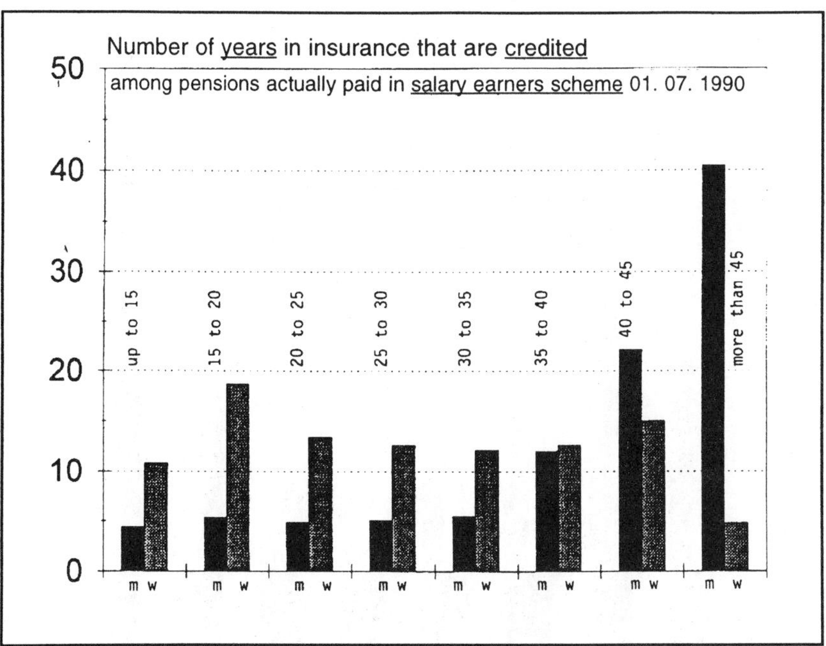

In the German Democratic Republic, no equivalent of the Federal Republic's old-age insurance system and the pension formula existed. Yet since 1990, this formula has been applied 'retrospectively' to all working lives of people in the former

GDR. This regulation actually privileges women, because in the GDR continuous work for women was normal, even if there were children in the family. (Publicly organised child-care made this possible') This has a surprising effect: in the 'poorer' part of Germany, women have a higher average pension than women who live in the Länder of the former Federal Republic of Germany. This is striking proof of the importance of the time factor!

***Figure 9** Number of years ...salary earners' scheme*

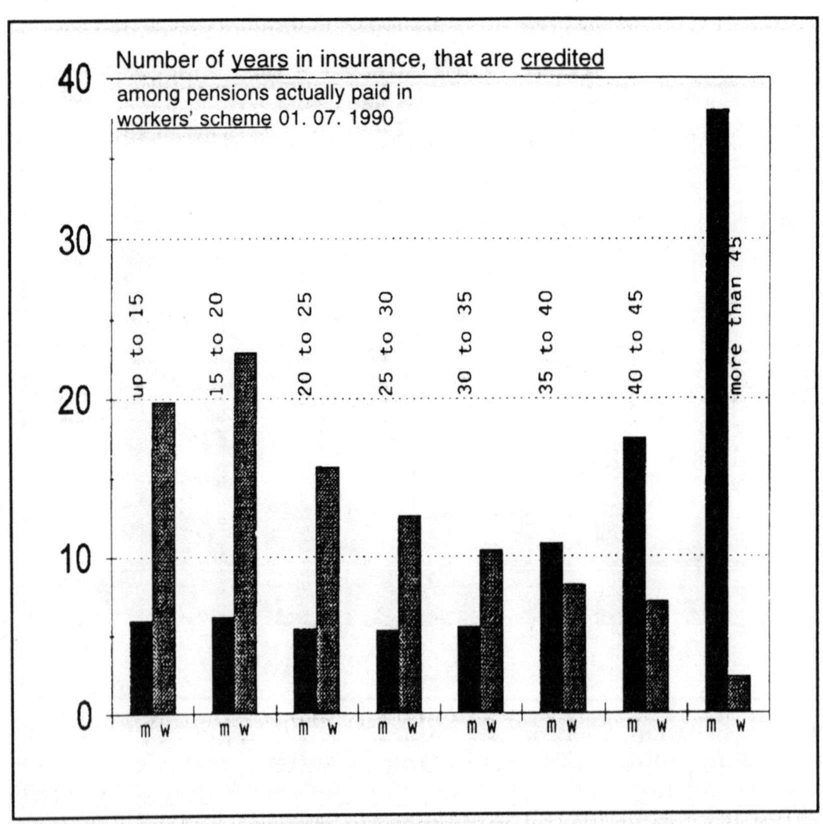

If we look around Europe, we find some countries where women would fulfil the conditions of the German pension formula better than German women themselves do. The proportion of women in the labour market in certain age groups in various countries is higher than in Germany. In Britain, there is a sharp rise in the group between 34 and 49 years; in France, there is only a slight decline (maybe the effect of *Ecole maternelle*); and in Denmark, housewives 'have died out' — because they are gainfully employed in the care of the elderly, other social work, and care for children!

***Figure 10** Development of credited years*

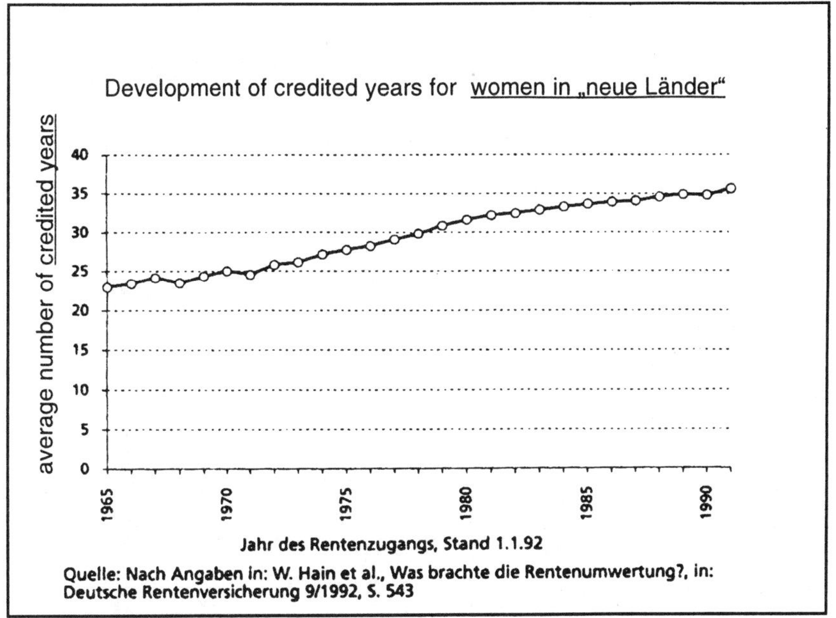

Quelle: Nach Angaben in: W. Hain et al., Was brachte die Rentenumwertung?, in: Deutsche Rentenversicherung 9/1992, S. 543

Put it to the Test

If we compare the standard figures for men and the typical deviations for women and their working lives, the formula reveals the fact that pensions for women will only amount to 25.2 per cent of the average income instead of 60 per cent as intended. This means that the pension formula fails to do justice to the majority of elderly people – the women!

Figure 11 *Result: Comparing available Insurance Pensions in the old and new Länder since 1990*

Key-date	**Available Insurance Pensions**		**New vs**
	Old	**New**	**Old in %**
	Länder		

Stichtag	verfügbare Versichertenrenten Alte Bundesländer (DM)	Neue Bundesländer (DM)	Verhältniswert der verfügbaren Renten in den neuen zu den in den alten Bundesländern (v.H.)
Männer			
30.06.1990	1.511	572	37,9
01.07.1990	1.558	739	47,4
01.01.1991	1.558	870	55,8
01.07.1991	1.635	992	60,7
01.01.1992[2)]	1.635	1.145	70,0
01.07.1992[3)]	1.691	1.242	73,4
01.01.1993[3)]	1.691	1.295	76,6
01.07.1993[4)]	1.757	1.468	83,6
Frauen			
30.06.1990	637	432	67,8
01.07.1990	658	524	79,6
01.01.1991	658	620	94,2
01.07.1991	693	716	103,3
01.01.1992	693	764	110,2
01.07.1992	728	826	113,4 !
01.01.1993	728	861	118,2
01.07.1993	757	950	125,5
Männer und Frauen			
30.06.1990	1.032	475	46,0
01.07.1990	1.064	590	55,5
01.01.1991	1.064	697	65,5
01.07.1991	1.117	802	71,8
01.01.1992	1.117	881	78,9
01.07.1992	1.161	956	82,4
01.01.1993	1.161	997	85,9
01.07.1993	1.206	1.113	92,3

Figure 12 Employment ratio

RATIO OF EMPLOYMENT IN AGE GROUPS **1983**

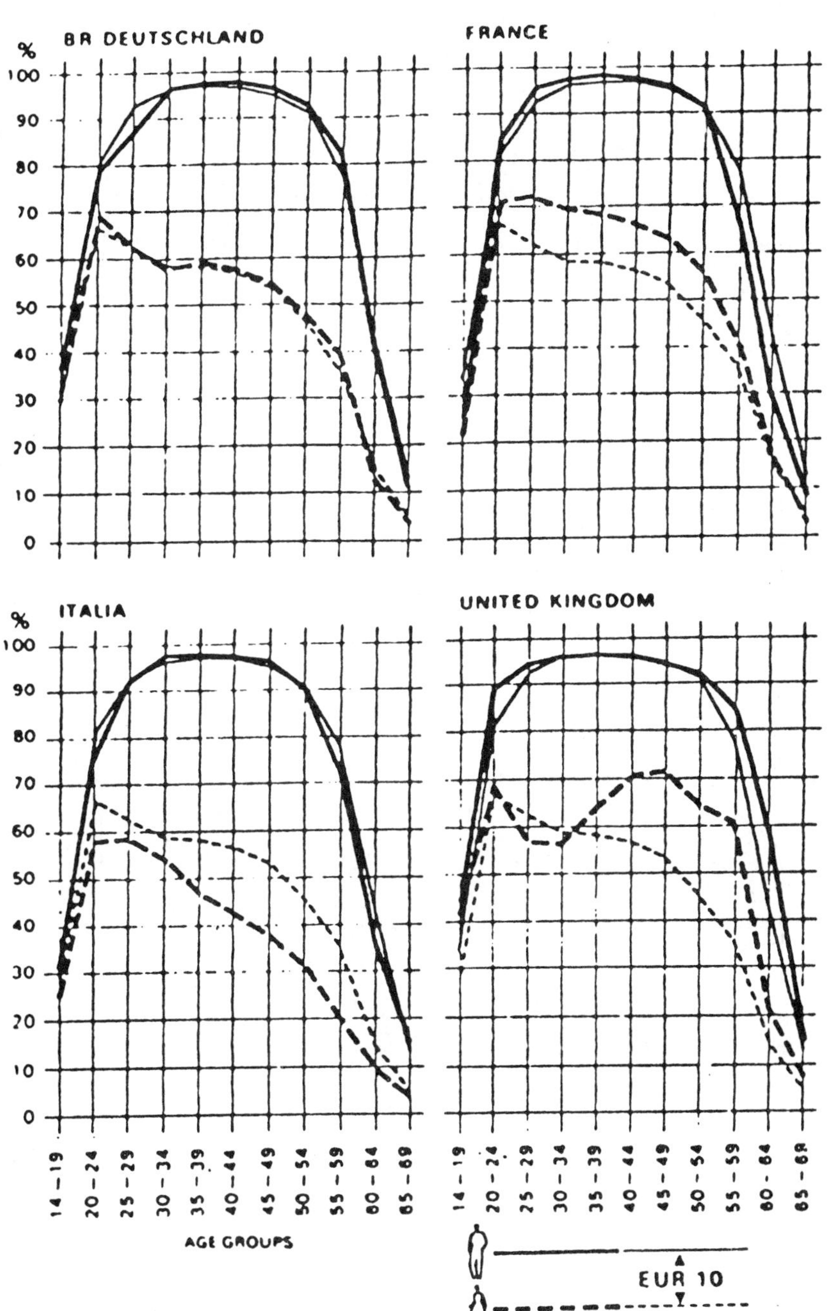

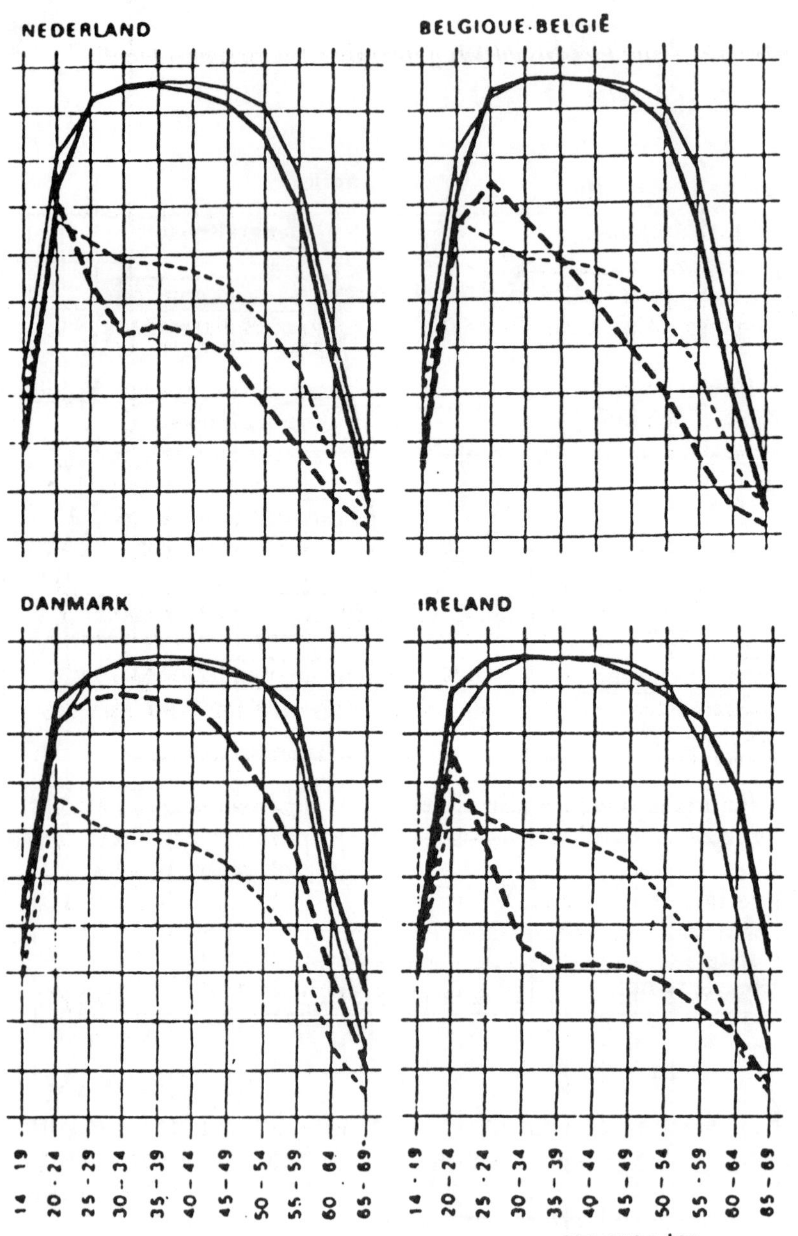
NEDERLAND
BELGIQUE-BELGIË
DANMARK
IRELAND
14 - 19
20 - 24
25 - 29
30 - 34
35 - 39
40 - 44
45 - 49
50 - 54
55 - 59
60 - 64
65 - 69
GROUPES D ÂGE

Figure 13 Four factors which determine the pension level (Version 2)

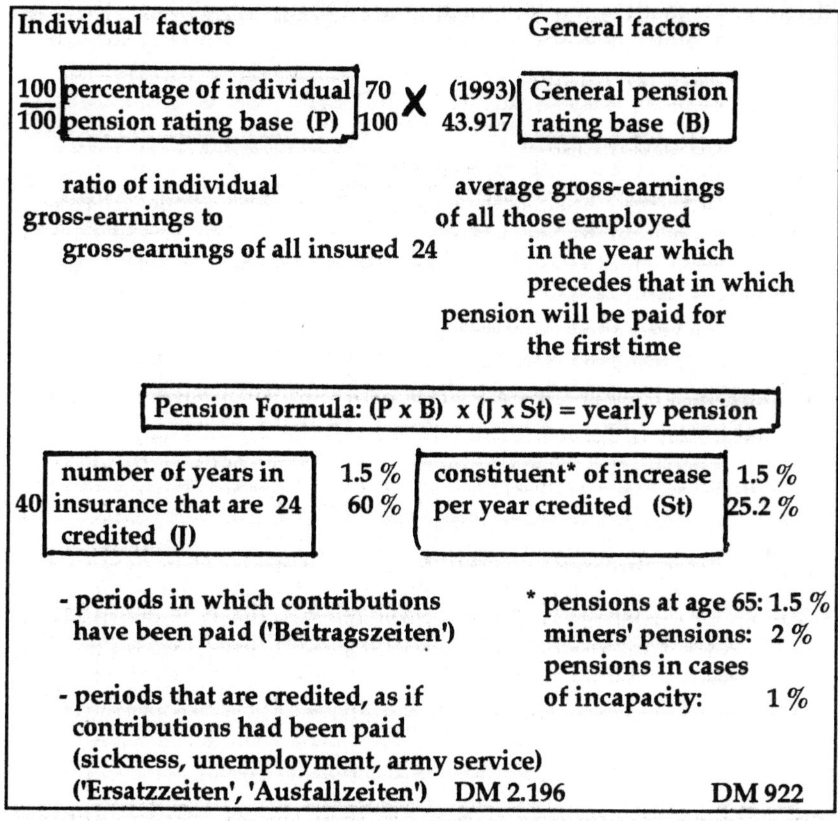

A look at the real figures of the different women pensions proves the theoretical argument: on average, most pensions for women are under the poverty line – which makes these women eligible for social welfare payments.

Figure 14 *Structure of verage pension level for women compared with social assistance benefits*

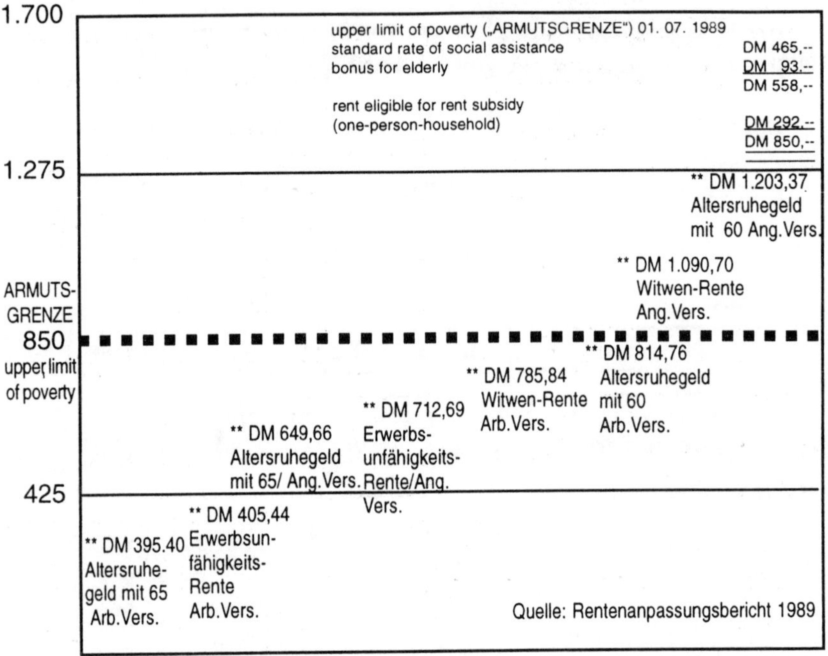

Finally, a survey concerning the strata of pensions, differentiating between men and women, corroborates assumptions about the distorted distribution of income in old age.

Figure 15 *Pension levels, 1989*

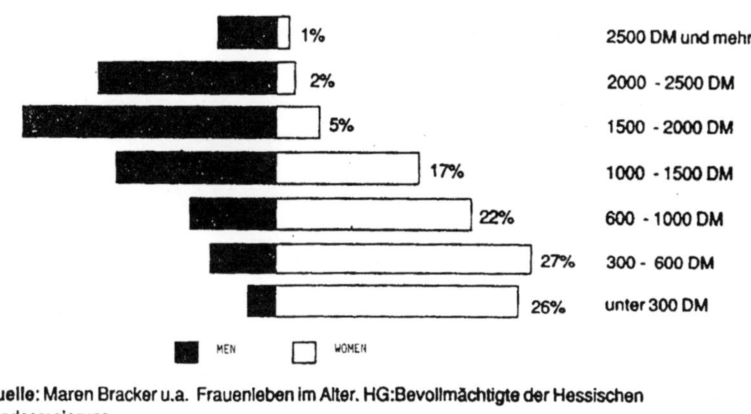

Quelle: Maren Bracker u.a. Frauenleben im Alter. HG:Bevollmächtigte der Hessischen Landesregierung

Seventy-five per cent of women's pensions do not reach the level of DM 1,000; 53 per cent are below DM 600.

Thus the five women whose lives I sketched at the beginning of this chapter are by no means deplorable exceptions; they constitute a representative sample of old women in Germany.

I am, finally, also afraid that the current generation of young women will not be much better off in their old age, due to the following factors: there is an insufficient number of apprenticeships in vocational training; there are the general difficulties in the labour market with soaring unemployment rates, particularly for women who want to return to work after raising their children; and a large number of women are single parents.

Female Emigration from Ireland[1]

Patricia Conlan

General Background

The Irish are a people with a long tradition of migration. The reasons are multiple.[2] Irish people are to be found in all continents with the USA, Britain, Australia and Canada being the most prominent countries by the beginning of the twentieth century.

Although emigration had been high at the beginning of the twentieth century,[3] it trailed off in the 1930s[4] due to the Depression (in the host countries). As the economic situation improved, emigration again increased, although this time saw Britain preferred over the USA.[5] The post-war period saw emigration increasing.[6] The 1960s – prior to accession to the EC – showed a reversal which continued throughout the 1970s to the point where there was net immigration[7] even though emigration was still taking place – but for different reasons than had previously been the case.[8] Unfortunately this was short-lived and by the end of the 1970s emigration was again gathering pace.[9]

The 1986 census showed the highest net emigration since the early 1960s for the period 1981-1986 – although these figures did attract some controversy.[10] This upward trend was again visible during the 1986-1991 intercensal period[11] – although women no longer make up the majority of emigrants,[12] as had been the case in earlier times.[13] The 1991 census showed the first decline in population since 1961.[14]

In the early years of the state there was an excess generally of males over females: this trend continued up to and including the 1981 census. Since the 1986 census there has been a reversal of this trend, and the excess of females over males in the popu-

Eberhard Bort and Neil Evans (eds), *Networking Europe*, Liverpool University Press 2000, 175-90.

lation seen in the 1986 census has been continued in the 1991 census.[15]

The effects of the gender imbalance arising from the high emigration rate among females and the general excess of males over females have been the subject of some debate in the past.[16] At the very least there has been the imbalance seen in the lack of suitable marriage partners – particularly in rural areas.

Census figures relate to the actual population recorded on a particular night – chosen to coincide with a period when movement of persons would be minimal.[17] The figures for net migration are estimated: after deaths and births are taken into account a calculation can be made on the numerical differences between the two census periods in question and this then is used as an estimate of net migration.[18]

There is no place in Ireland where statistics are gathered centrally[19] which could serve as reliable evidence of the background, gender or numbers of emigrants and their host countries. Attempts to establish numbers of emigrants within a particular period can draw on two main sources. These are the official census figures[20] – referred to above – or there are the surveys carried out among certain groups.[21] None provides irrefutable evidence. In the absence of 'direct administrative measures', the census system operates as a purely mathematical calculation and the surveys cover only a small group of people. Post-censal population figures are only estimated and depend for confirmation on the next census.[22] Realistically it is therefore impossible to speak with any great authority on who has emigrated or to where.

Ireland has no de/registration requirements unlike most other European countries: with few exceptions[23] there is no obligation to inform the authorities of one's address. In addition, the UK and Ireland form a common travel zone which means that travellers between both countries do not need passports and travel can be carried out without prior notification.

While the traditional host countries remain attractive to emigrants – not least because of the language and possible existing personal contacts – there are of course new alternative host countries as a result of EC membership and ensuing free movement of workers.[24] There has been increased emphasis on other member states – specifically Germany[25] – although given the difficulties of monitoring actual emigration and especially actual host countries,[26] the question of empirical evidence remains to be addressed. It is difficult to estimate what the future will hold for labour mobility given the unpredictability and complexity of factors which influence it.[27] What is clear is that there are new alternatives and it remains to be seen to what extent these new alternatives will be explored by Irish emigrants.

Background to Female Emigration

Early Irish emigrants included an unusually high proportion of women – by European standards – rarely falling below 50 per cent.[28]

Eighteenth-century Ireland was a country where wealth was based on land ownership and a pre-industrial society with a rising population whose rural economy was unable to cope with the growth.[29] Young women began to emigrate to America and later to Australia first in the 1790s and then in growing numbers in the early nineteenth century, and eventually in a steady stream throughout the following century to a world where they could hope to better themselves and their relatives.[30]

The position of women in Irish society weakened in the post-Famine era[31] because of the changes wrought in domestic industry, in agriculture and in the home. Emigration was preferable to the economic alternative facing young women.[32] This deterioration in the economic status of women affected their marriage prospects[33] and contributed to a high incidence of female emigration in search of marriage and a family – which would have been denied to them at home. Had they remained in Ireland it would not have been possible economically to dower more than one daughter, as to do so would have reduced the family's savings and consequently their status.[34] In the period 1850-1950[35] some one third of emigrants from Europe (as a whole) were women whereas the proportion from Ireland for the same period was 50 per cent.[36] A disproportionate number of those women who remained in Ireland either did not marry at all[37] or else married husbands much older than themselves.

An alternative to emigration was offered to women by Fr Guinan:

> How happy, in comparison, and how blessed would have been the lot of an Irish girl, the poor betrayed victim of hellish agencies of vice, had she remained at home and passed her days in the poverty, aye and wretchedness, of a mud wall cabin – a wife and mother mayhap[38] – her path in life smoothened by the blessed influences of religion and domestic peace until it ended at a green old age in the calm peaceful repose of God's just.[39]

We are told that those who emerged as the beneficiaries of the 'post-famine settlement had no urge to linger unduly on the implications of emigration'[40] and tended to seek to lay the blame elsewhere – anywhere – on anyone, including the emigrants themselves. In so doing they painted a rosy picture of Irish society at the time,[41] being left behind by these emigrants who would rue the day they left their homes. In particular the 'fickleness of females' was blamed for

> ...Irish girls, beguiled by hopes of fantastic wages abroad, give up more than they know when instead of the simple neighbourly village life or the friendly relations still existing in good Irish households, they choose at a distance the tawdry, uncertain splendours of a despised servant class, and take on themselves the terrible risk of utter failure faraway from all home help. It is surely true that scarcely one Irish girl abroad is ever happy again at heart.[42]

As Lee explained,[43] the concern with female emigration resulted from the fact that Irish emigration was unusual given (as we have said) that it was 50 per cent female: the ratio for other countries being 2:1 (males predominating). This concentration on female emigration allowed attention to be deflected from the male emigration and its underlying causes. The cinema was regarded as a particular *bête noir* – as having put ideas into the heads of flighty females – especially from the 1930s onwards. No consideration was given to the reality of life for women – as expressed by AE (the poet George William Russell) in 1912:[44]

> Many a young girl must have looked on the wrinkled face and bent back and rheumatic limbs of her mother, and grown maddened in a sudden passion that her own fresh young life might end just like this.

Whereas male emigrants had been in the majority during the 1936-1946 period – a period including the Second World War years – in the immediate post-war period[45] women emigrants were again in the majority. Concern for the threat, real and imagined, to the sexual morality of female emigrants resurfaced with the huge increase in the number of girls leaving. Of every 100 girls in Connaught aged 15-19 in 1946, 42 had left by 1951[46] and there were suggestions that restrictions be imposed unless the intending emigrants could prove that they were joining relatives. This suggestion was rejected by the Department of External Affairs.[47] The Department was inclined to the view that the reasons for the outflow were more than economic,[48] although the abnormal emigration of young girls was larger than the availability of employment openings in reasonable conditions in Ireland would seem to call for: it was also a fact that money wages and working and living conditions were generally less attractive than in Britain[49] – not to mention the greater personal freedom.

Of the various theories as regards the reasons for emigration and how it should be viewed, these include the view that:

> the weakness in [our] demographic experience is less the high emigration than the low marriage rate ... policies should be followed directed to removing the evil of a low marriage rate even if there were made inevitable by such policies a higher rate of emigration.[50]

This has been criticised as intellectually unsustainable given that the two[51] are historically intimately connected.[52]

The 1951-1961 period saw a brief reversal of the immediate post-war and pre-1936 trend. The period 1961-1979 was again a time when the majority of emigrants were women. However, since that time the more recent censuses have shown a majority of male emigrants[53] and, since 1986, an excess of females over males in the population at large.[54]

Recent studies into the causes and effects of female emigration[55] continue to refer to the economic factors – coupled with social pressures (repressive moral and social attitudes) – as influencing female emigration from Ireland.

Women and Work

Women have always worked,[56] whether on smallholdings or as domestic servants, although it cannot be said that they ever formed a homogeneous group. Opposition to married women in the workforce in the early days of the State remained constant until relatively recently. Only six per cent of married women in the Free State and in Dublin in 1926 were active outside the home – a statistic which did not change appreciably until the 1960s.[57] The marriage bar[58] in the civil service[59] did not disappear until after Ireland acceded to the EC.[60] In the early days of the State, disapproval of married women working outside the home was felt even among women trades unionists.[61] Attitudes to single women were somewhat different. However, this did not necessarily improve their lot as their wages were low and working conditions so bad as to encourage them to emigrate.[62]

Irish women easily found work in post-war Britain – to a large extent in the areas where native labour was less willing to work (domestic service, factory employees, hotels, catering) – but also in nursing and clerical areas[63]. Irish women did not have quite the same working-class image in Britain as Irish men had. Many of them were recruited directly from Ireland – especially nurses – and were supplied with hostel accommodation. This often provided them with a ready made social circle and springboard to more permanent accommodation.

Recent studies into female emigration[64] suggest that female emigrants in the main still occupy the lower end of economic activity – citing the domestic, au pair and catering occupations:[65] they, of course, are still represented among the middle-class professions like nursing, teaching, banking. The view is also held that Irish female emigrants (in London) are very well educated but unable to find jobs which make use of their educational achievements and skills.[66] There is the suggestion that women are faced with greater difficulties in finding work – and in coping with their role as mothers because they find themselves without a support system in their host country. There is a lack of empirical research into emigrants[67] and work outside the traditional host countries,[68] which limits informed discussion on the alleged brain drain – male and female.

It is difficult to estimate what the future will hold for labour mobility in general, let alone female emigration, given the unpredictability and complexity of factors which influence it.[69]

Ireland and Membership of the EU[70]

Ireland eventually acceded to the European Communities in 1973.[71] During the negotiation period the question of free movement of workers[72] did not receive a great deal of attention.[73] This lack of attention was described at the time as 'insular' given the perceived supply (in Ireland) and demand (in other member states) for workers.[74] Other less enthusiastic views on EC free movement of workers were held, especially given the historical significance of emigration in Ireland.[75]

In the intervening years a wider range of views on the merits and demerits of EC free movement of workers has been aired.[76] The official attitude has now changed to the extent that there is active participation in the EURES[77] (European Employment Services) by Irish officials. This is a means whereby would-be employers (in the various member states) and workers (in the various member states) are given access to information on available jobs and job seekers. It is still too early to comment on its efficacy – either in terms of numbers of successful job placements[78] or in terms of quality of work on offer. It does, however, show a complete reversal from the time when the official attitude was that Irish workers would not look to the mainland of Europe but would continue to concentrate on the traditional host countries.[79]

Female Migrants in the EU

The free movement provisions of the EC treaty (and secondary legislation) do not have a gender bias. Their focus is (in the first place) the worker[80] or the self employed[81] or provider of services[82] – as economic actors/factors of production. These economic actors/factors of production can be male or female. Among the many benefits accruing to workers[83] (and their families and dependants as defined[84]) who are nationals of member states are: the legal right to exit/entry, national (equal) treatment in relation to access to and conditions of employment, and the right to reside and to remain. These have been supplemented by secondary legislation widening the circle of those who enjoy the legal right of free movement[85] and by amendments to the EC treaty arising from the TEU (Treaty on European Union) which confer political rights on migrant citizens of the Union living/working in a member state other than their own.[86]

Non-nationals represent 4.2 per cent of the female population and 5.3 per cent of the male population in the EU. Two-thirds of non-nationals are non-EU citizens. The percentage of young women among female non-nationals is higher than it is among nationals – with, conversely, the proportion of older women being much lower. France, Germany and the UK are the favoured host countries for all migrants (EU citizens and non-EU citizens alike) – with the highest percentage of the population as a whole being found in Luxembourg and Belgium.[87]

Foreign women who are nationals of EU member states are spread very unevenly in the EU. Luxembourg, Ireland and Belgium have the highest percentage of EU citizens.[88] The most recent figures available[89] indicate that of the five[90] most prominent home countries among the twelve member states, Irish migrants are the only group where there are more female migrants than males represented:[91] this 'distinction' also applies taking the other[92] five 'leading' home countries for migrants moving to EU member states into account. This would seem to suggest that Irish female migrants as a total body within the EU represent a numerical majority over males. It must of course be remembered that a sizeable number of these would be in the UK, one of the well-established traditional host countries for Irish emigrants.

Irish Female Emigrants in the EU

The problem of the lack of centralised statistics in Ireland on emigrants and the actual host country has already been alluded to. There is also the problem that the host country statistics may not reflect the actual situation on the ground. Although there may be de/registration requirements in the host country – a normal feature of many European countries – it is not inconceivable that the requirements are ignored by some of the migrant population.

This can be for a number of reasons: the migrant worker may be working on the black market and thus not wish to draw the attention of the authorities to themselves: in itself this is an interesting reflection on the appreciation by the migrant worker holding citizenship of the Union of the benefits which the legal right to free movement confer. It may of course be that the migrant worker is unaware of the legal rights conferred which then begs the question as to how migrants can be best informed of their rights.

A migrant worker may choose to ignore the de/regulation requirements – especially the de-registration requirement. This may be because of the intention to return to the host country at a later date and a desire not to get caught up in bureaucracy. This may result in migrants being counted as still resident when in fact they have left the host country. This phenomenon is well known.[93] It can be exacerbated by the fact that the Irish would constitute only a fraction of the foreign population and thus

The most recent statistics[95] for Irish nationals in other member states are shown in Table 1:[96]

Table 1 *Irish nationals in other EU member states, 1992*

Belgium	2,000
Denmark	1,000
Germany	13,000
Greece	1,000
Spain	2,000
France	4,000
Italy	1,000
Luxembourg	1,000
Netherlands	4,000
UK	506,000

No figures were shown for the other member states.[97] Unfortunately, there is a lack of full-scale empirical research on Irish emigration to EU member states. Among the exceptions to this is research[98] carried out in 1988 in Germany.[99] This entailed a survey among Irish residents:[100] in addition, official German statistics were examined.[101] A discrepancy between those registered as paying social welfare contributions, in receipt of unemployment benefit or child benefit and nationals[102] was apparent. This discrepancy[103] continues to be seen in subsequent official – and unofficial – annual statistics.[104] Apart from the empirical research carried out in 1988 – referred to above – there has been no attempt to explain these discrepancies. This example is offered as grounds for urging caution when drawing on official statistics as regards numbers of migrants and their host country.

As has already been pointed out above,[105] the official statistics indicate that Irish female migrants are the only ones among the ten main home countries for migrants within the EU showing a majority over male migrants. However, given the general caveat discussed above, any discussion of actual female emigrants must be treated with the same caution.

Conclusion

Emigration as a general phenomenon has re-emerged in Ireland. Female emigrants no longer represent the majority of the outflow as was the case; they do, however, represent the numerical majority of the total number of emigrants in the EU. Figures are still a matter of calculation rather than empirical research; the question of host countries is still an open one – in the absence of direct monitoring measures – both in Ireland and in host countries. Without doubt, EC free movement of workers does confer legal rights on Irish migrants – male and female – moving to other member states and also provides alternative host countries. It still remains to be seen whether there will be a noticeable shift from the traditional countries.

Notes

1 This chapter was presented at the Freudenstadt Symposium of 1993; it has been largely left unchanged, which should be borne in mind in relation to statistics.

2 J J Lee, *Ireland 1912-1985: Politics and Society*, Cambridge: Cambridge University Press, 1989, pp.377 ff; pp.380 ff: Commission on Emigration and Other Problems, p.222 (A Fitzgerald, *Reservation No.2 to the Reports of the Commission on Emigration and Other Problems*), Dublin, 1956.

3 Kieran A Kennedy, Thomas Giblin and Deirdre McHugh, *The Economic Development of Ireland in the Twentieth Century*, London: Routledge, 1988, p.38.

4 *Ibid.*, p.47.

5 *Ibid.*, p.48. See Lee, *op. cit.*, p.227 for an official view of the positive aspects to emigration — safety valve, remittances, reducing demands on the Irish exchequer, unemployment assistance; p.260 on fear of returning

migrants and the knock-on effect on the weak Irish economy (which did not occur as Britain offered better prospects).

6 Lyons, *Ireland Since the Famine*, London: Weidenfeld and Nicolson, 1971, p.557; Lee, *op. cit.*, p.379.

7 CSO Census 91, Vol.1, p.16.

8 Kennedy *et al.*, *op. cit.*, p.141.

9 CSO Census 86, Table J, p.23.

10 Dáil Debates 1989, Vol.392, col. 1783 ff.

11 CSO Census 91, Vol.1, p.16.

12 *Ibid.*

13 See below: 'Background to female emigration'.

14 CSO Census 91, Vol.1, p.7.

15 *Ibid.*, p.8.

16 Jim Mac Laughlin, *Ireland: The Emigrant Nursery and the World Economy*, Cork: Cork University Press, 1994, p.69.

17 CSO Census 91, Vol.1, p.5.

18 *Ibid.*, p.15.

19 CSO Population and Labour Force — Projections 1991-2021, p.14.

20 *Ibid.*, p.215. 'Definitive estimates of net migration can only be made when census results become available. This absence of current information and the volatile nature of migration ... makes the projection of Irish population a very uncertain exercise even in the short term...'

21 HEA: universities on first jobs for third level graduates: Department of Labour, *Annual Surveys of Second School Level School Leavers*. These are regarded as 'useful pointers'; see Sexton, 'Recent Changes in the Irish Pattern of Emigration', in *The Irish Banking Review*, Autumn 1987, pp.31-44; p.34.

22 CSO Statistical Abstract 1994, January 1995, p.22.

23 Department of Social Welfare, *Guide to Social Welfare Service*, Dublin (issued annually)

24 EC Treaty articles 7a, 8a and 48 (as amended by the Treaty on European Union).

25 Patricia Conlan, *Die Bedeutung der EWG-Freizügigkeit für Irland: Fallstudie Irland-Bundesrepublik Deutschland*, Berlin: Duncker and Humblot, 1991, pp.97 *et seq*.

26 As indicated above.

27 EC Commission Beschäftigung, pp.152ff.

28 Gearóid O'Tuathaigh, 'The Historical Pattern of Irish Emigration: Some Labour Aspects', in Galway Labour History Group (ed.), *The Emigrant Experience*, Galway, 1991 (papers presented at the Second Annual Mary Murray Weekend), p.11.

29 M MacCurtain, 'The Historical Image',in Ni Chuilleanain (ed.), *Irish Women: Image and Achievement*, Dublin: Arlen House, The Women's Press, 1985, pp.37-50; p.43.

30 *Ibid.*, p.45.

31 Lee, 'Women and the Church since the Famine', in M Mac Curtain and D Ó Corráin (eds), *Women in Irish Society*, Dublin: Arlen House, The Women's Press, 1978, pp.37ff.

32 Daly, 'Women in Ulster', in Ni Chuilleanain (ed), *op. cit.*, pp.51-60; p.54.

33 Lee, *art. cit.*, p.38.

34 *Ibid.*, p.39.

35 For details on the role of the land in Irish society / Irish economy see, *inter alia*, Lee, *Ireland*, pp.390 *et seq.*

36 Lee, *art. cit.*, pp.38-39.

37 Liam O'Dowd, 'Church, State and Women: The Aftermath of Partition', in Curtin, Jackson and O'Connor (eds), *Gender in Irish Society*, Galway: Galway University Press, pp.3-36; p.23.

38 Despite the drop in the marriage rate given the post-Famine economic and societal changes.

39 Lee, *Ireland*, p 383; drawing on J Guinan, *Priest and People in Doon*, Dublin 1903, 6th edition 1925), as quoted in Lee, *art. cit.*, p.43.

40 Lee, *Ireland*, p.375.

41 i.e. 1908.

42 Lee, *Ireland*, p.376; drawing on the *Freeman's Journal* of 24 February 1908.

43 Lee, *Ireland*, pp.376ff.

44 *Ibid.*, p.376.

45 CSO Census 91, Vol.1, p.16.

46 Lee, *Ireland*, p.377.

47 Quoted in Lee, *Ireland*, p.377: 'nothing effective can be done to protect the moral and social interests of girls going to domestic service once they have left the country'.

48 *Ibid.*

49 *Ibid.*

50 *Ibid.*, p.381; citing A Fitzgerald, *Reservation to the Report of the Commission on Emigration*, p.222.

51 High emigration and low marriage rate.

52 Lee, *Ireland*, p.382.

53 CSO Census 91, Vol.1, p.16.

54 *Ibid.*, p.8.

55 K Kelly and T Nic Ghoille Coille, *Emigration Matters for Women*, Dublin: Attic Press, 1990, p 14; see Jim Mac Laughlin, *op. cit.*, pp 70ff.

56 Luddy and Murphy, 'Cherchez La Femme', in Luddy and Murphy (eds), *Women Surviving: Studies in Irish Women's History in the Nineteenth and Twentieth Centuries*, Dublin: Poolbeg Press, 1989, pp.1-15; p 8.

57 O'Dowd, *art. cit.*, p.27.

58 The marriage bar in the Civil Service also had a negative effect on single women as it was not seen as a worthwhile investment to promote (and train) single women who would only have a short career: see Daly, 'Women, Work and Trade Unionism', in MacCurtin and O'Corrain (eds),

Women in Irish Society: The Historical Dimension, Dublin: Arlen House, The Women's Press, 1978, pp.71-81; p.76.

59 Banks, insurance companies and other such private sector employers following suit.

60 1 January 1973.

61 Daly, *art. cit.*, p.75.

62 O'Dowd, *art. cit.*, p.28.

63 Ryan, 'Irish Emigration to Britain since World War II', in R Kearney (ed.), *Migrations: The Irish at Home and Abroad*, Dublin: Wolfhound Press, 1990, pp.45-68; p.54.

64 K Kelly and T Nic Ghoille Coille, *op. cit.*, 1990, p.14.

65 *Ibid.*, pp.71ff.

66 *Ibid.*, pp.72ff.

67 In general — not just female emigrants.

68 For examples of restricted research see MacEinri, 'The New Europeans: The Irish in Paris Today', in Mulholland and Keogh (eds), *Emigration, Employment and Enterprise*, Cork and Dublin: Hibernian UniversityPress, 1989, pp. 58-80 (Paris); Patricia Conlan, *Bedeutung*, pp.113ff (FR Germany).

69 EC Commission Beschäftigung, pp.152ff.

70 The Treaty on European Union (TEU), Title I, article A establishes a European Union on the foundations of the existing three Communities. As a political concept it is therefore deemed appropriate to refer here to EU, whose territory would be analogous to that of the European Communities (EC).

71 Conlan, *Bedeutung*, pp.80ff.

72 Article 48ff., EC Treaty and secondary legislation.

73 For comments from different perspectives, see, Government of Ireland, *White Paper* 1970 (Government view): Dáil Debates, 1971, Vol.252, Column 232 (Opposition view); see also K R Simmonds, *The Dublin Conference*, October 1970 (report), C.M.L.Rev.8 (1971), pp.266 ff. (general).

74 Jane Cochrane, *Implications for Ireland of Membership of the European Communities*, C. M. L. Rev. 7 (1970), p.340: for full discussion on this criticism and background see PConlan, *Bedeutung*, pp.83 ff.

75 For an insight into this thinking see Conlan, p.84; especially footnote 47.

76 See *ibid.*, pp.97ff. for some of the views.

77 Decision 93/569/EEC: see P Conlan, (ed.): *EC/EU Legislation in Ireland*, Dublin: Gill and Macmillan, 1994, pp.1002ff.

78 For comments on the role of the public employment service as a means for successful matching of potential job applicants/employers, see, OECD, *The Public Employment Service in a Changing Labour Market*, Paris: OECD, 1984.

79 Government of Ireland, *White Paper*, 1970, Chapter 6.7.

80 Article 48 ff. EC Treaty.

81 Article 52 ff. EC Treaty.

82 Article 59 ff. EC Treaty.

83 These legal rights are no longer confined to economic actors/ factors of production – emanating from article 48 EC Treaty and secondary legislation or self-employed (article 52ff) or providers of services (article 59ff.): for details of the wider circle see PConlan, (ed.), *EC/EU Legislation in Ireland*, pp.1188 ff. The TEU inserted an amendment into the EC Treaty (article 8-e) establishing 'citizenship of the Union' – which brings with it legal rights to free movement for all 'citizens of the Union'. Citizenship of the Union is conferred on all nationals of member states.

84 Regulation (EEC) 1612/68: see P Conlan, (ed.), *EC/EU Legislation in Ireland*, pp.977ff.

85 Students, retired, those of independent means — with families/ dependants as defined, Directives 90/364/EEC, 90/365/EEC and 93/96/EEC, in P Conlan,(ed.), *EC/EU Legislation in Ireland*, pp.1188 ff; in addition recipients of services — see Luisi v M. del Tesoro C 286/82 [1984] ECR 377.

86 Articles 8b-c, EC Treaty.

87 1992 (12), Office for Official Publications of the European Communities, *Women and Men in the European Union*, Luxembourg, 1995, p.29.

88 The most recent statistics available (1992) date from before the accession of Austria, Finland and Sweden in 1995: see *ibid.*, pp.29 *et seq.*

89 1992: see previous footnote.

90 Italy, Portugal, Ireland, Spain and Greece.

91 Office for Official Publications of the European Communities, *op. cit.*, p.33.

92 Turkey, Morocco, Former Yugoslavia, Algeria, and Poland; see previous footnote.

93 For an examination of the situation of Irish citizens/ workers in the Federal Republic of Germany and the phenomenon of the 'file bodies', see PConlan, *Bedeutung*, pp.110ff.

94 For an example of this in the Federal Republic of Germany, see P Conlan, *Bedeutung*, p.111.

95 Office for Official Publications of the European Communities, Eurostat Yearbook '95, Luxembourg, 1995, pp.66-7.

96 As of 1992.

97 Portugal. Austria, Finland and Sweden had not acceded to the EU in 1992.

98 Limited in its scope: see also MacEinri, in Mulholland and Keogh (eds.), *op. cit.*

99 Excluding the old GDR.

100 Workers *and* non-economically active.

101 Statistisches Bundesamt: Bundesanstalt für Arbeit.

102 P Conlan, *Bedeutung*, pp.110ff.

103 Between social welfare contributors (workers) and nationals with dependency ratios (residents:workers) being excessive and, given the age structure of those 'counted', requiring closer investigation.

104 Statistisches Bundesamt: Bundesanstalt für Arbeit.
105 See section on 'Female migrants in the EU'.

III

The Federal Republic of Germany – A Melting Pot? The Integration of Refugees after the Second World War

Mathias Beer

Introduction

The Federal Republic of Germany, it is frequently maintained, is no country of immigration. But if we look at the positive migration ratio and the development of immigration figures since the end of the Second World War, then such a statement is revealed as untenable. Since 1945, over 25 million people have come to the Federal Republic.[1]

The bulk of those who have migrated to the Federal Republic since the Second World War can be classified into several groups according to circumstance, reason for, and actual time of, migration as well as origins. Chronologically speaking – albeit with overlappings – there are the following groups.

First, the expellees and refugees who came to Germany in consequence of evacuations, flight and expulsion – as a result of the fascist regime and the Second World War. Both German states had received more than 12 million refugees by the early 1950s.

A second group would be the 'Gastarbeiter', recruited in the Mediterranean countries since the mid-1950s to satisfy the needs of the labour market in the flourishing German economy. Today, as a result of this recruitment, about seven million foreigners live in the Federal Republic.

A third group involves ethnic German settlers. According to the German constitution this encompasses on the one hand

Eberhard Bort and Neil Evans (eds), *Networking Europe*, Liverpool University Press 2000, 193-215.

people of German ethnicity from eastern and south-eastern European states, who came to Germany since the beginning of the 1950s; on the other, citizens of the GDR who left the 'workers' and peasants' republic' in great numbers before the Wall was built in 1961, and then again towards the end of the 1980s. Since 1951 the Federal Republic has received about 2.5 million settlers from the eastern countries and about the same number from the GDR.

The fourth group involves asylum seekers. Their number has risen dramatically in the recent past and exceeded the figure of 200,000 per year at the beginning of the 1990s.

Taken all together, these figures show that nearly one third of the population presently living in the Federal Republic stems from immigration. There are no figures comparable to these in the second half of the twentieth century – neither among the industrial states nor among the classic overseas immigration countries. The emigration country that Germany was in the nineteenth and early twentieth centuries has been transformed, even if that may seem unacceptable to many, into an immigration country.[2] Immigration and integration situations are not the exception, they are the rule in the history of the FRG.

Even if the processes of integration of all immigrants into the Federal Republic are intertwined and have a lot in common, the differences prevail. In my paper I will restrict myself to a study of the largest group of immigrants into the Federal Republic, the refugees and the victims of expulsion. Using examples mainly from the south-west of Germany, my paper will deal with, first the preconditions and, in a second step, the development and, finally, the result of this integrative process which, despite the bulk of secondary literature,[3] has not yet been sufficiently researched.

Preconditions and Framework

A few years ago the French political scientist and expert on Germany, Alfred Grosser, stated with astonishment and respect that the integration of the war refugees was the biggest task in social and economic policy mastered by the Federal Republic.[4] This impartial judgement is only one among many which acknowledge the integration of refugees and expellees as nothing less than a miracle.

If we look at the preconditions we will see that 'miracle' was not an over-exaggeration. During the war, about one million ethnic Germans were – under the motto 'Heim ins Reich' (Home into the Empire) – planted in the conquered areas in the east, where the Polish population had been evicted.[5] Even before the end of the war, hundreds of thousands of Germans fled with the advancing front line from the areas beyond the Oder and Neiße rivers or were driven away from there. Added to them was a quantity of expellees running into millions.[6] The Allied Forces who had, during the war, basically agreed on a transfer of the German population, did not initially realise the size the stream of refugees and expellees would take. In retrospect, the American Division responsible for the transfer stated: 'Last fall, when the problem was beginning to develop ... the problem was completely underestimated.'[7] It was the Potsdam Conference, which cemented the European post-war order sketched at Yalta, that the 'transfer of parts of the German population according to order and humanity' from Poland, Czechoslovakia and Hungary to the four occupied zones was decided upon. At the same time, the Allied Control Council got the order to work out a 'just distribution of these Germans among the various occupation zones.'[8] According to this plan, which went into operation on 20 November 1945, the Soviet zone was supposed to receive 2.75 million Germans from Poland and Czechoslovakia, the American zone 2.25 millions evicted from Czechoslovakia and Hungary, the British zone 1.5 millions expelled from Poland, and the French zone 150,000 refugees from Austria. Yet the plan and its execution differed considerably. A 1947 report on the refugee problem in the American occupied zone states: 'These figures have already been by far surpassed because unexpectedly, the largest number of Germans from east of Oder and Neiße have been expelled by the Polish government.'[9] But the figures were also surpassed because Yugoslavia on its own authority expelled its German citizens.[10] At the census of 13 September 1950 the ratio of evicted refugees was 16.5 per cent of the total population of the Federal Republic, which in absolute figures amounted to about eight million people. Roughly two-thirds originated from the eastern provinces of the Reich, the remaining third from a number of states in the eastern parts of central Europe where large German minority communities lived.[11] The distribution of refugees in the Federal Republic was, other than anticipated by Allied planning, uneven. Whereas, for example, Schleswig–Holstein, which together with Lower Saxony and Bavaria was among the main receiving Länder, counted thirty-three refugees per hundred inhabitants, the Rhineland-Palatinate at the same time had only three per hundred. At the time of this census in the Federal Republic, over four million 'transfer settlers' ('Umsiedler'), as the evicted were officially called there, lived on the territory of the GDR – a fact that had not been recognised for a long time.[12]

This was not the first, but the biggest forced population transfer in the history of the twentieth century.[13] The aim of it was, as Winston Churchill once said, to get a settlement once and for all. Through the 'transfer', quoting the Greek–Turkish population exchange of 1923 as a precedent, a national purification in the evacuated areas was to be gained. On that basis a lasting solution of the minority and ethnic conflicts in east-central Europe was expected.

As new as the extent of the population transfer were the questions about coming to terms with its consequences. The reception of such a huge number of people in such a short time would have confronted a functioning state apparatus with barely soluble problems. All the more difficult was the reception and accommodation of the millions of refugees and expellees who, generally speaking, possessed no more than their own life, in a defeated, occupied and destroyed country like Germany. The American Julian Bach appropriately summed up the situation in Germany after unconditional surrender:

> America, Britain, Russia and France, speaking three different languages among themselves, are trying to rule a fifth nation, Germany, which speaks a forth different language. All this is taking place in the world's largest collection of worthless ruins.[14]

The Expellee and Refugee Problem before the Foundation of the Federal Republic

The American military government made it clear right from the start that it considered the integration of expellees and refugees as an exclusively German problem.[15] In its view, the expellees and refugees were a result of the presumptuous policies of the Nazi Reich. Quite in contrast, for instance, to the millions of forced labourers who had been deported to Germany – displaced persons[16] – who were taken care of by the allied forces directly, accommodation and catering for the refugees and the expellees was the sole responsibility of German authorities. Had Germany not attacked and had the evicted been loyal to the governments of their places of residence, then, according to General Lucius D Clay, the deputy governor and later military governor of the American occupied zone, then the refugee problem would not have occurred in Germany.[17]

Notwithstanding such statements, the American military government exerted a considerable influence upon the development of the refugee problem in Germany. The USA had agreed to Article XIII of the Potsdam Agreement because they had expected that by doing away with the German minorities in east-central Europe, this area would be pacified. For that, a lasting accommodation of the expellees was an absolutely necessary prerequisite. Simultaneously, the task was to avoid the situation where, in the reception areas in Germany, the refugees and expellees would develop into a new minority with pronounced leanings towards left- or right-wing movements. The means of achieving this goal was the rapid and total assimilation of the refugees and expellees.[18] 'These persons will be absorbed integrally into the German communities and will be subject to all laws, regulations and will be entitled to all privileges therein.'[19] This total assimilation into the West German population – sharing the same language and culture was seen as a good starting point – was to lead to an amalgamation with the West German population of expellees of different origin, background, experience and traditions. In the shortest possible time the refugees and expellees were, according to American policy targets, to become indiscernible from the native West German population: 'United States policy is directed toward the full assimilation, political, social and economic, of all refugees in the communities to which they are assigned.'[20] Based on the American historical experience, they obviously used the 'melting pot' as their point of reference. The American military government did its utmost, following the maxim of 'Make the Germans do it', to direct the efforts of the German authorities responsible for integrating the refugees towards assimilation. Laws and restrictions, the enactment and observation of which were controlled, were supposed to help achieve the target of assimilation.

The German administrative authorities, such as were left after the collapse or were in the process of reconstituting themselves, followed these demands reluctantly. The Stuttgart Ministry of the Interior, for example, took until November 1945 to appoint a provisional refugee administrator, upgraded in March 1946 to government official for refugees (Staatsbeauftragter für das Flüchtlingswesen), although he was charged with only a few responsibilities.[21] Accordingly, the measures taken were scanty. They were only related to 'directing and looking after the refugees'. And this purpose, it was generally assumed in early 1946, could be achieved within the bounds of general care. The refugee problem had not yet gained the attention it deserved. The refugees were looked upon, analogous to the evacuated Germans, as an alien group of people, here today and, hopefully, gone tomorrow, and thus as a temporary problem. This estimate led to a continuation of the state of administrative inertia which stemmed from the emergency situation after the total collapse at the end of the war.

When regular mass transports commenced in 1946, the number of expellees to be accommodated rose dramatically. Thus, beginning in February 1946, 18 transports with, all in all, 20,000 expellees were directed into the Borough of Leonberg (just outside Stuttgart).[22] Because of war casualties and the enforced retention of men able to work in the areas of expulsion, the number of women and children exceeded by far the number of men. The expellees and refugees were sent predominantly to rural, agricultural areas. This was because it was thought that channelling the expellees to areas that were as thinly populated as possible, only peripherally touched by the destruction of war, would benefit the fast execution of the transfer.

This inadequate framework, reluctantly installed, led to severe problems, beginning with accommodation and distribution. The boroughs objected strongly to the increasing influx of eastern refugees. In May, the Ludwigsburg Borough administration demanded that the transfer of eastern refugees into the borough must end immediately, because such an accommodation of eastern refugees was no longer possible.[23] This was not a lone voice: in a number of boroughs in the German south-west the quota of expellees and refugees reached the thirty per cent mark. In those communities to which refugees from the chronically–overcrowded borough transit camps were allocated, without consideration of economic, social or denominational factors, the picture was the same. We read in a letter from a vicar, 'the purely Protestant village of Neubronn [has] received 116 Catholic and seven Protestant refugees, while over 70 and over 200 Protestant refugees were directed, respectively, to the purely Catholic villages of Hohenstadt and Abtsgmünd.'[24] Often the expellees could only be moved into the confiscated rooms, according to the Accommodation Act No. 18, with the help of the police. Camps had to be installed to offer the newcomers at least a roof over their heads.[25]

These inadequacies and the increasing gravity of the situation were also recognised by the occupying forces. A report of the sub-department for Food and Agriculture, OMGUS Berlin, dating from 1946, states that neither in Württemberg-Baden nor in Hesse or Bavaria had there been any serious effort to:

> create coordinated plans for the accommodation, care or distribution of the refugees ... The problem has not been recognised as a general problem of uprootedness, abolition and settlement of whole communities, but as an emergency problem of poverty relief.[26]

The unsatisfactory handling of the refugee problem, the non-existence of a targeted plan, and the continuing number of 20,000 expellees arriving in weekly mass transports led, in mid-1946, to an increase of pressure by the American military government on the German authorities. The Stuttgart Government was called upon to give priority to the accommodation of incoming refugees, and to work out a plan of immediate, short- and long-term measures ensuring the integration of the expellees. 'It is the responsibility of German government in this Land to resettle these refugees and expellees in a manner which will cause a minimum of unrest and dissatisfaction.'[27] The plan produced in reaction to this was rejected by the military government as not being appropriate to achieving its goals and principles. The amalgamation of the expellees and the refugees with the indigenous population – 'they must be absorbed' – could not be guaranteed in a plan whose principle was separating expellees and resident citizens.

> The organization as outlined in the plan submitted, appears to be built somewhat on the principle of separation: separate budgets, separate staff, separate schools, separate societies of settlers, separate industries. The basic principle approved by the Military Government is one of assimilation, not separation.[28]

In accordance with these principles the military government issued a so-called coalition ban. Expellees and refugees were banned from founding their own parties: 'Expellees and refugees should express their political needs by joining the established political parties and political groups rather than seeking to create their own separate parties and groups.'[29] The military government categorically vetoed the repeatedly articulated demand for the licensing of expellee parties. 'To facilitate the assimilation of expellee and refugee elements into the life of the German people, political parties whose primary aim is judged to be the furtherance of expellee and refugee interests will not be authorized.'[30] They not only assumed that special parties for the expellees would hinder the assimilation process, but also feared that 'such a party might well become the focal point for irredentist movements which would again menace the peace of Central Europe.'[31]

The massive demands and clear-cut ideas of the military government, aiming at assimilating the expellees to make the expulsion irreversible and thus promote the pacification of Europe, were not without consequence. They resulted in, among other things, the relevant laws of the Land Württemberg-Baden. The 'Provisional Guidelines for the Care of Refugees', issued on 26 September 1946, postulated the creation of a new home for the expellees and refugees as an aim. Refugees and expellees were put on a par with the indigenous population in every respect. They were granted all citizens' rights and duties – equal to any other German, with one exception: they were not allowed to create their own political parties. The guidelines explicitly speak of a new home to be created for the refugees and expellees in the South West.[32]

Even more clearly expressed is the aim of assimilation, aspired to by the occupying force and unwillingly followed by the German administration, in 'Act No. 303 Concerning the Accommodation and Integration of Refugees (Refugee Act)', issued on 14 February 1947: 'The integration of refugees and expellees shall safeguard their organic merging with the indigenous population.'[33] Along with the acceptance of the aim of assimilation and its increasing manifestation in law-making, a new term for the expellees turned up: new citizens ('Neubürger'). That term had not existed before and was introduced following the explicit wishes of the military government. In mid-1947, for instance, the State Commissioner for Refugees organised an exhibition in the Messeturm in Bad Cannstatt. Its programmatic title was 'Our New Citizens: New Citizens – New Hands – New Home'.[34] The exhibition aimed at 'awakening and furthering the understanding for the integration of the new citizens' and at showing the indigenous population the high culture and economic values the new citizens brought with them. The mayor of Wertheim, a town in North Baden, addressed the expellees of his community by the end of 1947: 'New citizens, you stay here.'[35]

The term 'Neubürger', which was fast spreading, embodied the goal to transform expellees and refugees into fully accepted citizens, equal to the indigenous population. It stood for the attempt to make, by law, full citizens of eastern refugees and expellees.

Local Circumstances

Yet the social and economic situation was far from fulfilling the promise implied by the term 'Neubürger'. In accordance with its strict advocacy of assimilation, the military government gave the order that the expelled population from one community or village was not to be settled together, but severally in the whole area of settlement. 'In order to prevent minority cells from developing ... the German authorities will distribute and resettle expellees from any one community abroad among several German communities, to the greatest extent practicable.'[36] Accordingly, the 2,000 inhabitants of the Hungarian village of Nagykovacsi, for instance, were settled far from each other. Two of the three transports, in which the whole German population of the community was expelled, were directed to the Baden boroughs of Sinsheim and Buchen, the third to two Bavarian boroughs. The former inhabitants of the village now, in 1947, lived in 158 different communities.[37] Anyone familiar with the circumstances and relationships prevalent in a village community will know the lasting damage inflicted by such a splitting up of communities. It was not a question of uprooting, but rather a cutting off of roots that had been growing for decades and centuries.

In addition, the expellees and refugees, despite repeated appeals and threats of punishment – 'the native population will be subject to severe penalties for discrimination or agitation against the newcomers'[38] – were not seen and accepted as German fellow citizens. They remained, in the eyes of the native population, the 'so-called new citizens'. They spoke differently, wore different clothes, very often had a different creed, and they were without possessions and, in most cases, without work and thus competitors in the work market. In various opinion polls of the time, many of the expellees said that the native population did not regard them as Germans but as human beings of minor value, as strangers or even beggars.[39] A woman expelled from Budaörs, a village near Budapest, stranded with her family in Schorndorf, east of Stuttgart, said that in the beginning she had not understood the natives and vice versa. She had once been asked if she (herself a Bavarian dialect speaker) was speaking

Hungarian, whereupon she had answered she was speaking German. Even greater were the difficulties when natives and refugees were forced to live side by side in a narrow space. Then scepticism and rejection could turn into open hostility against the new arrivals.

To the deficiencies in accommodation was added the catastrophic economic situation. Most of the expellees were directed towards rural areas. In 1949, still more than half of the refugees and expellees lived in communities of under 2,000 inhabitants.[40] These offered very few jobs. In the area of agriculture, workers were needed, but this meant in many cases an alien occupation for the refugees and expellees, accompanied by a decline in social respect. Those jobs were taken up with great reservations and only to secure nourishment for the family. The poor food situation could be mitigated with the help of the Act for the Provision of Land Settlement and the Land Reform Act as well as the Initiative for Garden Land, but could not be effectively improved.

The disorganised communities, the uprootedness, the stressful accommodation situation and the difficulties in the labour market meant that a large proportion of the refugees and expellees still regarded their sojourn in West Germany as temporary. In 1946, for example, the Director for Work and Welfare in Karlsruhe complained about unwillingness to work among the male refugees from Yugoslavia and Czechoslovakia: 'They believe in building a state within the state and harbour thoughts of returning very soon with their families to their homeland.'[41] In the founding contract of a firm formed by refugees in 1946 we read:

> The company has been formed for the duration of the sojourn of eastern refugees in North Württemberg-Baden. It will have fulfilled its purpose as soon as the complete return of the eastern refugees is decreed by the authorities.[42]

Even in a 1948 poll, ninety per cent of the refugees and expellees expressed their wish to return to their homeland.

Miserable housing, the tense situation in food supply and sometimes fierce competition in an underdeveloped labour market led 'here and there to an actual war between old and new citizens'. Even in the graveyard the new citizens were not tolerated among the ranks of the natives. In the boroughs of Waiblingen and Aalen, east of Stuttgart, a broadsheet made the rounds with a poem in the form of a prayer:

> Father in heaven, look down on our plight,
> We farmers have neither larder nor bread.
> Refugees dine, get round and fat
> and steal our last bed.
> We die of hunger and suffer great pain,
> Lord father, send home the pack.
> Send them back to Czechoslovakia,
> Lord god, set us free from that pack.
> They have neither creed nor name
> The thrice-damned, forever amen.[43]

These catastrophic circumstances did not escape the eyes of the occupying force:

> Swabians from Hungary and ethnic Germans from Czechoslovakia are culturally different from natives of Württemberg or of Baden and subject to discrimination and aversion as foreigners. The implications of the situation are becoming more fully realized each passing month. There are real economic, social, political and religious differences. It is not yet certain which process – of assimilation or of estrangement and discrimination – is making the most headway.[44]

They had learned that they had overestimated the common linguistic, social, economic and cultural features of old and new citizens and underestimated the existing differences between the two groups and between the different expellee groups.

> It is certain that these cultural differences have been largely ignored in the urgent efforts to secure a minimum of a single room for each family unit. The efforts of settlement have been greater than was anticipated... In

> general the difficulty of assimilation increases with the time elapsed.[45]

The ban on coalitions was loosened so that New Citizen Societies – only allowed to pursue economic, social and cultural interests – were mushrooming. The course taken up to then came under review.

> Rapid assimilation within a generation demands ruthless, probably inhumane, scattering of these expellees over Germany. Some cultural and social loss will be involved ... On the other hand, any grouping for social satisfaction or political and economic protection from discrimination may perpetuate minority groups and identify classes considered socially and economically inferior, if not centers of trouble.[46]

But this did not yet mean a fundamental renunciation of the concept of assimilation. General Clay, in 1947, impressed on the minister-presidents of the three Länder within the American zone:

> These people are with you. They must be absorbed and your good citizenship in the future depends on the manner in which you absorb them. If matters continue as at present, you will be establishing a minority group fostering hatred and hostility for years. You should know the difficulties that minority groups have caused in the past.[47]

And this danger seemed to come true when the ban on coalitions was fully suspended in 1948. The developing refugee parties were growing fast, not least because the licensed parties had, up to then, hardly dealt with the affairs of the refugees. In the second land elections, Deutsche Gemeinschaft/Block der Heimatvertriebenen und Entrechteten (German Community/ Block of Expellees and Deprived People) returned 16 out of 100 mandates.[48] The successes of the refugee and expellee parties were a sure sign that the equal rights laid down in law were socially, economically and politically still far from being enacted.

Accordingly, the account which the State Commissioner for Refugees of Württemberg-Baden came up with was sceptical.[49] The expellees 'will only then find a new home among us when we succeed in giving them decent jobs and dignified housing.' Neither was the case for most of the population. Many expellees and refugees were occupied outside their profession. They were hit more severely than the indigenous citizens by the negative consequences of the currency reform.[50] The proportion of unemployed was always higher among the expellees than among the indigenous population. Towards the end of the 1940s, the number of unem-ployed rose massively among the expellees and reached peaks of up to nearly forty per cent.[51] Looking at the newly-founded refugee firms, the report of the Refugee Commissioner stated that turn-over and numbers in employment would not yet allow a judgement of the future importance of these firms. Even worse was the situation of the expellee farmers. 'The full integration of this group of persons is impossible, considering the structure of the Land.' With good reason the report finally speaks of an 'incipient integration'.

The 'Integration Miracle' in the Federal Republic of Germany

The much-hailed miracle of integration was to take place only after the foundation of the Federal Republic, when the essential responsibilities in refugee legislation were transferred from Land to Bund. The first federal government declared housing shortage, levelling of burdens and the care for war victims – in other words the removal of war consequences – as the most urgent tasks within the realm of social policy. With that, the integration of refugees and expellees was elevated to a state measure of the first rank. This was made obvious and documented *vis à vis* the public by the establishment of the Ministry for Expellee Affairs, unprecedented in German history.

As a first step, the lop-sided distribution of refugees and expellees caused by the post-war situation was corrected. In various resettlement programmes between 1949 and 1956, the main receiving countries – in the following order: Schleswig-Holstein, Lower Saxony and Bavaria – handed over refugees and expellees to Länder with a lower quota.[52] At the receiving end were, above all, Northrhine-Westfalia, Baden-Württemberg and Rhineland-Palatinate. With that, not only was an even distribution of refugees over the whole area of the Federal Republic achieved; increasingly, the demand for work and actual jobs could be matched up. These resettlements were supported by specific resettlement programmes of the Länder.

A second important measure was the *Lastenausgleichsgesetz*[53] (equalisation of burden act), which was passed after a long and difficult process in 1952. The fundamental concept behind it was to pay the refugees and expellees a compensation rather than reimbursing them for all properties (mobile and immobile) lost through expulsion and flight. This was supposed to improve their inferior economic and social position. Complicated proceedings of acknowledging losses and of securing the necessary means for the compensation funds were introduced. The Equalisation of Burdens Act did not lead to any change in the Federal Republic's social structure – wished for by some, feared by others; nor was the existing distribution of property touched upon. Still, it helped considerably in facilitating social and economic integration.

The third important measure, closely related to the Equalisation of Burdens Act, was a concentrated effort on housing. The stimulation of house-building mitigated the acute shortage of housing. In due course, one by one, camps and emergency accommodation, in 1955 still home to 250,000 refugees and expellees, even after resettlements, could be dissolved. This was not only helped by financial boons and other support, but also by the immense degree of self-help among the refugees themselves, in building houses. Refugee and settlement co-operatives built complete blocks of houses. They also participated in the building of whole suburbs and villages springing up all over the Federal Republic.[54]

'Little Korea' – the nickname coined by the people for some of these settlements – points towards a factor which was in fact the key to the success of the aforementioned measures: the emerging new geo-political situation, soon to be labelled the

'Cold War'. This improved the conditions for integrating refugees and expellees considerably, both in social and economic respects, and politically. The reconstruction of the German economy was accelerated considerably by the Korean War. And a now flourishing and expanding economy offered jobs for refugees and expellees, too. Alien occupations, and therefore lower incomes in comparison with the natives, were compensated by the expellees' proverbial hard work, their high professional and regional mobility, and their high degree of adaptability and willingness to work. This, in turn, was an important motivating factor for the dynamic and long-lasting growth process of the West German economy. Without any doubt the up and running economy sent out strong integrationary impulses. By the mid-1950s a state of full employment was reached. The still existing demand for workers could now only be satisfied by the recruitment of 'Gastarbeiter'.

The conditions of integration were further improved by the US interest, stamped – in view of geopolitics – by the confrontation of two blocs, in an economically strong, politically and socially stable Federal Republic, fully integrated within the Western alliance. It is in this context that we must see the changing American attitude towards the German refugee problem: '[T]he sound rehabilitation of Western Germany's economy and the solution of the Refugee problem are closely related. This relationship is one of interdependence.'[55] Moneys from the European Recovery Programme were now released for integration measures. This meant a mitigation of the concept of strict assimilation, which had prevailed until then, in favour of a 'two-way process of integration'. But the problem of integration is, of course, not only an economic question. If it is to last, integration must be social and cultural.

> ... assimilation in the sense of absorption, is the last thing that should happen at this time in Germany's life, when she has a matchless opportunity to enrich herself through the mutual process of sharing cultures to which many countries owe so much ... So the process of integration must be mutual.[56]

This way of looking at things by the United States was in agreement with the integrationary policies followed by the Federal Republic. In addition to referring to the task of economic and social integration, the 1953 'Expellees and Refugees Act'[57], which also defined the relevant persons belonging to this group, stated as its aim 'to keep alive the consciousness of the cultural values of the expulsion areas within the body of expellees and refugees as well as with the entire German population.' That this also meant keeping the 'German Question' open can hardly be doubted.

The unexpectedly rapid progress in social and economic integration in the 1950s and 1960s meant that the refugee problem was soon regarded as having been solved. Analogous to the 'economic miracle', this unexpected success in dealing with the consequences of expulsion and flight was soon also termed a miracle. There was also no sign of the apprehended radicalisation of the expellees and refugees. Whereas the 'Block of Expellees' was still represented in the second Bundestag, it failed to pass the five per cent hurdle in the next general election. When in 1969, in the period of the emerging new *Ostpolitik*, the Federal Ministry for Refugees, Expellees and War Victims was dissolved, this was seen as expressing the belief that the integration of expellees and refugees was now complete. In economic and social respects this was, given only a few exceptions, certainly true. A different picture emerges if we take into account the psychological dimensions, the dimensions of mental histories, of this process. The process of integration itself covers a broad variety of attitudes and approaches by refugees and native citizens, reaching from a total merging (assimilation) to total non-acceptance. And these processes, beginning with flight and expulsion, have effects to this very day, as is shown by recent German refugee research, oriented towards social and migrational history. Even in this case of a successful integration of refugees and expellees, it seems, we must reckon with a pattern embracing three generations.

Conclusion

That the integration was eventually successful is to do with the specific conditions of post-war Germany. The refugees and expellees arrived in a country which was undergoing a severe social transition and trying to find, under the authoritative guidance of the occupying forces, a new social, economic and political order. Everything was in transition, a melting pot, creating a new blend out of old and new citizens. There was perhaps less of an integration of expellees and refugees into the Federal Republic – the Federal Republic seems, rather, to be itself the product of this successful integration process.

Yet the integration of refugees and expellees, because of the specific conditions of the post-war situation, cannot offer a manual for the present and future migration into the Federal Republic of Germany. But the study of this process may raise awareness of patterns of behaviour which have left their imprint on West German society.

Notes

1 Klaus J Bade, 'Einführung: Wege in die Bundesrepublik', in K J Bade (ed), *Neue Heimat im Westen: Vertriebene, Flüchtlinge, Aussiedler*, Münster 1990, pp.5-13. Klaus J. Bade, *Homo Migrans: Wanderungen aus und nach Deutschland: Erfahrungen und Fragen*, Essen 1994.

2 Siegfried Bethlehem, *Heimatvertreibung, DDR–Flucht, Gastarbeiter-zuwanderung: Wanderungsströme und Wanderungspolitik in der Bundesrepublik*, Stuttgart ,1982. Klaus J Bade, *Vom Auswanderungsland zum Einwanderungsland? Deutschland 1880-1980*, Berlin, 1983. K J Bade (ed.), *Auswanderer – Wanderarbeiter – Gastarbeiter: Bevölkerung, Arbeitsmarkt und Wanderung in Deutschland seit der Mitte des 19. Jahrhunderts*, 2 vols., Ostfildern 1984. K J Bade (ed.), *Das Manifest der 60: Deutschland und die Einwanderung*, München, 1994. K J Bade (ed.), *Ausländer, Aussiedler, Asyl: Eine Bestandsaufnahme*, München 1994. Wolfgang Benz (ed.), *Integration ist*

machbar: Ausländer in Deutschland, München, 1993. Jürgen Fijalkowski, 'Die Bundesrepublik und das Migrationsproblem: historische Erfahrungen und aktuelle Herausforderungen', in Manfred Knapp (ed.), *Migration im neuen Europa*. Stuttgart, 1994, pp.113-128. Johannes Dieter Steinert, *Migration und Politik: Westdeutschland – Europa – Übersee, 1945–1961*, Osnabrück,1995.

3 Gertrud Krallert-Sattler (ed.): *Kommentierte Bibliographie zum Flüchtlings- und Vertriebenenproblem in der Bundesrepublik Deutschland, in Österreich und der Schweiz*, ed.. Bayrisches Staatsministerium für Arbeit und Sozialordnung in Zusammenarbeit mit dem Sudetendeutschen Archiv und der AWR-Forschungsgesellschaft für das Weltflüchtlingsproblem, Wien, 1989. Rolf Messerschmidt, 'Mythos Schmelztiegel! Einige Neuerscheinungen zur "Flüchtlingsforschung" der letzten Jahre', in *Neue Politische Literatur*,Vol.37, 1992, pp.34-53. Mathias Beer: '"Baden-Württemberg ist noch nahezu unbeackert geblieben": Literatur und Quellenlage zur Eingliederung der Flüchtlinge und Vertriebenen im deutschen Südwesten nach 1945', in Mathias Beer (ed.), *Zur Integration der Flüchtlinge und Vertriebenen im deutschen Südwesten nach 1945. Ergebnisse der Tagung vom 11. und 12. November 1993 in Tübingen*, Sigmaringen 1994, pp.27-48. Cornelia Schmalz-Jacobsen und Georg Hansen (eds), *Ethnische Minderheiten in der Bundesrepublik Deutschland: Ein Lexikon*, München, 1995.

4 Franz J. Bauer, 'Zwischen "Wunder" und Strukturzwang: Zur Integration der Flüchtlinge und Vertriebenen in der Bundesrepublik Deutschland', in *Aus Politik und Zeitgeschichte*, Vol.32, 1987, pp.21-33. Mathias Beer: 'Zur Datierung eines Wunders: Anmerkungen zur Eingliederung der Flüchtlinge und Vertriebenen im deutschen Südwesten nach 1945', in *Banatica*, Vol. VIII, No.3, 1991, pp.7–22. For the term 'Integration' see Volker Ackermann, 'Integration: Begriff, Leitbilder, Probleme', in Mathias Beer (ed.), *op. cit.*, 1994, pp.11–26.

5 Helmut Hecker, *Die Umsiedlungsverträge des Deutschen Reiches während des Zweiten Weltkrieges*, Hamburg, 1972. Robert L Koehl, *German Resettlement and Population Policy 1939 –1945: A History of the Reich Commission for the Strengthening of Germandom*, Cambridge, 1957. Rolf Dieter, *Hitlers Ostkrieg und die deutsche Siedlungspolitik: Die Zusammenarbeit von Wehrmacht, Wirtschaft und SS*, Frankfurt am Main, 1991.

6 Bundesministerium für Vertriebene, Flüchtlinge und Kriegsgeschädigte (ed.), *Dokumentation der Vertreibung der Deutschen aus Ost–Mitteleuropa*. Bearb. von Theodor Schieder u.a., 5 vols. and 3 Beihefte, Bonn, 1954–1962, new edition, München, 1984.

7 RG 260 OMGUS 22-39/1-1.

8 Alfred Maurice de Zaya, *Die Anglo–Merikaner und die Vertreibung der Deutschen: Vorgeschichte, Verlauf, Folgen*, sixth, enlarged ed., München 1981. Joseph B Schechtman, *Postwar Population Transfer in Europe 1945–1955*, Philadelphia, 1962. Wolfgang Benz (ed.), *Die Vertreibung der Deutschen aus dem Osten: Ursachen, Ereignisse, Folgen*, Frankfurt am Main, 1985. Dieter Blumenwitz (ed.), *Flucht und Vertreibung*, Köln, Berlin, Bonn, München, 1987.

9 *Das Flüchtlingsproblem in der amerikanischen Besatzungszone: Ein Bericht des Länderrats des amerikanischen Besatzunggebietes*, Ausschuß für Flüchtlingsfragen an General Clay, Stuttgart, 1945, p.12.

10 *Dokumentation* (see note 6), Vol.5, Bonn, 1961. Hans-Ulrich Wehler, *Nationalitätenpolitik in Jugoslawien: Die Deutsche Minderheit 1918–1979*, Göttingen, 1980.

11 Gerhard Reichling, *Die deutschen Vertriebenen in Zahlen, Teil II: 40 Jahre Eingliederung in der Bundesrepublik Deutschland*, Bonn, 1989, pp.30-33, 106. Werner Nellner, 'Grundlagen und Hauptergebnisse der Statistik', in Eugen Lemberg und Friedrich Edding (eds), *Die Vertriebenen in Westdeutschland: Ihre Eingliederung und ihr Einfluß auf Gesellschaft, Wirtschaft, Politik und Geistesleben*, Kiel, 1959, Bd. 1, pp.161-44.

12 Alexander von Plato, Wolfgang Meinicke, *Alte Heimat – neue Zeit: Flüchtlinge, Umgesiedelte, Vertriebene in der Sowjetischen Besatzungszone und in der DDR*, Berlin ,1991. Manfred Wille, Johannes Hoffmann and Wolfgang Meinicke (eds), *Sie hatten alles verloren: Flüchtlinge und Vertriebene in der Sowjetischen Besatzungszone Deutschlands*, Wiesbaden, 1993. See also Helge Heidemeyer, *Flucht und Zuwanderung aus der SBZ/DDR 1945/1949–1961: Die Flüchtlingspolitik der Bundesrepublik Deutschland bis zum Bau der Berliner Mauer*,Düsseldorf, 1994. Volker Ackermann, *Der 'echte' Flüchtling: Deutsche Vertriebene und Flüchtlinge aus der DDR (1945–1961)*, Essen, 1995.

13 Eugene M. Kulischer, *Europe on the Move: War and Population Changes 1917–1947*, New York, 1948. Hans-Joachim Hoffmann-Nowotny, 'European Migrations after World War II', in William Mc Neill and Ruth S. Adams (eds.), *Human Migration: Patterns and Policies*, Bloomington, London ,1978, pp.85-105. Michael M Marrus, *The Unwanted European: Refugees in the Twentieth Century*, New York, Oxford, 1985. Hans Lemberg, '"Ethnische Säuberung": Ein Mittel zur Lösung von Nationalitätenproblemen?', in *Aus Politik und Zeitgeschichte*, Vol.46, 1992, pp.27-38.

14 Julian Bach, *America's Germany: An Account of the Occupation*, New York, 1946, p.4. Quoted in Elisabeth Kraus, *Ministerien für ganz Deutschland? Der Alliierte Kontrollrat und die Frage gesamtdeutscher Zentralverwaltungen*, München, 1990.

15 'The reception, care, distribution and resettlement of dislodged Germans and expellees who arrive within U.S. area of control under the authority of Military Government, is a direct responsibility of the German authorities.' RG 260 OMGUS 3-165/ 1–11.

16 Ulrich Herbert, *Fremdarbeiter: Politik und Praxis des 'Ausländer-Einsatzes' in der Kriegswirtschaft des Dritten Reiches*, Berlin, Bonn, 1985. Wolfgang Jacobmeyer, *Vom Zwangsarbeiter zum heimatlosen Ausländer: Die Displaced Persons in Westdeutschland 1945-1951*, Göttingen, 1985. Eugene M Kulischer, *The Displacement of Population in Europe*, Montreal, 1943.

17 Lucius D Clay, *Entscheidungen in Deutschland*, Frankfurt am Main, 1950, p.30.

18 Thomas Grosser, 'Das Assimilationskonzept der amerikanischen Flüchtlingspolitik in der US-Zone nach 1945', in T Grosser, Christiane Grosser, Rita Müller and Sylvia Schraut, *Flüchtlingsfrage – das Zeitproblem: Amerikanische Besatzungspolitik, deutsche Verwaltung und die Flüchtlinge in Württemberg-Baden 1945-1949*, Mannheim, 1993, pp.11–54. Sylvia Schraut,

Flüchtlingsaufnahme in Württemberg-Baden 1945–1949: Amerikanische Besatzungsziele und demokratischer Wiederaufbau im Konflikt, München, 1995, especially pp.62ff.

19 RG 260 OMGUS 3-165/1-11.

20 United States Department of State (ed.), *Occupation of Germany: Policy and Progress 1945–1946*, Washington DC (Department of State Publication 2783, European Series 23, p.25).

21 Roland Müller, 'Der Staatsbeauftragte für das Flüchtlingswesen und die Anfänge der Flüchtlingsverwaltung in Württemberg-Baden: Politik und Verwaltung in der Nachkriegszeit', in *Zeitschrift für württembergische Landesgeschichte*, vol. 52, 1993, pp.253-399. Schraut, *Flüchtlingsaufnahme, op. cit.*, pp.149ff.

22 Thomas Beckmann "Alle wollen in die Stadt': Pendlertradition und Eingliederung der Vertriebenen im Altkreis Leonberg', in Mathias Beer (ed.), *Integration, op. cit.*, pp.129-46. Concerning the number of refugees received in Württemberg-Baden, see Gerhard Boranski, 'Vertriebene und Flüchtlinge 1950 und 1961', in *Historischer Atlas von Baden-Württemberg*, Beiwort zu Karte XII, Stuttgart, 1992. Erwin Müller, *Die Heimatvertriebenen in Baden-Württemberg*. Berlin 1962. Schraut, *Flüchtlingsaufnahme, op. cit.*, pp.302f.

23 Hauptstaatsarchiv Stuttgart (HSTAS) EA 1/920. Bü 667. See also Landkreis Ludwigsburg (ed.), *Eingliederung der Vertriebenen im Landkreis Ludwigsburg: Ein Bückblick auf vier Jahrzehnte seit 1945*, Ludwigsburg, 1986.

24 Mathias Beer, 'Alte Heimat – Neue Heimat: Das spezifische Verständnis von Kirche und Gemeinschaft bei den Vertriebenen aus Südosteuropa und dessen Auswirkungen auf den Eingliederungsprozeß im deutschen Südwesten', in *Jahrbuch für ostdeutsche Volkskunde*, Vol.36, 1993, pp.244-72.

25 For an example of one of the numerous camps, see Mathias Beer, 'Schlotwiese: Fremde auf der Suche nach Heimat', in M Beer and Paula Lutum-Lenger (eds.), *Fremde Heimat: Das Lager Schlotwiese nach 1945*, Stuttgart, Tübingen, 1995, pp.5-10.

26 Franz Bauer, *Flüchtlinge und Flüchtlingspolitik in Bayern 1945–1950*, Stuttgart, 1982, p.247.

27 HSTAS EA 2/960, Bü 667.

28 *Ibid.*

29 RG 260 OMGUS 1945–46/1–4. See also Max Hildebert Boehm, 'Gruppenbildung und Organisationswesen', in Lemberg and Edding (eds.), *op. cit.*, pp. 521-605. Johannes Dieter Steinert, 'Organisierte Flüchtlingsinteressen und parlamentarische Demokratie: Westdeutschland 1945–1949', in Klaus J Bade (ed.), *Neue Heimat, op. cit.*, pp. 61-80. Schraut, *Flüchtlingsaufnahme, op. cit.*, pp.399ff

30 United States Departement of State (ed.), *Germany 1947-1949: The Story in Documents*. Washington DC. (Departement of State Publication 3556. European and British Commonwealth Series 9), p.159.

31 RG 260 OMGUS 17-55/2-9.

32 HSTAS EA 1/920 Bü 667.

33 Gesetz Nr. 303 über die Aufnahme und Eingliederung deutscher Flüchtlinge (Flüchtlingsgesetz) vom 14.2.1947. In Innenministerium Württemberg-Baden (ed.), *Wichtige Gesetze*, Stuttgart,1947, pp.1-6.

34 HSTAS EA 1/920 Bü 667. Schraut, *Flüchtlingsaufnahme, op. cit.*, pp.368ff. Concerning the different terms, see Mathias Beer, *Flüchtlinge und Vertriebene im deutschen Südwesten nach 1945: Eine Übersicht der Archivalien in den staatlichen und kommunalen Archiven des Landes Baden-Württemberg*, Sigmaringen, 1993, pp.13-24.

35 Walter Rahn, *Das Schicksal der Heimatvertriebenen in Wertheim am Main: Herkunft – Flucht – Ankunft – Eingliederung: Eine Dokumentation.* unpublished Ms., 1991.

36 RG 260 OMGUS 3-165/1-11.

37 Johannes Künzig, 'Unsere Sorgen um die Heimatlosen', in J Künzig (ed.), *Kleine volkskundliche Beiträge aus fünf Jahrzehnten*, Freiburg, 1972, pp.175-182.

38 RG 260 OMGUS 11-38/3-6.

39 Anna J Merritt and Richard L Meritt.(eds), *Public opinion in occupied Germany: The OMGUS Surveys, 1945–1949*, Urbana, Chicago, London, 1970, pp.112-14, Report No.28, 14 November 1946.

40 Sylvia Schraut, 'Zwangswanderung nach 1945 und ihre sozialen Folgen: Die Aufnahme der Flüchtlinge und Ausgewiesenen in Württemberg-Baden 1945-1949', in Grosser *et al.*, *Flüchtlingsfrage*, *op. cit.*, pp.164-95, esp. pp.170ff.

41 Paul Sauer, *Demokratischer Neubeginn in Not und Elend: Das Land Württemberg-Baden von 1945 bis 1952*, Ulm, 1978, p.246.

42 HSTAS 2/801 Bü 309.

43 Archiv des Instituts für donauschwäbische Geschichte und Landeskunde Tübingen, Nachlaß Hamm 354.

44 RG 260 OMGWB 12-27/1-15.

45 *Ibid.*

46 RG 260 OMGWB 12-27/1-5.

47 Bundesarchiv Koblenz and Institut für Zeitgeschichte (eds), *Akten zur Vorgeschichte der Bundesrepublik Deutschland 1945-1949*, Vol.2, München, 1989, p.186.

48 Immo Eberl, 'Vertriebenenverbände: Entstehung, Funktion, Wandel', in: Beer, *Integration* , *op. cit.*, pp.211-34. Innenministerium Baden-Württemberg (ed.), *Flucht, Vertreibung, Eingliederung: Baden-Württemberg als neue Heimat. Begleitband zur Ausstellung*, Sigmaringen, 1993, pp.166-75.

49 Staatsbeauftragter für das Flüchtlingswesen (ed.), *Die Eingliederung der Heimatvertriebenen in Württemberg–Baden: Stand 31 . 12. 1951*, Stuttgart, 1952, p.7.

50 Ian Conner, 'Die Integration der Flüchtlinge und Vertriebenen in den Arbeitsprozeß nach 1945', in *Jahrbuch für ostdeutsche Volkskunde* Vol.32, 1989, pp.185-205.

51 Falk Wiesenmann, 'Flüchtlingspolitik und Flüchtlingsintegration in Westdeutschland', in *Aus Politik und Zeitgeschichte*, Vol.23, 1985, p.35-44.

52 Georg Müller and Heinz Simon, 'Aufnahme und Unterbringung', in Lemberg and Edding, *op. cit.*, pp.300-446.

53 Reinhold Schilling, *Der Entscheidungsprozeß beim Lastenausgleich, 1945–1952*, St. Katharinen, 1985. Immo Eberl, *op. cit.*, pp.188-95.

54 Hermann Bausinger, Markus Braun and Herbert Schwedt, *Neue Siedlungen: Volkskundlich soziologische Untersuchungen des Ludwig-Uhland-Instituts Tübingen*, Stuttgart ,1959. Elisabeth Pfeil, 'Städtische Neugründungen', in Lemberg and Edding, *op. cit*, pp.502-20. Erhard Holtmann, 'Neues Heim in neuer Heimat: Flüchtlingswohnungsbau und westdeutsche Aufbaukultur der beginnenden fünfziger Jahre', in *Jahrbuch für ostdeutsche Volkskunde*, Vol.30, 1987, pp.1-19.

55 *The Integration of Refugees into German Life: A Report of the ECA Technical Assistance Commission on the Integration of the Refugees in the German Republic*, Washington,1951, p.6.

56 *Ibid.*, p.8.

57 *Bundesvertriebenengesetz. Gesetz über die Angelegenheiten der Vertriebenen und Flüchtlinge*, Stuttgart, Köln, 1953.

Growing Old in a Strange Country: Some Results and Reflections Based on a Research Project in Stuttgart

Friederike Hohloch

Introduction

My paper is based on an *expertise* which I carried out, commissioned by the City Council of Stuttgart, entitled 'Living conditions of aged migrant workers who do not follow an occupation'.[1] For this *expertise* I interviewed staff members in about forty institutions specialising in working with ethnic minorities and staff members of general social services. My questions did not only concern the living conditions of older migrant workers, but I also gathered propositions from staff members as to the question of how to deal with future challenges regarding the elderly of ethnic minorities. In my paper I try to draw a connection between gerontological and migration research by exploring some major issues in regard to the social processes of the ageing of migrant workers in Germany. This paper is to give an insight into a group of migrant workers, using demographic data. Subsequently, some socio-economic aspects which influence the lives of aged migrant workers in Germany will be analysed. Then I will discuss the question of re-migration in old age and the option of returning as a lifelong attitude. Furthermore, I will look at resources within ethnic communities and family support in old age. I will then finish with some general remarks concerning social policy.

Eberhard Bort and Neil Evans (eds), ***Networking Europe,*** **Liverpool University Press 2000, 217-34.**

A German Paradox:
Immigration without being an Immigration Country[2]

To reflect upon immigration into Germany is a difficult enterprise. Estimations and political statements about this phenomenon are deeply divided. At the extreme poles of a continuum of attitudes and opinions are at the one end those which repeat stubbornly that 'Germany is not an immigration country' and often paint frightening visions of a country swamped by foreigners. The danger of 'Überfremdung' (over-alienation) is their catchword.[3] And there are those, at the other end of the spectrum, committed to idealistic conceptions of a multi-cultural society, praising all the advantages and possibilities of democratisation, liberation and the enrichment of the cultural diversity of a nation. Both representatives and their respective statements usually lack historical depth. Germany, as a country in the centre of Europe, has always been an objective of immigration, a fact that is often overlooked. I would like to concentrate on one phenomenon of post-war immigration which, historically, is particular indeed. The elderly of ethnic minorities I am talking about are members of post-war immigration, which started in the late 1950s.

I would like to give a short insight into the historical background of recruitment of 'guest-workers' in the 1960s. The post-war period of economic growth, the so-called German 'Wirtschaftswunder' (economic miracle), coincided with a shortage of workers caused by diminished middle-age groups as a consequence of the Second World War. Due to the falling birth rate during the war, the generation that entered the labour market in the 1950s was small in number. This was interrelated with the high proportion of elderly people in Germany. Many middle-aged people, who would have been the backbone of the work-force, had lost their lives in the war. In 1955, the Army of the Federal Republic of Germany was set up, and half a million young people, who normally would have entered the labour market, were recruited into the *Bundeswehr*. The building of the Berlin Wall in 1961 put an end to the wave of refugees from East Germany.[4]

These circumstances led to a post-war shortage in the labour force in the 1960s and became the starting point for the systematically-organised recruitment of foreign labour. Commissons composed of business executives, officers of the employment offices and appointed medical staff travelled, first to villages in southern Italy, then to Greece, Spain and Portugal and, in the early 1970s, to Turkey and former Yugoslavia. The migrant workers were submitted to a thorough medical check before they received their work permits.

Most of these first generation guest-workers remained, legally, 'Ausländer' (foreigners), which means foreigners without any political rights, vulnerable to the regulations of the *Ausländergesetz*.[5] Their legal status in terms of residence, working permission and social security varied with regard to their origin and citizenship in EC countries (Italy, Greece, Spain, Portugal) and non-EC countries (former Yugoslavia and Turkey). At the time I carried out my research in Stuttgart, about 80 per cent of the immigrants of the southern European countries had time-restricted residence permissions. As has been said: their career as German citizens has been that from 'guest-worker' to 'foreigner'.[6]

For the migrant workers themselves, migration – as a rule – was a provisional project. The proximity to the countries of origin, new communication technologies and transport systems supported the hope of return, as they were able to maintain close relations to their communities of origin. They were hard workers, sometimes with two different jobs simultaneously, in order to earn enough money to support families at home, sometimes to build houses in their villages, and to save money for the purpose of establishing a new business at home. Yet the date of the intended return 'home', for complex reasons, was deferred from year to year. Having grown old in the country of immigration, the ambitious project of a migration aiming to return 'home' as professionally successful persons was a failure.

In contrast to the countries in the Americas, whose national identity is that of an immigration country, the unexpected existence of aged migrant workers in our German society questions some taken-for-granted assumptions. Elderly people from ethnic minorities are definitely a falsification of the idea that migration of labour in Europe is temporary and that the migrant worker's life in Germany is a provisional project. The political intention to recruit an economically efficient labour force, prepared to return as soon as they are not needed any more, may be one of the reasons for the fact that the whole issue is discussed with a connotation of 'abnormality'. In publications of the 1970s which criticise the instrumental character of immigration politics one often comes across the quotation of the Swiss writer Max Frisch: 'We wanted workers, and human beings came.' In the 1990s, with a growing number of aged first-generation migrant workers, this statement has taken on a new dimension: human beings are growing old from the very beginning of their existence.

The elderly of ethnic minorities are certainly a very recent issue in social policy and in the social sciences. Looking at the literature in Germany, one will find publications resulting from conferences of professionals, mainly social workers, who at that time – in the late 1980s – were already confronted with ethnic minority elderly as clients. There has been some documentation produced by communal and federal state administrations in the 1990s. The city council of Stuttgart published my *expertise*. Since 1990, one finds a growing number of articles by social scientists in periodicals dealing with questions of migration and social work. The first theoretically elaborated monograph, which makes available a synthesis of migration, gerontology research and theories of adult education, was published in 1993.[7]

This focus on ethnic minority elderly has not found its way into social communal planning, as an overview of future concepts in Stuttgart revealed. First-generation guest-workers are either invisible or, if mentioned at all, always mentioned with the conclusion that, regarding provisions for the help-for-the-aged programmes, they can be neglected because they will return to their country of origin. The group of aged migrant workers is still, in absolute figures, a minor one, but its number is growing, particularly in Germany's urban areas. Some demographic developments, focusing on Stuttgart, need to be explained.

Demographic Aspects of Old-Aged Migrants in Stuttgart

With regard to falling birth rates and the proportional growth of the number of aged people, industrialised societies are described as 'ageing societies' with dwindling populations. The age composition of non-German citizens shows remarkable differences from that of the population in general: in 1991, 21 per cent of the population were older than 60, while among the population of the so-called foreigners only five per cent were older than 60.[8] The prognosis is that the 'foreign' population will assimilate to the age composition of the German population. There are projections available from the year 1987, predicting that in the year 2030 we will reach a proportion of 37.2 per cent of people older than 60 in the group of foreigners, which translates into 2.1 million persons in absolute numbers.[9]

In terms of the scale of its foreign population, Stuttgart ranks fourth amongst German cities. Stuttgart has 575,277 inhabitants, of whom 135,682 are, legally speaking, non-German citizens.[10] This amounts to 23.6 per cent of Stuttgart's population. The major group within the foreign population – 79.8 per cent (107,608) – are migrant workers from southern European countries.[11]

To conclude this section, I would like to give a short breakdown of the composition of the group of migrant workers, regarding relevant age-groups and national origin. We will find a continuing increase within the group of ethnic minority elderly from the year 1974 to the year 1993 (Table 1).

In absolute numbers, there were 23,400 non-German inhabitants, aged between 45 and 60, from southern European countries in Stuttgart. This is the group which will be growing old within the next years and will cause a disproportionate increase in the group of people older than 60, which contained only 5,990 persons in 1993.

Table 1 *Increase in number of non-German inhabitants in Stuttgart older than 60*

Year	Population older than 60	Non-German pop. older than 60	Percentage of pop. older than 60	Percentage of non-German population
1974	128,739	2,267	1.8	2.3
1982	132,772	2,748	2.2	2.7
1991	122,487	5,566	4.5	4.8
1993	122,125	7,681	6.3	5.7

Socio-economic Factors Influencing Quality of Life of Aged Migrant Workers

The socio-economic standard of living in old age is primarily a function of the social status and income level prior to retirement. It is a general phenomenon of the social ageing process that deficiencies and disadvantages will manifest themselves in middle age and cumulate in old age because the chances to improve standards of living will decline. Recent comparative studies about the living conditions of migrant workers confirm that, in comparison with Germans of the same class, a cumulation of disadvantages for migrant workers can be shown which will compound the problem and increase insecurity in old age.[12]

In terms of age and income, we have to distinguish two groups of aged migrant workers: those who loose their employment aged between 50 and 60, and those who are entitled to old age pensions.[13] Particularly the older long-term unemployed migrant workers are confronted with difficult problems and challenges, which will affect their quality of life in old age. And at the moment they are the main group that social workers in counselling services for immigrants are concerned with.

Their opportunities for re-entering the job market are minimised due to reasons which give an insight into the working conditions of first-generation migrants. Ninety per cent of the migrant workers are employed in manufacturing industries which are particularly sensitive to economic crisis and rationalisation.[14] The standard of occupational qualification is usually low. Within the group of unemployed migrant workers in the local unemployment office of Stuttgart, 80 per cent were without any qualifications.[15]

Employment in manufacturing industries also brings high health risks. While migrant workers started out as a select group with an above-average health record, there has been a steady process of assimilation into the population in general. Research since the late 1970s has found an increasing number of applicants for invalidity pension.[16]

Old and long-term unemployed people are left in a difficult situation, stuck between their insecure economic and vulnerable legal status. The procedures of being accepted as long-term unemployed or as a claimant of pension insurance – to get either an invalidity or a retirement pension – take an average of four to five years. The reasons for the long duration of medical and administrative examinations of the pension scheme are to be found in conditions specific for migration. The entitlement to a pension depends on the years of membership in the pension insurance scheme. Very often it is necessary to know the number of years of pension contributions in the country of origin in order to legitimise the claim for German insurance. Besides the fact of complicated international co-operation procedures between often widely differing structures of administration, migrants from rural areas often have difficulties to prove their times of membership, because they may have worked as casual labourers or members of family enterprises. Sometimes time-consuming proceedings by the social security appeal tribunal are necessary to clarify claims. To bridge that long period of insecure financial status, people not infrequently need supportive social benefit, which may either affect and endanger their legal status, or which is avoided for fear of legal restriction. Social workers reported that many clients in that situation spend all their savings, laid aside for life in old age and the envisaged return. This might not be a problem if the pension is eventually granted, but this is not the guaranteed outcome in all cases. Besides the danger of impoverishment in general, future re-migration might be made impossible, as it presupposes long-term and secure economic conditions.

The low income of retired migrant workers is another consequence of their careers. The amount of retirement pension in Germany is based on income and duration of employment. The migrant workers usually become members of the pension insurances in their late 20s and spend their entire working lives in low-paid jobs. Their average pensions were about 30 per cent lower than those of Germans in the same occupation group.[17]

Social gerontological studies demonstrate a correlation of quality of life and satisfaction with the accommodation provided in old age. In Stuttgart, we find a concentration of 30 per cent of the migrant population in the inner city area. Despite the fact that the immigrant population is, demographically, a young population, the immigrant population in this part of the city resembles the German one in its age structure: 37 per cent of those living in the inner city are older than 50.[18] The advantage may be that they grow old in their accustomed neighbourhoods and networks, but when loss of vigour jeopardises self-sufficiency, the low quality of housing may have dramatic consequences. Social workers in hospitals are reporting increasing numbers of migrant workers who would have returned to their homes, with the support of community nursing workers, but finally had to move to nursing homes because of bad housing conditions.

Rückkehrorientierung — Option of Re-migration, or: How to Grow Old with an Unsolvable Dilemma

For many of the migrant workers, life in Germany always was provisional. But in 1989 only one out of six migrant workers older than 60 re-migrated.[19] The reasons for retired migrant workers to stay in Germany are as follows: the children and grand-children have settled in Germany and have become an increasingly important focus of social life in old age. Confronted with the realistic possibility of return after retirement, many realise the alienation from their country of origin. They also realise that re-migration is, in fact, a second migration, with challenging consequences and burdens. If exacerbated by loss of vigour in old age, re-migration sometimes seems to be too demanding a project. A very important reason, too, is the well developed health service in Germany, which with growing age assumes an increasing importance. In some cases this means not only the wish for better quality, but is an existential need, particularly if regular medical treatment involves medical high technology which, especially in rural areas of the countries of origin, may not be available.

The findings of my interviews, backed up by socio-psychological studies of migration, suggest a strict differentiation between the concrete decision of re-migration and the orientation towards returning to the country of origin, the option of re-migration as a life-long attitude of first-generation migrants. This attitude is usually preserved into old age. It is the very heart of the migration-as-provisional concept of life.[20]

Earlier migration studies which usually follow deficit paradigms about migrants and their lives treated the wish of re-migration as an 'illusion', a cause of many problems for migrants. Recent research, based on Berger and Luckman's concept of 'social construction of reality',[21] changed perspectives and began to examine the meaning of this attitude within subjective worlds and migration contexts, questioning its instrumental character with regard to the development of internal ethnic support systems. In this perspective, the life-long option of return is seen as part of the complex strategies of people coping with migration.[22] The option of re-migration stands as a metaphor symbolising loyalty both towards the community of origin and the minority community in Germany. It can be described as an expression of one's intention to continue to remain a member of both communities. It is part of the system of self-perception and self-esteem. Regarded as part of one's own identity, this attitude may oscillate in its meaning and importance during the course of one's life. The meaning of the option of re-migration may reach a new importance in old age as an attitude which creates continuity in the biography and may correlate very closely with the intensity of ethnic identification and ethnic reminiscence in old age.

A certain undecidedness is the consequence. A solution for this dilemma can be described as a typical pattern of old migrant workers in European countries: 'commuting migration',[23] which means spending longer periods of time in both the adopted country and the country of origin, is a pragmatic and active solution for those whose health and financial situation will allow travelling between Germany and their country of origin. 'Commuting migration' should be perceived as a 'retirement pattern', a particular pattern known in all industrial countries. Among German elderly people we will, for example, find the so-called 'Mallorca pensioners'.

Retreat into the Ethnic Group: Provision of Support or Double Stigmatisation of Being Old and a 'Foreigner'

Gerontological theories and research emphasise the importance of non-material resources, like integration in social networks and subjective perceptions and expectations towards life in old age. Ageing represents one of many aspects that are socially defined, and old age is a category whose properties and problems are constructed within the context of shared expectations. In the next section I explore some general issues relating to these problems.

The discussion about 'retreat into an ethnic colony in old age' as resource or jeopardy is conducted against the background of two gerontological hypotheses. These two competing hypotheses about satisfactory adjustment to ageing are the activity theory and the disengagement theory. The activity theory holds that those who withdraw or disengage themselves from activities as they become increasingly older are more likely to adjust to old age. One aspect in this debate deals with the question of social integration. How is retreating within age-homogeneous groups to be understood? Either as a process of social disintegration and disengagement or an activity, a mobilising process which supports the active adjustment to old age? This is a complex question in the case of first-generation migrant workers.

The retreat to age-homogenic groups is generally interpreted as a reaction against stigmatisation and negative stereotyping of aged people in industrial societies. Because of its effect as a self-fulfilling prophecy, this approach has been criticised as supporting disengagement concepts. Recent developments in gerontological discourse have abandoned that dichotomy. First of all, the recognition of heterogeneity of the aged reveals that one has to differentiate with regard to particular groups of aged people. Furthermore, the mobilising effect of age-homogeneous groups, particularly with regard to an increase in self-consciousness and the development of new competences and social support systems, is also recognised.

This gerontological approach can be linked with sociological theories of 'ethnicity' and the growth of 'ethnic colonies'. Ethnicity as an important dimension of social differentiation in modern pluralist societies describes, within a dynamic concept of social identity, the feelings of belonging to the same region of origin or ethnic group and the reference to common language, traditions, history and belief systems. In a process of loss and revitalisation, ethnic identity gains changing connotations and meaning throughout the life-span. In Germany, we lack long-term research projects and findings, so a final and conclusive answer to the question of how membership of an ethnic group is influencing the social process of ageing cannot be given. American studies reveal that one has to differentiate strictly between different ethnic groups.[24]

However, we can state some tendencies. The first generation of migrants, in particular, moved in groups; sometimes members of the same village moved into the same regions and created support systems for overcoming initial problems in the new arrivals' new lives abroad. These were age- and, at the very beginning, gender-homogeneous groups, in which symmetric interaction in terms of status and language was possible. In my research, I found confirmation for the theoretical assumption that age as a 'stage of reminiscence' reinforces an orientation towards the past, which means towards 'cultural roots'. The loss of social roles after retirement, together with the decrease of social contacts with Germans, which in the case of first-generation migrant workers concentrated mainly in the 'world of work', reinforces the revitalisation of ethnic identity and stresses the importance of relations to one's own ethnic group. Ethnicity, together with the option of return, forms a system of strategies to cope with and adjust to old age. The double-negative stigma of being old in an industrial society and being a foreigner can thus be weakened. But in the interviews it became also obvious that those who have not created ethnic networks before their retirement or are alienated from their ethnic groups are prone to suffer extreme social isolation. The fact that many of them have very little knowledge of the German language closes the door to German peer groups. On the German side, social workers' reports speak of hostile attitudes towards foreigners within the older generation in their institutions, and they are not very optimistic that social integration of migrant workers could be successful.

In Stuttgart, social workers occupied in counselling and caring for different ethnic communities started groups for aged migrant workers. These, as far as age and ethnicity is concerned, homogeneous groups of Turks, Greeks and Italians have become important meeting points. The aims of these projects are to enable social contacts, to build networks of mutual support, to offer meetings on topics which can be subsumed under the broad field of adult education for the elderly (language classes, information classes on issues concerning pensions and social benefits in old age, but also excursions to, say, Stuttgart's museums or institutions of local administration etc.) and to organise inter-cultural meetings between different ethnic groups of old people. Weekend seminars on issues concerning old age have proved very productive. Practical developments of mutual support systems, like the foundation of a 'Telefonkette' (a private telephone network to be used in cases of emergencies at home) have been the first tangible results. The experiences of inter-cultural meetings between different minority groups and German groups of elderly people showed that such projects have to be well prepared by the organisers. Prejudices on either side are serious obstacles.

Family Support in Old Age

Particularly for the first-generation migrant workers reaching old age, core and extended family links will gain in importance. Young second-generation families thus are confronted with high expectations of financial and emotional support. I often heard the statement: 'The family is our little home country abroad'. Recent studies show that inter-generational relations are influenced by dramatic social and cultural changes within the junior generations. But one should not invent the image of 'cultural dramas' within families inevitably leading to a lack of inter-generational solidarity. Social position will enforce the 'normative solidarity' which means an obligation of family orientation and support. A 'functional solidarity', meaning the transfer of financial resources, is the most probable consequence.[25]

But I found in my research that we must also pay attention to the fact that caring for elderly family members is a question of material resources being a major factor for the realisation of good-will towards mutual family support. The sometimes meagre financial budgets of the second migrant generation, the double-employment of husband and wife, their restricted housing conditions plus their high mobility as a 'reserve army of workers' may be serious obstacles, particularly in cases of physical frailty of aged family members when intensive caring is demanded. These factors may affect particularly what is called 'affectual solidarity'[26] (the quality of emotions between family members) and the 'associational solidarity'[27] (the quality and intensity of inter-generational communicative interaction). The overburdening of caring female family members is an issue in help-for-the-aged programming in general.

Another, often ignored, aspect is the number of single persons within the group of aged migrant workers. In Stuttgart, 44 per cent of male migrants in the age group between 45 and 60 live without their wives.[28] After long periods of separation, a return in old age cannot be taken for granted. Cases of divorce in old age are well known to social workers. A total of 46.5 per cent of all migrants older than 50 live in one-person households – an amazing approximation to German structures: 47.7 per cent of Germans in the same group live in single households.[29] Groups of aged single persons, particularly, will have to depend on social services and institutions in times of sickness or chronic infirmity.

Some Implications for the Development of Help-for-the-Aged Programmes, which will Meet Needs and Reflect the Context of the Migrant Elderly

A crucial socio-gerontological premise is to avoid degrading old people to objects of professional care. Concepts of social services for the aged generally are in a state of transition. Conceptual premises like 'tailoring services to the users'[30] can build a basis for the integration of the new group of elderly in Germany. Pragmatic consequences are the support of self-help systems, giving people a greater individual say in the services they need, but also encouraging and enabling the elderly to participate in future planning. The aim of placing greater reliance on quasi-voluntary help and informal support is ambiguous, particularly in times of financial austerity concerning state budgets. In my interviews, I found a tendency within the groups of professionals in help-the-aged programmes and social planners to overestimate the possibilities and resources of ethnic communities. Unproven, taken-for-granted assumptions and over-estimations serve to legitimise neglecting the possibilities for and needs of these groups. An either-or strategy (self-help or professional help) is doomed to fail. The conceptual reliance of community care needs, generally speaking, both perspectives: 'professional care in community' and 'helping the community to care'.[31]

Co-operation between representatives of communal social policy and representatives of ethnic minorities has been rudimentary – and is so to this day. One reason for this can be found in the consciousness of the professionals still being occupied by various kinds of unreflective myths about first-generation migrant workers, as mentioned above: the 'myth of re-migration in old age' and the overestimation of ethnic resources.

The description of another myth surrounding my topic will offer the opportunity of presenting a final perspective. It is often said by professionals and politicians that the issue of the elderly of ethnic minorities will be a transitory problem concerning only the first generation of guest workers. With reference to a paper of the Council of Europe published in 1991, Maria Dietzel-Papakyriakou has pointed out that there will be, in all European countries, a fluctuation of the immigrant population, with the consequence that there will always be a first generation.[32] Due to different backgrounds, we may have to deal with different needs, but to find answers to inter-cultural challenges for social policy is a long-term issue; the area of help-for-the-aged programmes is just one example.

Another aspect is social-psychological in nature and touches upon the questionable paradigm of what is called 'integration': based on the assumption that identity is a life-long dynamic process, one cannot foresee how a second, third, or even fourth generation may develop. Biographical studies of subsequent generations support the idea of what is termed 'biographical reflexivity'.[33] Interaction between people of different national and cultural origin in immigration does not mean that different kinds of modernised and traditional knowledge are strictly demarcated, one against the other, nor that certain ways of thinking will, self-evidently, get lost in the so-called process of modernisation. What will happen in multi-cultural societies is a permanent change, loss, renewal and revival of different forms of knowledge, life-styles and references of belonging. This means that it would indeed be short-sighted, and an expression of a mechanistic approach, to assume that the development of an inter-cultural orientation in the realm of social policies would be an approach limited to a certain time-span. A social policy which strives to avoid creating objects of care must reflect the particular living conditions of the elderly of ethnic minorities and their 'cardinal biographic experience'[34] of migration as a long-term project.

Notes

1 Friederike Hohloch, *Situation älter gewordener, nicht mehr im Arbeitsprozeß stehender ausländischer Mitbürger: Gutachten im Auftrag der Landeshauptstadt Stuttgartt*, Stuttgart, 1990.

2 See K J Bade (ed.), *Deutsche im Ausland. Fremde in Deutschland. Migration in Geschichte und Gegenwart*, München, 1992, pp.393ff.

3 i.e. the perceived danger of too many foreigners in a nation.

4 The first post-war immigration began as early as 1944, after the occupation of East Prussia by the Red Army. After 1945, flight and expulsion led to immense immigration movements, particularly into the West of Germany. A census of 29 October 1946 showed that 9.6 million refugees and evacuees had immigrated into West Germany (Wolfgang Benz, 'Fremde in der Heimat: Flucht - Vertreibung - Integration', in K J Bade (ed), *op. cit.*, p.382). Between the end of the Second World War and the reunification of the two Germanies in autumn 1990, about 15 million evacuees and refugees from Eastern Europe and East Germany (GDR) immigrated into the "old" Federal Republic of Germany. One third of the whole population of West Germany can be seen as resulting from post-war immigrants. (K J Bade, 'Einführung', in Bade, *op. cit.*, p.16). See also Mathias Beer's chapter in this volume.

5 The law which regulates issues of permission of residence and work, rights of social security etc.

6 In linguistic terms, the German language provides a clear order to classify 'them' and 'us' by exclusive categories of Inländer (Deutsche/ Germans) and Ausländer (foreigners). A socio-linguistic analysis would reveal that the term 'Ausländer', in its everyday use, has undergone a major redefinition since the 1970s. 'Ausländer' became more and more

confined to those without German citizenship but living in Germany. Apart from that, its use is more or less synonymous with the definition of guestworker from southern Europe and their descendants. Regarding subsequent generations, the term 'Ausländer' is highly ambiguous, because they are people born in Germany, living their whole lives in Germany, speaking a German dialect rather than the mother tongue of their parents, and perhaps have never been in their parents' home countries. For an anthropological study on German-ness and foreign-ness, see Diane Forsythe, 'German Identity and the Problems of History', in E Tonkin and M McDonald (eds), *History and Ethnicity*, London: ASA Monographs, 1989, pp.137-56.

7 Maria Dietzel-Papakyriakou, *Altern in der Migration: Die Arbeitsmigranten vor dem Dilemma: zurückkehren oder bleiben?* Stuttgart, 1993.

8 Maria Dietzel-Papakyriakou, 'Ältere Ausländer in der Bundesrepublik Deutschland. Zwischen Ausländersozialarbeit und Altenhilfe', in *Informationsdienst zur Ausländerarbeit*, Vol.3 , 1993, pp.43-53; p.45.

9 *Ibid.*, p.44. To use these projections is questionable because many basic variables which have been used are historically non-valid. But they do show rough tendencies.

10 The sources of all the demogaphic data about Stuttgart are: Statistisches Amt der Landeshauptstadt Stuttgart, *Bestandstabelle Nr.5: Bevölkerung nach Staatsangehörigkeit, Geschlecht und Altersgruppen*, Stuttgart, 1993.

11 National groups of non-German inhabitants from southern European countries: former Yugoslavia: 44,738; Turkey: 25,807; Greece: 16,550; Italy: 15,298; Portugal: 2,855; Spain: 2,360.

12 Axel Schulte and Dan Tursan, 'Zur Lebenssituation ältерer Ausländer in Niedersachsen', in Niedersächsisches Sozialministerium - Ausländerbeauftragte (ed.), *Alt werden in der Fremde: Probleme der älteren Ausländergeneration*. Hannover, 1990; Maria Dietzel-Papakyriakou, *Das Alter der Arbeitsemigranten*; Friederike Hohloch, *Situation älter gewordener...*

13 The official age limit for the entitlement to old age pension in Germany is 60 or 65. There are different possibilities to receive pensions at an earlier age, depending on job market and regulations.

14 Hohloch, *Situation älter gewordener...*, p.144.

15 *Ibid.*, Anhang 9/Table 16.

16 Maria Oppen, 'Ausländerdiskriminierung und arbeitsbedingte Gesundheitsrisiken', in *Argument Sonderband*, 146, 1987, pp.97-108; Maria Dietzel-Papakyriakou, *Krankheit und Rückkehr. Frühinvalidität ausländischer Arbeitnehmer am Beispiel griechischer Rückkehrer*, Berlin, 1987.

17 Hohloch, pp.182ff.

18 *Ibid.*, pp.110ff.

19 *Ibid.*, p.38.

20 Dietzel-Papakyriakou, *Altern in der Migration*, p.115.

21 Peter L Berger and Thomas Luckmann, *Die gesellschaftliche Konstruktion von Wirklichkeit: Eine Theorie der Wissenssoziologie*. Frankfurt am Main, 1979.

22 Dietzel-Papakyriakou, *Altern in der Migration*, pp.97ff.

23 Hohloch, pp.71ff. Legally, the reform of the *Ausländergesetz* facilitates this pattern of life for members of non-European countries as well. If they have spent more than eight years in Germany and are entitled to a German pension and do not need social benefits, they have the legal 'option of return' to Germany, even if they stay abroad longer than six months.

24 Vern L Bengtson, 'Ethnicity and Aging: Problems and Issues in Current Social Science Inquiry', in Donald E Gelfand and Alfred J Kutzik, (eds.), *Ethnicity and Aging: Theory, Research and Policy*, New York, 1979, pp.9-32; Vern L Bengtson and James Dowd, 'Aging in Minority Populations: An Examination of Double Jeopardy Hypothesis', in *Journal of Gerontology*, Vol.3, 1978, pp.427-436; Jaquelyne Jackson, 'Race, National Origin, Ethnicity and Aging', in Robert H Binstock and Ethel Shanas (eds), *Handbook of Aging and Social Sciences*, New York, 1985, pp.264-303.

25 Dietzel-Papakyriakou, *Altern in der Migration*, pp.46ff.

26 *Ibid.*, p.47.

27 *Ibid.*

28 Hohloch, p.40.

29 *Ibid.*, p.29.

30 Alan Walker, 'A Cultural Revolution? Shifting the UK's Welfare Mix in the Care of Older People', in Adalbert Evers and Ivan Svetlik (eds), *Balancing Pluralism: New Welfare Mixes in Care for the Elderly*, Avebury, 1993, pp.67-88.

31 *Ibid.*, p.72, where Walker discusses British concepts and initiatives in community care.

32 Maria Dietzel-Papakyriakou, 'Ältere Ausländer in der Bundesrepublik Deutschland. Zwischen Ausländersozialarbeit und Altenhilfe', in: *Informationsdienst zur Ausländerarbeit*, Vol.3 , 1993, pp.43-53; p.49.

33 Ursula Apitzsch, 'Jugendkultur und Ethnizität', in Rainer Brähler and Peter Dudek (eds), *Fremde – Heimat: Neuer Nationalismus versus interkulturelles Lernen* (*Jahrbuch für interkulturelles Lernen*), Frankfurt am Main, 1992, p.175.

34 Maria Dietzel-Papakyriakou, 'Das Alter der Arbeitsmigranten: ethnische Ressourcen und doppelte Benachteiligung', in *Zeitschrift für Gerontologie*, Vol.23, 1990, pp.345-53; p.347.

Can We Compare Racisms? Nations, Regions and Europe[1]

Neil Evans

I

Researchers who undertake intensive work on particular places face problems when they attempt to produce more general conclusions. Much of my own detailed research has considered racism and the experience of ethnic minorities in Cardiff, a city with one of the oldest black communities in Britain, and subsequently I have placed this within the wider framework of Wales and Britain.[2] When faced with a conference on ethnic issues and racism in Europe it seemed necessary to interrogate this research so that in some way it might speak to the whole continent. The best approach to this seemed to be through the problematic which underlay my work. Did Cardiff – or Wales – deserve its reputation as a place of exceptional tolerance for ethnic minorities? A chance find of material on the 1919 race riots in Cardiff had led to my original questioning of this belief and prompted further investigation. This work produced a rather different story from the familiar one. Cardiff's reputation for tolerance is hard to reconcile with a reality which includes a serious anti-Irish riot in 1848, innumerable conflicts between the multiple European and black groups which composed its inner-city population through the second half of the nineteenth century, an anti-Chinese riot in 1911 and clearly the worst – in terms of deaths and bitterness – of the wave of anti-black riots which swept across Britain in 1919. A cynic might conclude that where there is a local tradition of speaking of tolerance it often cloaks a history of conflict. This is true of Nottingham in the 1960s and 1970s. It was held to be tolerant and integrated – but

Eberhard Bort and Neil Evans (eds), *Networking Europe*, Liverpool University Press 2000, 235-62.

in reality it was one of the sites of white attacks on blacks in 1958, the scaled-down version of the 1919 outbreaks in post-war British history.[3]

What was true of Cardiff turned out to be true of Wales in general. Welsh people think of themselves as tolerant – much more so than the English. Yet this viewpoint is not sustained by any close examination of Welsh history, particularly in the nineteenth century. We need to add Cardiff's tumultuous history to the record which can be assembled for the rest of Wales which includes nine other significant anti-Irish riots, the last of which was in Tredegar in 1882, the most serious British anti-Jewish riots (in 1911, with their epicentre in Tredegar), a few anti-Italian riots in 1940 and much evidence of intolerance of minorities in word rather than deed. This last is apparent, for instance, in resolutions of the South Wales Miners' Federation during the First World War and proposed ones after the Second.[4] One element of this is a strand of hostility to the Spanish community in Abercraf. Another seems to be as much hostility to gypsies as in any other Western European society.[5]

What happens when we move beyond Wales to the British Isles in general? It is remarkable that much the same pattern is repeated. Britain is seen, generally, as a tolerant society in which ethnic conflicts are minimal, if at all present. There are arguments about Scotland which are similar to those in Wales but they are not entirely sustained by the record, including hostility to Lithuanian (in fact Jewish) immigrants in the Lanarkshire coal field in the years before the First World War, and towards Asians in Glasgow during the inter-war period. Society in the West of Scotland became organised in almost tribal groupings around nuclei of native Protestants and immigrant Irish and they clash ritually at Rangers *vs* Celtic matches. For Britain generally, Colin Holmes has posed the question as to whether it is *A Tolerant Country?* (London: Faber, 1991) and generally found it wanting. Holmes goes so far as to reject any comparisons of national traditions of racial attitudes and hostility, on the grounds that they tend towards complacency and that ideas of relative tolerance cannot be sustained by historical or contemporary evidence.

When people make comparisons between British attitudes to race and to minorities and those of other countries, it is often left unclear just what is the object of comparison. There is usually a vague notion of superiority but less often a specific and detailed comparison. One benchmark is clearly the United States, towards which a sense persists that the mother country manages these things better than its upstart former colonies. Another, particularly for more recent times – though with similar import – is South Africa. Yet in British attitudes to this issue we can guarantee that Germany is not too far in the background. The avoidance of fascism is still popularly associated with British moderation, tolerance and fair-mindedness. Germany is seen as lacking all these qualities. Such attitudes inform the outbursts of odd British cabinet ministers and the approach of Prime Ministers who need briefings on Germans and their attitudes. What we have here is a nice case of an argument that Britain is a tolerant society which manifests itself as a species of racism! As Ian Kershaw has pointed out, all the early twentieth-century British attitudes towards Prussian militarism and the inherent expansionism/megalomania of Germans still persist in some people's minds. The main change is that they are dignified by the name of Euroscepticism now.[6]

II

The attentive reader may have noticed that we have begun to play a game. It is the old British party game of pass the parcel. Scots and Welsh people claim they are not racist (or a least not *very* racist); they leave that to the English. The English, on the other hand, think they are models of tolerance and integration which can be held up as a beacon for the rest of the world to navigate by. They leave racism to Americans, South Africans (and the Afrikaners amongst them at that!) and to Germans.

The nature of its twentieth-century history probably has not allowed a German idea of tolerance towards other peoples to develop. There is, of course, the tradition of free access to Germany for refugees which has grown up since 1945 in reaction to the history of the earlier part of the century. That is now under siege but it is real nonetheless. Similarly, Green attitudes to outsiders owe a great deal to reactions to a perceived past. Yet it is difficult to construct an idea of German tolerance which holds of all periods of its history. In some ways an attempt to do this – or something similar – underlay the *Historikerstreit*. The assertion is not so much of relative tolerance but of comparative guilt.[7] The crimes of the Third Reich were massive, but so were those of Stalin, and our century has not in general been a very edifying one.

The same kind of argument can also be made – and rightly in my view – about anti-Semitism. In the late nineteenth century and the early part of the twentieth century, Germany was hardly the fount of the creed. That was not even the case as far as western Europe was concerned. It was turn-of-the-century France which was driven by a political and cultural dispute in which anti-Semitism played a central role. When we turn to the east, the position is even clearer. Russia was the land of the pogrom in the nineteenth century, and it was the Russian secret police who invented the Protocols of the Elders of Zion and hence the idea of the Jewish world conspiracy. It was Arthur Rosenburg, fleeing like so many Baltic Germans from the Russian Revolution, who introduced Hitler to this particular refinement to his beliefs. We have evidence from Jews that Austria had worse anti-Semitism than Germany, and while it may be unwise to follow Keynes in his view that 'Jew-baiting' was Poland's only industry, it seems clear that in Poland anti-Semitism was more pronounced and more central politically.[8]

Recent approaches to the holocaust – those which the late Tim Mason dubbed 'structuralist' – build on these insights. Blame is now more broadly apportioned. Hitler and the Nazi Party remain centrally responsible, but the murder of six million people would not have been possible without wider complicity. The list is long and includes the *Wehrmacht*, those European countries which assisted in the rounding up of Jews, the Swiss who knowingly closed their borders to refugees, and the British and Americans who refused to bomb the installations at Auschwitz and elsewhere.[9] If we want to extend this chain of examples and argument into the present, we can add that despite the prominence which the British press and television give to incidents of racial violence in Germany, there are more racially motivated attacks in Britain than in Germany.[10]

None of this adds up to a tradition of German tolerance, but it does point in the same direction as the sceptical approach now being taken to British tolerance. If Britain is not seen as being notably relaxed in its attitudes, neither is Germany seen as being notably racist. The German parcel has been passed in a different direction from the British one, but with similar effect.

Space and knowledge do not allow the sketching of the position for other European countries. But some indication of the generality of the problem can be given by looking at two other cases. France is the European country which has the longest tradition of substantial and sustained migration from outside its borders.[11] This has not led to notable integration of communities. Indeed the French tradition has been the revolutionary one of 'the Republic, one and indivisible' and has stressed the assimilation of individuals rather than the integration of communities. That intolerance of difference is one of the manifestations of racism in France. Its positive side is the relative acceptance of French citizens from the overseas departments of the West Indies. Its negative side is the hostility displayed by many towards west Africans and Moslems from north Africa. French traditions, revolutionary or not, have not been ones which have avoided conflict.[12] There were tensions in France in the era of the First World War over immigrant workers which were similar to those which produced riots in Britain. Now France sports Europe's largest racist party and it is one which can even draw on the support of some blacks from overseas departments who are citizens and see the removal of immigrants as the solution to all their, and France's, ills.

The other case is the Netherlands. It is famed for its liberalism and tolerance, and this reputation is rooted in the way in which it has handled the potential conflicts between strongly entrenched Catholic and Protestant communities in the context of a sharply experienced drive to secularisation. Dutch sociologists talk of successful 'pillarisation' – what elsewhere is called consociational democracy. The three pillars, Protestant, Catholic and secular, organise distinct bodies throughout the range of social activities, but the aims of these pillars are reconciled by effective negotiation within the political system. The integration of the communities is effectively achieved.[13] There is no conflict of anything like a Northern Ireland intensity nor is there the effective break-up of the state into sub-states in which each ethnic group rules supreme as is the case in Belgium.

Whatever has been achieved here has not been passed on to the black minority population which has generally arrived in the post-war period, adding a significant diversity to what was once seen as one of the most homogeneous populations in Europe. The reaction to this change has not been total tolerance and benevolence. Blacks in the Netherlands in the early 1990s faced the highest unemployment rate in Europe and great pressure to assimilate rather than to integrate. One instance of conflict is the triptych presented to the church by the Guild of Vorstenbosch to mark its 350th anniversary in January 1990. The temptations of St Anthony include a black devil which its opponents say – and surely they are right – belongs only in an exhibition on racism. As one black man commented, no one would use the equivalent Jewish stereotype, but clearly many people were prepared to defend the black man as a symbol of the temptations of the spirit – cocaine, suicide, abortion, etc.[14]

So revolutionary France and tolerant Holland also fall by the wayside. What should we conclude about the nature of European racism from this brief survey? The obvious conclusion to be derived from a survey of European attitudes to minorities would seem to be that they are characterised by irredeemable racism. We might be pushed further in this direction by looking at the origins of racism. In 1968 the American historian Winthrop Jordan did just that and published a huge book on *White Over Black: American Attitudes Towards the Negro 1550-1812* (Harmondsworth: Penguin, 1971). His thesis was a fairly simple one: European racism was predetermined before the encounter with significant numbers of blacks. European culture in the middle ages was so impregnated with hostility to blackness and associations of whiteness with virtue that racism was the inevitable outcome. Slavery was an 'unthinking decision'. Some of the fear came from the unknown depths of European forests; much of the rest from sexual unease. Jordan's analysis is a Freudian one: he gives the game away in his main title. What he seems to provide is an underpinning for what I have been describing. It is not surprising, in this view, that any search for tolerance within Europe is futile. Europeans displayed hostility to black people from the very beginning and to do so, if it is not implanted in their genes, it is certainly deeply embedded in their culture.

We might view the tightening of European immigration controls in recent years in the same light. The freer movement of Europeans around the countries of the Union[15] has been paralleled by restrictions on the movements of non-EU citizens. A Federal Europe may have failed but a fortress Europe has been constructed anyway. Seen in this light, 1992 might seem to be an inevitable consequence of 1492. It is not surprising that a modern rush of European sentiment has been accompanied by hostility to those who are not Europeans. After all, one of the ways that Europeans first became aware of themselves as a distinct human grouping was through the contacts with non-Europeans which came through the process of conquest. The post-modernist way of putting this would be that every discourse has to be defined against its 'Other'.[16]

III

Some commentators want to go beyond this. It has been claimed that people are simply xenophobic and show hostility to any group of people which they perceive to be different from themselves. This is close to saying that racism is human nature and the implication of that is that there is little that can be done about it.[17] It seems then that the quest to compare racisms, to find islands of tolerance in the oceans of xenophobia, leads to counsels of despair. Nobody is more tolerant than anybody else and we seem to end up like Candide cultivating our gardens, confined by political impotence.

The issues which have been broached in my own research can therefore be shown to fit in with a wider tradition of writing, and when they are placed in this context they might seem to propose the conclusions which have been suggested in the last few pages. It will be argued in the remainder of the paper that we should reject the terminus to which the first part of this paper took us. It should not be the end of the journey for a number of reasons.

The first of these is political. The implication of seeing a timeless, unchanging, never-varying Western racism is that there is little we can do about it. It is the obverse of the particularistic optimism which also stultifies political action. If there is no problem in Cardiff, Wales, Scotland, Britain, etc., there is no need to do anything. If the problem has been around for over 500 years and is more or less the same wherever westerners have encountered non-westerners, there is little point in political action. No one should be comfortable with a situation in which racial and ethnic discrimination exists. Whatever our vision of the Good Society is, we want to eliminate that from the present one.[18]

The second reason is that black people often experience differences in the intensity of racism in various societies – or at least perceive that there are some western countries where they can live more comfortably than others. In the television series 'Black on Europe', shown in 1991 in Britain, this was a noticeable feature. In the programme on Germany three black people thought they would be better off in Britain, and two separate reasons were given for this: a longer tradition of black organisation – Brixton was seen as a place where black organisation had made life better – and better opportunities for a happy life for children and a normal life. The programme on Portugal ended with a woman of African ancestry emigrating to the Netherlands where she thought there would be better opportunities for education, better houses and jobs. Of course, when we turn to the Netherlands itself we find the kind of situation that has already been described. Yet there probably are differences: Portugal's immigrants are 50 per cent illegal, often live in shanty towns and frequently have no political rights. Illegal immigrants live in constant fear of police checks on papers that they do not have, work for lower wages and have to resist the bulldozers regularly sent to demolish huts erected as a temporary measure twenty years ago; but still in use. What is being expressed here is a manifestation of the distinction between *Gastarbeiter* with minimal or no rights and the colonial immigrant who has full citizenship rights. This rift runs right through France, as we have seen, and the distinction is of more general relevance to understanding the situation in Europe in the recent past and now.[19] Other evidence is more anecdotal. I once spoke to a black woman in London who told me she had enjoyed a visit to Wales because she had not been racially abused on the streets there. There is more substantial evidence of variations within states too. The 1960s Institute of Race Relations report on *Colour and Citizenship* included surveys on racial attitudes which showed considerable variations. They were very complicated and indicated that there were complex attitudes and prejudices lying behind the answers to survey questions.[20]

A third reason for thinking more seriously about variations in racism within Europe is that comparative studies of non-European societies have revealed a good deal about the nature of racism, and there is no need to think that this will not be true within Europe too. American historians and sociologists turned to looking at South America in the 1950s and 1960s because they thought that the experience of slavery and exploitation had not left the same legacy of racism and social division there. They generally came away from their studies with a more sober view of South America which turned out to be less tolerant than it seemed at first sight, but also confirmed in their view that racism and community relations were not uniform things. Comparative studies have also shown some of the differences between the highly segregated societies of the American South and South Africa. They do not yield startling theories or the light of brilliant illumination which suddenly makes everything clear to us, but they do gain something from holding one case against another for the magnification that they can provide.[21]

The rejection of comparison in racism also comes from a counsel of academic despair which parallels the political despair referred to earlier. It is very difficult to find workable explanations of the incidence of racial conflicts. The right often puts forward the 'numbers game' – a certain number of blacks/immigrants are acceptable – always, magically, the number that currently exist, or just below it – but beyond that there will be conflict. It is not always the right which advances this argument. In Britain it was Roy Hattersley who coined the famous formula:

> Without integration, limitation is inexcusable;
> Without limitation, integration is impossible.

In 1970s France it was François Mitterand who spoke of a threshold of tolerance being passed – though it was Margaret Thatcher who said in 1978 that people were understandably concerned about their culture being swamped. She was, of course, developing a theme which Enoch Powell had adumbrated a decade earlier in his notorious 'Rivers of Blood' speech.[22] The left has rejected the numbers game both because it is tainted with racism, and because it has limited explanatory power. There are plenty of cases of very small minorities being bitterly attacked – perhaps because their small size made them vulnerable. There are many other problems in trying to explain variations in racism, and this has become a powerful reason for the emergence of the idea of what has, rather grandly, been called 'transhistorical racism'. The rejection of this idea is a convenient summary of the objections made in the past few pages.[23]

The idea enshrined in the phrase is the idea that racism is essentially constant and unchanging. By contrast, the most sophisticated research now seeks out variant forms of the phenomenon. The simplest distinction is between forms of racism which are derived from culture and forms which are rooted in biology. The latter was a late nineteenth-century phenomenon and became an attempt to find a scientific way to explain variations in society. That quickly failed, but it endured as the kind of pseudo-science which ran through Nazism – remember that students and teachers were eager recruits to the party. To take another example, slavery in the United States did not rest on constant ideological defences. Before the American Revolution it seemed to need few of them, and only when the conflict against Britain raised the issue of the equal rights of all men did it begin to need defenders. They tended to be pragmatic: the South simply could not manage without the 'peculiar institution'. Only with the attack on slavery mounted in the early nineteenth century did an articulated theory of racial inferiority really emerge. It had not been necessary in the past.[24] This reinforces the political point: if racism varies, it can decline as well as intensify. It can be combated.

IV

What is needed is a more flexible, contingent and variable notion of racism. If we can look at its development in one place/country over a period of time there is no logical reason why we cannot look at variations between places. Colin Holmes has done fine historical work in this field in Britain – clearly the finest that we have. He rejects transhistorical racism, stressing instead historical shifts in the idea. Yet he is opposed to comparisons of national traditions of racism. It is hard to see why this is the case. If we make comparisons we will not find tolerant British and intolerant Germans, but we might find evidence and ideas that will help us to understand better the ways in which racial antagonism waxes and wanes. We do not want to compare simply racial attitudes but also the circumstances in which they become vital and politically significant. There may be a lowest common denominator: Western racism which assumes a basic superiority over peoples of non-western backgrounds. The ways in which this becomes manifest are highly varied – and some of these have already been discussed. The circumstances which provoke this are also varied, but in principle at least capable of analysis and explanation. This is my attempt to sum up the pressures which produced the south Wales race riots of 1919:

> Resentment at increased prosperity, at the houses and girl friends which the war put in the coloured men's way did not in themselves lead to riot. Such attitudes were largely passive until the severe economic depression and housing crisis, which coincided with the badly mis-handled demobilisation of troops and sailors, made them active and querulous. Pre-existing racial stereotypes enabled the multifarious tensions of the post-war world to be focused on a convenient scape-goat.[25]

Oddly, perhaps, in view of what I have written above, Colin Holmes took up this passage in his article on the Jewish riots in South Wales and almost turned it into a theory.[26] Perhaps we can go a little further along that road and develop it more generally – as a basis for regional and national comparisons. The fact that

W E B DuBois made a similar formulation in trying to explain the East St Louis race riot of 1917 is a further encouragement along the path.[27] Paul O'Leary astutely summarises my more general approach to racism in Wales in these words:

> while hostility was more common than is often supposed, historical circumstances prevented this from becoming an engrained tradition.[28]

The Welsh evidence points to this conclusion in a particular way. In the nineteenth century, Wales attracted large numbers of immigrants of diverse backgrounds as its economy boomed. It was also a period when there were a good number of ethnic and racial conflicts. In the twentieth century, by contrast, there have been no serious outbreaks of violence. There have also been relatively few new immigrants as the Welsh economy collapsed between the wars, and it was not a vastly expanding region in the post-war period. The exception – which proves the rule – is the black community in Cardiff which expanded greatly in the First World War, and which was violently attacked in 1919 and faced massive discrimination from a whole range of social institutions in the inter-war period. The point is not that Wales is tolerant in the twentieth century but that its social and economic development did not multiply the potential occasions for conflict with newcomers. This means that a version of the numbers game is important though it is not *simply* a matter of numbers.

Similar conclusions arise from important work which Robert Miles and his various collaborators have done on post-war Scotland. The central conclusion of this is not that Scots are particularly tolerant, despite a relative absence of racial antagonism. His conclusion is that there is plenty of racism in Scotland but that it has not led to politics becoming *racialised*. There are four major reasons for this:

- Nationalism became central to Scottish politics, and central control of the economy in London has been blamed for many ills, rather than immigrants.
- There are relatively few immigrants and therefore they do not come to the forefront in politics. They are not conspicuous.

- Scottish society is deeply divided into Orange and Green components. It is therefore difficult to see which culture immigrants are 'threatening'.
- There is no strong tradition of fascist politics in Scotland and therefore they have not played the same role in shaping the political agenda as they have in England.

This begins to provide a framework in which we may analyse some broader European trends. But perhaps we need an excursion back to colonial America just to reinforce the point first. Earlier, mention was made of Winthrop Jordan's work and the way in which it could be seen as underpinning a whole body of writing which finds unvarying racism throughout four or five centuries and across the continent of Europe and into its various fragment societies. At the other end of the spectrum in American writing in this period we have Edmund Morgan. In his book, *American Slavery, American Freedom: The Ordeal of Colonial Virginia,* published in 1975, he examines the experience of Virginia from its foundation in the early seventeenth century to the American Revolution. Where Jordan sees racism as inevitable, and as underpinning slavery, Morgan sees the situation as being more fluid and with more open possibilities. In the last analysis it is slavery which creates racism rather than the other way round. Where Jordan sees slavery as an 'unthinking decision', Morgan sees more consideration. In early seventeenth-century Virginia there were no slave laws. The turning point was Bacon's rebellion in the 1670s. The planters turned themselves into a class in its aftermath; they became Virginians as opposed to Nabobs. In the 1690s a wedge was driven between servants and slaves. As slavery was institutionalised, so racist attitudes were consciously inculcated. American freedom rests on a relatively equal white society which is supported by a totally unfree black one. As with all *Herrenvolk* situations, race is used to reduce class antagonisms.[29] Morgan sees the situation as having many possibilities and that, initially, the English settlers wanted to prove they could do better than the Spaniards. Only in the longer run did the kinds of deep anxieties which so concern Jordan become manifest, and this was the result of particular political circumstances. Attitudes are not enough!

We are now on a track which will allow us to compare racisms. It is not the view that Germans are more racist than British people. But it will be an examination of the contrasting ways in which racial attitudes enter British politics and German politics. It is sometimes argued that British and German approaches to racial issues differ because of their very different experience of empire. The argument usually runs like this. Germany had a very brief moment as an imperial power – just slightly over thirty-five years, from 1884 to 1919, when its colonies were forfeited under the Treaty of Versailles. It follows that it therefore had uneasy relations with Africa and did not learn to rule it effectively. Two particular episodes can be pointed to – the brutal repression of the rising in German South-West Africa in the early twentieth century, which became a rallying point for the right against social democracy in the so-called 'Hottentot election' of 1907, and the law which banned and annulled African-German marriages in 1908. The outcome of all this within Germany has been what one black observer has described as a Prussian style of racism, worse than South Africa. Black people have been treated worse than dogs, as non-human, as *Untermenschen.* They were seen only as labourers, with Germans as masters. Medical research was conducted into people of mixed parentage and they were known as 'bastards'. These attitudes survived the loss of colonies and were built upon under the fascist state. In 1937 younger African children were sterilised and in the course of the regime older Africans were socially ostracised. Many disappeared into concentration camps. To complete the argument, the post-war experience of blacks in Germany can be added. The stationing of black American troops in Germany after 1945 led to the birth of some children of German/black-American parentage. Often they lived in rural areas where they became adult before they saw another black person. These 'occupation babies' were often very badly treated within their families and ostracised socially. That experience for black people has continued up to and beyond the fall of the Berlin Wall. Easterners who rarely saw 'foreign-looking' people take out the resentments that they feel about their situation against the blacks who were imported by the SED (Socialist Unity Party/GDR) regime to work in unsavory places like abattoirs. Since 1989 racist attacks and murders have multiplied.

In 1989 Easterners gained not only freedom from the oppressive regime of Erich Honecker but freedom to be racist: the GDR regime had forcibly repressed the expression of racial antagonism. There was not even a brief respite in this racism in the honeymoon period when the old regime collapsed. Black Germans who wanted to lend their weight to the push against the wall were often told to leave: it was not their celebration.[30]

The general thrust of this argument does not seem to be wrong. What is certainly dubious, however, is the contrast with Britain which is frequently made or implied. This argument of German intolerance can be contrasted with British tolerance: a long imperial tradition, the development of attitudes of 'effortless superiority', the relative absence of formal/legal segregation in the British Empire and the open door policy on colonial immigration which was adhered to up to 1962. Some of these things can be questioned, but they all have an element of truth in them. The mistake is in seeing them as a total picture of British imperialism and racial attitudes. Certainly, in the long history of the British Empire there was time for a variety of attitudes to develop. There was plenty of brutal repression, and the punitive expedition against recalcitrant tribes was a fairly constant feature. It carried on into an era where modern technology made it even more terrifying. If the Luftwaffe, famously, perfected dive bombing in Spain, and the Italian armed forces honed their skills against Abyssinians, the RAF tried out its new equipment on Sudanese, Iraqi and Afghan rebels against the Empire.[31] Yet there was also a tradition which was frequently powerful in British politics of defending native peoples, and it can be traced back at least as far as the campaigns to abolish the slave trade and slavery. Much of this had its own brand of 'protective' racism within it, but it is different in its implication from the punitive expedition.

Perhaps even more important was the pragmatic, rather than principled, tradition of softer rule which developed. The vastness of the British Empire was a good thing for imperial celebrants, but it was a military and naval headache. Territories spread so widely seemed to be permanently in open season for the predators amongst Britain's European rivals, of which there was an increasing number. Added to this, there was the challenge of nationalism within the Empire which rarely became a concerted attack but was always a potential threat. Black politicians often put this with a brutal simplicity. It was an Empire of four hundred and fifty million people, and white people were very much outnumbered within it. This fact did exercise some restraining influence on repression as a weapon in the arsenal of imperial defence. In many ways it led to hypocrisy rather than tolerance. Between the wars there was an effective ban on black immigration from the Empire, but it operated by denying that these black people were British subjects rather than by adopting the much riskier strategy of open restrictions on the movements of colonial peoples.[32] This tradition continued into the post-war period when discussions of restricting Commonwealth immigration always foundered on the problems of maintaining what remained of the Empire, and when pressure was exerted on the governments of India and Pakistan to restrict immigration. The declining imperial power did not want to be seen to be restricting immigration. Alongside this, there ran a genuine commitment on the part of some politicians to maintain free entry. Restriction, in 1962, was agonised over by the more paternalist Tories and opposed by Labour. Sadly, the populist element in both parties came increasingly to the fore after that.

The point to stress is not that the British imperial tradition is inherently less racist and violent than the German one, but that it is more diverse. That diversity has opened up the space for a black political tradition which now has deep roots. Perhaps what is important is not so much the diverse tradition but the opportunity which its spaces give to black organisations to get their crowbars in and to exert leverage.

Thinking about imperial traditions and black politics provides a route for returning to the numbers game that we were playing earlier. It is clear that numbers alone do not determine race relations. There are too many cases of small and defenceless groups being attacked for that to be the case. Equally, a large and well-organised minority can be too big to be easily challenged. There is, therefore, no guarantee that small numbers lead to harmony and large ones to conflict. Despite this, it is a mistake to dismiss analytical concerns about numbers entirely. Anyway, that is what the Welsh experience seems to show, when considered overall, rather than in respect of particular incidents. In the twentieth century the relative absence of immigrants has reduced the number of potential occasions for conflict. Two of the attacks on tiny minorities happened in a period of intense industrial conflict and against minorities which could both be seen as in some way threatening in that heated context. In Tredegar, in 1911, some Jews were possibly involved in rack-renting, and there was some background of hostility from the more evangelical religious denominations.[33] In Cardiff, the Chinese had been accused of running vice operations in their laundries, and in the seamen's strike they were felt to be recruiting centres for blacklegs. The other case of an attack on a small minority, the fairly minor assaults on otherwise well accepted Italians in 1940, fits into a similar context. Italian entry into the war was seen as opportunistic, and some of the Italians in South Wales had connections with fascist groups. They could be seen as the enemy within.

Whether large minorities are a source of violent conflict may depend on whether or not the issues of their presence enter the political arena or not. Belfast and Glasgow both have deeply entrenched Orange and Green divisions, but only Belfast has a long – and seemingly insoluble – problem of violent conflicts over this. The divisions have pervaded the social life of Glasgow, but seem to be expressed in football matches as much as anything. Antagonisms clearly existed, and the whole shape of society was moulded by the rift, but class politics triumphed in Glasgow, unlike in Belfast, or (until the post-war period) Liverpool. This is an analysis which is related to Robert Miles' view of post-war Scotland where politics have not become racialised despite the prevalence of racism.

Perhaps this also points to the key contrast between Britain and Germany. In inter-war Germany, for a whole complex of reasons far too extensive to be considered in detail here, politics became racialised. Defeat in the Great War, the lack of legitimacy of the new Republic, economic collapse and the lack of a strong, well organised conservative party were some of the reasons why a maniac with two obsessions, both of them racial, could come to power and begin realising his dreams. The conquest of eastern Europe with the consequent reduction of Slavs to the drones of Teutons also made possible the second objective, the elimination of the Jews from the racial struggle with the Aryans. Yet even here, where the whole panoply of Western racism in its worst, pseudo-scientific, form came to its apogee, it is hard to say that large numbers supported the whole array of Nazi policy. The Nazi Party had to become a political party rather than an anti-Semitic sect in order to achieve power. In the process it cultivated a certain degree of respectability and for electoral purposes toned down its racism. It offered '*Tod dem Marximus*' (Death to Marxism) to its potential supporters much more frequently than the annihilation of the Jews. Hitler was a substitute for the Kaiser and the party a substitute for the broadly-based conservative party that had failed to develop in Germany.[34]

In Britain these circumstances, apart from the depression which was anyway less catastrophic than in Germany, did not apply. Particularly the Conservative Party recovered from its disastrous flirtations with protection in 1906 and 1923 and became the ruling group for most of the period. This took away much of the space for fascist politics, and the marginality of Oswald Mosely was the result. Broadly the same has been true of British politics since 1945, though with the exception that minuscule fascist groupings have had more effect on the general political landscape. In the 1950s they alone were agitating for immigration controls. By the 1960s these were part of the consensus in British politics. Both major parties have played the racial card and, when fascism revived in the 1970s, arguably Mrs Thatcher did at least as much to defuse it as the Anti-Nazi League. Her 'swamping' speech of 1978 was calculated to draw voters worried about race away from the National Front and back to the Conservative Party they had deserted over Heath's 'unsound' decision to allow entry to Uganda Asians in 1973. Perhaps Helmut Kohl and the whole new phenomenon of Christian Democracy in post-war Germany also have had their uses.[35]

Racial issues have again become prominent in European politics in the past ten years. The deep recession has clearly been one reason for this but so has the process of European integration. It has influenced the situation in two, perhaps contradictory, ways. Firstly, it has challenged the identities of people who are wedded to the old nation states. In Britain this has deep roots: the decline of the economy and the Empire threw up many doubts about just what it means to be British when

Britannia no longer ruled the waves. One clear answer, attractive to some, was that it involved being white. Secondly, the more that Europe comes to consider just what unites it and how it can think of itself as a political entity, the greater is the danger that skin colour will become an all too readily available criterion.

We have seen the process around 1992 and Maastricht. Fortress Europe is the nightmare that invades the dreams of European unity. One way of avoiding this will be to foster greater awareness of European history and the way this connects with the history of those areas which are now providing immigrants to Europe. Europe's dominance over the world was of quite brief duration, say 1500 to 1914 or 1940. Initially it was based on little more than superior fire power though, of course, other elements later emerged. Culturally and economically it drew on the rest of the world and reshaped that world to meet its needs. It defined itself against that world. Imperialism is one thing that all Europeans have in common, and some of the anxiety which Germans feel about their particular past would profitably be extended to the whole continent in respect of the rest of the world. The slave trade is not quite the African Holocaust but it comes close enough to concern us all. European integration is an attempt to rebuild a powerful position for Europe in a world which it can no longer dominate in the old ways. But unless we want to build a racist citadel we need to acknowledge the nature of that past. A good part of what we think of as European is derived from the wider world. African art has been plundered almost as much as African labour. European museums are full of artefacts from earlier civilisations which were largely collected at the height of European dominance in the nineteenth century. They seem to say two things about Europe and the world: that Europe is the inheritor/successor of the lost glories of the past, and that it exists and can display these creations while the creators have vanished. The idea of Europe was a selective process applied to past cultures. Greece and Rome were singled out as ancestors (despite the fact that what is now seen as Europe was rather peripheral to their concerns) and for the element of spurious continuity which any essentially new civilisation needs. It was these 'white' civilisations which were seen as living on in Europe. 'Black' ones like

Egypt or Mesopotamia may have been impressive in their time but were now dead.

V

Let me begin to draw the threads together. Overall it has been stressed that we need to distinguish racial attitudes from the circumstances in which racism flourishes as a political force. The former runs through European history, and no one brought up on this continent can escape imbibing at least some of it. Of course it varies from place to place and from time to time, but the ideas are an ever-present potential. It is rather futile to compare this, and the quest itself is potentially racist. Are Germans more racist than the British? Posed in this way the question should suggest its own answer. The best way to deal with issues like this is through educational work. Racism is an idea, a deeply rooted one, and it has to be combated with other ideas. Germany has confronted this through its facing up to the challenges offered by Nazism and the Holocaust. Britain has only recently started to come to terms with the slave trade, but Liverpool's Maritime Museum does now, finally, recognise that pillar of its existence, and slavery has been the subject of a crop of recent novels, one of which has won the Booker Prize.[36] Phillippa Gregory's more popular novel about the slave trade in Bristol, *A Respectable Trade,* has just become a TV serial attracting over eight million viewers, and the hope has been expressed that it will bring issues to prominence which many would prefer to leave swept under the carpet.[37]

The political and economic circumstances in which racism flourishes are another matter. The more we make comparisons here, the better hope we have of understanding, and hence of combating, racist movements. Comparison is a means of analysing and drawing general arguments out of varied phenomena. It has already been indicated just how difficult it is to account for the outbreak of incidents of racial violence. We know this because we can compare differing incidents within one nation or culture. Potentially, we can learn much more if we take a wider field. Well-defined comparisons within this can produce deeper insights and perhaps resolve issues which currently seem to be insoluble within a purely British context. Europe is a good field to take as it offers a good range of variations within a relatively limited space. The cultures also have enough in common to make comparison realistic, so the methodological conditions for comparative studies are met.[38]

Clearly, immigration is not a novel phenomenon in Europe. In many ways it can be seen as quite central to the European experience. An outline of this complex process would include the following elements:

- The continent was formed in what we used to call the 'Dark Ages' by waves of migration which were superimposed upon each other in complex ways.[39]
- Subsequent expansion, for instance of Normans into Italy and Germans into eastern Europe, stirred the mixture again.
- The process of statebuilding created ethnic minorities within states – none of which were ethnically exclusive national states, and some were multi-national empires.
- The persecutions which followed the Reformation created religious and cultural minorities in many parts of the continent.[40] To give just one instance, the Huguenots moved from France to Britain, Prussia and Holland in the wake of the Revocation of the Edict of Nantes.
- Added to this was the long-range migration caused by industrialisation which put Poles into the Ruhr and mixed up the peoples of eastern and southern Europe in a manner which contributed to the area's seething tensions in the period before the First World War.[41]
- The Nazis moved, at least temporarily, large numbers of workers across European borders as slaves for their racial empire.[42] The Second World War led to a vast shifting of populations which aimed at producing more ethnically homogeneous states.
- Imperialism produced an admixture of more exotic cultures, especially in the present century.[43] Some of the potential tensions to arise from this could be seen after the First World War when the French occupying forces in Germany em-

> ployed black troops and a European-wide controversy ensued.[44]

Given this history, one of the attractions of Europe as a field of ethnic research is the complexity of the patterns that it has generated. European and non-European minorities abound in a setting in which host communities are highly variegated. It provides two valuable perspectives, both the reactions of Europeans to other Europeans who differ in culture and religion, and their response to non-Europeans in their midst and abroad. Understanding these circumstances better may enable us to take more effective political action against racist movements.

So can we compare racisms? Probably not if we think of this as a process of ranking European societies on a scale of tolerance and intolerance. Racism is so pervasive within Western cultures, and the process carries many risks. What we can certainly compare – and indeed it is imperative that we do – are racist movements and the circumstances in which they flourish and fail. It may be the case that the appropriate approach to be employed here is a regional one. That will take us away from the thorny and dangerous issue of national stereotypes and attitudes and will lead to a focus on the economic, social and political circumstances which obtain. Regions are the particular knot of these and tackling them at this level will raise the issue of what circumstances produce different intensities of racial violence. The answers will not come in the form of national characteristics so much as in terms of industrial traditions and social and political structures. Paul O'Leary has argued – from the other end of the telescope – that studies of the Irish in Britain would benefit from moving away from an intensely local focus to a more regional one, and his point has a more general application.[45] The three sides of the industrial triangle around the Irish Sea – Ulster, Lancashire and western Scotland – have different configurations of ethnic politics, and analysis of these has been advanced far more by looking at their varied social and political structures than by trying to account for them by means of the supposed national characteristics of Irish, English and Scots. Indeed, thinking of these particular regional cultures raises questions about the integration and validity of the national complexes to which they belong. It may be that particular regions and cities – for reasons which are essentially social and economic – have cultures and styles of politics which are more open, welcoming and tolerant. If we find this to be the case we are less likely to explain it as the inherent character of the people of (say) Lorraine, Provence, north-east England, the East End or Brandenburg than we are to seek an understanding through considering the way that social relations and politics have been shaped in those particular contexts. Nations have a much stronger association with engrained ideas of national character and even of race than do regions.[46]

Racism poses the greatest danger to the idea of Europe – or at least to one which will carry us forward. Ever since 1945, advocates of European integration have celebrated the cultural, political and economic achievements of its civilisation. They have frequently done so by constructing a myth which refuses to recognise the downside of European history. Racism and imperialism have been central to this. If we want to create a European culture to which we can genuinely feel an allegiance, it will need to be one which has eliminated racism. Famously, Mahatma Gandhi, when visiting London, was asked by a journalist what he thought of western civilisation. He replied wryly that he thought it was a marvellous idea. Until the idea of Europe passes Gandhi's test it will clearly have failed.

Notes

1 I would like to thank Ed Countryman for his advice on the issue of origins of racism in America and Logie Barrow for his extremely careful reading of a draft. The notes are intended to provide an English language bibliography on the topic; the text is not always based upon them. Generally I have not repeated references which are available in my article, 'Immigrants and Minorities in Wales' (note 2, below) where full references to studies in the British Isles are given.

2 Neil Evans, 'The South Wales Race Riots of 1919', in *Llafur: Journal of Welsh Labour History*, Vol.3, No.1 ,1980; pp.5-29; N Evans, 'The South Wales Race Riots of 1919: A Documentary Postscript', in *Llafur*, Vol.3, No.4, 1983, pp.76-87; N Evans, 'Regulating the Reserve Army: Arabs, Blacks and the Local State in Cardiff, 1919-1945', in *Immigrants and*

Minorities, Vol.4,. No.2, July 1985, pp.68-115; N Evans, 'Immigrants and Minorities in Wales, 1840-1990': A Comparative Perspective', in *Llafur*, Vol.5, No.4, 1991, pp.5-26; N Evans, 'Voices of the Unheard: Contemporary British Urban Riots in Historical Perspective', in Ieuan Gwynedd Jones and Glanmor Williams (eds), *Social Policy, Crime and Punishment: Essays in Memory of Jane Morgan*, Cardiff: University of Wales Press, 1994, pp.35-50.

3 Ira Katznelson, *Black Men, White Cities: Race, Politics and Migration in the United States 1900-1930 and Britain 1948-1968*, New York: Oxford University Press, 1973, ch.10; Daniel Lawrence, *Black Migrants, White Natives: A Study of Race Relations in Nottingham*, Cambridge: Cambridge University Press, 1974.

4 South Wales Miners' Federation, Minutes, 17 July 1908; 25 March and 9 November 1916; 23 November 1917, 25 March 1918. My thanks to Alun Burge and Dot Jones for these references.

5 *Western Mail*, 12 August 1919.

6 Ian Kershaw, *Germany's Present, Germany's Past*, (Bithell Memorial Lecture, University of London, 1992), p.2.

7 Michael Marrus, *The Unwanted: European Refugees in the Twentieth Century*, Oxford: Oxford University Press, 1985, looks at the background to the issue of refugees. The literature on the *Historikerstreit* is immense: see James Knowlton and Truett Cates (eds), *Forever in the Shadow of Hitler?*, Atlantic Highlands, New Jersey: Humanities Press, 1993, for an English translation of the key texts, and Ian Kershaw, *The Nazi Dictatorship* (3rd ed.), London: Arnold, 1993, chs 8 and 9, for a bibliography.

8 Michael Marrus, 'French Jews, the Dreyfus Affair and the Crisis of French Society', in Robert Bezucha (ed.), *Modern European Social History*, Boston: Heath, 1972, pp.335-53; and his *The Politics of Assimilation: French Jews at the Time of the Dreyfus Affair*, Oxford: Oxford University Press, 1971; Lucy Davidowich, *The War Against the Jews*, London, 1975; Harmondsworth: Penguin, 1977; George Clare, *Last Waltz in Vienna*, London: Macmillan, 1981; Keynes, cited in R J B Bosworth, *Explaining Auschwitz and Hiroshima: History Writing and the Second World War, 1945-1990*, London: Routledge, 1993, p.16.

9 Kershaw, *Nazi Dictatorship*, chs 5 and 8; Michael R Marrus, *The Holocaust in History* (1987), Harmondsworth: Penguin, 1989.

10 Roger Eatwell, 'Fascist and Racist Revival in Western Europe', in *Political Quarterly*, Vol.65, No.3, July-September 1994, p.314.

11 Don Dignan, 'Europe's Melting Pot: A Century of Large Scale Immigration into France', in *Ethnic and Racial Studies* (henceforth *ERS*), Vol.4, No.2, April 1981, pp.137-52; Judy A Reardon, 'Belgian and French Workers in Nineteenth-Century Roubaix', in Louise A Tilly and Charles Tilly (eds), *Class Conflict and Collective Action*, London: Sage, 1981, pp.167-83; Jeanne Singer-Kerel, 'Foreign Workers in France, 1891-1936', in *ERS*, Vol.14, No.3, July 1991, pp.279-293; Tyler Stoval, 'Colour-Blind France? Colonial Workers during the First World War', in *Race and Class*, Vol.35, No.2, 1993, pp.25-55; Gary S Cross, 'Towards Social Peace and Prosperity: The Politics of Immigration in France during the Era of World War 1', in *French Historical Studies*, Vol.XI, No.4, Fall 1980,

pp.610-32; John Horne, 'Immigrant Workers in France during World War 1', in *ibid*, XIV No.1, Spring 1985, pp.57-86; Donald Reid, 'The Limits of Paternalism: Immigrant Coal Miners' Communities in France, 1919-45', in *European History Quarterly*, Vol.15, No.1, January 1985, pp.99-118; Christoph Kleesmann, 'Comparative Immigrant History: Polish Workers in the Ruhr Area and the North of France', in *Journal of Social History*, Vol.20, No.2, Winter 1986, pp.335-51; Vasoodeven Vuddamalay, Paul White and Deborah Sporton, 'The Evolution of the Goutte d' Or as an Ethnic Minority District of Paris', in *New Community*, Vol.17, No.2, January 1991, pp.245-58.

12 Martin Demming Lewis, 'One Hundred Million Frenchmen: The "Assimilation" Theory in French Colonial Policy', in *Comparative Studies in Society and History*, Vol.4 ,No.1, January 1962, pp.129-53; John M Mackenzie, 'European Imperialism: Comparative Approaches', in *European History Quarterly*, Vol.23, No.3, July 1992, pp.415-29.

13 J Bank '"Verzuiling": A Confessional Road to Secularisation, Emancipation and Decline of Political Catholicism, 1920-1970', in A C Duke and C A Tamse (eds), *Britain and the Netherlands, Vol.VII: Church and State since the Reformation*, The Hague: Martinus Nighoff, 1981, pp.207-30.

14 Hans van Amersfoort and Boudewijn Surie, 'Reluctant Hosts: Immigration into Dutch Society, 1970-1985', in *ERS*, Vol.10, No.2, April 1987, pp.169-85; Louk Hagendoorn and Joseph Hraba, 'Social Distance towards Holland's Minorities: Discrimination against and among Ethnic Outgroups', in *ERS*, Vol.10. No.3, July 1987, pp.317-33.

15 Frederico Romero, 'Cross Border Population Movements', in William Wallace (ed.), *The Dynamics of European Integration*, London: Pinter, 1990, pp.171-91.

16 Paul Gordon, *Fortress Europe? The Meaning of 1992*, London: Runnymead Trust, 1989; and his 'Fortress Europe: Policy and Identity', in *Studies in the Education of Adults*, Vol.23, No.2, October 1991, pp.121-32; Steve Cohen, *Imagine There's No Countries*, Manchester: Greater Manchester Immigration Aid Unit, n.d. (c. 1990); Glyn Ford, (ed.), *Fascist Europe: The Rise of Racism and Xenophobia*, London: Pluto, 1992; *Race and Class* Vol.32, No.3, January-March 1991, special issue on 'Europe: Variations on a Theme of Racism'; Luciano Cheles, Ronnie Ferguson and Michalina Vaughan (eds), *Neo-Fascism in Europe*, London, Longmans, 1991; Marie Macey, 'Greater Europe: Integration or Ethnic Exclusion?', in Colin Crouch and David Marquand (eds), *Towards Greater Europe? A Continent without an Iron Curtain*, Oxford: Oxford University Press, 1992, pp.139-53; Neil Evans, 'Beyond Nationalism? The Construction of Ideas of Europe', in David Sullivan (ed), *Nationalism and Community*, Harlech: Coleg Harlech Occasional Paper, 1994), pp.77-115.

17 For forceful critiques of this position, see Barbara Jeanne Fields, 'Slavery, Race and Ideology in the United States of America', in *New Left Review*, No.181, May-June 1990, pp.95-118; and Thomas C Holt, 'Marking: Race, Race-Making and the Writing of History', in *American Historical Review*, Vol.100, No.1, February 1995, pp.1-20.

18 I am much influenced here by remarks which Eric Foner made in the final session of the VIth Biennial Conference in Early American History at the University of Milan in June 1992.

19 Stephen Castles and Godula Kosack, *Immigrant Workers and Class Structure in Western Europe*, Oxford: Oxford University Press, 1973; and their 'The Function of Labour Immigration in Western European Capitalism', in Theo Nichols (ed.), *Capital and Labour: Studies in the Capitalist Labour Process*, London: Fontana, 1980, pp.117-37; S Castles, Heather Booth and Tina Wallace, *Here for Good: Western Europe's New Ethnic Minorities*, London: Pluto, 1984; H Stuart Hughes, *Sophisticated Rebels: The Political Culture of European Dissent, 1968-1987*, Cambridge, Mass.: Harvard University Press, 1988, ch.3.

20 E J B Rose *et al.*, *Colour and Citizenship: A Report on British Race Relations*, Oxford: Oxford University Press, 1969, ch.28.

21 George M Frederickson, *White Supremacy: A Comparative Study in American and South African History*, New York: Oxford University Press, 1980; John W Cell, *The Highest Stage of White Supremacy: The Origins of Segregation in South Africa and the American South*, Cambridge: Cambridge University Press, 1982; Carl N Degler, *Neither White Nor Black: Slavery and Race Relations in Brazil and the United States*, New York: Macmillan, 1971; Pierre L van den Berghe, *Race and Racism: A Comparative Perspective*, New York: Wiley, 1967; 2nd edn 1978.

22 For analyis of the impact of this, along with the text of the speech, see Stuart Hall *et al.*, 'A Torpedo Aimed at the Boiler Room of Consensus', in *New Statesman*, 17 April 1998, pp.14-19.

23 Holmes, *Tolerant Country?*; Robert Miles and Annie Phizacklea, *White Man's Country: Racism in British Politics*, London: Pluto, 1984. p.57; Robert Moore, *Racism and Black Resistance in Britain*, London: Pluto, 1975, ch.2.

24 Peter Kolchin, 'In Defense of Servitude: American Proslavery and Russian Proserfdom Arguments, 1760-1860', in *American Historical Review*, Vol.85, No.4, October 1980, pp.809-27.

25 Neil Evans, *art. cit.*, *Llafur*, 1980, p.10.

26 Colin Holmes, 'The Tredegar Riots of 1911: Anti-Jewish Disturbances in South Wales', in *Welsh History Review*, Vol.11, No.2, December 1982, pp.214-25, esp. p.225.

27 DuBois, cited in Holt, 'Marking', pp.6-7. See also the perceptive Henry Louis Gates, *Loose Canons: Reflections on the Culture Wars*, New York: Oxford University Press, 1992.

28 Paul O'Leary, 'Articles Relating to the History of Wales, Published Mainly in 1991', in *Welsh History Review*, Vol.16, No.4, December 1993, p.600.

29 Kenneth P Vickery, '"Herrenvolk" Democracy and Egalitarianism in South Africa and the American South', in *Comparative Studies in Society and History*, Vol.16, No.3, June 1974, pp.309-28.

30 Michael Burleigh and Wolfgang Wippermann, *The Racial State: Germany 1933-1945*, Cambridge:Cambridge University Press, 1991; D K Fieldhouse, *The Colonial Empires: A Comparative Survey from the*

Eighteenth Century, London: Weidefeld and Nicholson, 1966, pp.364-71; Dieter Groh, 'The "Unpatriotic" Socialists and the State', in *Journal of Contemporary History*, Vol.1, No.4, October 1966, pp.151-77.

31 David Omissi, *Air Power and Colonial Control: The Royal Air Force, 1919-1939*, Manchester: Manchester University Press, 1990; Channel 4 TV Programme, 'Birds of Death', screened summer 1992.

32 Neil Evans, 'Across the Universe: Racial Conflict and the Crisis of Imperial Britain, 1919-1925', in *Immigrants and Minorities*, Vol.13, Nos.2 and3, July-October, 1994, pp. 59-88.

33 Ursula R Q Henriques, (ed.), *The Jews of South Wales: Historical Studies*, Cardiff: University of Wales Press, 1993.

34 Ian Kershaw, 'Ideology, Propaganda and the Rise of the Nazi Party', in Peter D Strachura (ed), *The Nazi* Machtergreifung, London: Croom Helm, 1983, pp.162-81; Larry Eugene Jones, 'The Dissolution of the Bourgeois Party System in the Weimar Republic', in Richard J Bessel and E J Feuchtwanger (eds), *Social and Political Change in Weimar Germany*, London: Croom Helm, 1981, pp.268-88; Heinrich August Winkler, 'German Society, Hitler and the Illusion of Restoration, 1930-33', in *Journal of Contemporary History*, Vol.11 , No.4, October 1976, pp.1-16.

35 Michael Newman, 'Democracy vs. Dictatorship: Labour's Role in the Struggle Against British Fascism, 1933-1936', in *History Workshop Journal*, No.5, Spring 1978, pp.67-88.

36 Barry Unsworth, *Sacred Hunger*, Harmondsworth: Penguin, 1992.

37 *Radio Times*, 11-24 April, 16-22 May 1998.

38 Max Haller, 'The Challenge for Comparative Sociology in the Transformation of Europe', in *International Sociology*, Vol.5, No.2, June 1990; Neil Evans, 'Think Continentally, Research Regionally: Reflections on the Rise of Regional Europe', *Journal of Regional and Local Studies*, Vol.14, No.1, Summer 1994, pp.1-9.

39 Hugh Miall, *Creating the New Europe*, London: Pinter, 1993, ch.1.

40 Hugh Trevor-Roper, *Religion, the Reformation and Social Change*, London: Macmillan, 1967, chs1 and 2.

41 Jan Lucassen, *Migrant Labour in Europe, 1600-1900*, London: Croom Helm, 1987; Frieda Wunderlich, *Farm Labour in Germany, 1810-1945: Its Historical Development within the Framework of Agricultural and Social Policy*, New Haven: Yale University Press, 1961; John J Kulczcki, *The Foreign Worker and the German Labour Movement*, Oxford: Berg, 1994; Pieter van Duin, 'Ethnicity, Race and Labour, 1830s-1930s: Some Irish and International Perspectives', in *Soathar: Journal of Irish Labour History*, Vol.19, 1994, pp.86-103; Z A B Zeman, *Pursued by a Bear: The Making of Eastern Europe*, London, 1989, pp.23-37.

42 John H E Fried, *The Exploitation of Foreign Labour in Germany*, Montreal, 1945; Edward L Homze, *Foreign Labor in Nazi Germany*, New Haven: Yale University Press, 1967.

43 Ulrich Herbert, *A History of Foreign Labor in Germany, 1880-1980: Seasonal Workers/Forced Laborers/Guestworkers*, Ann Arbor: University of Michigan Press, 1990.

44 Robert Reinders, 'Racialism on the Left: E D Morel and the "Black Horror on the Rhine"', in *International Review of Social History*, Vol.13, 1968, pp.1-28; Keith L Nelson, 'The "Black Horror on the Rhine": Race as a Factor in Post-World War I Diplomacy', in *Journal of Modern History*, Vol.42, No. 4, December 1970, pp.606-27; Sally Marks, 'Black Watch on the Rhine: A Study in Propaganda, Prejudice and Prurience', in *European Studies Review*, Vol.13, No.3, July 1983, pp.297-334.

45 Paul O'Leary, 'A Regional Perspective: The Famine Irish in South Wales', paper prepared for a forthcoming volume edited by Sheridan Gilley and Roger Swift.

46 However, some recent works have managed to use national frameworks as the basis of comparisons with notable success: David Feldman, *Englishmen and Jews: Social Relations and Political Culture, 1840-1914*, New Haven: Yale University Press, 1994; Rogers Brubaker, *Citizenship and Nationhood in France and Germany*, Cambridge, Mass.: Harvard University Press, 1992.

IV

Why the Social Democrats do badly in the South West of Germany: An Essay on Regional Political Culture

Horst Glück

Introduction

Electoral behaviour in Baden-Württemberg shows, particularly in its highly-industrialised, dominantly Protestant core regions in northern Württemberg, some remarkable peculiarities. More than a quarter of Baden-Württemberg's population lives in this industrial region around Stuttgart – anything between three and four million people, depending on where you draw the boundaries. One noticeable fact are the bad results – in comparison with its overall performance in the Federal Republic of Germany – the Social Democrats (SPD) have been reaping there, in the past as in the present, despite the fact that the social structure, according to all common determining factors for electoral behaviour such as, for instance, ratio of denominations, proportion of the working class within the population, density of population, would point towards a favourable environment for social democracy.

Different electoral results obtained by the two big parties in different regions of Germany have been explained, albeit with receding ability of offering an all-encompassing explanation, by empirical research into electoral behaviour as resulting from an uneven distribution of determining factors within the social structure of regional electorates along, roughly, the following lines:

- The more Catholic a region, the more votes for the CDU (Christian Democrats);

Eberhard Bort and Neil Evans (eds), ***Networking Europe,*** **Liverpool University Press 2000, 265-76.**

- The higher the proportion of workers in a region, the higher the vote for the SPD;
- The more urbanised a region, the better the result for the SPD.

These statistical correlations, according to election researchers, correspond with historical lines of conflict in nineteenth-century societies, resulting in the establishment of parties of interest and, eventually, the political party system.

Conflicts between urban and rural areas, centre and periphery, church and state, labour and capital brought about their specific parties of interest as well as more or less homogenous social, economic and cultural milieux. R M Lepsius described four such structure-constituting main-milieux for Germany: the rural-conservative milieu, the urban-bourgeois milieu, the Catholic church milieu, and the socialist working-class milieu. These supported, respectively, the conservative, liberal, Catholic and socialist parties.

These milieux have been characteristic for the political landscape of the Federal Republic far into the 1960s, and are still – in (West) Germany – the sociological basis for the electoral heartlands of the two big parties, CDU/CSU (Christian Social Union/Bavaria) and SPD.

The particular electoral behaviour in the industrialised Protestant areas of Baden-Württemberg is the puzzling exception to this rule, and thus a 'deviating case' in special need of explanation.

Although Baden-Württemberg exemplifies, in terms of social and structural data and in comparison to other federal Länder, the average norm as no other Land does, the SPD's electoral results have constantly ranged between six and seven per cent below its federal average.

That this should be so and that the Social Democrats in Baden-Württemberg should be structurally thus disadvantaged against the CDU – as expressed in election result after election result – has, in spite of various attempts and approaches, never been fully explained. Baden-Württemberg being, structurally speaking, the German norm par excellence, explanations for the sub-average SPD results, based on social and structural data, have not been convincing.

Well-aired Arguments for the SPD's Bad Results in Baden-Württemberg

A High Proportion of Catholics in Closed Rural Social Milieux

The proportion of Catholics in Baden-Württemberg is 47.4 per cent (Census of 1970), and is thus closest of all Länder to that of the Federal Republic *in toto* (43.3 per cent). Catholics make up 73.8 per cent of the Saarland population, in Bavaria they account for 69.9 per cent, in Rhineland-Palatinate 55.7 per cent, and in Northrhine-Westfalia 52.5 per cent.

Even a superficial glance will show that the SPD, not only in the Saarland and in Northrhine-Westfalia where, particularly within the traditional industrial working class, trade union and Catholic-denominational orientation have conflicted in the formation of electoral behaviour but, in the end, have favoured – in the course of secularisation – the SPD structurally, but also in a comparatively low-industrialised Land like Rhineland-Palatinate – despite larger Catholic rural areas – is well within the range of the federal average in terms of election results (Federal Election 1987: 37.1 per cent). The SPD in Baden-Württemberg trails these results by more than seven per cent.

Smaller-scale Settlement Structures and Lower Proportion of Population in Cities over 100,000 People

On average, 34 per cent of the population within the Federal Republic of Germany lives in cities bigger than 100,000 inhabitants, whereas in Baden-Württemberg the relative figure is only 17.8 per cent (1987). The figure for the Federal Republic, though, is highly problematic. If we exclude the highly urbanised Northrhine-Westfalia, where over 50 per cent of the population live in big cities, the federal average plummets to 19 per cent, with Schleswig-Holstein (17.4 per cent) and Rhineland-Palatinate (15.6 per cent) even below the Baden-Württemberg figure, and Saarland (18 per cent) and Lower Saxony (19.2 per cent) only marginally above it. Yet in all these Länder the SPD enjoys a far greater share of the vote. Only in Bavaria, with 21.4 per cent living in cities, are the results worse for the SPD.

The density of population figure for Baden-Württemberg (258.5 inhabitants per square kilometre) and the average size of communities (8,318 inhabitants) are both slightly higher than the overall average on the federal level.

An Economic Structure Characterised by the *Mittelstand*

The average size of firms in manufacturing (counting firms with more than 20 employees) in Baden-Württemberg in 1984 was 136, as compared with 152 in the Federal Republic, and with Schleswig-Holstein, Rhineland Palatinate and Bavaria below the Baden-Württemberg level. The difference, however, is too small to serve as a sound explanation for diverging voting patterns – particularly as Baden-Württemberg differs from the federal norm in having a higher employment rate and an above-average emphasis on manufacturing industry. For every 1,000 people, in 1982, Baden-Württemberg had 230 employees in manufacturing; the federal average was 190. Baden-Württemberg is still the most industrialised Land (not counting the city states) in the Federal Republic.

This is also expressed in the annual reports of the Labour Exchange Office (*Bundesanstalt für Arbeit*). In 1985, manufacturing employed 55.7 per cent of workers covered by the social security system; the federal figure was 49.1 per cent. Connected with this is the higher proportion of workers among insured employees, 54.2 per cent in Baden-Württemberg, 51.1 per cent in the Federal Republic.

A Lower Degree of Trade Union Membership

The proportion of trades unions' members among the workers is below average in Baden-Württemberg. The proportion of DGB (*Deutscher Gewerkschaftsbund* – the 'German TUC') members among employees in Baden-Württemberg was 30 per cent (in 1984); in the Federal Republic it was 32.9 per cent. In addition to that, the employment rate is well above average. The low degree of trade union organisation, though, is directly connected to that higher employment rate, particularly the high rate of employed women – as women employees make up only about a quarter of the DGB membership. However, if one puts the number of trades union members (DGB) in relation to the number of population in a Land – a sensible thing, if we assume in our sociological attempt at explaining election results, that union membership favours the SPD vote – one would find for Baden-Württemberg a proportion of 12.4 per cent, very close to the federal average of 12.6 per cent (by comparison, Rhineland-Palatinate has 10.4 per cent; Northrhine-Westfalia 14.5 per cent; Bavaria 9.8 per cent; Hesse 13.2 per cent).

Thus, Infas – one of the leading German polling institutes – conceded, reasonably resignedly, in 1980: 'In general, the known political analytical categories in Baden-Württemberg lack selectivity and focus.'

Towards the end of the 1980s, Infas developed a new approach to explain regional voting patterns. According to this, workers in prosperous regions with secure jobs would vote in the majority for the CDU, while workers in economically stagnating regions with more severe labour market problems would generally favour the SPD.

Historical Roots

But he SPD's problems in the south-west are much older than the turbulences in the labour market of the past 15 years. Almost exactly one hundred years ago, the following appeared in the SPD's paper, *Sozialdemokrat*:

> Württemberg is regarded in Germany as that part in which the economic condition of the *Mittelstand* and the working classes cannot yet be termed utterly unbearable; that is why the proletarian working-class movement there is not progressing as rapidly as in north Germany with its overload of big industrial centres.

And indeed, Württemberg at that time rather trailed behind industrial developments in other parts of the Reich. A rapid, disproportional industrial growth process, though, brought Württemberg into the top group of highly industrialised regions of the German Reich by the end of the Weimar Republic, yet without any linkage to political success for the 'proletarian working-class movement'. Compared with the average socialist vote in the Reich, Württemberg still lagged quite a few percentage points behind. And, as we have seen, this was and has been the case since 1945 in the context of the Federal Republic of Germany.

The historical continuity of these 'atypical' voting patterns in Württemberg suggests that there might be a particular political tradition, a geographically-delineated political culture, which formed a political view specific to this region, which in turn finds expression in voting behaviour. A political culture has become historical; it mirrors the background and the interpretative patterns of the people, handed down from generation to generation. A key role in this process is played by the specific economic and social history of such a region.

Württemberg's idiosyncratic way of industrialisation was determined by, above all, two factors:

- Hereditary subdivision of land in Old-Württemberg led to increasing fragmentation and permanent diminution of farmers' acreage, with the consequence that earnings from the farmland were no longer sufficient to maintain a livelihood, and complementary sources of income had to be found (home trade, forestry, crafts). The farmer thus became a part-time farmer and, in the course of industrialisation, a worker-farmer. And as these worker-farmers still ploughed their small fields, they did not move to the industrial cities, but commuted daily between home and work. In addition to that, as from the mid-nineteenth century, the state heavily sponsored emigration for impoverished Württembergers. Both, the creation of worker-farmers and emigration prevented the rise of a dispossessed and landless mass proletariat.
- Württemberg is not rich in resources, so that the coal- and steel-based process of industrialisation in Germany between

> 1850 and 1900 severed Württemberg from the prospering coal regions of the Reich. Another consequence of this was the initial dependence of Württemberg's tentative and belated industrialisation on water power, which reinforced a tendency towards decentralised industrialisation along rivers. Württemberg's development was thus characterised by a belated industrialisation, centred around manufacturing, and a work force containing a high proportion of commuting worker-farmers.

The evolution of election-determining milieux hinges on both common interests and the spatial proximity of a common neighbourhood, forming a somewhat coherent set of values, opinions and convictions. Just that, though, was much less the case in the Württemberg industrial regions than in other industrial areas of Germany. Within the Württemberg working classes, a close context of life and work was the exception rather than the rule. Despite a high degree of industrialisation, there did thus not emerge a strong tradition of working-class milieux.

For the formation and evolution of a regional political culture, the history of settlements is of at least as much interest as the history of industrialisation. The relatively high concentration of towns in the south-west of Germany during the late middle ages led – due to the limits of urbanisation set by the stagnation of agriculture – to the fact that for a long period (in comparison with the densely-populated areas of the old Federal Republic, really, until today) no dominant urban centre of agglomeration developed. The German south-west retained its small-scale spatial structure. The combination of hereditary land-division and decentralised industrialisation became the breeding ground for small-town bourgeois and rural-agrarian, estate-bound liberalism – less reminiscent of the bourgeois revolutions, but rather restorative, anti-absolutist, a liberalism grown in Württemberg over centuries, invoking until far into the nineteenth century the 'good old right' of the estates against absolutist despotism. This Swabian liberalism is characterised by a deeply-rooted individualism based on land, directed – on the one hand – traditionally against the 'high and mighty', then the absolute sovereign, but now against all who parade their wealth all too openly. On the other hand, this liberalism is conservative and cautious where collective social visions based on solidarity are concerned. In the past centuries, the sovereigns of Württemberg ruled and regulated their subjects to a degree that we might well speak of an institutionalised way of life. Of particular impact, in this context, seems to have been the *Generalrescript* of 1781, targeting '*Übelhäuser*' (bad houses). According to this law, any farmer who did not look properly after his farm could be disowned and conscripted to military service. Whoever informed on such '*Übelhäuser*' was rewarded by the sovereign with one third of the confiscated farm. To this day, laziness ('*Nicht schaffen*') is among the worst crimes known in the Swabian-Württemberg part of the Land! Still today, neigbourhoods watch each other suspiciously. Exaggerated industry and lack of solidarity are to this day the consequences in the everyday culture of this region.

This small-scale liberal political tradition in Württemberg is coupled with an above-average distancing from anything to do with party politics. Particularly in local politics, looking back on a long history of local self-government, so-called '*Sachpolitik*' (issue-oriented politics) and '*Persönlichkeitswahl*' (voting for personalities) range way before '*Parteipolitik*' (party politics). In Württemberg, the Land of the '*Freie Wähler*' (independent groupings, in contrast to parties), independent councillors, not bound to any of the parties, are still exerting major influence in local politics. This singles out the region of *Alt-Württemberg* from all other regions of the Federal Republic. The strength of the '*Freie Wähler*' may decrease corresponding to the increasing size of town, yet even in the regional cities they return, with about 30 per cent of the vote, regularly one of the three largest council representations, rivalling CDU and SPD.

A Specific Regional Political Culture

The particular weakness of the SPD in Württemberg has become a historical fact and cannot be explained on the grounds of the present social structure. The same can be said – albeit with a considerably younger phase of growth – about the particularly strong performance of the CDU. We must remember that the SPD after the war was not in any diaspora situation, out in the wilds, far away from government. Until 1960, the SPD was part of some kind of 'all party government', and from 1966 to 1972 part of the Land government in a grand coalition with the CDU. The SPD may never have provided the Land prime minister, but it did bring forth a series of respected ministers. The social and political climate in Baden-Württemberg until the late 1960s was, for that reason alone, hardly polarised. The SPD in Württemberg, until the mid-1960s, did relatively badly in elections with a great turn-out (federal elections), and relatively well in elections with low turn-outs (Land elections). The situation was reversed for the CDU. That means that the SPD remained reduced to its core following, whereas the CDU, as a bourgeois, Christian and anti-communist movement, could mobilise additional support in important elections.

It is the proportion of traditionally loyal socialist voters which has been relatively small in Württemberg, due to the idiosyncratic way of industrialisation with their specific lack of working-class milieux. Württemberg (not Baden) is, in terms of local elections, regarded as the homeland of the '*Freie Wähler*'; their continuing influence distinguishes Protestant Württemberg from all other parts of the Federal Republic.

Even in the elections of mayors or lord mayors, elected directly by the people in Baden-Württemberg, this predilection for 'independent candidates' is shown, interestingly in contrast to Baden, which has a completely different political tradition and thus a completely different regional political culture. If we compare mayoral elections between Württemberg and Baden in 1948, this characteristic difference becomes evident. Of the 963 mayors in Württemberg, 90.8 per cent are non-party members, whereas of the 489 mayors elected in Baden only 47.7 per cent did not belong to any party. And even 40 years later, in September 1989, the differences between Baden and Württemberg are still distinctive: Of the 31 towns with lord mayors (towns over 20,000 inhabitants) in Baden 14 were affiliated with the CDU, 13 with the SPD, and four were non-party members; of the 49 towns with lord mayors in Württemberg, 24 were not members of parties, 13 belonged to the CDU, nine to the SPD and three to the FDP (Liberal

Democrats). This points towards a different understanding of the office of the mayor. But it is also an expression of above-average distance in Württemberg from the political parties.

In contrast to the centre-right parties which, until the beginning of the 1980s, resembled in character a party of Honourables (not unlike the *Freie Wähler*), the SPD was a traditional membership and functionary party. The traditional Württemberg disinclination for joining organisations and distance from parties hit all parties, but in particular the SPD, whose character was geared towards a political public and party membership. The Baden-Württemberg SPD (again, especially Württemberg) has the lowest membership-population ratio of all Länder (including Bavaria).

In the Stuttgart region, compared with other areas of the Reich, individual political interpretative patterns were formed far less by political macro-organisations (like political parties). The influence on the formation of voting norms and patterns of well-known personalities, lord mayors or local representatives of the estates, was far greater. The long tradition of local self-government in Württemberg prevented the emergence of a political party monopoly on offering political views and interpretative patterns. Instead, the small-scale and comprehensible nature of Protestant Württemberg, even in its industrial core areas, favoured the personalised 'party of Honourables' approach. This made it a tough terrain for membership parties, centred around organisation, like the SPD. Yet it is not only the SPD which has its lowest membership figures in Baden-Württemberg, the CDU as well, despite its permanent majority-cum-government position, is below average in terms of membership, compared with its performance elsewhere in the Federal Republic.

Given these socio-cultural and organisational conditions, the SPD in Baden-Württemberg has fallen far short of its socio-structural expectations. The general election of 1957 saw the SPD here at 25.8 per cent and thus at the end of the scale including all Länder (even Bavaria) with the exception of the newly-reintegrated Saarland. In the following phase of 'Comrade Trend' until 1972, the Baden-Württemberg SPD grew below its federal average growth rate; from 1972 to 1987 it lost above the average growth rate.

The SPD's erosion in the south-west, particularly in regional and local politics, since the 1970s is, I think, closely linked to the wide-spread distance to parties found here. The SPD was, in Baden-Württemberg too, perceived by the voters as the party of change against the conservative, rooted parties of the Honourables of the CDU and the '*Freie Wähler*'. As the SPD in Baden-Württemberg, as we have seen, had only a relatively small number of members, the rapid rise at the beginning of the 1970s, relying mostly on young, leftist and post-materialistic new members, changed the party's profile in the communities considerably, effecting increasing alienation between the SPD and those rather conservative traditional majority cultures of the Land.

That is the reason why the years of strong party-political polarisation between 1970 and 1976, noted by the electorate on a left-right dimension of scale, connected with the SPD's claim for substantial change of social conditions through politics, did not, in Baden-Württemberg, fall on any conceivable fertile social-democratic ground.

It seems as if a historically-caused lack of rootedness within the milieu, coupled with particular shortcomings as to party membership, in itself pointed the SPD in the south-west towards a relatively strong 'post-material' political orientation, which in turn strengthened the trend towards a minority party. From this minority position, the SPD in 1975/76 lost a relatively high proportion of its traditional following to the CDU and, after 1979, again considerably, from its new 'post-material' electorate to the new party of the Greens. The capability of keeping together differing party wings and electoral milieux depends – as the example of the SPD in the northern *Länder* shows – on a certain foundation of strength: capacity to lead opinion, rootedness in the milieu and organisational power – qualities which the SPD simply did not possess in the south-west.

In the 1970s, a period of strong political polarisation between the progressive and the conservative political camps, the CDU managed to bind its formerly loose Christian-centre-right electoral following closer together and, furthermore, gained the refugee vote, the old-liberal milieux, the nationalist vote and the apolitical supporters of the '*Freie Wähler*' as part of its broadened loyal electorate. The SPD, on the other hand, drifted into a hopeless minority position, lacking any option of exerting power on any level. The CDU's strength, however, is still not based on organisational power, nor is it tied up with docking on to a particular dominating milieu; it is based rather on its anti-socialist and anti-progressive collective pooling character.

With the weakening party-political and general political polarisation, the CDU has lost cohesion as a focus of pooling. Since the mid-1980s, the dominant regional party has suffered painful losses: having gained 56 per cent of the vote in 1976, its result declined to 39 per cent in 1992 – but without a strengthening effect for the opposing SPD. On the contrary, the SPD in 1992 suffered further losses and landed only 29 per cent of the vote.

It is the small and the new parties who profited from these developments. The traditional liberal FDP still performs above average in Baden-Württemberg; Baden-Württemberg was the first of the Länder that returned Greens to the *Landtag*, in 1980, and the Greens still perform well here. The far-right populists of the so-called *Republikaner* were most successful in Baden-Württemberg: in 1989, gaining 8.7 per cent in the European Elections, and in 1992, at the *Landtag* elections, they gained third rank with 10.9 per cent of the vote.

All these peculiarities are expressive of the weak identification with political parties, compared with other areas of the Federal Republic, in the Württemberg core region around Stuttgart. This lack of identification, in turn, is a long-term product of, above all, the specific history of industrialisation in this region.

As I have tried to show in this paper, these regional peculiarities and idiosyncrasies cannot be pinned succinctly down to the regional social structure. In order to understand the 'deviating voting patterns' of this region, we must turn our eyes to the historical development of a specific regional political culture.

The Culture and the Economy of the Gaeltacht

Frank Conlan

The Gaeltacht Region – Background

The Gaeltacht is the collective name for those geographically dispersed rural areas in Ireland where the Irish language (known as Gaelic) is spoken. The Gaeltacht areas are legally defined[1] and are located mainly along the western seaboard with a population of 83,268 and an area of 5,600 sqare kilometres (see Table 1). This means that the Gaeltacht accounts for less than 2.5 per cent of the national population and under eight per cent of its land area. In these respects, it is not a very significant entity in quantitative terms. However, as the region where Irish is the primary language of the community and in the home, the Gaeltacht has a central role in the realisation of the national ideal of promoting the wider use of Irish as a spoken language throughout Ireland. The special position of the Irish language is recognised in the constitution.[2]

The county structure was established in Ireland in the twelfth century and its modern equivalent provides the basis for the local government of the country immediately below the national parliamentary level (see Fig. 1). Within this structure, the Gaeltacht regions are designated in the counties of Donegal, Mayo, Galway, Kerry, Cork, Waterford and Meath. The old provincial structure, which predates the establishment of the counties, no longer serves any administrative function. However, in the Irish language there are three dialects – associated with the provinces of Ulster, Connaught and Munster.

Eberhard Bort and Neil Evans (eds), ***Networking Europe,***
Liverpool University Press 2000, 277-96.

***Table 1** Gaeltacht population by county*

County population	Total	County area km^2	Gaeltacht population
Donegal	128,117	4,830	24,504
Mayo	110,713	5,398	11,868
Galway	180,364	5,940	32,578
Kerry	121,894	4,701	8,116
Cork	410,369	7,459	3,578
Waterford	91,624	1,837	1,368
Meath	105,370	2,335	1,256
		Total	83,268

Source: Census 1991, Vol. 1 (Central Statistics Office).

The background to the special status for the Gaeltacht can be traced to the establishment of the Congested Districts Board in 1891 during the period of reform in the ownership of land before Independence. It was recognised at that time that particular problems existed in the counties of Donegal, Leitrim, Sligo, Roscommon, Mayo, Galway, Kerry and West Cork arising from the small land tenancies and high population density. During that period, up to five million people lived in overcrowded conditions along the western seaboard.

The main activities of the Congested Districts Board included:

- the promotion of local industries such as spinning, weaving and knitting with subsidies and technical assistance;
- improving the standards of farming by providing instruction in modern farming techniques;
- purchasing land and reselling it to farmers to improve the size of farm holdings;
- helping farmers resettle from poor land to more productive farms in other areas; and

- promoting fishing by supplying boats and tackle and by building piers and harbours.

The work of the Board was considered successful because of the level of financing made available for its work by the Government, its semi-independent status, its powers of compulsory land purchase and the quality of the technical experts it employed.

In the late nineteenth century and early in this century, a tradition of emigration had been established and this had reached a stable level. The predominant source of these emigrants was the relatively poorer agricultural areas of the country. This can be seen from the census returns for the period 1881–1901 (see Fig. 2). It is noteworthy that there is a gradation of increasing emigration in the country from east to west. This pattern has persisted to the present day and political expression has been given to the concerns voiced regionally by the appointment of a Minister of State in the present Government, in the office of the Taoiseach, for 'Western Development and Rural Renewal'.

After Independence in 1921, the responsibility for the work of the Congested Districts Board was allocated to new Departments which were set up by the new State. The position of the Irish language was weakened by internal migration of the population from country to towns and also by the patterns of emigration from the Western counties where the language was more vibrant at the beginning of the century (see Fig. 3).

The modern Gaeltacht is not a homogeneous rural region, having no legally defined towns (that is an urban centre with over 1,500 persons). It spans a number of local authorities (counties) without encompassing any of them completely. The settlement pattern is characterised by a densely populated coastal fringe surrounded by a more sparsely populated upland zone. Due to a combination of peripherality, lack of urban development, and topographical considerations, the region has a very underdeveloped infrastructure, particularly road networks. There are no rail connections and none of the country's major ports are situated on the western coastline.

Economy and Employment

Historically, the economic base of the Gaeltacht was subsistence farming and inshore fishing, and it had very high rates of emigration and unemployment. The population of the area that is today defined as Gaeltacht fell from 126,059 persons in 1911 to 71,521 persons in 1971, a decline of 43 per cent. This population decline was arrested in 1971 and overall the population increased to 83,430 persons in 1986, an increase of 17 per cent. This was brought about by a reversal in the historic pattern of outward migration, largely as a result of the successful implementation of an economic development programme for the region. The census of population in 1991 indicates a slight decline.

Twenty-nine per cent of those at work in the Gaeltacht are employed in industry, a relatively high proportion for a rural region. Engineering, textiles and clothing, and food processing are the main manufacturing sectors. While net employment in manufacturing has increased over the last decade (in contrast to the situation in Ireland as a whole), the sector faces a number of challenges, including a heavy dependency on traditional industries such as textiles and clothing, a size profile which is skewed towards small industry, and a reliance on domestic markets. Efforts to diversify this industrial base have been successful in developing such sectors as engineering and electronics.

The primary sector – agriculture, forestry and fishing – provides employment for 30 per cent of those at work. However, because of the poor quality of the land and its unsuitability for agricultural purposes, there is considerable underemployment in the agriculture sector. Fishing and aquaculture are, however, important in the region's employment structure.

The service sector employs 41 per cent of the working population, mostly in public and professional services. Due to the absence of urban centres, commercial services are not significant employers in the region. The unemployment rate is estimated at 25 per cent – considerably higher than the national average.

Part-time and seasonal employment, especially in tourism, aquaculture, fish processing and other resource-based industries, plays a very important role in the socio-economic life of the Gaeltacht where a family's total income is often generated by incremental contributions from a variety of economic activities in which different members of the household are engaged.

The Legal Basis of Údarás na Gaeltachta

Údarás na Gaeltachta (The Gaeltacht Authority) is the Government agency which is responsible for the economic, social and cultural development of the Gaeltacht. It is established by legislation and came into effect in 1980[3], taking over the responsibilities of its predecessor agency, Gaeltarra Éireann. Gaeltarra had operated since 1958.[4] Its establishment at that time represented the first significant attempt by the State to implement an interventionist programme of economic development in the region. Prior to the establishment of Gaeltarra, official policy had concentrated on social development – improvements to housing and other social amenities, administration of welfare services and some infrastructural improvements. Because emigration had persisted at a high level and the population was falling rapidly, it was recognised that there was a need for a more direct economic development programme, specifically aimed at promoting employment.

Structure and Operations

Údarás na Gaeltachta is responsible to the Minister for Arts, Culture and the Gaeltacht, who ranks as a full member of the Cabinet. The Gaeltacht is the only geographical entity in Ireland which is the exclusive responsibility of a Minister in the national government, a recognition of importance which the region's development commands at national level.

Fig. 1 *The county structure in Ireland, showing the Gaeltacht areas*

The board of Údarás has thirteen members, seven of whom are directly elected by the people of the Gaeltacht in elections that are held every five years. The electorate is based on the register of electors for the Gaeltacht and polling takes place in three constituencies for the seven elected members. The remaining six members, including the Chairman, are appointed by the Minister for the Arts, Culture and the Gaeltacht.

Údarás na Gaeltachta is unique among state organisations in Ireland by virtue of this democratic representation, which allows Gaeltacht communities to have a voice in the decision-making process regarding the development of their region.

The management structure of Údarás is headed by a chief executive, who reports to the board. Four deputy chief executives, with respective responsibilities in the areas of industrial development, investment, administration and corporate affairs and legal and secretarial services, report to the chief executive.

The organisation has a staff of 110, mostly located at headquarters in Furbo, near Galway city. Increasingly, decision-making has been decentralised to regional committees of the board, and to support this structure the regional management and administrative structure has been strengthened. Regional offices are now located in Derrybeg in County Donegal, and Dingle in County Kerry, with sub-offices in Belmullet in County Mayo and Ballingeary in County Cork.

Enterprise Development

The principal aim of Údarás na Gaeltachta is to create an economically viable employment base as a prerequisite for the economic, social and cultural development of Gaeltacht communities.

Údarás na Gaeltachta implements its enterprise development programmes within the overall framework of national industrial policy. The emphasis is on promoting commercially viable enterprises with a focus on export markets, or on import substitution opportunities. A range of incentive packages are used for this purpose. These may include capital grants or per capita employment grants; training grants; rent subsidies; and research and development and feasibility study grants. In addition, equity participation is sometimes used in combination with these support measures and a wide range of advisory and support services (business planning, finance, marketing, legal and construction) are also available. Factory buildings may also be provided at subsidised rents. Údarás can directly initiate and establish subsidiary companies for the development of innovative projects.

Údarás aims to achieve this by implementing programmes which promote local industrial initiatives, develop indigenous resources and entrepreneurial abilities and attract mobile investment to the Gaeltacht. Small and medium-size enterprises (SMEs) are a specific focus of these programmes.

The strategy pursued is aimed at:

- Attracting new industries to establish in the Gaeltacht.
- Supporting the start-up and development of small, local enterprises.
- Developing the full potential of established enterprises, including its own subsidiary (wholly–owned) and associate companies (companies in which a minority investment has been made).
- Initiating and supporting the development of enterprises in sectors that offer the potential for growth, including resource-based industries.

This strategy represents a continuation of varying degrees of intervention, ranging from support for proposals brought forward by third parties to a more entrepreneurial role, taking the form of a direct initiation of enterprises in targeted sectors. Each of the elements of this strategy are outlined here in turn.

Inward Investment

Grant support for inward investment represents about 20 per cent of the total grant aid paid out by Údarás na Gaeltachta and employment in these companies accounts for 25 per cent of the total employment in Údarás-assisted enterprises. These figures are low by national standards.

Much of the overseas investment in manufacturing industry in Ireland has been from the United States, and American companies have shown a clear preference for locating in larger urban centres, in close proximity to major infrastructural facilities such as airports. Companies from continental Europe, by contrast, are more willing to consider rural and more peripheral locations. A further aspect of the Údarás experience has been that, while it is very difficult to attract 'green field' investment projects to the Gaeltacht, overseas investors are more disposed to taking over and developing established enterprises, even in cases where a business may have been experiencing trading difficulties.

Local Enterprise Development

Small local enterprises account for the bulk of the projects supported by Údarás na Gaeltachta in any one year. They represent about one-third of the employment in Údarás-assisted industries. These enterprises tend to be very small-scale and are often family-based. They embrace a broad sectoral classification, including manufacturing and craft activities, service businesses and resource-based enterprises.

Micro-enterprises of this type make a valuable contribution to socio-economic development and job creation in the Gaeltacht region. They represent a key element in bringing about sustainable development. However, as the basis for an enterprise strategy the sector presents a number of difficulties, including the fact that many of the backers of such enterprises have limited aspirations for the growth of their businesses and they suffer from key managerial skills deficiencies. Such enterprises also tend to be concentrated in a limited number of product sectors characterised by over-capacity and dependency on the small domestic market. Micro-enterprises are also perceived to have a high-risk status and this creates difficulties in raising loan finance from banks. Even where bank finance is available, these projects often prove to be under-funded from the outset as their backers typically underestimate their financing requirements and/or are unable to provide the required equity.

Fig 2 *Annual average emigration (by county) in the intercensal period from 1881 to 1901*

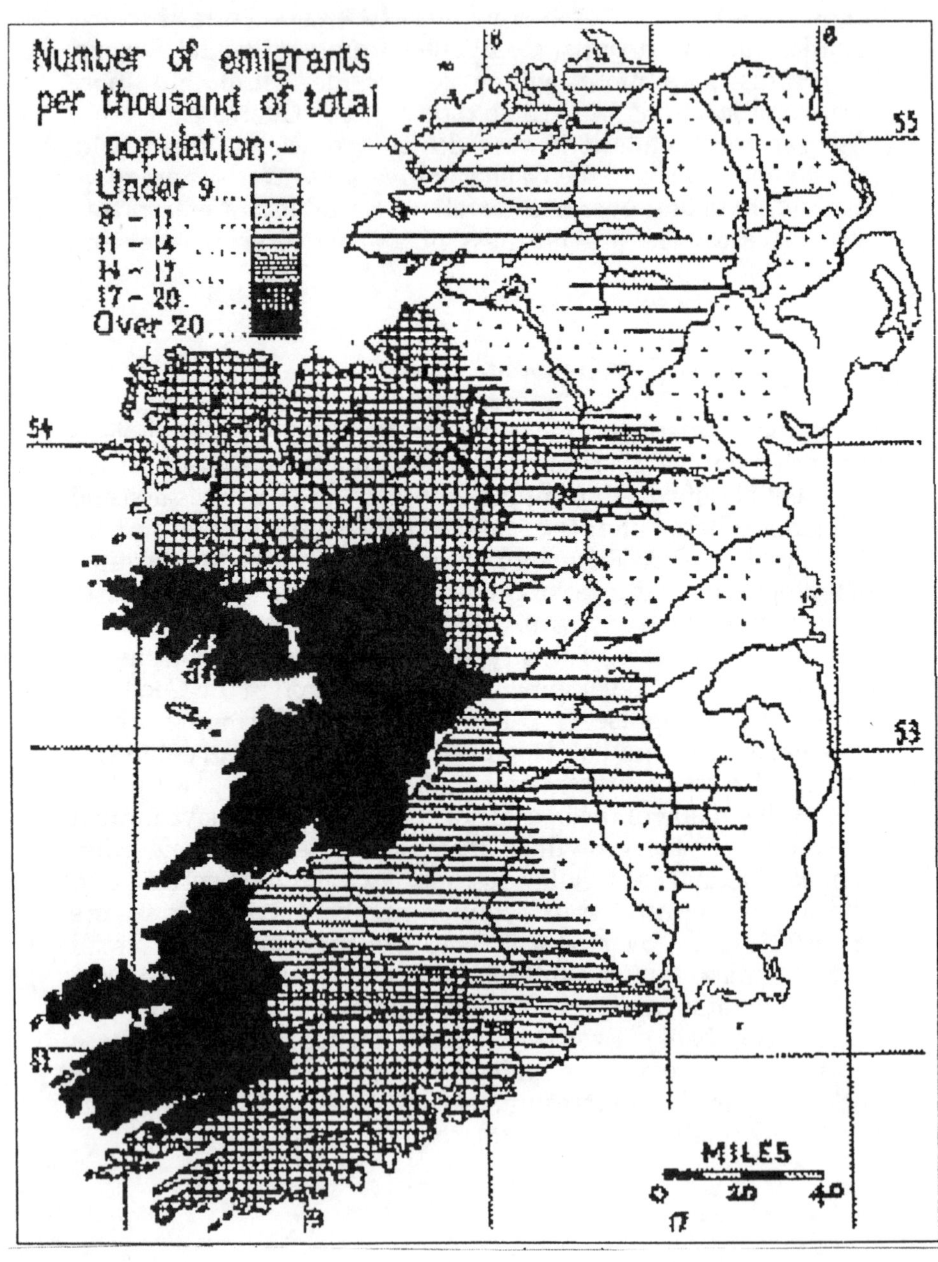

Development of Established Industries

On its establishment in 1980, Údarás na Gaeltachta inherited a portfolio of investments from its predecessor, Gaeltarra Éireann.

This portfolio included many loss-making enterprises, necessitating a programme of rationalisation, involving closures and restructuring. Where it was judged that the potential for a viable business did not exist, closure was seen as the best option. The political difficulties associated with implementing this programme of wide-scale closures and job losses were considerable and the situation demanded much skill in communicating the policy rationale in terms of releasing resources which could be used to seed new enterprises.

The restructuring of potentially viable enterprises involved a number of elements, including injection of fresh equity, bringing in new partners with finance and access to markets and technology, installing experienced management (including specialist personnel seconded from Údarás na Gaeltachta) and providing a range of advisory, business planning and support services. A key factor in successful restructuring was refocusing management's attention on market opportunity and away from a dependence on state support as the primary factor in the firm's survival. In a number of cases, successful restructuring led to management buy-outs or the sale by Údarás na Gaeltachta of its shareholding to a third party.

In an environment such as that of the Gaeltacht, which could be considered relatively unattractive to private capital, direct equity investment by a state agency like Údarás offers advantages as a means of enterprise development. Such investment accommodates a longer-term view of expected returns and it facilitates the funding of the working capital requirements (which are very often under-estimated). Furthermore, it allows the agency to acquire an in-depth knowledge of the business and of the associated market opportunities which is beneficial, particularly where a broad sectoral strategy is being pursued.

In the experience of Údarás na Gaeltachta, a minority equity participation is the most undesirable situation for a state agency as it leaves one without control and vulnerable to demands by majority partners. A more hands-off approach, in the shape of providing non-repayable grant aid as a means of support for a

Fig 3 *Distribution of the Irish language (census of population, 1901)*

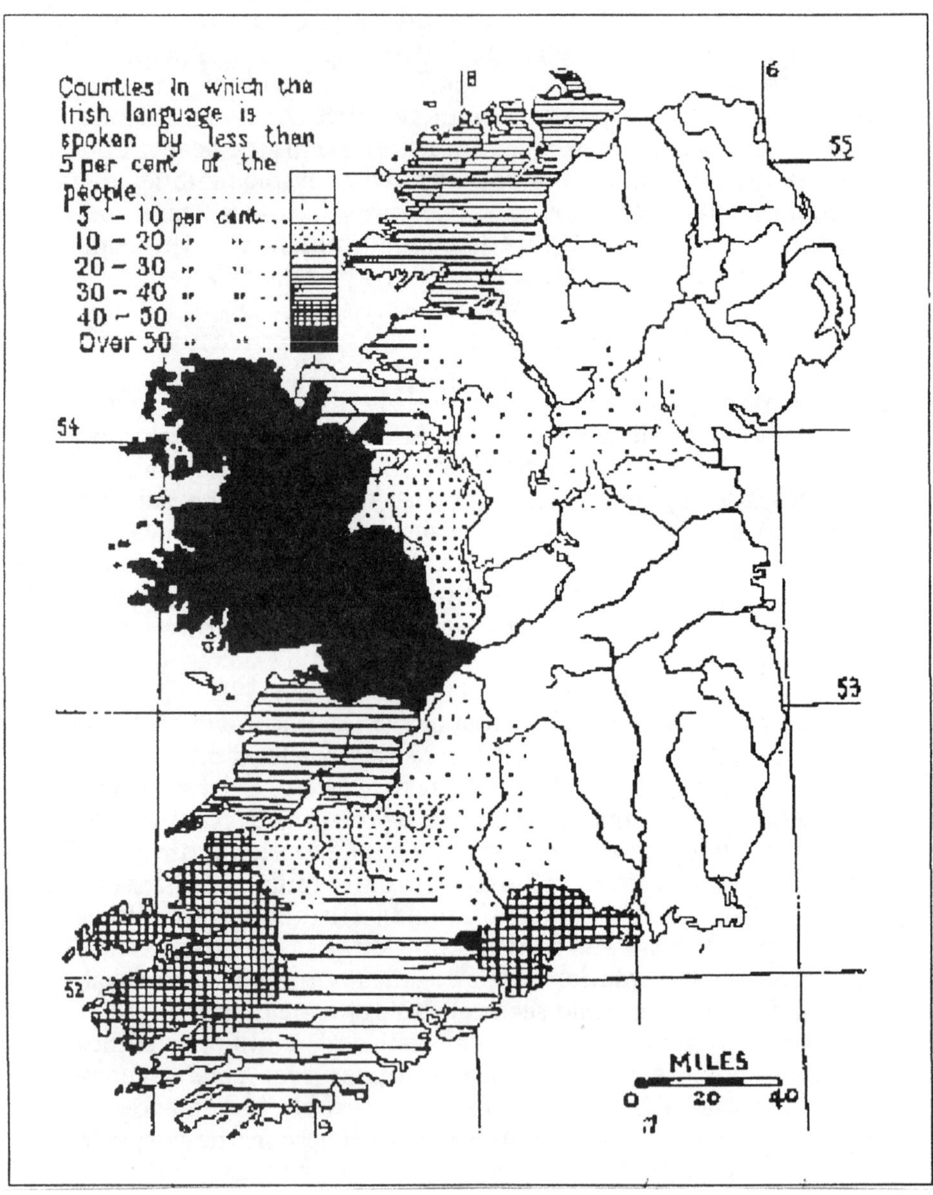

company's development, is preferable to investment as a minority equity partner.

Development of Enterprises in Sectors with Growth Potential

This element of strategy for enterprise development involves the state agency in the role of entrepreneur in its own right, targeting specific sectors with growth potential and directly initiating and stimulating enterprises aimed at realising that potential. It is a relatively high-risk strategy which does not rest easily in an environment of bureaucratic control. However, when planned and executed with commitment, skill and conviction, it is a very effective means of promoting employment and enterprise creation in a disadvantaged rural region which may involve a wide range of external players.

The Cultural Dimension

These represent the orthodox approach to the problems of unemployment and job creation in a relatively sparsely populated rural region on the fringe of the European market. However, the role of Údarás na Gaeltachta is not confined to the question of economic development alone. The distinguishing feature of the organisation is that its 'territory' is defined in terms of a language which is still used as an everyday part of life in the Gaeltacht. This cultural dimension finds its expression not in the language alone, but also in the cultural heritage, literature, music and folklore of the people of the Gaeltacht. In addressing the question of the cultural role of the organisation, the objective has been to create an environment in which the Irish language can flourish as part of a vibrant community.

Taking this wider community responsibility into account, Údarás na Gaeltachta has been proactive in inaugurating a number of community-based initiatives. These have extended over a wide range of activities and, by way of illustration, the following will give some idea of the scope of the schemes and projects.

Irish Language Pre–schools

More than 70 *naíonraí* (Irish language pre-schools) operate throughout the Gaeltacht with the support of Údarás na Gaeltachta. The objective is to ensure that the Irish language becomes a natural part of the lives of children before entering the primary school cycle in the Gaeltacht where all subjects are taught through Irish. Údarás na Gaeltachta has been active over the years in providing the structures and support for locally-based groups to establish *naíonraí.* This includes the co-ordination with national accreditation and certification bodies and also providing for the training of the staff for the pre-schools.

Schools

The principal developmental work in the primary and secondary schools includes curriculum development, such as the preparation of new course material in Irish, and commissioning career development material for the secondary schools in the Gaeltacht, including information about the apprenticeship schemes in companies operating in the different Gaeltacht areas. This introduction to work experience is extended to placements in companies and short courses organised to integrate into the school curriculum, such as in the computer science and information technology fields. Údarás na Gaeltachta maintains close contacts with the Department of Education with regard to the curriculum development needs of the Gaeltacht schools.

Youth Clubs

These clubs constitute an important resource in rural communities for the development of recreational activities and for personal development outside the more formal educational environment. Údarás na Gaeltachta supports up to 50 youth clubs throughout the Gaeltacht in their activities, particularly in providing them with advice about structures and administration. Training courses are organised and inter-club competitions are staged annually. As part of this on-going youth development programme, representatives of a range of youth clubs from the Gaeltacht take part in a sail training cruise along the west coast of Ireland on board the *Asguard* – a national sail training vessel.

Community and Cultural Heritage Projects

Much of Údarás na Gaeltachta's efforts in promoting Irish language and culture concentrates on the local community and in fostering a spirit of community enterprise. The provision of recreational facilities or community centres helps to strengthen the sense of local identity, thus giving a firm base for the development of a co-operative teamwork at local level where the survival of the language is most critical. Údarás na Gaeltachta provides support by giving recognition to locally-based representative groups which act as co-ordinators and a central representative voice for each community when dealing with statutory bodies and other agencies.

'Cultural Tourism' may form an important feature in combining a range of existing activities in a locality which reinforce the cultural and linguistic character of a community. A broad spectrum of activities ranging from environmental and educational (including Irish language summer schools) to the development of the arts and music can play a part in the community's own efforts to determine the development of their future. This has the added advantage that the distinctiveness of the region in its language and culture is the resource base on which the local people are able to build.

Údarás na Gaeltachta tries to ensure that its initiatives in the area of cultural tourism are in harmony with the strategies being followed by other bodies and agencies in the public and private sectors, such as national and regional tourism bodies and local authorities.

'An Pobal Beo' Community Competition

A number of these initiatives are combined in an enterprise competition for community groups and organisations which is hosted annually by Údarás na Gaeltachta. The main aim of this contest is to introduce a spirit of competition in fostering an awareness of the cultural heritage in the community and its value as a resource for their own development efforts. An annual prize is awarded by Údarás na Gaeltachta and individual private sector sponsors also contribute prizes for projects on specific themes (environment, tourism, music etc.). The competition has been run for a number of years and has contributed greatly to the sense of identity in the communities and fostering the link between the language and economic activities in the Gaeltacht.

In order to illustrate how some of these strategies have combined in practice in the Gaeltacht, a case study may help to illustrate the approach.

Case Study – Media/Audio-Visual Industry

Background

The Gaeltacht has no tradition in the media/audio-visual industry and no significant facilities other than a local radio service, Radio na Gaeltachta, operated under the aegis of the national broadcasting company, RTÉ. Against this background, Údarás na Gaeltachta felt that the industry had much to contribute to the objectives for all facets of Gaeltacht development: cultural, linguistic, social and economic.

National television broadcasts less than three hours per week in the Irish language, mostly news and current affairs. This lack of any significant Irish-language programming means that the language lacks modern contemporary status, particularly for children and young people. Údarás na Gaeltachta saw this as a major threat to its future. It was also seen as an opportunity to build an industry based on the creative talents and high standards of educational achievement of local young people with significant socio-economic spin-offs in the shape of enterprise development and employment opportunities.

Initiatives

In late 1986 Údarás na Gaeltachta started with an internal study group which analysed the situation, consulted previous reports and looked at the experience in other regions, including S4C, the Welsh-language television service which had been established at that time. This group favoured a national Irish-language television service but considered that, because of its high cost, it was unlikely to be funded in the short term. However, the group did identify some feasible options. It was evident that within RTÉ there was a lack of facilities and personnel for Irish-language programme production, in particular for voicing-over and dubbing bought-in programmes. This was seen to present an opportunity for establishing an embryonic production industry.

RTÉ was asked to participate in a joint venture. After protracted negotiations, agreement was reached and in 1989 Telegael Teo. was established in premises owned by Údarás na Gaeltachta as a post-production facility. An investment of £1 million was made in the very latest technology and facilities. Today, Telegael employs nearly fifty people and is trading profitably in a highly competitive industry which demands the highest standards.

Another important initiative was the provision of skills training. Workshops were organised to which experts were invited to discuss the industry and the skills involved in script writing, production, editing, camera work, and sound and lighting. These workshops, which were intended to stimulate local interest, produced a tremendous response. They led to the organisation of an intensive training course, covering script writing, production, direction, camera, sound and graphics. Twelve young people graduated from the first four-month course, during which participants produced broadcast-quality material.

In order to provide the first of these trained personnel with an opportunity to market their skills, RTÉ was encouraged to commission a series of six half-hour programmes to be produced by a group of eight of the newly-qualified personnel. An experienced director from RTÉ was seconded to the project and, under his supervision, the young people did all of the work, including story lines, script, production and post-production. The series was broadcast on national television to wide acclaim. On completion of this series, a number of the participants set up their own independent television production companies with assistance from Údarás na Gaeltachta.

This success led to a second course, and the training of a further twelve audio-visual professionals. The availability of trained personnel of high quality has spurred RTÉ to invest in a pilot programme for a 'soap opera' in Irish. An initial set of programmes was made in its entirety in the Gaeltacht. If this pilot is successful there will be an investment of £1.5 million in the production of a full series, which will take three years to complete and provide employment for up to 60 people. Once again this initiative is based on a joint venture between Údarás na Gaeltachta and RTÉ, and it has led to a decision to invest in a television studio in the Gaeltacht.

Achievements

As a result of these initiatives, an embryonic media/audio-visual industry has been established in the Gaeltacht. Today, there are thirty small production companies providing nearly 150 jobs, where none existed five years ago. Local young people are the back-bone of this industry, which is using the very latest technology and is competing to international standards. One company is currently negotiating a co-production agreement with four European television stations for a children's series. Another has been supported by the European Community's EUROFORM programme in developing co-production skills between European producers in the area of puppetry. This particular initiative was based on transnational partnerships with other minority-language communities in Europe.

Under the current round of Community Initiatives (1995–1999), individual companies and community groups have been approved to undertake projects in the ADAPT programme for the development of enterprise skills for the growing number of entrepreneurs in the Irish-language television sector; in the HORIZON programme for the training and development of young people in traditional craft skills; and in the YOUTHSTART programme for the training of young people for the skills needed in television production. The Gaeltacht has an established LEADER programme which has put an emphasis on enterprise development within the context of the cultural heritage of the geographically dispersed communities in the Gaeltacht.

Irish-Language Television Service

The future of this industry is closely tied to the establishment of an Irish-language television service, a key market for the industry's output. While the process of building the industry and providing the skills was taking place, Údarás na Gaeltachta was also actively promoting the establishment of this new television service. With professional assistance and co-operation from RTÉ, and with financial support from the European Community's MEDIA programme, Údarás na Gaeltachta carried out a feasibility study which was submitted to the Government in 1990. The study's outcome was a costed proposal for the establishment of an Irish-language television service, broadcasting nationally from a Gaeltacht base, and generating up to 200 jobs. This study has been the subject of subsequent discussions at Government level and a decision has been taken to establish an Irish-language television channel. Operating details have not yet been announced.

Critical Success Factors

A number of factors can be attributed to the successful efforts at enterprise creation in the media/audio-visual sector. Firstly, there was the existence of an organisation (Údarás na Gaeltachta) with the credibility to attract support and co-operation from key players, and with access to sources of finance. Secondly, the industry was seen as relevant and compatible with the region's needs. This ensured local commitment, a vital component for success.

Thirdly, early on a clear-cut but feasible goal was identified and a framework of support was established. Fourthly, the initial investment in training and skills development provided a pool of available people for the start-up. Fifthly, helpful partnerships at local, national and European levels were developed and promoted by Údarás na Gaeltachta. Finally, Údarás na Gaeltachta persevered in the face of setbacks and was prepared to improvise in finding innovative solutions as problems arose.

The approach which Údarás na Gaeltachta has taken in developing the media/audio-visual industry, and in other targeted sectors like aquaculture, is not particularly innovative but it has delivered results. In each case the model may be transferable to other locations and to other sectors which have potential for enterprise creation. This can be summarised as having an emphasis on capacity building and training within an integrated strategy encompassing all components of the sector. An aim of the strategy is to maintain harmony between the needs of commercialisation and profitability, on the one hand, with marrying the traditional skills and cultural heritage of the region with modern innovative technology, on the other. Finally, the development of partnerships creates the environment in which the resources of the Gaeltacht – cultural, human, and commercial – enable the various participants together to strengthen the future economic base of the Gaeltacht and the well-being of its community.

Notes

1 Determined by order under Section 2 of the Ministers and Secretaries (Amendment) Act, 1956.

2 Bunreacht na hÉireann (Constitution of Ireland); Article 8.1 'The Irish language as the national language is the first official language.'

3 Údarás na Gaeltachta Act, 1979 specifies the role 'of promoting the linguistic, cultural, social, physical and economic development of the Gaeltacht'.

4 First established under the Gaeltacht Industries Act, 1957.

Multiculturality in Wales[1]

Robin Reeves

Thanks to recent research we now know that Wales has had its share of anti-Irish riots, anti-Jewish riots and anti-Black riots, denting a belief which the Welsh political classes, at least, have liked to cultivate about Wales – namely, that it is wholly tolerant society. Blemishes are not only inclined to be brushed under the carpet, but also vehemently fought over.

Reviewing a history of the Jews of South Wales in the *New Welsh Review* recently, the former Welsh Labour MP, Leo Abse, accused the book's editor, a (Jewish) professor of history, of playing up the importance of the 1911 anti-Jewish riots in Tredegar, the Valleys hometown of that famous Welsh socialist, Aneurin Bevan.[2] Abse, himself a member of a well-known Welsh Jewish family whose ancestors came to Wales from Poland in the last century, was in no doubt that the Jewish shopkeepers hit by the riots were 'a bad lot', who had deserved their fate as a result of their extortionate money-lending activities. His grandfather had told him so. The book's very incensed editor, in turn, accused Abse of trying to play down the only event 'to cast the shadow of the Russian pogrom on the Jewish population of Britain'.[3]

In talking about multiculturality in Wales, I could discuss Wales' easily identifiable ethnic minorities? Cardiff's black community is one of the longest–established in Britain, a consequence of Cardiff's growth during the nineteenth century into the world's biggest coal export port. One of Cardiff's black sons, Colin Jackson, is a world champion hurdler and just one of a long line of black Welsh sporting heroes. Cardiff's black community is a melting pot in its own right with its ancestral roots and modern-day connections ranging from Yemen and Somalia, to Cape Verde Islands and the West Indies. But within any society there are other, less obvious, minority cultures.

Eberhard Bort and Neil Evans (eds), *Networking Europe*, Liverpool University Press 2000, 297-310.

During the Second World War, the *lingua franca* of managers on some industrial estates in south Wales became German. Refugee businessmen fleeing Nazi Germany to Britain in the 1930s were told in London that if they wished to relaunch their businesses they should do so in south Wales and help alleviate the terrible unemployment there. And after the war, rural Wales had a sizeable Polish community with its own institutions. It was made up of war-time soldiers and refugees who feared the consequences of returning to live under communism and found in Wales a place that reminded them of home.

Any comprehensive study of multiculturality in Wales needs to include parts of Wales that have not spoken Welsh for 1,000 years, such as South Pembrokeshire, known as Little England beyond Wales, and the southern side of the Gower peninsula. It gives rise to interesting insights into the matter of identity. A farmer in English-speaking Gower, asked if he was Welsh or English, replied: 'I suppose if travelling to London, you could say that when we arrive in Swansea to catch the train we feel English, but by the time we reach Paddington, we feel Welsh.'[4]

Perhaps because of its cultural and geographical divisions and the political relationship with England, Wales is a more tolerant place than most. The Welsh have survived living next to a powerful, imperial neighbour by being devious rather than aggressive. There were bombs and arson attacks on holiday homes in the 1980s and early 1990s, but nobody has been killed. And such activities do not begin to compare in aggressiveness with the bloody campaigns of the IRA, or even the incidence of racial attacks in big cities in England and the attacks on Turkish residents in Germany. The fact that there are differences of geography, class and language, as well as ethnic and (less important these days) religious background that have to be accommodated in any body claiming to represent Wales or Welsh interests is why Wales' archetypal basic unit of political organisation is the committee – only a committee structure can ensure all sections of society are represented. Welsh committees can be very quarrelsome. It is famously said that the first item on the agenda of a new Welsh committee is 'the split'! Nevertheless, without a governing committee representing Wales' geographical and cultural diversity, any institution claiming to represent Welsh interests in a country which has no separate citizenship and which in some ways is ruled like a colony from London lacks legitimacy.

For many outsiders, though, Wales's dominant cultural characteristic is that it has both an English-language and a Welsh-language culture. Social and cultural perceptions within each group vary enormously. A Welsh-speaking Welsh person would usually say, in Welsh, that 'Wales is a bilingual nation'. But Welsh-speakers living in rural areas have traditionally described anyone who doesn't speak Welsh as English, even if they were from English-speaking south Wales and their immediate ancestors spoke Welsh. It reflects the fact that in Welsh-speaking Wales, language is so often the crucial divide. It is nothing to do with where you came from or your racial or ethnic characteristics. If you live in Wales and speak Welsh, you are Welsh.

This is not true of English-speaking Wales. The great majority of the 80 per cent of Wales' population born in Wales but not brought up in Welsh-speaking households would nevertheless describe themselves as Welsh, and react indignantly to any suggestion otherwise. Indeed, opinion surveys suggest that a higher proportion of the population of the predominantly English-speaking industrial Valleys regard themselves as Welsh first and British second than does the population of Welsh-speaking rural Wales. At the same time, others find the whole business tiresome and take refuge in calling themselves British.

But these cultural complexities have practical consequences. My qualification for talking about the subject of 'Multiculturality in Wales' is, I suppose, that I am a cultural worker. I edit a magazine called the *New Welsh Review*, a magazine subtitled 'Wales's leading literary quarterly in English'. The magazine is jointly promoted by the English-language section of the Welsh Academy and the University of Wales Association for the Study of Welsh Writing in English, and subsidised by the Arts Council of Wales. Yet despite its pedigree and purpose, when I tell non-Welsh-speaking people in Wales I edit the *New Welsh Review*, they very often assume it is a Welsh-language magazine. They know that Wales has produced some famous poets and writers who wrote in English and will probably be familiar with Dylan Thomas. They also know that as a non-Welsh-speaking person they are among the majority in Wales. Nevertheless, they don't expect a literary magazine produced in Wales to be anything other than in Welsh. They tend to believe literary magazines in the English language are only produced in the cultural power centres of England, that is, in London, Oxford and Cambridge.

Why is this, you may ask. One of Wales' leading English-language literary critics, Tony Conran, sought to explain the problem – perhaps it would be better to call it a cultural situation rather than a problem – to the Arts Council of Great Britain. It wanted to know what should be its literary strategy for the 1990s and he was asked by the Welsh Union of Writers to write its reply. He began by first trying to identify the character and composition of the audiences for Welsh language and English-language publications supported by the Arts Council of Wales as follows:

> The Welsh language culture, though smaller in numerical terms is relatively cohesive, organised and politicised and very conscious of its responsibility to the Welsh past. Welsh language culture therefore does not require much leadership from official bodies. What it wants are concessions, recognition of its rights both as a national and as a minority culture, and some protection (at least) against the monopolistic juggernaut of English; and of course, being a small culture, money to subsidise its culture and educational products.[5]

He went on to point out that the Welsh Office – that is, the British Government department responsible for Wales – feels that Welsh language culture as a whole, and not simply the fine arts, ought to be supported.

> This may be simply a cynical attempt to contain nationalist agitation which would otherwise result in another Northern Ireland, but the benevolence, for the moment, is certainly there.
>
> I suggest the only thing to do is to milk it for all it is worth. The English speakers may be jealous in that it favours the minority at the expense of themselves, but the alternative is to have Wales treated as a region of

> England. For all the wealth of independent bureaucracy in Wales, Wales is perceived as different by the parliament in Westminster because of the provisions which have to be made for the Welsh language and culture.

The use of Welsh culture as a weapon with which to confront English governments is well established. Another distinguished Welsh historian, John Davies, in recalling Herman Goebbels' famous quotation 'Every time I hear the word culture I reach for my gun', likes to relate the occasion when the War Office in London wanted to clear part of the Preseli mountains, west Wales, to create a gunnery range. There were political protests – people said it was a militarist affront to Wales. It would destroy a number of Welsh-speaking communities including that of Wales' great twentieth-century pacifist poet, Waldo Williams. The protests were effective and the plan was withdrawn. 'So you could say,' John Davies concludes, 'every time the Welsh hear the word gun, they reach for their culture!'

But to return to Tony Conran, who went on to describe the cultural requirements of the non-Welsh-speaking Welsh who make up the majority of the population in the following way:

> Compared with the Welsh speakers, the English-speaking majority in Wales is a lot more heterogeneous. There is great disunity of purpose and outlook and very little cohesion as a specifically Welsh group. Among the more sympathetic to Wales are a fair number of middle-class incomers, who often try to learn Welsh. Other incomers are belligerently anti-Welsh, however, as are still a fair number of Welsh people themselves. It is not simply a matter of having a positive or negative attitude to the language, though in Welsh-speaking areas this often dominates to the exclusion of other factors. Many people from all walks of life seem quite content to regard living in Wales as living in a region of England, and are upset when events show them that their contentment is misplaced.[6]

So while the potential constituency for Anglo–Welsh literature in general, and the *New Welsh Review* in particular, is at least the whole population of Wales – for everyone understands English – the actual audience tends to be smaller than for Welsh, and in fact tends to include many of the same people. 'Only in rare cases, almost always validated by the London market first, are Anglo-Welsh literary works or magazines accepted by educated English-speaking Welsh people as belonging to themselves. It almost seems as though the loss of the Welsh language implies a disinterest in all home-produced culture and a complete acceptance of your own provincial status,' Conran added.

This gives a small but significant insight into Wales' cultural complexities. But how have they arisen? The first reason is geography. In a recent exploration of the relationship between landscape and identity, Ioan Bowen Rees, a retired local authority chief executive of Welsh nationalist persuasion, quotes approvingly an observation of a prominent Welsh Labour historian, Dai Smith, that 'any definition of Welsh experience, native or otherwise, is inseparable from a sense of place'.

He drew attention to a late nineteenth-century description of Wales by O M Edwards, a leading writer and administrator of that time who, amongst other achievements, was responsible for introducing the teaching of Welsh into schools in Wales.

> Wales [O M Edwards said] is a land of mountains, its mountains explain its isolation and its love of independence; they explain its internal divisions; they have determined through its history, what the direction and method of its progress were to be. It goes on: Wales is not the home of one ancient race; it is not the home of one ancient language. Many races have reached its glens and hills, some have died away, some remain. Many languages have died on its mountains: many may be spoken again and pass away. But while races and languages go, the mountains remain. And they give a unity of character to the people who live among them. Purity of race, continuity of language we have not but we can trace a continuity of character. Geography ever triumphs over history, climate affects the bent of the mind. A land of mountains which forms the character of

> those who come to it, giving them a vague similarity of ideas which makes unity possible in history and literature? That is the abiding fact in the history of Wales.[7]

Geographical determinism may not be so popular a historical explanation today as it was at the turn of the century. But it is impossible to get away from Wales' geography when considering its history and cultural experience. Some would maintain the unity of which O M Edwards talked was pure romantic invention, in keeping with the rise of nationalism in the nineteenth century: Wales' divisions were the reality. The people may have spoken the same language but their only unity was in being descendants of the original Britons who defined themselves as being in opposition to the Saxons and Normans (they have also been described as the Irish who couldn't swim). It is also the case that mountain peoples have rarely been able to maintain independent states of their own: they have been conquered for crude geopolitical reasons by their more prosperous neighbours settled on the plains. But it is also a fact of geography that without the rich coal and iron deposits in the Valleys of the south and slate and coal in the mountains and hills of the north, Wales would not have been thrust into the forefront of the industrial revolution and been in a position to modernise its economy, culture and society in the nineteenth century. Instead, it would have been hit by the same mass emigration and draining of vast human resources as Ireland and the Highlands of Scotland.

Welsh men and women did cross the Atlantic or emigrate to the colonies of the British empire in search of a better life. One shipload famously went to Patagonia. My Welsh grandfather left Harlech, north Wales, in 1889, at the age of 17, to settle in America. Happily for me, he was homesick and returned after two years.

However, such migrations from Wales were the exception rather than the rule. The late Professor Gwyn A Williams, noted that between 1846 and 1914, over 43 million people emigrated from Europe to the Americas, helping to build the USA into the greatest capitalist power on earth. But in proportion to population, English emigrants to the USA were four times as numerous as the Welsh, the Scots seven times as numerous, and the Irish twenty–six times as numerous. During the 1880s, over 1.25 million people left rural Germany for America, as cheap American grain exports drove European agriculture into depression. Welsh rural areas suffered a comparable depopulation over the same period, but those affected merely went to the south of their country to work in the rapidly expanding Welsh coalfield. As a result, the population of Wales rose from a little over half a million in 1801 – the date of the first population census – to 2.4 million by 1911, just prior to the outbreak of the First World War.[8]

As well as keeping Welsh people in Wales, exploitation of the iron and coal reserves also attracted immigrants in large numbers from England and Ireland, and from as far afield as Italy and northern Spain. In broad terms, it transformed the south Wales valleys into a densely-populated, multicultural, increasingly English-speaking, industrial society which saw its future salvation in trade union solidarity and the philosophy of socialism. At the beginning of the nineteenth century, Welsh had been overwhelmingly the language of Wales. By the 1911 census, Welsh speakers accounted for only 43.5 per cent of the population. But it was also the case during the period that the number of people who spoke Welsh was actually increasing dramatically – it was soon to reach nearly one million, the highest level ever. It was just that the scale of inward migration was such that, also for the first time in history, the Welsh-speaking Welsh became heavily outnumbered by the English-speaking Welsh.

In terms of exports, the south Wales coalfield peaked in 1914. In that year, the coalfield produced a total of 53 million tons, of which 35 million tons were exported. The peak in terms of employment occurred in 1925 when the south Wales coalfield employed 270,000 miners, or one-third of the total Welsh male working population. Winston Churchill's insistence upon Britain returning to the Gold standard, combined with the 1926 General Strike, lost Welsh coal many of its traditional markets to oil and set the scene for a catastrophic economic and social collapse in the 1930s Depression. As unemployment soared, a total of nearly half a million people emigrated from south Wales in the 1920s and 1930s – or about one fifth of the whole population of Wales –

in order to find work in the new consumer industries of the English Midlands and London and the South-East. Few ever returned.

As Gwyn A Williams remarked of that period:

> The Depression played the same role in Welsh history as the famine played in Irish history. Not until 1961 did the Welsh population precariously regain the level of 1921. The industrial valleys of South Wales became, and to a large degree remain, a problem area, while into the rural west and north began that flow of the largely non-Welsh population which started the cultural transformation of those areas, ultimately to precipitate a crisis of Welsh language culture, a crisis of arson and bombs.[9]

In the 1961 census, to which he was referring, the proportion of the population of Wales which was Welsh-speaking had fallen to 26 per cent, and from the age structure it was clearly set to decline even more dramatically in the years ahead. In February 1962, one of the founding father of Plaid Cymru, Saunders Lewis, gave a famous radio lecture in which he warned that – assuming there were still people left in the British Isles by then (the Berlin Wall had only just been built and the threat of nuclear war loomed large) – 'Welsh would cease to be a living language, assuming the present tendency persisted, by the beginning of the twenty-first century.'

Lewis went on to say that the Welsh language could only be saved by a revolution. 'By adopting revolutionary methods alone will we succeed,' he declared, urging his listeners to make it impossible for local authority or central government business to be conducted in Wales without the Welsh language.[10]

It was this call which led to the foundation of *Cymdeithas Yr Iaith Cymraeg*/The Welsh Language Society by a group of young nationalists. They began with a day of mass law-breaking in Aberystwyth designed to secure court summonses in Welsh, before turning their attention to the use of Welsh in the post office, on car licences and on road signs. Signs in English only were painted out and, failing remedial action by the authorities, were then removed altogether. Society members became involved in a host of court cases and periods of imprisonment.

While those who participated were almost exclusively young people, large numbers of older Welsh speakers viewed their activities with tacit approval. Others found it upsetting, were indifferent or hostile.

Today, some 30 years on, Saunders Lewis' prophecy has not come to pass. Welsh is not only very much alive but in many ways fighting back lost ground. Over the past 20 years there has been an explosion in demand from parents in Wales wanting their children to be educated through the medium of Welsh. The strongest demand has come from the Anglicised industrial valleys of south Wales where parents want their children to recapture the language which they remember being spoken by one or more parent or grandparent but which they were denied the opportunity to learn. But no part of Wales has been immune from a burgeoning demand for bilingual education. In my short lifetime, parents who bring their children up Welsh-speaking have moved from a position of being accused of holding their children back – from getting on in the world – to one where they are accused of being élitist and of wanting to give their child an unfair advantage.

Jobs are now advertised in which an ability to speak Welsh is put as desirable or essential. Wales has its own television channel and radio station in Welsh. The teaching of Welsh to adults has developed into a big industry all over Wales. It is becoming almost commonplace for people moving to Wales to make an effort to learn Welsh. Road signs are becoming bilingual as a matter of course, and Welsh is increasingly visible on official forms from public bodies and, in some instances, is being used by private industry in their advertisements etc. Travelling around Wales today, it is visibly becoming a bilingual country. Thirty years ago this was not the case. There was hardly a Welsh sign to be seen anywhere, apart from outside Nonconformist chapels.

The 1991 census revealed that half a million of the inhabitants of Wales, 18.7 per cent of the population over the age of three, claimed to have a knowledge of Welsh. This was a very slight fall on 1981, indicating the decline had been halted. Even more important was the advance among the younger age groups. In 1981, 18 per cent of those between the age of three and fifteen claimed to be able to speak Welsh, a figure which had risen to 24.9 per cent in 1991. For the first time since 1891, when the census first concerned itself with language, knowledge of Welsh was more widespread among children than it was amongst the population as a whole.[11]

Another major change, however, is that the majority of Welsh-speakers now live in areas where the language is not that of the majority. Maps showing the percentage of population speaking Welsh give the impression that the strength of the language still lies in the western inland areas of Wales. But those showing the absolute numbers suggest its strength lies along the northern and southern coasts. Yet the fact that Welsh is no longer the predominant community language in many parts of Wales does no mean it is not being used. Rather it has become a network language, spoken within particular groups and in particular circumstances.

At the same time, it enjoys widespread goodwill. According to a recent public opinion survey of attitudes in Wales, commissioned by the Welsh Language Board, over 70 per cent of those questioned supported the use of the language, three out of four (77 per cent) agreed it was 'an asset to Wales', and the overall percentage of those who thought the Welsh language was 'something to be proud of' was as high as 88 per cent.[12]

What has been the impact of all these changes upon the politics of Wales? Traditionally Wales has been a country of safe seats and big majorities for MPs going to Westminster. That is not true of the Conservatives. They have not held a majority of seats in Wales since 1868 when the franchise was extended. In the 1906 Liberal landslide, the party of David Lloyd George won all but five of Wales' 33 seats, and the fledgling Labour Party the remainder. The Conservatives lost every seat. By 1966, however, it was Labour that had established almost complete dominance. In the general election that year Labour captured 32 of the 36 seats, leaving the Conservatives with just three seats and the Liberals with one. But Labour's hegemony went unchallenged for only a few months. In July 1966, the Welsh Nationalist Party leader Gwynfor Evans defeated the Labour candidate in Carmarthen to win Plaid Cymru's first seat in Westminster.

Plaid Cymru improved its position during the 1970s, winning two more seats at the expense of Labour. But the home rule cause suffered a serious setback in 1979 when Labour's proposals for establishing a Welsh Assembly were firmly rejected in a referendum, and its plans for a Scottish parliament did not go ahead. In the general election which followed soon afterwards bringing Mrs Thatcher to power, the Conservatives shocked other political parties by capturing half a dozen Welsh seats. Not only did it seem as though the nationalists had fatally overplayed their hand, but that a separate sense of Welshness had weakened to the point where Wales was now embracing Mrs Thatcher's brand of British nationalism.

It was also against that background of defeat that the new Conservative Government introduced policies which in 1980 led to more than 20,000 redundancies in the Welsh steel industry in a matter of months. In succeeding years, a programme of coal pit closures culminated in the great 1984–85 miners strike and the final rundown of that industry. On assuming power in 1979, Mrs Thatcher's government also proposed reneging on its election promise to establish a Welsh-language TV channel. The decision was only reversed after Gwynfor Evans threatened to go on hunger strike.

It was in this atmosphere that the infamous holiday home arson campaign designed to discourage the English from moving into Welsh-speaking rural Wales also got under way. It was to continue off and on for much of the 1980s, happily without loss of life, petering out with the collapse of property market prices in the early 1990s.

Now, after years of being governed by a party which enjoys only minority support in Wales, the idea of establishing a Welsh Parliament or Assembly to protect Wales from right-wing governments in London and interface with Europe in much the same way as a German Land, has gathered fresh appeal.

Labour has said it will introduce legislation to establish a Welsh Assembly within its first year in office, though some fear that Wales' geographical and cultural divisions, which led to the massive rejection of the 1979 Welsh Assembly proposals, could reassert themselves and lead to the proposal being dropped. Others argue that the proposed powers, far less than those planned for a Scottish Parliament, will render the Assembly no more than a 'talking shop'. But any assembly, whatever its powers, is bound to have responsibility for health, economic matters, education and cultural affairs and there will be many who will hope it provides the impetus for turning Wales into a truly bilingual nation – one in which the overwhelming majority speak both of Wales' languages – in the twenty-first century.

This is by no means guaranteed. Others recall the example of Ireland where everybody was rushing off to their Irish classes until the Irish Free State was established in 1922 and then stopped bothering. After all, Welsh is not necessary to get around in Wales or for most forms of employment. The days of the monoglot Welsh speaker have passed. Those who speak Welsh also understand and speak English. If Welsh is to survive and prosper alongside Anglo-American cultural predominance, it will require an act of political and cultural will akin to the establishment of Hebrew as the national language of Israel.

Is this likely? Ioan Bowen Rees, the retired chief executive whom I mentioned earlier on, I thought put his finger on why this is possible during the course of a presidential address he gave to the National Eisteddfod, Wales' great annual cultural festival, in 1989. He was speaking in Welsh, so this is a translation:

> We bring up our children to speak Welsh, not for the sake of the language, but for the sake of our children. And not in the main for them to enjoy literature – however unreasonably superb that literature may be, considering we are such a small tribe. To many of us, the Welsh language has become a symbol of things more important than the language even, and that may be our salvation. Welsh has come to symbolise neighbourliness, brotherhood and equality. More fundamentally, every minority language symbolises the right to think in a different way, to express that difference and to be different and free – to use a phrase of Ivan Illich, 'a domain on which a certain kind of power cannot trespass'.[13]

Illich was comparing vernacular dialects with self-sufficient non-market economic activities. The Welsh language offered a similar domain to the people who inhabit the mountainous western peninsula of one of Europe's main offshore islands.

Notes

1 This paper is an abridged version of my address to the Freudenstadt Symposium in June 1994.

2 Leo Abse, 'A Tale of Collaboration not Conflict with the "People of the Book"', in *New Welsh Review*, No.22, Autumn 1993, p.18.

3 Ursula Henriques's letter of reply, *New Welsh Review*, No.23 , Winter 1993–94, p.85.

4 Recounted by Dr Prys Morgan, Depart.ment of History, University of Wales, Swansea, in a lecture on the history and social economy of Gower at Plaid Cymru's 1981 summer school, Trinity College, Carmarthen, Dyfed.

5 Tony Conran, 'A Welsh Strategy for Literarure', in *New Welsh Review*, No.15, Winter 1991–92, p.52.

6 *Ibid.*, p.53.

7 Ioan Bowen Rees, 'Landscape and Identity', in *New Welsh Review* , No.25, Summer 1994, p.19.

8 Gwyn A Williams, *The Welsh in their History*, London: Croom Helm, 1982, p.175.

9 *Ibid.*, p.178.

10 Saunders Lewis, 'The Fate of the Language', an English translation of the 1962 BBC Cymru annual radio lecture, in *Planet* , No.4 . 1971, pp.13–27.

11 Janet Davies, *The Welsh Language*, Cardiff: University of Wales Press, 1993.

12 *Public Attitudes to the Welsh Language: A Reseach Report Prepared by NOP Social and Political for the Central Office of Information and the Welsh Language Board/Bwrdd Yr Iaith Gymraeg*, November 1995.

13 Ioan Bowen Rees, 'Wales Today: Nation or Market?', in *Planet*, No.79, 1990, p.78.

A Degenerate View of Re-generation, or Side-stepping the Heritage Question

Dai Smith

Introduction

In 1985, the twelve-month-long miners' strike was, in grass-roots form anyway, a social rebellion and a communal defence ground inexorably to its agonising close. South Wales had been a region of unparalleled solidarity even within its own traditions. Arguably, the effects of that struggle will, as with 1926, take a generation to emerge from the sullen carapace of defeat under which the former mining communities now cower. Inarguably, that defeat signalled the utter material destruction of the distinctive working-class culture, both popular *and* proletarian, that had been painfully wrought since the 1880s.

The Miners' Institutes' Welfare Halls and well stocked libraries (Aneurin Bevan's Tredegar Library subscribed in 1949 to *Pravda* and the *New York Herald Tribune* but not the local, hated *Western Mail* which the young Bevan had publicly burned in 1926) were proud bastions of culture, homes to societies, debating clubs, brass bands and public lectures ranging from women's rights to contraception and Indian independence. Independent working-class education, at local and national level, was enthusiastically supported by the surest test of all, voluntary financial contribution. At its peak, in the early 1920s, the South Wales coalfield contained a mining work force of over 270,000 and a vast ancillary dependent economy of workers besides. The collapse into economic depression and mass unemployment notwithstanding, this society, and its union

Eberhard Bort and Neil Evans (eds), *Networking Europe*
Liverpool University Press 2000, 311-20.

leaders and politicians, dominated the whole agenda of Welsh life well into the 1960s. It is, of course, all too easy to idealise and romanticise those valley communities or to argue, correctly of course, that the travel writer H L Morton, who overheard two unemployed miners discussing the theory of relativity on a street corner in 1932, was only recording an impressionistic (yet surely revealing) moment. Certainly this is the reality *and* the myth of South Wales' popular culture: indigenous and cosmopolitan, localised and internationalist, widespread and elitist.

The problem I have with it, historically and now in contemporary terms, is that it is all too readily separated out or only given accredited validity for the parts that those alternatives to 'popular' – i.e. 'mass', 'vulgar', 'commercialised' – allegedly did not reach. I would suggest that a willingness to re-examine what was, and is, thought to be 'degenerate' in working-class culture (i.e. what is *truly* popular) might lead us, then and now, to a more hopeful perspective than the industrial ruins of South Wales, tarted up with theme parks on mining history, currently allow.

Re-examining Working-Class Culture

During that 1984-85 strike, Raymond Williams did me the honour of reviewing a book I had written about modern Welsh sensibilities in the *London Review of Books* (a rare enough niche for *any* Welsh writer!). He was, as always, thoughtful and courteous but clearly had a difficulty with my degenerate optimism. He wrote:

> ... the industrial Welsh by-passed the muted tones of English culture for their version of the brash expansiveness of North Americans ... From Welsh-language Wales this was often seen ... as a vulgar, Anglicised betrayal of 'Welshness'. Yet Anglicised, at least, it was not. The work of the English-language writers of industrial South Wales is unmistakably in-

> digenous; its English in tone and rhythm is not an English literary style ... In these writers and in everyday speech of the valleys ... a distinctive culture is using that diverse and flexible language for its own unmistakably native writing and speech.
>
> (But) ... there are moments ... when the gesture towards North America, the intellectually and emotionally sophisticated movement outwards from the confines of a narrow inherited, sits uneasily besides the simple and heartfelt proletarian continuities. This is especially so at a time when many of the same external forces are directly allied in their presentation of a desirable social world, with the forces which are working to break up not only a restricted working-class culture but all the values which have gathered, under long pressure, around both class and place.

To most of that argument, including the end, I would nod assent. Its too easy assumption of 'continuities', however, is a suspect one. At one level it is equally possible to point up fractures and fragmentation throughout the history but, more importantly, the formation of that now highly-prized and widely-acknowledged working-class culture was never an immaculate one, never separate from those 'external forces' and often directly entangled with them. This extends from questions of public rhetoric and communal aspirations right across the intricate history of crowd behaviour, carnival or fancy-dress Jazz bands parading in the streets in the middle of the great strikes of the 1920s, down to the social ostracism or even violence meted out to those who transgressed the general concept of what was 'fair' as opposed to what was legally permitted under the law. In other words, it is the totality of 'lived experience' to which we should refer, and not only to its manifestation in the abstracted, partial shape of a 'Culture'.

Some of the despair which settles like a pall over those who depict a diverse, contemporary working class as a permanently stalled vehicle comes from an unwillingness to abandon the idea of social process as a journey. A progressive, enlightened notion of time here, unnecessarily in my view, conflicts with the equal reality of space in which people must also live and struggle. In South Wales today if time (class) appears frozen or derailed it is because we have not recognised how space (place) is being appropriated. Assuredly, the atomistic consequences of domestic privatisation are everywhere apparent. Less clear is that the abandonment of public space or shared, collective life in any number of guises has not left us with a vacuum but with an alternative, organising, corporate world, geared to secure us as receptive consumers on a uniform, yet individual, basis within a society whose once formal, institutionalised, opposition channels are all closed or diverted. To be specific: annual Miners' Gala days (celebratory demonstrations of this once powerful presence) or the Miners' Eisteddfod (dignified portrayals of variegated cultural skills) are, within this past decade, consigned to oblivion, and no other union or political group has re-invigorated their efforts. The old 'popular culture' is, to all intents and purposes, gone, and no amount of special interest – rainbow – cultural politics can disguise the fact, nor lay claim to any widescale involvement.

Even so, the *popularity* of culture is not in question or at risk, only whether the net result is closure or liberation. Let me return to the actual history once more since, in a different context, this is not a new experience within South Wales, and a grasp of our own complex inheritance is essential if the 'Heritage Industry' is to be a facilitator in the popular control of space rather than a lobotomised time capsule.

A Nation of Degenerates?

A senior Welsh educationalist, Sir Alfred Davies, one of the band of stout Edwardian Liberal patriots who 'controlled' Wales until the 1920s and who were increasingly horrified at the immigrant, novel society developing all round them, wrote in 1916, the year in which that other populist Welshman, David Lloyd George, became Prime Minister of the British Empire:

> One may as well expect to gather grapes off thorns as expect the younger generation of Welsh boys and girls to become good patriots if they are left to draw their views of life from the gutter press, to associate manliness with the deeds of banditti, or courage with the conduct of the apache. Nor are they likely to become citizens of the highest type if the relaxations of the cinema, the excitement of the boxing ring and football field or the attractions of the public house, are the only respite Young Wales is taught to know from the fatigues of the pit ...

The expressed concern, in this and many other such reports of this time, is for the preservation (meaning creation) of 'national characteristics' to hold up against the 'alien' influences of class-divisive politics and the ideology of socialism. The belief, interchangeably explicit and implicit, is that the 'base' tendencies intrinsic to popular culture not only 'de-nationalise' but also 'de-humanise'. A nation of degenerates seemed to be in the making. Between 1909 and 1917 Wales (or rather its distended southern appendage), already supreme in rugby football, addicted to professional soccer and to foot-racing, produced world boxing champions at featherweight, lightweight and flyweight, three world champion professional cyclists, three major urban riots involving the use of imported police and troops, serious coalfield-wide strikes, a number of highly influential syndicalist writers, thinkers and activists and, in Ivor Novello, the most popular song writer of the age: begging for and getting parody of his saccharine sweetness in the soured trenches.

Or, to put it another way: in 1917 a young miner, one who had, aged 15 in 1903, in his home town of Aberdare, watched Buffalo Bill and Sitting Bull parade through the streets, played amateur rugby for covert payment for his local team, been to Ruskin College, Oxford, on a miners' scholarship and seen his brother Twm arraigned on a manslaughter charge for accidentally killing his opponent in an illegal bare-knuckle prize fight, stood up at the South Wales Miners Conference in Cardiff and successfully moved that, in future, the second object of the Federation should be 'the abolition of capitalism'. The man was W J Edwards, clearly an unpatriotic degenerate who understood better than many subsequent historians the intricate filaments of connection that gave *his* working class a consciousness rather than a control button. He wrote in his autobiography:

> A wonderful period was on the horizon [of the 1890s] ... a period of change. The gramophone, the cinema, the internal combustion engine which made the motor car a possibility and, later, the aeroplane, with speed and still greater speed on the earth and in the air.
>
> There were mushroom growths of political parties, great trade unions developed, there were strikes and lockouts, and out of all this social travail, new ideas were born as new problems developed.

To move through the new times which men such as W J Edwards envisaged as possible and as necessary it was essential to occupy the space that had become available, and to do so with all the new, popular, cultural means at their disposal. Technology is a neutral factor until given social usage: then its control becomes another site of contention. For a while cinemas, for instance, were considered intrinsically subversive. The audiences were overwhelmingly urban and working-class. Theatres and operettas did not long flourish but the surreal realism of the screen projected the immigrant society to itself, in South Wales as well as in Pittsburgh or Chicago. Above all, in the 1930s and 1940s, it was not the tortured inanities of home-grown British cinema that delighted but the breezy, wise-cracking and more open-ended lives depicted in American cinema. Not so much escapism as escapology.

Those weary old arguments about 'social control' as being instrumental in cultural production are, I contend, extremely weak when we come to examine the actual lives, minds and deeds of those exposed to and allegedly corrupted by the 'Poppy' of the masses.

In South Wales even Marx was served up with style. Thus Councillor Murray Williams, in the mid-1930s, held street meetings to discuss Thesis, Antithesis and Synthesis. The crowd would grow restless after a few blasts from Murray's monotone rendition of *Das Kapital*, so he would unroll a little wooden mat that he had kept from his previous career as a music hall artiste and, accompanied by a mouth organ, tap dance his way back to a larger crowd before he concluded with his triumphant philosophical conclusion. The trouble was that his listeners everafter confused Utopia with the ultimate terpsichorean synthesis of the 1930s: the films of Fred Astaire.

Jokes, black laughter, slapstick comedy and absurdist humour were survival techniques. Jesters could be unlicensed judges in a world that had been stood on its head. The Marx Brothers were more long-lasting and successful agents of social subversion than the *soi-disant* Marxists who also, all too often, looked for 'citizens of the highest type'.

The novelist Gwyn Thomas wrote:

> ... during the recent revival on television of almost all the Marx Brothers' films they found a vast and zealous following among younger viewers. Indeed it is likely that the idol-smashing buffoonery that set the cinema of the thirties by the ears is more intelligible and appealing now than it was the first time round.
>
> As the brothers approached the end of their big creative period the world was setting its hand to lunacies that made the bizarre romps of Chico and Harpo and the radical savageries of Groucho seem as mildly sane as a magistrate's bench. Give a king-sized jester a total freedom of expression and humanity will clutch its heart first in laughter, then in fear...
>
> ... I was reminded of three bachelor brothers who lived near my home (in the Rhondda Valley) when the Marx films began landing like shells in the Valley stockades.
>
> These men were withdrawn; they had drifted into Glamorgan from Cenarth, near Cardigan. They spoke a soft purring kind of Welsh, designed not to upset coracles or alert water bailiffs. They never ceased to ache for the safe tranquillity of Cenarth. The Rhondda they regarded as a catalogue of rate-paying outrages. The sounding cinema, as the Spaniards called it, struck them as just another antic of industrial man at his vilest.

> I persuaded them to go and see *Duck Soup*. They were conservative in politics and the raking fire of Jacobinical irreverence from the screen drove them time and again to the cloister of the convenience. By the time we got to the Anthem they were in a state of screaming confusion and had to be steered home. They wanted to charge the cinema manager with conspiracy to dement and defraud the Celt. But I persuaded them that legal action can often be even more inscrutable than the Marx Brothers. Never had the Atlantic of the spirit that separates the Teifi from the Bronx been so neatly bottled.

'Imagine the Past: Remember the Future'

And now, in the 1990s, with slate 'museums', underground 'experiences', Heritage 'trails', woollen mills as 'craft boutiques' and all the bric-a-brac paraphernalia of a profit-fixated Heritage Industry we, in Wales, are indeed in danger of becoming what a colleague of mine predicted in the early 1980s: 'A Nation of Museum Attendants'. It is a kind of 'safe tranquillity', patriotic employment and enjoyment for 'citizens of the highest type', notionally committed to harmonising a discordant, post-industrial society.

If the Single Market, however gratuitously, destroys *that* smug, fearful, regional complacency, I would applaud. If popular culture across Europe, though it seems to me impossible to confine its definition to European terms, alights on universals, makes direct connections, disassembles particularisms in their parochial guise and introduces uneasy energies, then I would be delighted and say that it did once happen that way before. If, however, an expressed distaste for collective and popular culture by the Guardians of Taste and the Custodians of Characteristics has any historical precedent, then those Nose Wrinklers will prove to be, no matter what their nobility of purpose, the objective enemies of any regenerating working class.

Yet, to side-step the Heritage Industry in anger at its falsity, its kitsch presentation and its wilful purpose in avoiding the very process of history, and especially of working-class struggle, is to miss the chance to seize a potentially popular form and thereby to reach out to an atrophying historical imagination. The anger and prideful indignation we might elicit from the actual history is the only effective catalyst for real change and popular involvement, at least in so far as a working class is concerned. A dreamworld of spreading future betterment is, at best, a social palliative, one which truly wishes to cotton-wool a history it did not ever fully control and which still threatens its hegemonic cultural pretensions.

'Imagine the Past: Remember the Future' is a dictum that should be engraved above the portals of every Heritage Centre. In turn, I still think they *could* vivify a history whose real legacy to us is not the vanished institutions and formal organisations that have increasingly been appropriated as emblems, but the life stories and relationships whose complex experience they ought to probe and present. And that would mean an attention to the shared, proletarian and popular culture whose multi-dimensionalism they are so ill-equipped to narrate and whose present needs they are so reluctant to admit.

It is inconceivable that Heritage can be transformed into Culture (to become a part of Raymond Williams' 'whole way of life') without the active participation of a Labour movement empowered nationally and locally and comprehending of its role as a mere facilitator. The impetus will need to come from and be sustained by those in the regions able to use and work through whatever cultural agencies they can (print, radio, video, speech, television, etc.) to expose the history-in-aspic we are currently given for the insubstantial sham it is. In its place, surely, should come a 'pop' history to place alongside on-going and connected 'pop' cultures. Community needs and development ought to override *all* tourist-orientated considerations. For that we can always have Disneyland. Real learning and real living do not need to be dismissive of the latter but nor should they be warped into a mould they can never fit. Paradoxically it is of course the Disneyworld model that is never anarchic like reality, always sanitised unlike reality and deliberately comforting in its unchanging state. All that is solid can be flushed away. Degenerates of the world unite; you have nothing to pull but their chains.

Imagining Scotland: A Heritage Industry Examined

David McCrone

Heritage is a thoroughly modern concept. Much as sexual intercourse was, according to Philip Larkin, invented in 1963, so heritage belongs to the final quarter of the twentieth century. It is true, of course, that heritage, like sex, is as old as the world itself. All property which is not forcibly taken by conquest but has been passed on by means of some contract or other is heritage. Strictly speaking, heritage refers to that which has been or may be inherited, anything given or received to be a proper possession, an inherited lot or portion. But heritage has outgrown its legal definition. It has come to refer to a panoply of material and symbolic inheritances, some hardly older than the possessor. We have constructed heritage because we need to do so. Heritage is a condition of the late twentieth century.

First, it is necessary to establish that heritage is now part of our modern consciousness. The past twenty years or so have seen the rapid growth of 'heritage' centres and heritage-based attractions. When the British parliament passed the Ancient Monuments Act in 1882, it listed 68 monuments deemed to be significant. A century later, these numbered over 12,000. There were, in addition, 330,000 listed buildings, and in excess of 5000 conservation sites.[1] This growth in heritage, however, is largely a feature of the 1970s and 1980s. Half of Scotland's 400 museums have been opened since the late 1970s, and these attract around 12 million visitors annually.[2]

By the mid-1980s, tourism had become the UK's second biggest earner of foreign currency. By the late 1980s, 330 million site visits were being made, compared with 200 million in 1984. Scotland has its own version of this heritage explosion. The key sites are Edinburgh Castle, and Glasgow's Art Gallery (with one million visitors each), the Burrell Collection (750,000), around

Eberhard Bort and Neil Evans (eds), *Networking Europe*, Liverpool University Press 2000, 321-61.

half a million to the People's Palace in Glasgow, the same number to Edinburgh's Royal Museum of Scotland, and a third of a million to Holyrood House, to say nothing of the 350,000 which the Loch Ness Monster Exhibition claims to have had through its doors.

The consumption of heritage has its involved cadres as well as its infrequent foot-soldiers. Bodies such as The National Trust (covering England, Wales and Northern Ireland), the National Trust for Scotland, English Heritage, and Historic Scotland have large and important memberships. The National Trust enrolled its two-millionth member in 1990 (its membership doubled in the 1980s) and is the largest conservation organisation in the world, which needs £80 million per annum just to keep going at its present level, with a staff of over 2,000, supplemented by 20,000 volunteers. By 1993, the Scottish organisation (NTS) had over 230,000 members, an annual income of over £13 million of which over £3 million came from membership subscriptions.

Museums too have moved out of their musty past, and have been a major growth area in post-industrial Britain, with its attendant academic spin-off, 'the new museology'.[3] The Scottish Museums Council, for example, which is the main channel of central government support for the sector, supports over 300 local museums in Scotland, and has seen its annual allocation of grant aid rise from just £6,000 in 1975/76 to almost £400,000 in the early 1990s.

Understanding Scottish Heritage

Scotland, then, mirrors the explosion in heritage which is taking place across the western world. There is another deeper and more important reason for studying heritage here. To put it simply, the whole idea of heritage has its origins in nineteenth-century Scotland and the revolution in the writing of history brought about by Sir Walter Scott.

Figure 1 *Propping up heritage*

Scott's lifetime spanned a period of great historical change. In the words of Marinell Ash, he lived through 'the tensions and contradictions of a traditional Scotland merging into a great world empire'.[4] Scott spent part of his childhood on his grandfather's farm at Sandyknowe, near Smailholm in Roxburghshire, and at an early age was exposed to the oral history tradition of the Borders. These early childhood experiences were to provide the inspiration for his novels. In these, Scott created a highly romantic and fictitious picture of the Scottish past. He then encouraged nineteenth-century Scottish historians to recover and study historical documents and records and recreate for themselves similar pictures of the past. It was this activity which led the Hungarian philosopher Georg Lukacs to describe Scott's work as the first literary expression of world-historical consciousness.

Scott's historical revolution gave birth to a new way of thinking about the past which turned out to be extremely important in the context of nineteenth- and early twentieth-century European social development.[5] It introduced the idea of past and present as two very different entities. In the words of David Lowenthal:

> This new past gradually came to be cherished as a heritage that validated and exalted the present. And the new role heightened concern to save relics and restore monuments as emblems of communal identity, continuity and aspiration.[6]

We will argue that there are special benefits to be had by looking at heritage from a Scottish perspective. Scotland is clearly a nation which is not a conventional state, and in which for much of its history of the last three hundred years its population has been very aware of the difference between its cultural and political identities. The view from the periphery is likely in this instance to be more insightful of processes taken for granted at the core.

We might even argue that Scotland suffers from too much heritage rather than too little. Its iconography includes tartan, Glencoe, Bonnie Prince Charlie and Culloden, Bannockburn, Burns, Mary Queen of Scots, whisky, Edinburgh Castle and much more. It has become an *idée fixe* of many Scottish intellectuals that Scotland suffers from a deformation of its culture, that it has sold out its political birthright for a mess of cultural pottage.[7] It is argued that instead of a rounded thought-world in which culture and politics work together in gear, the images of Scotland which have been let loose are adrift from their political moorings. All manner of imaginings have been allowed to gather around the representation of Scotland, of which perhaps the best-known is the Hollywood concoction, *Brigadoon*. Genuine Scottish culture has truly been 'eclipsed'.[8]

Even the Scottish Tourist Board is reported as having tired of the Tartanry and Tourism image.[9] In a campaign to attract English visitors north of the border, the Tourist Board in its search for 'Scotland the Brand' launched an advertising campaign which played down the images of kilted bagpipe players in favour of Scotland's poetry, music and landscape. It is now a commonplace to assert that much of tartanry is Victorian fabrication,[10] that it owes more to the heritage industry than to history. Some, like Beveridge and Turnbull, argue that much of conventional Scottish culture is so utterly tainted that it is best left alone. However, it is also clear that most Scots are ambivalent about Scottish heritage icons like tartan. For example, it is frequently worn at sporting events, notably at Hampden and Murrayfield, in assertions of Scottish sporting nationalism. Even those central icons of the British imperial past, the Highland regiments, have their vociferous defenders in the Scottish National Party. All is not what it seems. The heritage icons are leaky. They take on radical as well as conservative meanings.

At the centre of Scottish heritage stands the country itself, Scotland as theme-park. Its landscape is a social and cultural product. It is, in the words of Denis Cosgrove:

> ... a way of seeing projected on to the land, and having its own techniques and compositional forms; a restrictive way of seeing that diminishes alternative modes of experiencing our relations with nature.[11]

Figure 2 *Modelling* Brigadoon.

The capture, both materially and culturally, of Highland estates in the nineteenth century for sporting purposes has bequeathed an iconography of Scottish landscape which is largely bereft of people. Landseer's best selling painting, the *Monarch of the Glen,* is a 'pastiche of the sublime'[12] which nevertheless sets the framework for our expectations. Raymond Williams has pointed out that a working country is hardly ever a 'landscape'.[13] Neither is it likely to be 'heritage'. The material power of the nineteenth-century aristocracy and its monarchy was translated into the cultural representation of Scottish landscape. The 'stag at bay' image of the Highlands is probably so deeply embedded in our reading of the landscape that it makes radical land reform to restore it to a 'working' landscape all the more difficult. Cleared estates have come to represent landscape in Scotland, just as soldiers in kilts inform our image of what it is to be a Scot.

The power of heritage seems unduly onerous in Scotland. It seems at times as if Scotland only exists as heritage. What singles it out for distinction is the trappings of its past. Its modernity seems to make it little different from elsewhere. At a lecture in Aberdeen, I was once asked why I thought it had been so difficult to establish a heritage centre in the city devoted to North Sea oil. My answer was that this would not happen unless and until North sea oil was 'over' as an economic phenomenon. If Scotland is heritage-rich, then it could be because it has a past but not present or future. That is perhaps why many Scottish writers attack the cultural representations of Scotland as overly obsessed with what has passed, and why the nationalist party presents itself as a modernist, economistic one. Heritage in Scotland seems to many to be too tainted, too heavy.

It is, however, a crucial cultural repository for answers to the identity question. Like many 'stateless nations' such as Catalonia and Quebec, Scotland cannot rely on a pragmatic definition in terms of its political statehood. Indeed, given that it currently has no meaningful level of democratic control over its administration, it has even more of an identity crisis than the other two nations. There is no shortage of cultural accoutrements, however, in this search for collective identity. In spite of the high degree of institutional autonomy afforded to Scotland,[14] there is a continuous questing for identity. The old joke has it that Canadians are defined as a people who constantly pull up their roots to find out who they are. How much more does this apply to Scotland (and to Quebec and Catalonia) who do not have formal political sovereignty?

In the quest for national (as opposed to state) identity, heritage is a vital source of legitimacy. The iconography of nationalism is replete with sacred objects and places – flags, emblems, sites – often contested and fought over (like Jerusalem in Israel/Palestine, and Kosovo in Serbia/Albania). In asking who we are, the totems and icons of heritage are powerful signifiers of our identity. We may find tartanry, Bonnie Prince Charlie, Mary Queen of Scots, Bannockburn and Burns false descriptors of who we are, but they provide a source of ready-made distinguishing characteristics from England, our bigger, southern neighbour.

Heritage of this sort also communicates a powerful sense of glamour. We have grown accustomed to thinking of glamour as a fairly superficial show-biz quality of the late twentieth century. It also has its deeper, more Scottish meaning of magic or delusion. The glamour of an object originally referred in the eighteenth century to its magical powers, to enchantment and witchcraft, even the power to bamboozle or deceive. Its etymology derives from the same root as 'grammar' – 'grimoire' – a sorcerer's book (*Oxford English Dictionary*). The painter Allan Ramsay is quoted in *OED* as defining glamour as follows: 'when devils, wizards or jugglers deceive the sight, they are said to cast glamour o'er the eyes of the spectator',[15] and Sir Walter Scott, who did so much to create Scottish heritage, is attributed with using it to refer to delusive or alluring charm.

All of this may seem highly suspicious to late twentieth-century rationalist eyes. If heritage has to do with 'glamour', with deceit and fabrication, then 'history' is much to be preferred. To make such a distinction, however, would be to ignore the secularisation of glamour afforded by modern tourism. The Australian writer Donald Horne has referred to modern tourist guidebooks as 'devotional texts', to the sightseer as pilgrim, the object as relic, and the photograph as the equivalent of holy icon.[16] The modern tourist, he argues, relies on 'authenticity', the 'magical glow' which 'can illuminate meanings that justify power or claim prestige'.[17] Above all, authenticity is conferred by interpretation, not the object per se. Central icons – what Horne calls monuments – acquire a special glamour to convey their special status, and all has to do with presentation and interpretation. Most of us have had the deflating experience of queuing to see a sacred icon only to wonder what all the fuss was about. To see the Black Madonna of Monserrat without knowing the icon's significance for Catalan identity, religious and national, is to miss the point. The key to heritage is to sacrilise its objects. The anthropologist, Annette Wiener, put it this way:

> An individual's role in social life is fragmentary unless attached to something of permanence. The history of the past, equally fragmentary, is concentrated in an object that, in its material substance, defies destruction. Thus, keeping an object defined as inalienable adds to the value of one's past, making the past a powerful resource for the present and the future.[18]

Heritage and Authenticity

History like heritage becomes less and less synonymous with professional historians and the realm of books. It is reflected in the shift from narrow scholarly appreciation towards history as a form of entertainment – or 'info-tainment' in the jargon. It also has employment pay-offs. To quote Robert Hewison, the heritage movement has been a godsend to the Manpower Services Commission, creating 'jobs that otherwise would not have existed, such as weaving, grinding corn, and living in a reproduction Iron Age round house at Manchester Museum.[19] Heritage presents new challenges as well as problems for academics such as historians and archaeologists. It is no longer enough to let the artefacts speak for themselves; indeed, it is vital that the artefacts speak. The demand is for authenticity rather than 'fact'. Peter Fowler points out that this frequently runs the risk of creating a past that never existed, and he quotes Joseph Heller's observation about a statue that 'it was an authentic Hellenistic imitation of a Hellenic reproduction ... for which there had never been an authentic original subject'.[20] But then again, he comments, 'there is more to the past than authenticity'.[21]

The search for the authentic through heritage is aided by technological advances which allow more active participation for the spectator. People are now much more willing to 'dress up and do', by taking part in enactments of battles by joining the Sealed Knot Society, or role-playing in country house reconstructions.

At its extreme, there is double reflexivity; tourists and natives perform their allocated roles for each other in the context of 'watching me watching you'. The Zuni Pueblo Indians in North America, according to MacCannell, have developed a typology of tourists – a New York type, a Texas type, a Hippy type, a 'save the whale' type. These figures have begun to be represented in Indian dances. Texas types wear cowboy boots and drive Cadillacs. Hippies wear tie-dyed T-shirts, and join uninvited in the dancing, while the 'East Coast' tourist is played by a male Indian wearing high heels, wig, dress, mink coat, dime-store jewellery, clutch purse and pill-box hat. Ex-primitives', MacCannell comments, 'knowingly overdose tourists with unwanted pseudo-authenticity'.[22] We may find that far-fetched and overly cynical until we remember the instance closer to home of the authenticity of tartan and the 'Scottish experience'. The desire to believe appears to overcome without much difficulty the counter-evidence that much of this 'tradition' is of recent origin. We can acknowledge pastiche while believing in it at the same time. Somehow, simulacra – what passes for the real – like the Scottish *ceilidh* experience have the power to overcome our cynicism.

Such talk of pastiche and the simulacrum has helped to develop a fresh interest in the culture of tourism in the late twentieth century. The commercialisation of culture may be obvious enough, but perhaps more insidiously, as MacCannell points out 'it is also an ideological framing of history, nature and tradition'.[23] In other words, when people are defined as tourist attractions, do they not tend to relate to each other by way of commercially enforced stereotypes of themselves? Do they have any meaningful identity beyond that which is required by the touristic framework?

Figure 3 *Reconstructing History: the Sealed Knot Society re-enact the Battle of Fyvie, August 1993.*

MacCannell ties this threat into the power of 'spectacle' over 'sights'. Mass tourism in its early twentieth-century phase required tourists to observe in a fairly passive manner – to see the sights, as it were. Late twentieth-century tourism is much more focused on spectacle, on a degree of active involvement, whether it is joining in a make-believe version of a 'native' dance, or having a go at pot making.[24] In these events re-enactment is a form not only of remaking the past but doing so for the purposes of the present.

As a result of the demand for active involvement, the traditional custodians of heritage are placed in a dilemma. They are forced to choose between defending their traditional activities and sites – letting stones speak for themselves, as it were, or becoming more interpretative of what they guard. So a controversy develops as to whether it is acceptable to build a replica of a Roman fort at Vindolanda – to give visitors a sense of 'what it must have been like to be a Roman soldier' – or to take refuge in the strictly scholarly and dry account. Opponents of 'conceptualisation' point out that this notion of heritage simply and quickly deteriorates into pastiche and 'Disney-fication'. They argue that what is created is simply an archaeological zoo, a theme park mentality which threatens the careful and scholarly attempts to build up knowledge from fragmentary evidence. It takes liberties with time and telescopes history, as in the action-packed and breathless experience on offer at Timespan (sic), a Highland heritage centre at Helmsdale in Sutherland (a centre financially assisted by Highland and Islands Enterprises):

> Experience our Highland heritage, fashioned over centuries. From Picts and Vikings, murders at Helmsdale castle, last burning of a witch, the harrowing Highland Clearances, the 19th century Sporting Scene, the Kildonan goldrush, and through our crofting and fishing past to the present day and our neighbouring oilfields.

Figure 4 *Festive Edwardian evening at Fyvie Castle, December 1991.*

Whether we are talking about actual or invented heritage sites, they have key features in common: they are, of course, places out of time for they operate in this time; they involve visits to 'time past'; they allow and encourage us to play for a time in another time; they seem to deny the possibility of decay and death for the passage of time is not allowed to occur between 'then' and 'now', and by implication 'we' and 'they' are not separated in time or, by definition, place.[25] In this view, 'in these changing and disturbing times historic theme parks and heritage centres probably tell us as much about ourselves as about the past – indeed probably more'.[26]

Heritage as Commodity

First of all, we are interested in the commodification of heritage, how it has been mobilised by private and public capital, in the context of a rapidly changing economy. It is clear that something very fundamental has happened to economic structures and relations in the last few decades of the twentieth century. We may choose to call it a 'post-industrial' or a 'service' economy, but it manifestly is one in which manufacturing industry is far less significant as an employer. The process whereby service sector jobs have replaced those in manufacturing has been variously described as 'de-industrialisation' and 'post-Fordist' in recognition of the fact that large-scale omnibus production is no longer the norm. A key part of this argument is that culture itself becomes a commodity in this new economy which is now internationalised – or 'globalised'.

Another aspect of this commodification of heritage and culture relates to the process of economic regeneration, especially at the local level. Local authorities in particular have not been slow to recognise the economic and political potential of heritage. In many British cities, the talk is of the 'heritage option' as a means of economic regeneration, and the 'culture economy' as a way of achieving post-industrial city status. These culture industries include traditional ones like museums and cathedrals, but also art galleries, concert halls, orchestras, community arts, TV franchises and the performing arts.

Closely connected with urban images are industrial ones. These are not simply images to escape from, but ironically in a post-industrial age, to recover, albeit in a sanitised form. A direct result of the French Minister of Culture expanding the definition of heritage in 1979 and cutting it free from its attachment to beauty was the development of industrial heritage. Hoyau sees this as 'the infrastructure taking its revenge'. The result is that:

> By being assimilated into the nation's heritage, material production once again finds its place in the cultural landscape: efforts are then made to prevent the destruction of factories, industrial archaeology sight-seeing tours are organised, and children are initiated into the mysteries of hydraulic pumps.[27]

In Britain examples of industrial heritage abound. Ironbridge Gorge Museum, Beamish Open Air Museum, The Black Country Museum, and The Scottish Mining Museum are among the most well known. Industrial heritage has attracted considerable criticism both from academics and from people working within the museum business. The historian Robert Hewison sees industrial heritage in general as a poor attempt to cope with industrial decline. Bob West is critical of the way the Ironbridge Gorge Museum (the first of its kind) has become part of the historical tourism 'business'. Tony Bennett regards the Beamish Museum in north-east England as exemplifying a British ability 'to transform industrialism from a set of ruptural events into a mere moment in the unfolding of a set of harmonious relations between rulers and people'.[28]

The urban and industrial opportunities have been matched by rural and agricultural ones. Cookson Country, Hardy Country, even Land O' Burns, have been virtually created by local councils and entrepreneurs as places which do not actually exist, sometimes, as the playwright Alan Bennett pointed out, with alarming consequences:

> The village in Yorkshire where I spend all too little of my time now sports one of those DoE brown heritage signposts declaring it a 'Dales Village' and it's only a matter of time before the inhabitants start playing it up as 'Dales Folk'. We're fortunate not to be in 'Herriot Country' or the temptation to act the part may be even greater. But it's toytown now on every hand, dignified and stately barns converted into bijoux residences with bottle glass windows and carriage lamps that bring with them a view of the countryside that is equally folksy. The Village shop becomes The Village Shop, the confectioners The Village Bakery; it won't be long now before some well-meaning parish council will be employing some of those turfed out of psychiatric hospitals as Village Idiots.[29]

There is, of course, more scope to elaborate heritage themes in rural areas, because as Raymond Williams observed, 'the country' is more easily treated as the essence of The Country or nation. It is but a short step from there to the use of heritage as a means of 'cultural capital', a symbolic resource with a capacity for power. Life styles may come with implicit social values built into them. Peter Fowler coins the term 'Ashleyism' to refer to the ethos one 'buys' with the Laura Ashley product: 'It harks back from an urban viewpoint not just to a rural underpinning of a former life-style but to assumptions about, a reading of, social hierarchies and the mores which went with it.' To underscore his point, he cites the producer herself: 'I did not set out to be Victorian but it was a time when people lived straightforward, balanced lives, when everything was clear-cut and respectable.'[30]

Yorkshire is also the home of possibly one of the most bizarre heritage sites in Britain, a reconstructed prisoner-of-war camp near Malton, North Yorkshire. Making use of huts left over from the war, it advertises itself as 'the only modern history theme museum of its type in the world', in which the visitor will be transported back to wartime Britain: 'You will experience the sights, the sounds, even the smells of those dangerous years', it promises, and the 29 huts become mini-theme parks, each devoted to a war battle, or specific feature such as 'the eden camp music hall', and '1946 prefab'. Given war nostalgia, this reconstruction of war heritage seems to be a sure-fire success.

Heritage as Consumption

Our second theme, and one related to its commodification, is the consumption of heritage. The concept of 'the heritage industry' implies a product, a set of entrepreneurs, a manufacturing process, a set of social relations structured around this process, a market, and, of course, consumers. The transition from a manufacturing to a service-based economy helps to forefront the consumption of culture and heritage. Using the ideas of Bourdieu, John Urry identifies a 'new middle class' as especially susceptible to heritage because as a class it is stronger on 'cultural' than on 'economic' capital.[31] By implication, those who work in the cultural and education industries – what have been termed the 'service class' – would seem to be likely consumers of heritage given its potential for linking economic and social interests, that is, class and status or life style.

Heritage as Politics

The third theme is that of the politics of heritage. It is this one which probably attracted most attention in the 1980s. In 1985, Patrick Wright published his book *On Living in an Old Country*, the somewhat horrified observations of an Englishman returning to Thatcher's Britain after living in North America. His point was not that heritage was unknown in the United States (after all, this was the culture which gave us Disneyworld), but that heritage in modern Britain had taken on deeply conservative and Conservative resonances. In the context of economic restructuring, Wright argued, heritage not only represented a cultural capital to be exploited for commercial gain, but was used by the regime to paper over some fundamental ideological and political cracks in the fabric of the state. Wright's book was followed two years later by *The Heritage Industry: Britain in a Climate of Decline*, by the journalist Robert Hewison. This book remains the most explicit commentary to date on the public's apparently growing obsession with the past, and its desire to consume cultural events and artefacts which reflect the past in ways relevant to the present. For Hewison, like Wright, the cultural and political perspective dominates. He stresses how Mrs Thatcher and the New Right have been able to mobilise and manipulate a set of thoroughly conservative ideas: 'Nostalgia is profoundly conservative. Its emphasis on order and tradition relies heavily on appeals to the authority of the past'.[32]

As regards the Scottish dimension of heritage, it is obvious that it is doubly peripheral to the dominant but often implicit English one. It is plainly not English, but it also escapes hierarchical ordering in a way the north of England ('The North') does not. It has the capacity to generate an alternative political and cultural consciousness, and it will be an important part of our argument that this capacity has grown rather than diminished in the late twentieth century. This is not simply because the cultural and political power of the British state has waned, although it undoubtedly has, but because most modern state formations are under scrutiny. Globalisation of the economy, supra-national political agreements (such as the European Union), and the impact of multinational media on 'national' cultures have all eroded the power of national states to control their own economic, political and cultural affairs. In the context of this broad debate, we can place the revival of regionalism and nationalism. The latter, and even the former, have a capacity to mobilise aspects of heritage for political purposes, and it is this process perhaps more than any other which has helped to foreground heritage. In the late twentieth century, when issues of identity become especially problematic, the search for roots, discovering where we have come from, the focus on heritage is bound to be one expression of this search.

Heritage as Ideology

The final central theme focuses on the ideology of heritage. We have already seen that heritage lends itself to pastiche, to reconstruction if not to construction *de novo*. The concept has also become caught up in a wider debate about modernism and post-modernism. Heritage seems to express neatly Baudrillard's statement that the real is no longer real, as well as Umberto Eco's observation that 'absolute unreality is offered as real presence'. The key association between heritage and the post-modern lies in MacCannell's notion of 'staged authenticity', where the sign and the real are treated as equivalent; indeed, the sign has priority over the real if it carries more magic or authenticity. MacCannell picks up the idea of front/back stage from Erving Goffman, and implies in his work that the 'unstaged' authentic lies in the back region where things are not arranged for tourists, and are therefore 'real'. There are considerable criticisms to be made of MacCannell's work, but it has undoubtedly been influential. I will not be arguing for a post-modern conception of heritage, but I will argue that the revival of academic interest in heritage reflects its ideological potential in the late twentieth century.

Understanding Scottish Heritage: The Iconography of Place

There is little doubt that Scotland has marketing integrity. In 1994 the Scottish Tourist Board appointed a new chief executive who had learned his trade in food marketing. 'Scotland is a very rich country in the sense that it has many points of uniqueness; whisky, textiles, meat,' he said: 'They all have in common the environment'.[33] When it comes to tourism, as Rojek points out, the Scottish tourist industry presents Scotland as a 'land out of time', as an 'enchanted fortress in a disenchanted world'.[34] This, of course, is a ploy common to all tourist bodies in all countries.

What is the point of selling the same as back home? Baudelaire, Rojek comments, defines a 'foreign' country as the opposite of the immediate conditions of 'home'; the exact contrary of disorder, tumult, the unexpected.

Scotland has one major feature which allows this presentation: its association with the 'wilderness'. And wilderness is presented as the antithesis of culture, as the quintessential escape area in modern society. After all, the claim is that Scotland is the last great European wilderness.

The key to the 'wilderness' tag is that it is a social construction. By the end of the eighteenth century, the Highlands were discovered as a scenic game park replete with 'nature' – and its game – salmon, deer and grouse. Such has been the reconstruction of the Highlands in particular that we find it impossible to 'see' them in any other way. They have, in Womack's words, been 'colonised by an empire of signs'.[35] He points out that whereas 'botanically no doubt "calluna vulgaris" [heather] is exactly as it was in the 1730s, semiotically it has been irrevocably hybridised',[36] namely that it has been given a social meaning evoking Highland and, through it, Scottish culture.

From even a cursory reading of Scottish and Highland history it is clear that the cultural construction of the region was the result of political and commercial forces, often acting together. What undoubtedly had been a distinctive region in geographical, linguistic and economic terms before and after the Union of 1707 was invested with cultural qualities and meanings. These meanings were not generated randomly but were the result of double defeats – first from a lowland-dominated Scottish state, and after 1745 and the Culloden defeat, by a wider British political system. The distinction between the Lowlands and the Highlands has always been a shifting and contentious one in practice, given that the linguistic, economic and geographical boundaries do not coincide with each other. There is, however, little doubting the cultural divide in the sense that the Highlands were invested with symbolism of being 'foreign' and exotic. The irony is that by the end of the eighteenth century Scotland as a whole was being colonised by this powerful sign.

By the end of the eighteenth century, then, the elements were in place for the construction of modern tourist icons. From then on, and especially in their literary exploitation by Walter Scott in the early decades of the nineteenth century, the Highlands in particular became the focus for 're-discovery' of the wilderness. Mairi MacArthur observes that visitors in 1883 remarked that 'the farther we went the more we were reminded that to travel in Scotland is to travel through the Waverley novels'.[37] Guidebooks and travel memoirs highlighted three themes: the wild grandeur of the landscape, remoteness and peace, with a dash of romantic (preferably tragic) history.

We are dealing here with what the geographer Denis Cosgrove has called 'terrains of power'.[38] He observes: 'Nature, landscape and environment are semiotic signifiers, deeply embedded in the cultural constitution of individual European nations and integral to the distinctive identities of Europe's peoples'. The point he is making is that these 'constitutions' relate to systems of power, not in any predetermined way, but as ideological constructs which reflect, often in attenuated ways, its operation. The 'imagined geography' of England focuses on 'woods of downland pastures of SE England's "home counties", "Constable" country in Suffolk and Wiltshire water meadows, and the hawthorn-squared ploughlands of the Midland counties'. On the other hand, 'Welsh and Scottish nationalisms have constructed their own meaning from mountain landscapes, valleys and glens, drawing as heavily on the natural world as upon their separate language to construct differences from England'.

Here Cosgrove is making an important point. It is not simply that the iconography of the Highlands or of Scotland carries a unique message which speaks only to the powerful who might use it as a holiday playground. The iconography 'leaks' in such a way that it can be turned to radical uses, in respective nationalist and oppositional discourses. 'The wee bit hill and glen' of the anthem 'Flower of Scotland' may make weak poetry but strong politics. The ability of different political forces to 'read' into the landscape a suitable message is the key here. It is not that only one message can be read off the heritage signs, or that the viewer can read in what he or she wants. The signification is not 'depthless'. Rather, as Cosgrove comments, the imaginative bonds between 'nature' and 'nation' are deep across Europe.

The nub of our argument is that heritage is significant in Scotland because it rests on a national, cultural, dimension. Heritage is a reflection of nationalism in its widest sense. It may not, and frequently does not, carry political overtones, as the observations of life-members of the National Trust for Scotland make clear. You do not have to be a Scottish Nationalist to be a cultural nationalist although, as will be argued later, it has become increasingly more difficult to separate the cultural and political realms in modern Scotland. The conclusion of some writers that 'her [Scotland's] political identity lost, her cultural identity began to be absorbed'[39] does not strike us as a proper reading of the evidence.

Manufacturing Scottish Heritage

There are three major competing discourses on Scottish heritage. First, it is treated as a product to be sold in the marketplace. This manipulation of heritage evokes the vocabulary of commerce, and is largely the preserve of the Scottish Tourist Board (STB). We will examine the assumptions about and presentations of Scottish heritage by STB. The second discourse concerning heritage is that of inheritance, or *'patrimoine'*. This evokes a vocabulary of social and cultural order, and is most closely associated with the National Trust for Scotland, with its strongly patrician ethos and culture. In the broadest sense, this is a 'political' discourse on heritage. The third discourse is more strongly associated with the 'academy', with the vocabulary of technique and knowledge, and we will examine the role of Historic Scotland and its concern with artefacts and ruins as a fitting representative of this discourse.

These three bodies constitute the 'holy trinity' of Scottish heritage: the Scottish Tourist Board, Historic Scotland, and the National Trust for Scotland. They work alongside each other, but have distinct aims and purposes, and quite different organisational cultures. They are set within a political and cultural framework which includes government departments and private operators. At the state level, The Scottish Office provides most of the funding for heritage which it dispenses indirectly through its public agencies such as the Scottish Tourist Board, which receives three-quarters of its budget from the Scottish Office, Historic Scotland (80 per cent), Scottish Museums Council (72 per cent), and Scottish Natural Heritage (100 per cent). Only the National Trust for Scotland (NTS) does not receive funds directly from the state, although it is a major recipient of grant in aid from Historic Scotland for the upkeep of many of its properties. Further down the heritage chain, private and commercial operators of 'stately homes', independent as well as local authority museums, receive grants from state agencies like Historic Scotland and the Scottish Museums Council. The heritage industry in Scotland has a strong 'voluntary sector' ethos (in contrast, for example, to that in France with its historic sense of national *patrimoine*), but it is clear that it would not survive without public funds.

The Scottish Tourist Board and Heritage

We can gauge the STB's approach to heritage from two sources: the images it presents; and what it says about Scotland's heritage. STB advertising campaigns stress landscapes and locations. Its television projects recently include the 'talking eagles' whereby two eagles fly down a Scottish loch discussing why there is no better place to be; and 'Mull early closing' in which a shopkeeper closes early in order to go fishing with friends – this also has a Gaelic version, and both are on offer in mainland Scotland. The STB has also exploited the posters industry under its campaign, 'One Visit is Never Enough'. The poster industry is a lucrative and important part of late twentieth-century tourism, indicating (or implying) the message of 'been there, done that', and posters become the accoutrements of travel, like T-shirts and key rings.

STB posters attempt to convey particular images of Scotland

- Peopleless places – the landscape: this is the stuff of Romantic representations with 'nature' presented as wild, rugged, barren, beautiful. The dominant colours are blues, browns, white. The lochs are deep, calm, and always brooding.
- Majestic Scotland: castles, kilts, pipers. Edinburgh Castle is the icon associated most strongly by tourists and by natives with Scotland.
- 'Everyday' Scotland: the posters of post boxes and of curlers convey the everyday melding into the exotic. Strange games played on ice by men in kilts; post boxes miniaturised in strange locations. Low and high heritage blur: '... it is no longer cold stones or of exhibits kept under glass in museum cabinets. It now includes the village wash-houses, the little country church, local songs and forms of speech, crafts and skills'.[40]

The other insight into the STB conception of heritage comes from a major report it commissioned in 1989 from an associate member of the international consultants Arthur Young International. This report formed the basis of an STB publication *Visitor Attractions: A Development Guide,* aimed at entrepreneurs interested in setting up or developing visitor attractions, including heritage sites. The remit of the heritage study is worth reproducing in full because it indicates the STB's definition of heritage. Heritage attractions, it spells out:

- are intrinsically related to the Scottish
    - landscape
    - history or
    - way of life
- can be presented in a way which will
    - attract and satisfy visitors
    - generate income and employment and
    - help to conserve the features to which the attractions relate.

Figure 5   *Representing Scotland.*

The key elements of this definition are that heritage attractions:

- must have core elements which are intrinsic to Scotland in some significant way;
- *need to be concerned solely with history and the past* (my emphasis); and
- must be linked directly to visitor use and economic benefit and to conservation.'[41]

This account is interesting for a number of reasons. First, it gives priority to commercial aspects ('generate income and employment', versus '*help to* conserve the features ...'). Second, and more significantly, there is a curious contradiction between the terms of reference for the Heritage Attractions Study commissioned by the STB International and Planning Division, and the subsequent publication whose definition of heritage is spelled out above. Whereas one of the key elements in the above is that heritage attractions 'need to be concerned solely with history and the past' (see italicised point above), the terms of reference for the study itself says precisely the opposite: 'need *not* be concerned solely with history and the past'. We have been unable to find out how this *volte face* arose, but from the tenor of the consultants' report, it is plain that 'history and the past' are not deemed necessary in developing heritage attractions. We can only surmise that in the final publication, its producer assumed that history and heritage were the same thing, whereas the gist of the consultants' report was that the economic potential lay precisely in the *lack* of correspondence between heritage and history.

There are other ideas for heritage projects:

- A 'living memory' exhibition based on a UK rather than simply a Scottish experience, but sited in the west because 'the vernacular feel of the product strongly suggests Glasgow' and because it would fit in with that city's project to become a major tourist destination;
- The 'Scotland in Fire and Ice Experience', telling the 'real [sic] story of Scotland's geological formation and its scenic sculpting'.

Are we to assume that these are simply 'creative ideas' to stimulate the consultants' sponsors about heritage? The fact that the STB included it in the remit perhaps implies that these ideas are the wider reaches of the heritage industry, but not by much. The using of 'living history' techniques, with the stress on 'the magic of the real', authenticity rather than history, historic enactments, actor role-playing and outdoor theatre are to be found in many other heritage projects and in other societies. Thinking the unthinkable out loud is frequently a device for testing the waters in the marketplace, especially if we remember that the development guide produced by the STB is aimed at developers and operators of what it calls 'heritage attractions'. We might think that we are looking at the Scottish heritage experience of the millennium. However, in 1994, a proposal was announced to open a £3 million neolithic heritage park near Oyne, a village of 200 people, in Aberdeenshire. The main attraction is to be a 900 square metre grass-covered dome, which will be approached by a time tunnel to put visitors in the pre-history mood using interactive displays, laser shows and video walls. The park itself will include mock Iron Age houses, a neolithic long house, and a Roman camp. The whole project is to be funded by the local council and Scottish Enterprise.[42] About the same time, Historic Scotland announced that its prehistoric hill-fort and burial mound at Cairnpapple near Bathgate would not be open in the coming season as the number of visitors was unlikely to warrant it. Fiction, it seems, is more palatable, or profitable, than truth.

Managing the State's Heritage: Historic Scotland

> Scotland has a rich legacy from the past – a heritage of monuments and buildings which bear silent witness to our proud history stretching back over 5000 years, which are a delight to us today and which we must carefully preserve for future generations.

In using these words in its first framework document, the Conservative Secretary of State for Scotland, Ian Lang, was setting the agenda for this executive agency to manage the nation's built heritage. If the Scottish Tourist Board treats heritage as a product, and uses the vocabulary of commerce, then Historic Scotland defines heritage much more as artefact, and speaks the vocabulary of technique. Historic Scotland, however, has, like British Rail, succumbed to business-speak by referring to its users as 'customers'

Although it was not christened Historic Scotland until 1991, this body, along with English heritage and CADW Wales, came into being in 1984. All three bodies were products of the National Heritage Act 1983 which was fuelled by Mrs Thatcher's desire to make the organisations responsible for protecting traditional heritage more commercially-minded.

Historic Scotland avoided sounding like a belated carbon-copy of English Heritage, something which the organisation actively wished to avoid. Similarly in keeping with the new times, the defensively sounding 'warders' of properties became user-friendly 'custodians', swapping prison officers' garb for more informal tartan trews and jumpers.

Historic Scotland has a budget of some £30 million (80 per cent from the state, and rest self-generated) which has virtually doubled since 1984, with running costs for 1993-94 at £12.7 million. These figures put it on a par with the Scottish Tourist Board. Visitors to its seventy sites have risen in that period from 1.8 million per annum to 2.4 million, and its membership organisation, Friends of Historic Scotland, stands at around 30,000.

The popularising of Scottish heritage has focused on literature and advertising, both press and television. The 'Scotland' which is presented in the literature is clear-cut and action-based. What kind of Scotland is it? It is described thus:

> Scotland is a land of castles. Mighty fortresses on rocky heights, isolated keeps, elegant homes for great families and grim strongholds set on towering sea cliffs.
>
> These were the stages on which the dynasties of Bruce, Douglas and Stewart played out their power struggles;

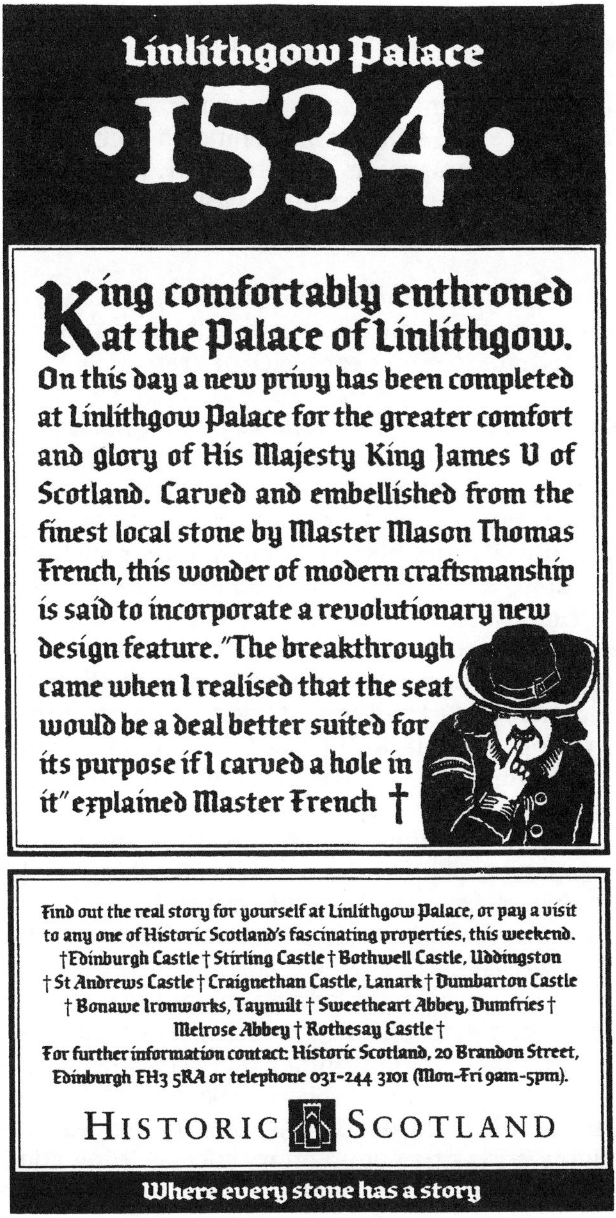

Figure 6 *Historic Scotland: a good day out.*

> where William Wallace fought for Scotland's independence, and Mary Queen of Scots fought for her life.
>
> In the great halls, great men discussed affairs of state against backdrops of regal splendour. Behind the scenes, whispered plots and counterplots were hatched, while in the gloom of the dungeons, unfortunate wretches ended their lives in misery and despair.
>
> Noble men and tyrants, kings and queens, lords and commoners all made their entrances and exits, and now only the stones remain to speak centuries of drama.[43]

This pamphlet, with its revealing title 'The Popular Choice', is a long way from the technicalities of medieval ruins. The text continues with descriptions such as: 'ruthless political intrigue', 'buccaneering raids', 'wayward churchman', 'burning and looting', 'a rare sense of tranquillity'. Its history is fairly nationalist and masculinist: the Jacobite Risings are not 'rebellions'; there is 'the ruthlessness of the Hanoverian forces', the Highlanders were 'too loyal to take the gold offered for Bonnie Prince Charlie'; there is whisky-smuggling, harsh punishment for soldiers, and all in all, 'real stories for real men' (sic). The implicit message seems aimed at fathers taking young sons on boisterous days-out at castles. This is backed-up by the agency's own focus-group research: it shows that 'the "stories" of the history of Scotland are of great interest to the audience. The message should use 'colour', fun, and excitement rather than text-book style teaching.' The research showed that there was less difference between AB social categories (managerial and adminstrative workers) and C2s (skilled manual workers).

The research led to a series of television and newspaper adverts. These ads were designed to be witty and eye-catching. The TV campaign which ran in the summer of 1991 showed two gargoyles engaged in witty repartee. Historic Scotland's budget did not stretch to a 1992 campaign. The newspaper adverts used cartoon drawing and witty commentary such as 'King comfortably enthroned at Linlithgow Palace', 'What kind of person carves his name on the wall of a 16th century abbey?' (answer: the architect); and 'Waverley man finds Crown jewels in spare room' (Walter Scott's discovery of Scotland's Crown Jewels at Edinburgh Castle in 1818). Examples of adverts used in the popular press (*The Daily Record*) appear in Fig. 6.

Historic Scotland appears to be protected by a broad nationalist discourse in Scotland which extends to the Conservative politicians who run the Scottish Office. It would be hard to envisage a similar controversy to the one which engulfed English Heritage in 1992 when it proposed to sell off its less profitable assets. This is not because Historic Scotland does not have any of these, because only Edinburgh Castle, and to a far lesser extent Stirling Castle, are profitable in their own right. Given the weakness of the Tory Party in Scotland, the Scottish Office would also have found it very difficult to appoint a Conservative businessman to lead Historic Scotland in the way that it did south of the border.

Nation in Trust: The National Trust for Scotland

If the Scottish Tourist Board represents heritage as product, and Historic Scotland heritage as artefact, then the National Trust for Scotland (NTS) interprets heritage as inheritance. Its vocabulary is that of organic order, and contrasts with the STB's language of commerce, and Historic Scotland's vocabulary of technique. For example, the chairman of the NTS council commented in his foreword to the 1993 annual report: '... our heritage – whether it be the built heritage or the heritage of countryside and wilderness – is part of the soul of the nation and we ignore the nation's soul at our peril.'[44]

It is hard to imagine either the STB or Historic Scotland making a play to be keepers of the national soul. What makes this doubly odd is that the NTS is not an agency of government but a charitable 'trust' (in setting up the National Trust in England in 1895, Octavia Hill preferred the word 'trust' to 'company' in order to stress the benevolent aspect of the operation). It is this ethos of voluntarism which helps to give heritage in Britain its image of good works and service, although in terms of funding it is likely that the state is by far the major contributor.

From the outset, the NTS has had a strong aristocratic and landed domination of its council. Its first president was the Duke of Atholl (1932-1942), who was succeeded by Sir John Stirling Maxwell (1944-1954), who had served as a vice-president from 1932 until 1943, and who was also chairman of the Royal Commission on the Ancient and Historical Monuments of Scotland (RCAHM) from 1940 until 1949. There was no president of the council after Maxwell until the Earl of Wemyss and March succeeded in 1968 and served until 1991 (Wemyss succeeded Maxwell as chairman of RCAHM in 1949 until 1985 when he in turn was succeeded by the Earl of Balcarres), when he gave way to the Marquess of Bute. Neither can we interpret the presidency as mere figure-head. Chairmen of the Council have all been male, and titled persons served for the first fifty years of the Trust's history: Sir Iain Colquhoun (1932-1945), the Earl of Wemyss and March (1946-1968), and the Marquess of Bute (1969-1984). He was succeeded by W M Cuthbert (1985-1989), and by R C Tyrell (from 1990 until 1994). The chairman-designate of the NTS, Hamish Leslie Melville, is an Eton and Oxford-educated financier who owns an estate in Garve, Ross-shire.

Vice-presidents have also been drawn heavily from lairds and gentry. Only in more recent years have non-titled persons begun to appear on the council. The remarkable feature of this list is the overwhelming preponderance of the titled, the landed and the powerful. Only three women have been vice-presidents, and only from the late 1970s.

In a country like Scotland where the land question has been an integral part of its political agenda, it might seem to be a disadvantage for the Trust to be so dominated by lairds and gentry. The Trust has worked to offset this by stressing its ideology of stewardship and social responsibility. The Trust presents an ethos of organic conservatism, and of a society in which the laird's house and the little houses are integrated in an organic whole so that all have their part to play in the scheme of things. This does not mean, of course, that all mix freely.

What sort of image of Scottish heritage does the Trust convey? In keeping with its patrician image, it is a traditional, 'respectable' one, eschewing any downmarket iconography of Scotland, as befits a gentry-led organisation. Its magazine, *Heritage Scotland,* is douce and worthy. An editorial by the director in the 1993 Summer edition begins:

> We regularly read newspaper headlines denouncing the 'moral sickness' within our society. It is therefore important to all of us to know that somebody cares. It is also important to know that there are caring organisations like the National Trust for Scotland, which not only preserves and protects buildings and inanimate objects, but also cares for the people and the communities at its properties. *The Trust is very conscious of its responsibilities in its role in the community. The Trust is, itself, a community but it is also part of a wider community which it seeks to serve through its duty to act 'for the benefit of the nation* '. (my emphasis)[45]

I have focused on the key agencies involved in Scottish heritage. Each has its own carefully constructed rhetoric and vocabulary. Whereas the Scottish Tourist Board is closest to a market conception of heritage and the vocabulary of commerce ('Scotland's For Me!'), Historic Scotland forefronts the heritage of artefacts ('Don't believe it when they tell you stones can't speak'), while concentrating on technical expertise. As we have seen, the National Trust for Scotland employs the language of conservative nationalism ('our heritage is part of the soul of the nation').

Status and Heritage

An examination of heritage sites in the Scottish Borders reveals an apparent conundrum. Why, in this most fertile part of Scotland, does the National Trust for Scotland have so few properties? The answer to our puzzle is not that the border-lands are bereft of heritage, but that the key ones are in private hands. They are the great stately homes of those whom Checkland called the 'mighty magnates' of Scotland. Here is the private face of heritage.

What is more important for our purposes is that these estates contain some of the finest 'stately homes' in the country, and these form some of its prime heritage attractions. From east to west, the country houses lie across the border country, from the Earl of Wemyss and March's Gosford House in East Lothian, Lord Binning's Mellerstain, Douglas-Home's The Hirsel, the Duke of Roxburghe's Floors Castle, Maxwell-Stuart's Traquair House, and above all Buccleuch's two estates of Bowhill near Selkirk, and Drumlanrig Castle in Dumfriesshire. All are an integral part of the stately home business, and help to form one of the most lucrative tourist trails in the country. Their public access is, however, of recent provenance.

By the late 1970s, at the point at which the heritage industry was created in its modern form, the border landowners were in a prime position to exploit their heritage potential. Why should this be? The conventional answer has been to see it as the result of economic necessity.

Heritage and the Landed Elite

The conventional way of explaining the capture of heritage for commercial purposes by the owners of the stately homes industry is that this has become an economic necessity in a modern world which is not of their financial and ideological making. There is truth in this, but we will argue that there is more to it than that.

If we consider landowners in general as a status group rather than as a class per se, then we can begin to chart their continuous struggle to hold the line of social privilege. Without denying that they have used their property assets as productive resources, it seems that their social behaviour can be better understood within the framework we have outlined. For example, concern with lifestyle of the 'gentleman', with the proper ways of behaving, with 'noblesse oblige', and correctness of rituals and beliefs does reveal the principles of status honour rather than class advantage.

The conventional wisdom about the 'stately home' industry is that it is largely a financial device to maintain the great houses by state and voluntary means. There is clearly truth in this, but not the whole of it. The inclusion of the word 'home' helps to evoke the private as well as the public domains, just as 'house' describes the family and its name as well as its relationship to its property – titles, residences, heirlooms and land. The word 'seat', for example, clearly implies residence. But many lairds have their homes elsewhere, often in London. Nevertheless, as Wright points out, the symbolism of 'home' has been used to romanticise the patriarchal family, to idolise domestic drudgery, and to vaunt a national heritage of 'stately homes'.[46]

The stately home heritage industry allows the lairds to insinuate their own history into that of the Scottish and British nations. While having distinct identities as Scottish lairds – 'authenticated' by family names, crests, mottoes, tartans and clans – they have much in common with great landowners south of the border. It is not uncommon to find a Scottish laird owning land in England, and vice versa.

Stately home guidebooks provide the ideal format for this interweaving, with their manicured family trees, tracing family antecedents back in genealogical time to the great figures of Scottish and English history. If the nation's history can be told through the medium of the family biography, then one cannot destroy the one without the other. The family and the country become one.

The Duke of Buccleuch 'owns' the land around Ettrick Forest because it was bestowed upon his ancestors in return for services to Robert the Bruce (Scottish credentials) in the fourteenth century. At the same time, the duke is, in the words of the Buccleuch guidebook, only 'a life trustee dedicated to the constant improvement of a vital asset to the benefit of everyone concerned, as well as further generations of his own family, on whom the responsibility for future progress rests.' The guidebook, then, is not simply a guide to the layout of the family property, but a chronological narrative of how the dynasty came to occupy the positions it holds. The guidebook continues:

> Once the links in the chain of continuity are broken, through the irreversible process of the break-up of estates, the merits of multiple land-use are lost forever. The advantage of continuity spanning many generations apply just as much to the families of those who occupy let farms and estate employees. On Buccleuch estates some family partnerships between landlord and tenant go back possibly as far as the 12th century.

Thus, the ideology of land and landownership is intricately connected and interwoven with a theory of history in a vernacular and informal sense, and with a theory of everyday life. The Buccleuchs are able to exploit the ambiguity of the term 'nation'. While their works of art are part of the British 'national' heritage, their connections with Bruce and with Douglas (the family name associated with Drumlanrig in the western borders) make their Scottish credentials abundantly clear. The Buccleuchs and their fellow lairds see themselves as champions of 'history' rather than as captains of a heritage industry. In this regard, Sir Walter Scott played a crucial role not simply in 'heritagising' Scotland, but in weaving into the 'story' of Scotland the Buccleuchs whom he vested with the (inauthentic) honour of being his own 'clan chief'. Whereas those who had access to the trappings of a Highland culture could play the clan chief, Scott was investing his own lowland namesake with the title too. To do so may have made poor history, but good politics.

In a country where the lairds and the land question have a salience in politics of some significance, and in the context of Scotland's place in the British state being questioned as never before, Scotland's lairds appear to have succeeded in converting their own and the nation's history into commodities whereby they can save themselves.

Ethnicity, Identity and Heritage

Heritage has uncommon power in Scotland because it is a stateless nation. It is not the case that only formal political power, ultimately sovereignty, is the only guarantee of nationhood. The political slogan 'A nation once again' is inaccurate because since the Union of 1707 Scotland has not ceased to be a nation. In large part its institutional autonomy as a distinctive civil society, with its holy trinity of law, education and religion, has helped to underwrite the continuing and strong sense of national identity north of the border.[47]

In Scotland the weight of identity has been placed conventionally since the Union on cultural rather than political matters. We might reflect, for example, on Ian Lang's claim for Bannockburn as the key event in Scottish history he would most wish to have been present at. As we pointed out earlier in this chapter, it seems to us somewhat strange to find the representative of a Unionist party claiming this sacred nationalist icon. The key lies in his final comments:

> From then on [after Bannockburn] as a nation, we have never looked back. So much so that it was our king James IV [sic] who succeeded to the throne of England in 1603: and it was his great grand-daughter – another Scot – who oversaw the Union of the nations of Scotland and England in 1707. This is the real legacy of Bannockburn, and it is one of which I am very proud. That is why I would like to have been there in 1314.[48]

This claim that Unionism and Nationalism are reconciled in this way may strike our eyes in the late twentieth century as somewhat odd. We have grown accustomed to an antithesis between them, at least as they are expressed in conventional political forms, between the Conservative party and the Scottish National Party. The dominant wisdom in contemporary Scotland is that Scottishness and Conservatism are strange bedfellows.

Recent historical work, moreover, shows that 'unionist-nationalism' has a central pedigree in Scottish life.[49] Graeme Morton has argued convincingly that in the mid-nineteenth century a view prevailed that only because Scotland won and retained its independence in 1314 was it able to enter the Union of 1707 as an equal partner, with England, in the British state. The National Association for the Vindication of Scottish Rights, for example, which was founded in 1853, expressed a sense of patriotism which allowed it to proclaim admiration for its partner England. Similarly, the erection of the monument in Edinburgh to Walter Scott which was begun in 1833 stresses the Scottish contribution to English heritage. And perhaps more surprisingly (given Scott's political Toryism), those who raised funds for the erection of monuments to the two prime Scottish patriots William Wallace and Robert the Bruce did so by stressing the contribution to the Union.

Such a discourse seems to contemporary Scottish ears anachronistic, because political developments in the twentieth century make the separation of 'nation' from 'state' less and less possible. We have grown used to the state encroaching on civil society, and civil society making increasing demands on the state. The cultural and political dimensions become increasingly fused. We have seen that there is a considerable body of opinion which celebrates Scottish heritage while giving allegiance to Conservatism. We have seen too that heritage is not some distant cultural hobby, but has the power to define who one is in a historical sense. Heritage in Scotland has the power not only to mobilise politically but to define who people are to themselves and others. In this respect Scotland's past has a vibrant if indeterminate future.

Credits

Fig.1 Propping up heritage, courtesy of *The Herald and Evening Times.*

Fig.2 Modelling *Brigadoon*, coutesy of Niall McInerney.

Notes

1 See R Hewison, *The Heritage Industry: Britain in a Climate of Decline*, London: Methuen, 1987.

2 Scottish Tourist Board, *Heritage Attractions Survey*, Edinburgh: STB, 1992, p.15.

3 The title of a collection of essays by P Vergo (ed.), *The New Museology*, London: Reaktion, 1989.

4 M Ash, *The Strange Death of Scottish History*, Edinburgh: Ramsay Head Press, 1980, p.13.

5 See Tom Nairn, 'Old Nationalism and New Nationalism', in G Brown (ed.), *The Red Paper on Scotland*, Edinburgh: EUSPB, 1975.

6 D Lowenthal, *The Past is a Foreign Country*, Cambridge: Cambridge University Press, 1985, p.xvi

7 See Nairn, *art. cit.*; and C Beveridge and R Turnbull, *The Eclipse of Scottish Culture*, Edinburgh: Polygon, 1989.

8 Beveridge and Turnbull, *op. cit.*

9 *The Herald*, 17 August 1994.

10 See H Trevor-Roper, 'Invention of Tradition: The Highland Tradition of Scotland', in E Hobsbawm and T Ranger (eds), *The Invention of Tradition*, Cambridge: Cambridge University Press; and H Cheape, *Tartan: The Highland Habit*, Edinburgh: The National Museum of Scotland, 1991.

11 D Cosgrove, *Social Formation and Symbolic Landscape*, London: Croom Helm, 1984.

12 *Ibid.*, p.233.

13 R Williams, *The Country and the City*, London: Chatto and Windus, 1973.

14 L Paterson, *The Autonomy of Modern Scotland*, Edinburgh: Edinburgh University Press, 1994.
15 *Oxford English Dictionary*, Oxford: Oxford University Press, 1983, p.855.
16 D Horne, *The Great Museum: The Re-presentation of History*, London: Pluto, 1984.
17 *Ibid.*, p.34.
18 A Wiener, 'Inalienable Wealth', in *American Ethnologist*, Vol.12, No.2, 1985.
19 R Hewison, *The Heritage Industry*, p.102.
20 P J Fowler, *The Past in Contemporary Society: Then, Now*, London: Routledge, 1992, p.13.
21 *Ibid.*, p.17.
22 D MacCannell, *Empty Meeting Grounds*, London: Routledge, 1992, p.31.
23 *Ibid.*, p.1.
24 Note the extension of this into 'activity holidays', and the denial of the orthodox tourist role in favour of the persona of 'the traveller'.
25 C Sorensen, 'Theme Parks & Theme Machines', in P Vergo (ed.), *The New Museology*.
26 *Ibid.*, p.65.
27 P Hoyau, 'Heritage and the "Conserver Society": The French Case', in R Lumley (ed.), *The Museum Time Machine*, London: Routlege, 1988, p.29.
28 T Bennett, 'Museums and "The People"', in R Lumley, *The Museum Time Machine*, pp.72-73.
29 A Bennett, 'Back-to-Back to the Future', in *The Guardian* (*Weekend*), 16-17 December 1989.
30 P J Fowler, *The Past in Contemporary Society: Then, Now*, p.40.
31 See J Urry, *The Tourist Gaze: Leisure and Travel in Contemporary Societies*, London: Sage, 1990.
32 R Hewison, *The Heritage Industry*, p.47.
33 *The Herald*, 29 March 1994.
34 C Rojek, *Ways of Escape*, London: Macmillan, 1993, p.181.
35 P Womack, *Improvement and Romance: Constructing the Myth of the Highlands*, London: Macmillan, 1989, p.1.
36 *Ibid.* p.2.
37 M MacArthur, 'Blasted Heaths and Hills of Mist'. in *Scottish Affairs*, No.3 , 1993.
38 D Cosgrove, 'Terrains of Power', in *Times Higher Education Supplement*, 11 March 1992.
39 M Pittock, *The Invention of Scotland: The Stuart Myth and the Scottish Identity, 1638 to the Present*, London: Routledge, 1991, p.72.
40 P Hoyau, *art. cit.*, p.28.
41 Scottish Tourist Board, *Visitor Attractions: A Development Guide*, Edinburgh: STB, no date, 47pp.

42 *Scotland on Sunday*, 17 April 1994.

43 Historic Scotland, *The Popular Choice*.

44 National Trust for Scotland, *62nd Annual Report*, Edinburgh: NTS, 1993, p.2.

45 *Heritage Scotland*, Vol.10, No.2, Summer 1993, p.10.

46 P Wright, *On Living in an Old Country: The National Past in Contemporary Britain*, London: Verso, 1985, p.11.

47 See L Paterson, *The Autonomy of Modern Scotland*.

48 *The Scotsman*, 27 November 1993.

49 See G Morton, *Unionist-Nationalism: The Historical Construction of Scottish National Identity, Edinburgh 1830-1860*, PhD Thesis, University of Edinburgh, 1993.

Developing Cultural Tourism in the European Regions

Brian Jones

Introduction

This brief paper seeks to summarise some of the issues and ideas which arose from a discussion of the nature of and possibilities for the development of cultural tourism as part of a wider consideration of the development of a regional Europe.[1]

It is estimated that by the year 2000 the increase in paid leisure time will make tourism the No.1 industry worldwide. The implications of this development are profound. Mass tourism has already had a significant impact on the social economic and cultural lives of those 'fortunate' enough to be recipients of the largesse that tourism can bring to a favoured destination. However the impact is not always beneficial or sustainable. Mass tourism has the power to transform destination environments into simulacra of reality, designed to satisfy and not to challenge, a post-modern Baudrillardian vision of 'hyperreality'.[2] Where more elite forms are practised, the effect can be that of a 'cargo cult' where for a brief time largesse is distributed and attention given until a new, more 'unspoilt' destination is found, leaving raised expectations, cultural and economic disruption and a sense of longing for better times to come again.

This paper will consider the cultural aspects of tourism in a European context and will argue that sustainability must include our cultural heritage and aspirations. It directly attacks the concept of tourism before moving on to consider our particular European culture and how this can be shared and understood more widely without destroying its richness and diversity. The term 'tourism' itself is not beyond criticism. As with other terms,

Eberhard Bort and Neil Evans (eds), ***Networking Europe,*** **Liverpool University Press 2000, 363-72.**

such as 'racism, sexism, voyeurism', it implies an attitude which should, at the very least, be questioned.

Sustainability

The notion of sustainability is not new: our forebears pollarded trees and rotated crops in order to achieve sustainable yields. However, a more recent awareness that we are consuming the Earth's resources faster than they can be replenished has found a voice in the *Brundtland Report* of 1987, the Rio Earth Summit of 1992, which led to Agenda 21 and, more recently still, the Chicago Summit of 1997. Although the principal focus is on the headline issues of deforestation, global warming and atmospheric pollution, other issues such as the effects of tourism are forming part of the wider agenda.

The issues of maintaining biodiversity, with their explicitly environmental imperatives, rightly dominate the agenda but, taken in the wider context, culture forms part of the environmental web which enmeshes us all. Indeed it may be argued that our attitude to our environment is shaped by a set of cultural values which supports self-interest at the expense of reciprocity, individual gain rather than the collective good, and in doing so allows capital supremacy over the common interest. Culture is therefore inseparable from the arguments for sustainability, and it may be argued that a deeper understanding of our culture reinforces the broader case for a sustainable future.

The following definition of sustainability can be found in the *Brundtland Report* of 1987:

> sustainable development is development that meets the needs of the present without compromising the ability of future generations to meet their own needs

Culture may be defined as 'a system of shared meaning',[3] and that shared meaning has an importance for an understanding of the present. However, a cultural understanding is also important for future generations. To understand where you are requires an understanding of where you came from. Too-rapid cultural shifts or the destruction of a culture can lead to culture shock and feelings of isolation, disorientation and loss of identity. The commoditisation of culture as yet another consumable would appear to pose clear dangers. Alvin Toffler used the notion of culture shock to develop his concept of 'future shock',[4] commenting on the disorientating potential of rapid irreversible change. In his analysis, cultural identity provided a safe conceptual space to return to. Culture as 'hyperreality', constructed to meet consumer demand, denies that safe space and adds to insecurity.

Jacques Derrida suggests that organisations as social constructs are not so much instruments of control, but ways of concealing our uncertainties.[5] Their functionality lies in their ability to distance us from a potentially hostile world.

Organised mass tourism, with its emphasis on homogeneity, standardisation and a voyeuristic cultural view, also tends to insulate whilst pretending to engage. The 'hyperreal' provides the frisson of engagement without the risk and our uncertainties are manipulated by the managers of our experience. The vicarious becomes reality, and reality is redefined. This tourist as 'post-Fordist mass consumer' involves a distancing from reality and promotes a self-interested, supremacist value-set. These values derived from individualistic consumerist norms which are the antithesis of the collectivist 'common good' sustainable ideal. In this sense, the purpose of 'sustainable cultural tourism' is to safeguard cultural diversity in the same way that biodiversity is the key to sustainable physical environment.

To borrow von Bertalanffy's concept from the disciplines of the natural sciences, culture may be viewed as sub-system in a comprehensive and interlocking set of socio-environmental systems.[6] Culture, encapsulating as it does the norms and values that inform our behaviour and shape our attitudes, holds an immediate importance for us. An awareness therefore of threats to our culture may help us appreciate more fully the significance of threats to the other sub-systems that form our wider environment. The development of sustainable cultural tourism may serve as a cipher through which we may learn the language of sustainability to inform our actions in other spheres.

Europe of the Regions: A Cultural View

It is perhaps no coincidence that the development of the European Union as a supra-national ideal, given substance through institutions which encourage homogeneity, has seen the parallel development of a Regional Europe recognised and reinforced by the establishment of the Committee of the Regions. The result has been an explicit challenge to the hegemony of the ideal of the 'nation-state', as re-emergent regional identities have demanded an independent 'voice'. A supra-national/regional dialectic has developed as the political, economic and cultural space once occupied by territorially bounded nation states becomes more fluid. It would appear that where once the nation state was able to promote a national culture designed to dominate regional cultures and buttress its own supremacy,[7] the entry of the EU as a player on the European field has provided an arena for resolving many of the inter-state antagonisms which fuelled 'nationalism' and has weakened the historic rationale for the 'nation-state'. A specifically German, French or Spanish cultural identity is becoming less distinct as regional cultures become more assertive and confident. In a sense, instead of a few bland colours we now see a more vivid multi-coloured tapestry of rich cultural diversity, the product of more than a millennium of linguistic and cultural development.

Culture cannot be discussed ahistorically: the great civilisations of Greece and Rome provide the dominant backdrop to European cultural development and, to the extent that the present EU boundaries contain much of the Roman Empire, this is perhaps to be expected. However, Celtic cultures are still extant on the fringes of the EU; Spain retains significant Moorish influences; and the dark-age migrations of the Germanic tribes and Viking raiders have left their linguistic and cultural marks.

European culture may be described as a series of cultural overlays as peoples have moved, conquered, dominated and become assimilated. Another way of describing cultural change, adaptation and assimilation is to return to the systems model and to describe particular cultures as sub-systems within an overall cultural system.

However, it is a system with permeable boundaries. Over time, values and beliefs cross the boundaries between sub-cultures creating new cultural forms, some bearing the heavy imprint of a newly-dominant culture, others scarcely changing at all. In one sense it is misleading to talk of a European culture except in the most general terms; it is perhaps more appropriate in the context of 'Cultural Tourism in the European Regions' to refer to a common European cultural heritage. As Europeans we share in this heritage and, whilst valuing, accepting and learning from its diversity, understand what it means to be European.

Europe also has considerable linguistic diversity. Language is the medium through which we interpret the world and may be described as the DNA of culture; therefore its significance in the context of cultural diversity cannot be ignored. The inclusion of languages as part of the development of 'Cultural Tourism in the European Regions' should be regarded as an integral element.

It is perhaps relevant, in terms of what follows in this paper, to acknowledge a debt to the first European Union, the Roman Empire. It too had a 'euro', a system of laws, weights and measures, citizenship (restricted, but not exclusive) and sought unity, but it is also fair to observe that religious, cultural and linguistic diversity were tolerated within a provincial framework of devolved authority. Its enduring legacy was the Roman Church which, until the Reformation, remained a unifying force through the continuing use of Latin. Through this use of Latin, which provided a common language through which scholars could communicate, and through the great religious houses they passed on accumulated knowledge prefiguring the universities of today. The Roman Church, the living remnant of the Empire, has thus provided us with an infrastructure of learning across Europe. Although today most universities are secular institutions, they are to be found in every major centre in Europe, maintaining the scholarly links established over more than a thousand years, but also reflecting their distinctively regional perspectives.

The universities of the European Regions occupy a unique role as repositories, propagators and interpreters of our European cultural heritage. They are the nodes of a network which spans Europe, but which are individually embedded in, and have access to the assets of, the regional cultures of which they are part. This is not the place to attempt a detailed definition of culture, only to observe that it is an inclusive rather than an exclusive term, reflecting as it does the present and the past, what is spoken and what is written, what is consumed and that which is preserved, the intangible and the tangible. Above all, culture is to be experienced as a precursor to understanding.

Developing a Model of Cultural Tourism

In developing a model of sustainable cultural tourism within the European Regions the rationale, purpose and values which inform the model should have a coherence which distinguishes this model from other types of tourism. From the discussions at Freudenstadt a broad consensus emerged around the following:

- Rationale – As citizens of the European Union we have access to a rich and diverse regional cultural heritage which both links us as Europeans and defines us as individuals. By exploring this cultural heritage, and by valuing its continuing significance for us, we will come to learn more fully what it means to be European.
- Purpose – To enable individuals to develop a deeper, richer and more integrated understanding of the distinctive culture of the region they are visiting.
- Values – In order that the richness of cultural diversity remains sustainable, the role of the cultural 'tourist' be constructed as that of a 'visitor' or 'guest', implying respect for the host, a reciprocity in understanding and meeting needs and a humility and willingness to learn from rather than to change others.

The above intentionally breaks away from conventional notions of 'tourism' to provide for a 'leisure' activity which is non-invasive, intellectually stimulating and which, by recognising the need to sustain cultural diversity, challenges the accepted values of mass tourism. It is suggested that the above provide a sound platform for the development of a workable proposal.

A Framework for the Development of Cultural Tourism in the European Regions

Regional universities, in this concept, are seen as focal points. The universities of Europe provide the basis of a network around which regionally-based cultural tourism can be organised. They have the knowledge, expertise and contacts to co-ordinate cultural tourism in their area. Recent developments in Information Technology (IT) are enabling them to communicate more easily with each other and disseminate information with increasing speed.

The universities are able through their extensive local networks to construct databases of the cultural assets in their area. These databases can be interrogated by subject or theme using standard search engines.

Interpretation of local cultural assets can be provided by academic and other contacts, and the integration of culture and community can be provided through the universities' local networks. Again, these can be constructed as databases, to be used in conjunction with the data on cultural assets.

In terms of accommodation, visitors could stay in halls of residence during college holidays, particularly during the winter and spring; at other times, alternative accommodation could be arranged, again using local networks. The latter would also facilitate community contacts.

Because the universities form nodes on a network, there would be no need for a central co-ordinating structure. There would, however, be a requirement for a project team in the start-up phase to establish common data-handling and exchange protocols and, subsequently, a management board to oversee the strategy for future development. All participating universities would need staff for whom handling bookings and billing would be a priority task.

It is envisaged that the project would be heavily dependent on IT. It would depend on networked access to the databases at the regional universities, allowing on-line access to facilitate enquiries by subject or theme. It is further envisaged that the system would accommodate a 'customer' booking and invoicing system.

This would mean that an individual could book a 'visit' to the region of their choice to explore such cultural aspects as are of interest to them, in the depth and detail they required, simply by approaching the staff responsible for bookings at their local university. They could choose from a menu of options or construct their own 'trail', following their particular interests.

Market research will be essential, but there is evidence from the research of Frieder Stadtfeld that a market for a provision of this nature exists.[8] The initial start-up costs, constructing the databases, establishing the network and its protocols and staff training would be significant. The recurrent costs would be those of administration and would be borne by the participating universities and would be recoverable from revenue from their 'visitors'. Ongoing central development costs could be met by a licensing or franchising arrangement with participating universities.[9]

Given the significance of this project to the European Regions, the EU should be approached. It is understood that the EU is interested in developing a 'tourism-management' programme in order to relieve the pressure on the 'honey-pots' of London, Rome, Paris, Madrid etc. This proposal would contribute to such a development. The whole initiative could even be marketed under an EU banner, as it supports and promotes the European ideal.

A detailed business plan will need to be prepared to provide the capital, cost and revenue structures and to assess viability. A suggestion has been made that universities already on the 'Freudenstadt' network should be approached to take part in a pilot scheme. A timetable for action will need to be prepared and a project team appointed.

Conclusion

It is believed that this paper reflects the broad thrust of discussions at Freudenstadt and presents an idea of ways in which a model of sustainable cultural tourism could be achieved. It is hoped that this paper moves the concept of cultural tourism beyond the narrow confines of the ticklisted, managed experience, the 'Excursion to...'. By providing a way of supporting those who wish to explore and learn from our cultural heritage, it complements the established networks of summer schools. By accessing the degree of interpretation and integration that the universities and their networks are uniquely placed to provide, it opens up the possibility of offering a rich and sustainable range of cultural experiences which, whilst valuing our cultural diversity, encourages our collective identity as Europeans.

Notes

1 The discussion on which this paper is based took place at the 1997 Freudenstadt Symposium and the author is indebted those colleagues whose ideas and insights inform this paper.

2 J Baudrillard, *Simulations*, New York: Semiotexte, 1983.

3 S P Robbins, *Organisational Behaviour*, Englewood Cliffs: Prentice Hall, 1989.

4 A Toffler, *Future Shock*, New York: Bantam, 1970.

5 See J Derrida, *Speech and Phenomena*, Evanston: North Western University Press, 1973; also J Derrida, *Writing and Difference*, London: Tavistock, 1978.

6 L von Bertalanffy, *General Systems Theory*, New York: George Brazillier, 1968.

7 D Beetham, 'The Future of the Nation State', in G McLennan, D Held and S. Hall(eds), *The Idea of the Modern State*, Milton Keynes: Open University Press, 1984, pp.208-22.

8 Frieder Stadtfeld gave a presentation at the 1997 Freudenstadt symposium. (A marketing plan will need to be developed as part of a detailed business plan.)

9 Detailed costings will require further detailed analysis.

V

The Welsh Assembly 1979 and 1997

John Osmond

Given the result of the last devolution referendum in 1979, those advocating a Welsh Assembly have a cliff to climb in September. The four-to-one defeat of the Assembly proposals in 1979 was, on the face of it, the end of the devolution story so far as Wales was concerned. Why, then, has the issue resurfaced once again so quickly and with such renewed force? To answer that question we need to examine why the result went the way it did in the 1970s and, more to the point, look at what has changed in Wales in the intervening eighteen years.

The first thing to say is that the 1979 referendum was fought in extremely unfavourable circumstances for those arguing for change. An Assembly was being advocated by an unpopular Labour government at the fag-end of its administration. The pay-round 'Winter of Discontent' was well under way, with many of the public-sector unions on strike: black rubbish bags were piled high on dirty mountains of snow across Wales (it was a bitterly cold winter) and in some areas the dead were unable to be buried because the grave-diggers had abandoned their posts.

All of this accentuated an anti-government – anti, that is to say, to any government – mood that was particularly strong at the time. Mrs Thatcher's version of Conservatism was in the ascendant, with its rallying cries of 'Roll back the frontiers of the state' and 'Get the government off your backs'. Yet here was a proposal involving what its opponents were effortlessly allowed to describe as 'more government'.

The Labour Party, the supposed advocate of the change, was badly split, with its most articulate and charismatic leaders in Wales leading the 'No' Campaign. Neil Kinnock, in particular, was building the foundations of his later career as Opposition Leader on the high profile he achieved as leader of the 'No'

Eberhard Bort and Neil Evans (eds), ***Networking Europe,*** **Liverpool University Press 2000, 375-88.**

Campaign. On the other hand, the 'Yes' forces were divided, not least in the way they put the arguments for change, and found co-operation difficult. The main advocates of an Assembly in 1979 were over-identified with the nationalists who were, then as now, a minority electoral force. In turn, this reinforced the claims of those who said devolution would be a first step on a' slippery slope to separatism'.

All of these conditions were equally valid in Scotland, yet the vote there resulted in a narrow majority in favour of the change. What accounted for the difference? The answer can be described with one word – citizenship.

Scottish identity is closely bound up with institutions, structures, moreover, that have survived the Union of 1707 relatively intact: separate legal and education systems and a separate Scottish church, the Kirk. Together these have provided the Scots with a sense of self as a whole, with an ability to imagine Scotland as an entity with which they can identify and for which they feel some holistic responsibility. In short, and mainly because of their institutional infrastructure, they can imagine Scotland as nation to which they can relate in terms of citizenship.

An underlying sense of specific identity is as powerfully felt in Wales as in Scotland. However, it is less easily expressed in terms of institutions to which an idea of citizenship can be attached. Being Welsh is much more diffuse and fractured than is the case in Scotland. There are, in fact, many different Welsh*nesses* – for some symbolised by the language and the striking differences between the regions of Wales – rather than one Welsh*ness* as such.

The Welsh find it difficult to imagine Wales within an institutional framework, or even as a single entity. Communications in Wales run east to west, along the southern and northern coasts, rather than north to south in a way that would naturally unify the country. Many people in southern Wales, for instance, have never, or rarely, been to the north, and vice-versa. Instead of Wales as a whole, the Welsh tend to identify first and most strongly with their locality – their valley, town, village or *bro* (as the Welsh language more clearly states it) rather than with a sense of Wales as a whole.

Compared with Scotland, Wales has an under-developed national press. Wales' 'national newspaper', the *Western Mail*, hardly circulates in north Wales, while the Liverpool-based *Daily Post* does not penetrate below a line drawn eastwards from Aberystwyth. Only 13 per cent of Welsh households take a daily morning newspaper published and printed in Wales; in Scotland the figure is 90 per cent.[1] The broadcast media have a greater claim to national coverage, especially BBC Wales. However, the broadcasters are hampered by what are called the 'overlap' regions, that is to say those parts of Wales that can receive English transmissions, from Granada in the north say, or BBC West rather than BBC Wales in the south. It is estimated that some 30 per cent of the Welsh audience in north-east Wales, the south-east and along the border tune in to English rather than Welsh television channels. When in answer to opinion polls on devolution some 30 to 40 per cent of Welsh respondents regularly say they 'don't know' what to think, that is genuinely the case. They literally have not heard the arguments.

Welsh institutions do, of course, exist – most saliently the Welsh Office and the all-Wales quangos whose numbers have more than doubled to around 80 in the last 20 years. However, they are relatively recent. The Welsh Office was only established in 1964, along with BBC Wales in the same year, the Wales TUC in 1973, and the Welsh Development Agency in 1975. For all these reasons, and certainly in comparison with Scotland, Welsh identity is relatively weak in terms of institutions, and relatively strong in terms of cultural markers such as the language.

Statements made during the 1979 referendum by key opponents within the Labour 'No' Campaign illustrate the point. *Facts to beat Fantasies* was the title of the manifesto published by the Labour No Assembly Campaign, whose leader was Neil Kinnock – one of the famous, or notorious, depending on your outlook – 'Gang of Six' Labour MPs of that era. A central passage declared:

> The view is put forward that Wales has a special identity and urgent needs which make Devolution necessary. The Nationalists and Devolutionists say 'We are a nation, that makes a difference', 'We have a Welsh Office, that makes

> a difference', 'We have a Wales TUC, that makes a difference'. But none of that takes account of the realities.
>
> We *are* a nation, proud of our nationality. BUT there is little or no desire for the costs, responsibilities of nation*hood* as the puny voting support for the Nationalists shows. We do not need an Assembly to prove our nationality or our pride. That is a matter of hearts and minds, not bricks, committees and bureaucrats.[2]

Or take this statement, from one of the shrewdest and most powerful opponents of the day, Leo Abse, then MP for Pontypool and another member of the 'Gang of Six'. Writing ten years on, in 1989 he recalled that:

> One of the important strands of Welsh socialism was its anarcho-syndicalist tradition ... The essential sense of locality; the small pit or forge where all worked, when work was available; the comparative isolation of valley villages or townships; the central role of the local miners' lodge; the cinemas and breweries owned by the miners; and the local health schemes which were to become the prototype of the National Health Service, all created a world – now sadly slipping away – where an intense loyalty was made to the immediate community ... Our allegiance was to the locality and to the world, and nationalist flag-waving, Russian, Welsh or English, was anathema to those of us shaped in such a society.[3]

The allegiance that Leo Abse revealingly failed to mention was, of course, to Britain, to being British. This is a nationality of a sort, though it strikingly fails to connect with citizenship in strict constitutional terms. British institutions do not allow for citizenship. The Welsh, and to a lesser extent the Scottish, have, in the past at any rate, felt comfortable with being simultaneously Welsh and British. Here, however, the English have a problem. Is their identity British in any kind that is different from being English? The key word to which we have to return in considering this question is, again, citizenship. For within British constitutional possibilities there is no room for citizenship. In Britain, sovereignty does not lie with the people. Instead, it lies with the Crown in Parliament in which the people are reduced to being subjects. This is the unitary state that the opponents of devolution feel, rightly, is so threatened by devolution. What a Scottish Parliament and a Welsh Assembly will achieve is the creation of a union state in which its constituent parts are recognised for what they are, separate nations with intensely strong connections, but separate for all that. Leo Abse's generation was unable to contemplate such a change. Instead, it opted in 1979 for subjecthood within a unitary state and a Welsh sensibility that was 'sadly slipping away.'

What has changed since 1979? The first, and most straightforward, reality is that a lot of people have died. A generation whose formative experience was the Second World War, the fight against fascism, and the consciousness and loss of Empire, has largely passed on. It is noteworthy in 1997 that the people most strongly against change are the elderly. This is demonstrated by the opinion polls. It is also borne out by the key leaders of the Just Say No Campaign – its President, for instance, is 88-year-old Viscount Tonypandy. However, most of his generation is no longer with us. In their place are 600,000 people who in the 1979 referendum were too young to vote. To this generation neither the Second World War nor the Napoleonic Wars are part of living memory, but share a place in the history books.

A second reality is that, since 1979, Wales has experienced eighteen years of Conservative government. As Conservative administrations went on, election after election, they intensified and dramatised what became known as the democratic deficit. The impact was symbolised by the present Secretary of State for Wales Ron Davies, who switched his position on devolution from opposition to support in the immediate aftermath of the 1987 election, the third general election Labour had lost. Looking back he explained his change in the following way:

> I felt the future was bleak. We had delivered in Wales, winning seats like Cardiff West and Clwyd South West. If England had performed as well we would have won the election. There was this very strong feeling that

> democracy was being undermined. A system of representation is contradicted when a country like Wales can vote one way and be delivered something completely different. Touring my constituency the day after the vote I came across graffiti on a railway bridge in Nelson – 'We voted Labour, we got Thatcher!' That summed the whole thing up for me. This question of democracy – the question of Welsh representation confronted me as a political reality which we had to address.[4]

The excesses of Conservatism that were washed across the border by such English Secretaries of State for Wales as John Redwood and William Hague did a great deal to sharpen an oppositional Welsh solidarity. Thatcherite conservatism corrupted a culture of potential citizenship into one that was merely a culture of consumerism. The majority of the Welsh (80 per cent in the 1997 general election) found the Conservatives' craving for market forces and individualistic consumerism to be deeply uncongenial and offensive to their traditions of collective responsibility. It led to such policies as the poll tax, opting out of schools, the internal market in the NHS, nursery vouchers, and the lottery (condemned by leaders of the Church in Wales). It was in reaction to such policies that the Welsh exercised a kind of collective unconscious response in their forensic rejection of the Conservatives in the 1997 general election.

The eighteen years of Conservative rule had a further, more instrumental impact. While in office in Wales, successive Conservative administrations paradoxically helped to prepare and clear the ground for devolution on two fronts. First they have enormously elaborated the Welsh bureaucratic machine – the actually existing Welsh state. The powers and budget of the Welsh Office were substantially increased. It now has full control over every aspect of Welsh education, for instance, taking responsibility for higher education. In the process it has created two new quangos – the Higher and Further Education Councils for Wales, with a budget between them of some £400-500 million. The total Welsh Office budget now is some £7 billion a year. More and more quangos have been created, for instance the Countryside Council for Wales, the Welsh Language Board, and Tai Cymru – Housing for Wales.

Secondly, the Conservatives reorganised local government, replacing a two-tier system – the eight counties and 37 districts – with a unitary tier of twenty-two. At a stroke this removed much of the force of the 'over-government' argument that was put in 1979. It has also cut the core from Labour's local government powerbase – the eight counties – that was a focus for much of the opposition in 1979.

Beyond these institutional changes the Welsh economy has been transformed and modernised in ways that are wholly positive from the point of view of devolution. The old smokestack industries have been largely replaced by a renaissance in manufacturing, driven by inward investment. These new firms look to world, and especially European, markets rather than just British ones. There are now more than 380 overseas companies with substantial investments in Wales, more than 170 from continental Europe, more than 140 from America, and more than 60 from Japan and the Far East.[5]

At the same time the notion of the British economy has been subtly altered. There is no *British* coal any more, no *British* steel; not even *British* Rail (in Wales we now have instead the Great Western Railway). By the end of the 1990s the Westminster Parliament, the British Armed Forces, and the British Broadcasting Corporation may be the only public sector bodies holding Britain together – apart from, perhaps, the Monarchy. And even that has been undermined during the 1990s with a speed of collapse that looks astonishing when compared with its position 20 years ago. From being a purely British institution, the BBC is presently transforming itself into a global player, confronting a pincer movement from Murdoch, BSkyB and the digital revolution.

Despite all this, it is the European dimension of Wales' affairs, together with the modernisation of the Welsh manufacturing economy within an essentially European rather than British milieu, that in the longer run will probably have the most far-reaching impact. In 1979, the place of Europe within the devolution argument was scarcely noticeable. Today it provides an ever-present backcloth to the debate.

Decisions made in Brussels increasingly have a direct effect on the Welsh economy. This is especially the case with changes to the Common Agricultural Policy and the EU Structural Funds. Acknowledgement that Wales needs to lobby more effectively to ensure its voice is heard came with the establishment in Brussels in the early 1990s of the Wales European Centre, supported by the Welsh Development Agency, the Welsh local authorities, the University of Wales and others.

There is a growing awareness, too, that Wales stands to benefit from forging regional alliances within Europe. Close ties, developing programmes of economic and cultural collaboration and exchanges, have been forged by the Welsh Office with the so-called 'Four Motor' Regions – Baden-Württemberg, Lombardy, Rhônes-Alpes and Catalonia. A 'Europe of the Regions' is beginning to emerge, with democratic representatives, from the regions in Germany, Italy, Spain, France and Belgium, all attending meetings of the new Committee of the Regions in Brussels, established under the Maastricht Treaty. Britain is the sole large member of the European Union which has no democratically elected regional representatives to participate. Yet a new regional vision of Europe is demanding attention, one that challenges the current Europe of the nation states and is likely to do so more strongly in the coming century. If it is to be democratic, this new Europe must have strong local and regional governments. It is a novel element that is increasingly permeating the debate over the creation of a democratic political culture in Wales.[6]

All these factors are coming together to promote, for the first time in Welsh history, a really felt and pragmatic sense of Wales as an entity which needs addressing in a practical, political way. One indication of this is the way the language issue has been taken out of the devolution debate. In 1979 it was undoubtedly a disruptive influence, with irrational fears about the domination of the projected Assembly by Welsh-speakers effortlessly deployed by the 'No' campaigners. It is difficult to imagine such a campaign being mobilised in 1997, though many of the No campaigners undoubtedly remain antagonistic to the Welsh language. They know instinctively, however, that to mobilise that argument in today's climate would be counter-productive. The shift in generation has been behind the change, encouraged by the success of S4C, the Welsh Fourth Channel, Welsh language rock groups, and the association of the language with modernity rather than as an icon of the past.

However, it is with the Welsh economy that a consensus is emerging that Wales as a whole needs to operate more effectively. There is a growing understanding that this can only be done by extending and improving Welsh institutions in a democratic direction. So in the 1979 referendum campaign the Wales CBI campaigned against; in 1997 it is taking a neutral stance, preferring to leave a political argument where it conveniently, for the purpose of this debate, belongs – with the politicians. Leading business leaders are growing increasingly conscious, and uneasy, about the prospect of Wales being left behind by a Scottish Parliament, a London Assembly, and development agencies in the English regions.

It is noteworthy that a central thrust of the 1979 Welsh Assembly proposals involved a separation of social and economic policy making in Wales. The Assembly then proposed would have had its main responsibility in social policy areas such as education, health and housing. Though control of the Welsh Development Agency was eventually conceded, following much negotiation between the Wales Labour Party and the Labour Government of the time, responsibility for the Welsh economic policy was left in the hands of the Secretary of State for Wales.

There is no such ambivalence in Labour's current policy for an Assembly, outlined in the White Paper, significantly entitled *A Voice for Wales*, published in July 1997. This makes it clear that an Assembly 'should take responsibility for the existing budget of the Welsh Office and its responsibilities', which include industry and economic development. The line was most clearly expressed by Ron Davies some years ago, in a keynote speech he made on the future of the Valleys (it is noteworthy, too, that at that time he was referring to a Welsh Parliament rather than an Assembly). A new approach was needed, Ron Davies said, one that relied on partnership between the public and private sectors, focused on harnessing development from within, and looking to continental Europe for inspiration:

> Creating a strong infrastructure demands extensive government intervention and European experience teaches us that public sector/private sector partnership can lead to success. I do not believe, however, that all this can be done by us taking a begging bowl to Westminster. It is something that we can and must do for ourselves, so we must have appropriate structures for local accountability and power. The present régime is thoroughly undemocratic and in the middle of it stands the Welsh Office. For a modern economy we need a modern democracy and this should be based on an elected Welsh Parliament and strengthened local councils. A more democratic and responsive Wales is not only right for democracy, it is also needed for the sake of industry, jobs and regeneration.[7]

By today this position sounds like so much common sense. Yet in terms of the devolution debate as it has been experienced in Wales over the last 20 years, it signalled an extremely radical break with the past and an adoption of an entirely new way of thinking. What it means is that an idea of Welsh citizenship, related to Welsh institutions, is coming to be seen as meaningful and important in hard, practical economic terms.

Many other changes are under way, not least in terms of Welsh culture – in particular and as has been noted, changes in the attitude of the majority English-speaking Welsh to the Welsh language. But the shift illustrated by Ron Davies' speech on the Welsh economy is the most fundamental and significant development in the devolution politics of the 1990s compared with the 1970s, and why an Assembly for Wales is now realistically on the Welsh political agenda in a way it has never been before.

So what is stopping Wales? Why is the outcome of the referendum in 1997 still felt to be so uncertain?

The short answer is: the Labour Party. Fundamentally, it is undemocratic in its structures and outlook, certainly in much of Wales. Here we have neither new Labour nor old Labour, just unreconstructed Labour. It wins around 50 per cent of the vote, and takes elections for granted. After the 1992 election defeat it refused to contemplate anything like a Convention on Scottish lines – despite a resolution to that effect from the Wales TUC. In a comment at the time, one member of the Welsh Labour Executive accused the Scottish Labour Party of contracting out its policy. One result is that the Welsh Labour Party has been extremely reluctant to take on board the kind of Welsh Assembly designed to capture the enthusiasm of those likely to support it.

- There is a reluctance to concede legislative powers – the kind of powers that would have made impossible the imposition of the poll tax in Wales.
- There is a reluctance to allow the Assembly the financial discretion and responsibility that would accompany tax-varying powers.
- There is a reluctance to concede proportional representation.
- There is a reluctance to take seriously the (under-) representation of women.
- There is a reluctance to envisage the Assembly being a strong voice for Wales within the European Union institutions.
- There is a reluctance to see the Assembly as anything other than an all-Wales tier of local government.

It is noteworthy that a new campaign within the party has emerged in the last few years – *Welsh Labour Action* – which is campaigning for a maximalist position on all these issues. It has a membership of around a hundred activists but has been cold-shouldered by the party's Welsh leadership. Its chairman, Gareth Hughes, is a member of the Welsh Labour Executive, but was voted off the Policy Commission that developed Labour's devolution policy.

On the whole, people in Wales do not like the Labour Party. They vote for it – in large numbers and especially in general elections – but they tend to resent its dominance. People in north and west Wales especially do not like what they see as the autocratic control of local government by Labour in the Valleys. The more Labour's Assembly is seen as being in the pattern of existing local government, the less popular it is likely to be. It will be especially unpopular with local government itself, as councils will see a relatively powerless Assembly as designed to take powers from local rather than central government.

The referendum will be decided by the large number of people who remain undecided: according to the polls a large block of somewhere between 25 per cent and 40 per cent. The evidence is, however, that once these people become aware of the key issues, they tend to come down in favour. This was the main message of a Beaufort Research poll, carried out for BBC Wales in June 1997, which probed not how people would vote in the forthcoming referendum, but their support or otherwise for the main arguments. So, for example, 68 per cent agreed with the proposition that an Assembly would 'provide a stronger political voice for Wales in the UK (17 per cent disagreed and 15 per cent were not sure). Again, 68 per cent agreed that an Assembly 'would make the Welsh Office and Quangos more directly accountable to the Welsh people' (13 per cent disagreed and 19 per cent were not sure). Seventy-one per cent agreed that it 'would pursue policies better suited to the needs of Wales' (14 per cent disagreed and 15 per cent were not sure). Fifty-six per cent agreed that the Assembly 'would give Wales a more direct voice in Europe' (22 per cent disagreed and 22 per cent were not sure); 51 per cent agreed that it 'would bring more investment and jobs to Wales' (23 per cent disagreed and 26 per cent were not sure).

On the other hand, 48 per cent of the sample disagreed with the proposition that an Assembly 'would lead to the break-up of the UK' (32 per cent agreed and 20 per cent were not sure); 50 per cent disagreed with the view that 'it would cause damage to the Welsh economy and loss of jobs' (27 per cent agreed and 23 per cent were not sure); 43 per cent disagreed that it 'would be dominated by Welsh language interests (37 per cent agreed and 20 per cent were not sure); and 43 per cent disagreed that 'Wales would have less influence with central government in London' (34 per cent agreed and 23 per cent were not sure). The only negative arguments that registered a majority in the poll were 50 per cent that agreed that an Assembly 'would increase the cost and bureaucracy of government in Wales' (21 per cent disagreed and 29 per cent were not sure), and the 39 per cent who agreed that the Assembly 'would be dominated by the Labour Party' (36 per cent disagreed and 25 per cent were not sure).

On the basis of this evidence, a positive result in September's referendum seems assured, so long as the 'Yes' Campaign effectively deploys the arguments. To a great extent, however, the arguments probed by the BBC Wales poll skate on the surface of the debate. Underlying them are much more powerful, subjective and largely unquantifiable considerations, reflected in the large number of people who remain unsure about which way to vote – the 'Don't Knows'. To some extent, as has been said, their large presence at the centre of the campaign reflects genuine ignorance. It also reflects uncertainty about taking a step into the unknown territory of identity politics, lack of confidence, timidity and even fear about such largely irrational matters as 'separation from the UK', 'an English backlash', 'the Welsh language' and 'Labour dominance'.

Yet the 1997 referendum is taking place in strikingly different circumstances from the one held in 1979. It is being promoted by a popular Labour government at the beginning rather than at the end of its mandate, and moreover, a government that is anxious for its policy to succeed. There will be an effective Labour 'Yes' campaign. There are Welsh Labour backbenchers opposed to the policy, but when compared with the leaders of the Labour Vote 'No' Campaign in 1979, they are much more emphatically representative of the older generation, they lack coherence, and they certainly lack charisma. At the same time the grassroots party is much more united. For instance a survey of Labour councillors, conducted by the magazine *Barn* (Opinion) for its August 1997 issue, found that 70 per cent were in favour, compared with only 40 per cent in 1979. Many councillors said that it was eighteen years of Conservative rule that had changed their minds.

More generally, the political context of the 1997 referendum is markedly different from 1979. Devolution is now a British-wide policy, with an Assembly for London being promoted and a rolling programme for the English regions as well as Wales and Scotland. A telling argument is that a 'No' vote in 1997 would mean that Wales would be out of step with the rest of Britain. Beyond that, the British context of Welsh affairs is having to be adjusted to take account of the emerging European dimension. The Welsh are still British, but they are also becoming European, an identity that has afforded them, for the first time with the Maastricht Treaty, constitutional citizenship. The extent to which the Welsh overcome their fears, discover confidence, and support an elected all-Wales institution, will demonstrate in Wales how far Welsh and European citizenship have advanced, and how far British subjecthood has retreated.

Notes

1 An analysis of these figures is provided in *The Road to the Referendum*, Cardiff: Institute of Welsh Affairs paper, October 1996.

2 Labour No Assembly Campaign, *Facts to beat Fantasies* (February 1979), Political Archive, National Library of Wales, Aberystwyth.

3 Leo Abse, *Margaret, Daughter of Beatrice: A Politician's Psycho-biography of Margaret Thatcher*, London: Jonathan Cape, 1989, p.173.

4 Quoted in John Osmond, *Welsh Europeans*, Cardiff: Seren, 1995, p.82.

5 See Gareth Jones, *Wales 2010 - Three Years On*, Cardiff: Institute of Welsh Affairs, December 1996.

6 See John Gray and John Osmond, *Wales in Europe: The Opportunity Presented by a Welsh Assembly*, Cardiff: Institute of Welsh Affairs, June 1997.

7 Quoted in John Osmond, *op. cit.*, p.87.

The Scottish Electorate and the Scottish Parliament

Paula Surridge, Lindsay Paterson, Alice Brown and David McCrone

Introduction[1]

The general election of 1 May 1997 saw a Labour government returned to office for the first time in 18 years and placed firmly on the agenda the prospect of a parliament for Scotland. In the run-up to the election, the Labour Party had promised Scotland a referendum on the establishment of a parliament and, shortly after taking the reins of government, passed legislation allowing the referendum to take place. Held on 11 September 1997, the referendum asked the Scottish people to vote on two issues: whether or not a parliament should be established and whether a parliament should have tax varying powers. Scotland awoke on 12 September to the news that the people had supported both propositions by impressive majorities.

In this chapter we deal with two main aspects of the debate about a Scottish parliament:

- The first is to examine three competing explanations of voting behaviour and assess how well they explain the result in the referendum of 11 September. The first of these explanations is a model of voting based on rational choice theory, the second is a claim that social location (for example, social class) can explain voting patterns, and the third is a model based on vote as an expression of national identity. We argue that understanding the vote in the referendum requires a model based not on economic rationality or on national identity but rather on welfare rationality. That is,

Eberhard Bort and Neil Evans (eds), *Networking Europe*,
Liverpool University Press 2000, 389-416.

the Scottish people voted for a parliament with tax-varying powers because they believed it would bring benefits to Scotland in terms of social welfare.

- The second aspect of the debate is to consider the role which the issue of a Scottish parliament played in the general election. In 1992, the Conservatives claimed that their defence of the constitutional status quo was a reason why their vote held up, and yet, in 1997 with the same policy, they lost all their seats in Scotland and a third of their remaining vote. Was the issue of a Scottish parliament a factor in this collapse?

Data

The data used in this chapter come from the 1997 Scottish Election Study (SES),[2] a representative study of 882 adults in all parts of Scotland. The survey fieldwork was conducted after the election and continued throughout the summer, covering May-August.[3] In this chapter, we focus primarily on the question of how people intended to vote in the referendum. The questionnaire contained two questions aimed at mimicking the referendum questions. These were:

> There are proposals to hold a referendum in Scotland to find out whether people want a Scottish Parliament to be set up. In such a referendum – supposing you had to vote 'yes' or 'no' to the following questions – how would you vote?
>
> Should there be a Scottish parliament within the UK?
> 1 Yes
> 2 No
> 3 (Would not vote in referendum)
> 4 Other answer (WRITE IN)
>
> Should a Scottish parliament be able to increase or decrease income tax within a limit of 3 pence in the pound?

1 Yes
2 No
3 (Would not vote in referendum)
4 Other answer (WRITE IN)

Table 1 shows how respondents to the 1997 Scottish Election Study answered these questions. This table suggests that many Scots had decided on their referendum voting intention well in advance of both the general election result and the announcement of the referendum itself; even opinion polls carried out well before the general election could predict the outcome of the referendum accurately. In addition, Table 1 shows that the Scottish Election Study, whilst still looking at *intended* vote, was remarkably close to the actual result. This is probably less surprising when we consider that the fieldwork for the survey was carried out during the period of the referendum campaign.

Table 1 *Intended vote in referendum on Scottish Parliament*

	May-Aug '96 (poll average)	Nov '96 (System 3)	SES 1997	Result
Parliament				
Yes	63	70	73	74.3
No	26	21	20	25.7
Don't Know / Not answered	11	8	8	
Tax-varying powers				
Yes	53	59	64	63.5
No	31	30	26	36.5
Don't know / Not answered	16	11	11	

In this chapter the questions above, on how people intended to vote on the two referendum questions, have been collapsed to give a five-fold measurement of intended referendum vote – Yes-Yes, Yes-No, No-No, No-Yes and Other (which includes all those who were undecided or said they would not vote on either question). By collapsing the questions in this way we are able to look at the likelihood of people choosing different combinations of vote intention. The proportions in these categories were 59 per cent Yes-Yes, 10 per cent Yes-No, 15 per cent No-No, four per cent No-Yes, and 12 per cent Other.

Models of Voting Behaviour

The models of voting used in this chapter were developed in the context of voting behaviour at general and local elections, at which the electorate are asked to choose between parties offering differing bundles of policy promises. As referenda are relatively infrequent and often assumed to be 'one-off' events, there are no general models of referendum voting on which to draw. It is usually assumed that vote in a referendum is a simple expression of policy preference. However, this is not necessarily the case and in the Scottish referendum is certainly misleading. In referenda voters are offered clear choices among preferences but not all the possible positions are offered. For example, in the Scottish referendum, independence from the UK state was not an option. Thus, in trying to understand the processes at work in people's decisions as to how to cast their vote at these referenda, we must look for explanations beyond a simple expression of policy preference.

Models based on rational choice theory, on the social location of voters in Scotland and on national identity have all been used to explain the distinctive pattern of voting in Scotland at general elections.[4] This chapter applies each of these models in turn to vote intention in the referendum.

Rationality and the Referendum Vote

Models of voting behaviour based on rational choice theory have become commonplace in recent years, both in academic circles and in the common-sense explanations of election results. Beginning in the 1970s, political commentators identified a 'decade of de-alignment'[5] during which, it was argued, voters became loosened from the anchors of social location and identity and started to choose parties on the basis of rational decisions. Several models of these rational decisions have been put forward. The earliest of these was the 'issue voting' model[6] in which voters line up their own attitudes and preferences against the policy positions of the parties and cast their vote for the party closest to their own choices. This model has proved difficult to test and substantiate at the level of vote in a general election as the level of knowledge of party positions among the electorate is often quite low. Moreover, the issue voting model is not appropriate for modelling vote at a referendum, when the electorate is asked to state its own position on a single issue and not to choose from bundles of policy positions put forward by parties.

More recent models of voting, based on rational choice theory, have focused on the economic evaluations voters make. These models can be divided into two types,[7] egocentric models and sociotropic models. The first of these, egocentric models, are based on economic evaluations of the voter's own position: that is, whether the individual voter feels that he or she would be better off with a given party in government. These models have been widely used to explain the electoral victories of the Conservative party in the 1980s. As the Conservative party was associated with lower taxation, people believed they would be better off (financially) under a Conservative government. These models also underpinned much of the Labour party's campaign advertising during the 1997 election campaign, when much of the advertising focused on taxation and tried to reassure people that taxes would not go up under a 'New Labour' government. The sociotropic models, on the other hand, are based on evaluations of the economic position of the nation as a whole: that is, whether or not the fortunes of the national economy are best served by a particular party. Again these models have been widely used to explain Conservative victories in recent elections and featured in their advertising during the 1997 campaign under the guise of 'Britain is booming'.

Earlier work on voting behaviour in Scotland has suggested that the Scottish National Party vote could be understood using a model of sociotropic economic voting, whereby a feeling of economic deprivation relative to the rest of Great Britain, coupled with a belief that independence for Scotland would improve this position, led to a vote for the SNP.[8] Can these economic models of voting be used to explain the outcome of the referendum in Scotland?

In order to test these propositions in relation to the referendum questions, we asked our respondents to answer a series of questions on their expectations of a Scottish parliament. These were 'Now supposing that a Scottish parliament within the UK were set up. As a result of this Scottish parliament, would unemployment in Scotland become higher, lower or would it make no difference?', with similarly worded questions about taxation, and (with 'better' substituted for 'higher', etc) the economy, education, the NHS and social welfare.

The results in Table 2 suggest that people in Scotland were aware that the introduction of a Scottish parliament was likely to make taxation higher, with 56 per cent expecting taxes to go up. These figures show quite clearly that the Scottish people were not going 'blindly' along the path to home rule as was suggested by the British Conservative leader William Hague during the campaign. Rather they were fully aware that the parliament was likely to increase taxes in Scotland (the much publicised 'tartan tax') and voted in favour of the parliament regardless. On other issues only a minority expected the position to worsen and in most cases a majority expected things to get better (the exception being on unemployment where 37 per cent expected there to be no change).

Using an egocentric model of voting we would expect to find that those who thought taxation would be higher after the introduction of a parliament were inclined to vote against the parliament, and especially against the parliament having tax-varying powers.

Table 3 looks at the intended vote in the referendum according to expectations of taxation if a parliament were introduced.

Table 2 *Expected effects of Scottish Parliament*

	Economy	Unemploy-ment	Education	NHS	Welfare	Taxation
Lot better	13	6	17	16	8	
Little better	41	32	45	44	40	9
No change	23	37	25	25	36	26
Little worse	11	10	3	4	5	48
Lot worse	3	4	1	1	1	8
Don't know/ Not answered	9	11	9	10	10	9
Unweighted N (=100 per cent)	882	882	882	882	882	882

Source: *1997 Scottish Election Survey.*
(For unemployment and taxation, 'better' corresponds to 'lower', etc.)

In this table we have collapsed the categories shown in Table 2 into two groups: those who expected taxes to be higher (either a little or a lot) and those who expected taxation to either remain unchanged or to be lower. This allows for a clear contrast between the pessimists and optimists on this issue. As the table shows, the expectations people held about taxation after the introduction of a parliament are not good predictors of intended referendum vote. Whilst a higher proportion of the group that expected higher taxes intended to vote No-No, this still only represents one fifth of this group: over half still intended to vote

Yes-Yes. These results seem to fly in the face of the models of rational choice discussed above. People in Scotland were not only aware of the likelihood of higher taxes but, in addition, this expectation did not lead them to vote No.

On the face of it, this evidence seems to suggest that rational-choice models of the vote do not explain the referendum result in Scotland. However, the position is altered if we look at rational voting as an exercise in cost-benefit analysis. Perhaps people are willing to pay more taxes if they perceive that the higher taxes will result in other benefits. That is, their egocentric evaluations may take second place to their sociotropic evaluations.

Table 3 *Expectations of tax rises and intended referendum vote*

	Yes-Yes	Yes-No	No-No	No-Yes	Other	Unweighted N (=100 per cent)
Taxes higher	59	9	20	5	7	491
Taxes unchanged/ lower	65	12	8	2	12	306

Source: *1997 Scottish Election Survey*

To test this proposition, a scale of benefits was constructed. Excluding taxation, each of the other five variables (as shown in Table 2) were collapsed to be either a positive response or no change and lower. The scale was then simply constructed counting each of the items on which people expected a benefit. Thus, the scale runs from 0 (where the respondent expected none of these items to improve) to 5 (where they expected all five areas to improve). The distribution of respondents on this scale is shown in Table 4. This table shows that, as well as the awareness of the 'tartan tax', people made distinctions about which areas would improve. There was not a simple divide between those expecting everything to get better and those who expected everything to get worse. Around a quarter of our respondents expected there to be no benefits from a Scottish parliament, whilst a fifth expected everything to get better.

In order to answer the question posed above, we need to compare the expectations people held on taxation with the benefits they expected from the parliament. Table 5 does this, looking only at those who expected taxes to increase.

It is quite clear from this table that people were prepared to support a parliament, despite expecting higher taxes, if and only if they expected the parliament to bring wider benefits. Of those who expected higher taxes but who did not expect any wider social benefits, just 10 per cent intended to vote Yes-Yes in the referendum. However, amongst those who expected higher taxes and one benefit, this proportion increased to 43 per cent, and amongst those expecting three or more benefits from the parliament, over 80 per cent intended to vote Yes-Yes.

***Table 4** Number of expected benefits of Scottish parliament*

	Number of benefits expected
0	24
1	9
2	10
3	14
4	22
5	20
Unweighted N (=100 per cent)	882

Source: *1997 Scottish Election Survey.*

This simple analysis suggests that the expectations which people held of a Scottish parliament were a key determinant of the referendum outcome. It also suggests that an expectation of a 'tartan tax' did not deter people from supporting the parliament. However, these claims need to be evaluated alongside other competing models of referendum vote. Models based on social location and on national identity are looked at below. However, in a more sophisticated statistical model of these processes, the findings described above were confirmed. A logistic regression model[9] was used to assess the relative impact of a number of factors on the likelihood of someone intending to vote Yes-Yes. This model showed that other factors, such as social class, gender and national identity, had only a small impact on intended vote, whilst the impact of expected benefits of the parliament remained significant even after taking these other factors into account. In addition, there was no significant impact of expectations of tax rises after the level of expected benefits was taken into account. These models and the evidence presented above suggest that an economic model of voting based on egocentric evaluations cannot explain the referendum outcome. A rational model based on a sociotropic evaluation of benefits of the parliament does explain the outcome. This is what we mean by 'welfare rationality': people supported a parliament because they believed that it would improve the quality of public welfare in Scotland.

In the 1950s and 1960s models of voting behaviour were based largely on the social location of voters. Put simply, it was argued that people in the working class voted Labour and those in the middle class voted Conservative.[10] There has been much debate in recent years about the extent to which these old alignments still explain voting behaviour in general elections.[11] However, models based on social location (and social class in particular) have been used to explain voting patterns in Scotland. Here it is argued that the Conservative party do poorly in Scotland as there are fewer of their 'natural' supporters (i.e. middle classes) than in other parts of Great Britain.[12] To explain the election victories of the Conservatives during the 1980s, many commentators pointed to the 'extension of popular capitalism',[13] in other words to the fact that Thatcherism as a project had converted many of those who had been 'working-class' into home owners and share owners – thus making them more ready to support the Conservatives. These particular social changes appeared to have less impact in Scotland (although reliable data sources are scarce). To what extent, then, can intended referendum vote be explained in terms of the social location of voters?

Table 5 *Expected benefits of Scottish parliament and intended referendum vote, among those who expected higher taxes*

Number of expected benefits	Yes-Yes	Yes-No	No-No	No-Yes	Other	Unweighted N (=100 per cent)
0	10	10	55	11	14	114
1	43	6	33	9	9	54
2	43	12	26	4	16	54
3	79	11	6	2	2	59
4	86	7	2	1	4	118
5	88	10		1	1	92

Source: *1997 Scottish Election Survey.*

Social Location

Table 6 looks at the sex, age, religion and social class of respondents to assess how, if at all, these are related to intended referendum vote. Social class is measured according to the categories developed by Goldthorpe.[14] The Table does show some differences among social groups, especially in terms of social class. However, despite these differences, the largest proportion of each group intended to vote Yes-Yes. Among the small group of petty bourgeoisie we find the highest likelihood of a No-No vote, at 30 per cent. However, even amongst this group, almost half intended to vote Yes-Yes. Perhaps surprisingly there are few differences among the religious groups in their intended vote, with a majority of both Catholic identifiers and Protestant identifiers intending to vote Yes-Yes. There is no strong tendency for young people to be more in favour of a parliament than older people: there is clear support on both questions in all the age groups apart from among those aged over 65.

The data in Table 6 suggest that a model based on social location cannot explain the referendum outcome. This is further confirmed by the statistical modelling described above, in which social class and gender were included alongside expectations of benefits and taxes and national identity. In these models, social class had only a small impact on the referendum vote, with members of the salariat and manual foremen being less likely to intend to vote Yes-Yes than members of the working class.

National Identity

National identity does not explain more than a small part of the referendum outcome either. There are good reasons to test such a model, because it is the dominant one both in political beliefs about what influences people's attitudes to the constitution, and in the academic writing on this subject. At the political level, all sides in the debate about a Scottish parliament over the last couple of decades have made some use of national identity in an attempt to increase their vote. This has been strongest from the opponents of any Scottish parliament and from those who favour independence. For example, when he was Prime Minister, John Major frequently spoke of the Britishness of Scotland and the history which Scotland had shared with England for three centuries.[15] Correspondingly, cultural nationalist have suggested that Scottish culture requires a Scottish parliament if it is to survive.[16] Even the supporters of home rule (as

Table 6 Social characteristics and intended referendum vote

	Yes-Yes	Yes-No	No-No	No-Yes	Other	Unweighted N (=100 per cent)
Sex						
Male	61	12	16	4	8	376
Female	58	8	15	4	16	506
Age						
18-24	69	12	12		8	129
25-34	68	9	8	4	11	157
35-44	63	9	13	3	12	154
45-54	57	9	24	3	8	159
55-64	58	12	12	5	13	118
over 65	44	8	22	8	18	156
Religion						
None	68	10	11	3	8	270
Catholic	59	14	12		15	126
Protestant	55	9	19	6	11	415
Social Class						
Salariat	49	12	24	5	9	211
Routine non-manual	66	5	15	5	10	188
Petty bourgeoisie	43		30	5	21	53
Manual Foremen and Supervisors	59	16	14	4	7	71
Working Class	67	11	6	2	14	298

Source: *1997 Scottish Election Survey.*

opposed to independence) have invoked Scottish identity as one argument for a parliament: this strand can be found in, for example, the Claim of Right for Scotland which preceded the setting up of the Constitutional Convention and which, therefore, led to the set of proposals that were voted on in the referendum.[17]

Similar views can be found among academics. Thus all the most influential writers about nationalism, despite the great differences among their interpretations, attach some importance to national identity as an explanation of why people support or oppose self government. The dispute between Gellner and Nairn on the one hand[18] and Smith[19] on the other, significant though it is, is about *how* nationalist movements mobilise national identity, not about *whether* they do so: they disagree over the extent to which that national identity was mainly invented along with industrialism (Gellner and Nairn), or was made up of much more ancient elements (Smith). Anderson,[20] too, does not question the importance of national identity: his contribution was to explain how it could be disseminated to a mass audience (through the new print media of the nineteenth century). Many other writers have explored the ways in which the political use of national identity is not only the preserve of opposition movements. For example, Kellas talks of the 'official nationalism' of the state:[21] in Scotland, an instance would be the rhetoric from John Major about Britishness. Billig[22] has pointed out that state-sponsored identity does not have to be strident to be politically effective. It can be the taken-for-granted background to every-day life.

Our data do not provide tests of all these theories in their full complexity: we are looking only at the immediate influences on people's vote on one specific set of proposals in the referendum in September 1997. Nevertheless, the data do allow us to examine the importance of national identity in explaining the positions which people take when faced with a crucial decision about the future of the overlapping nations in which they are living. One way of looking at it is through a question in the survey which asked respondents to say whether they felt themselves to belong to any of a list of national groupings. The options offered were (in this order) 'British, English, European, Irish, Northern Irish, Scottish, Welsh, Other, None of these'.

People found no difficulty answering this, and in naming more than one identity. Thus, 79 per cent said they were Scottish, 52 per cent British, 10 per cent European, and four per cent English; the other categories attracted negligible proportions. Among the Scottish identifiers, 45 per cent said they were also British and seven per cent European. Among the British, 13 per cent said they were also European.

Table 7 shows the intended referendum vote according to these non-exclusive categories of national identity. The striking conclusion, in the light of all the debate, is how unimportant national identity was in explaining the vote. For each category of allegiance, a clear majority intended to vote Yes on both referendum questions. Thus, even people who expressed some allegiance to an idea of Britishness voted 63 per cent in favour of a parliament, and 56 per cent in favour of its having tax-varying powers. Whatever weak effect Britishness may have had on the referendum vote, it certainly did not force people into opposition to the proposals. Furthermore, people who felt English apparently saw no incompatibility between that identity and supporting a parliament for the nation in which they had come to live.

Table 7 *Identities and intended referendum vote*

	Yes-Yes	Yes-No	No-No	No-Yes	Other	Unweighted N (=100 per cent)
Scottish	63	9	14	4	11	704
English	54	16	16	5	9	37
British	51	12	21	5	10	459
European	62	5	15	6	12	80

Source: *1997 Scottish Election Survey.*

Not surprisingly, in the light of the data in Table 7, the measures of national identity were much less powerful explanations of referendum vote than were the expectations of the parliament or party vote. Thus, in a logistic regression which analysed the intended vote on the first question in the referendum, Scottish, European and English identities had no effect at all beyond people's expectations of the parliament and their party vote in the general election. British identity was associated with being slightly less likely to vote Yes, but was a weaker predictor than expectations of the parliament for the economy, education, unemployment and the health service, and was much the same strength as age. The pattern was similar for the second question.

The essential irrelevance of national identity to the intended referendum vote is probably a signal of the success of Labour's strategy of associating its proposals for a Scottish parliament with renewing British democracy. Indeed, people who believed that Tony Blair was going to be an effective prime minister were more favourable to a parliament than people who did not, even after taking account of partisanship: thus, Labour supporters who admired Blair were more likely to intend to vote Yes than Labour supporters who were more sceptical of him. This success for Blair's approach can be seen further from Table 8, which shows intended referendum vote according to how the respondent felt about keeping the UK united. It is true that people who did care about this were more likely to oppose a parliament in the referendum than those who did not care about it: thus the No votes were between 30 per cent and 40 per cent among people who agreed or strongly agreed that the UK government should keep the Union together, in contrast to about 10 per cent or less among people who disagreed or strongly disagreed. Nevertheless, the resonance of Blair's strategy is seen in each of these groups. Even people who felt strongly that the UK should be kept united were evenly balanced in their attitude to a parliament, 53 per cent voting Yes on the first question and 46 per cent doing so on the second. Voting Yes was largely not seen as a way of breaking up the Union.

Table 8 *Views on 'government should do everything possible to keep Britain united'and intended referendum vote*

	Yes-Yes	Yes-No	No-No	No-Yes	Other	Unweighted N (=100 per cent)
Strongly agree	41	12	33	6	8	118
Agree	45	11	23	6	15	323
Neither agree nor disagree	60	13	7	1	19	130
Disagree	85	7	4	1	3	236
Strongly disagree	80	7	3	3	7	52

Source: *1997 Scottish Election Survey.*

The Constitution and the General Election

The Conservative party believed that their stance on the constitution in the 1992 general election had won them votes in Scotland, and that, in particular, it was the tactic which saved them from the collapse which both they and most observers expected.[23] In the 1997 general election, they therefore tried the same tactic again. Indeed, in the final few days of the campaign, the prime minister John Major toured Wales, Northern Ireland and Scotland, reiterating his belief that the Union was beneficial to all its partners, and that it was threatened by Labour's proposals for a Scottish parliament and a Welsh assembly.

Scottish Labour, on the other hand, had come to believe firmly and almost unanimously in its policy on home rule. That policy may have started expediently in the 1970s as a response to the rise of the SNP, but, by the time of John Smith's leadership between 1992 and 1994, it had become a matter of principle.[24] The main reason for the change was the party's work with the Liberal Democrats and various civic bodies in the Constitutional Convention between 1989 and 1995. The consensus which Labour could thus feel they were leading lasted through the referendum campaign itself, and, indeed, broadened significantly to include the SNP.

Labour also, however, feared that the Conservatives may have been correct that they had gained from their opposition to home rule in 1992. They also feared that the proposal to give a Scottish parliament powers to vary income tax would be used by the Conservatives throughout Britain to claim that Labour really believed in increasing taxes after all, despite protestations to the contrary by the Shadow Chancellor, Gordon Brown. That is one reason why, in the summer of 1996, they announced their intention to hold a referendum on their proposals, with a separate question on the proposed taxation powers.[25] They hoped that this would deflect Conservative criticism during the general election campaign: Labour would be able to say that decisions about home rule and about tax would be taken by the Scottish people themselves in a separate vote.

To many commentators, this move by Labour appeared to have worked. The constitutional issue seemed to play a less prominent role in the 1997 general election than it had done in 1992, despite Major's attempts to repeat his themes. The Conservative collapse in the election was taken by some opponents of home rule as confirmation of that: they claimed that voters felt safe about voting against the Conservatives because they knew that this would not automatically translate into a threat to the Union.

And yet the referendum delivered an emphatic endorsement of Labour's policy, and – as we have seen – this happened despite a widespread belief that taxes would rise. So was the constitution an issue in the election? Did it contribute to the Conservatives' losses? Did the Conservatives get their message about the effects of a parliament across?

The first point to note is that 50 per cent of people in the survey said that the issue of a Scottish parliament was important to them in deciding how they would vote in the general election. That does not suggest that the matter had been wholly removed from the election in the way that Labour had intended. But Table 9 shows that the effects of the issue were not as favourable to the Conservatives as they hoped and as Labour and the Liberal Democrats feared. This table displays the referendum intentions among three groups of people: those who recalled voting Conservative in 1992, those who still identified with the Conservative party in 1997, and those who actually voted Conservative in 1997. (Identifiers were those who chose the Conservatives in response to the question: 'generally speaking, do you think of yourself as ... '.) These can be taken as three increasingly strong measures of attachment to the party. For this purpose, it does not matter whether people were accurate in their recall of their 1992 vote: their response to that is merely a measure of some willingness to acknowledge a past association with the party. The main message of the table is that the Conservatives lost the votes of many of those among their supporters who intended to vote in favour of a parliament. Thus, whereas 41 per cent of people who recalled voting Conservative in 1992 intended to vote Yes on the first question, that proportion was only 36 per cent of those who still identified with the Conservatives, and a mere 23 per cent of 1997 Conservative voters. So a first inference from the table is that the Conservatives' stance on the constitution lost them votes.

This interpretation is confirmed by four further pieces of statistical analysis. The first is that, for the other three main parties, the referendum intentions were almost the same for their voters as for their identifiers or their previous voters. So people had already accepted these parties' stances long before the general election, and were not either attracted or deterred any further.

Second, people who identified in some way with the Conservatives in 1997 and who supported a Scottish parliament were more likely to say that the issue of a parliament was an important influence on their vote than people who identified with the Conservatives and who opposed a parliament. For example, among people who recalled voting Conservative in 1992 and who intended to vote Yes on the first question in the referendum, 43 per cent said that the issue was important; among those 1992 Conservatives who intended to vote No, only 34 per cent said it was important. Previous Conservatives who supported a parliament and who believed that the issue was important were faced with only two options in the general election: abandon their party or abandon the parliament. The fall-off in Conservative support among such people suggests that they tended to choose to abandon the party.

Table 9 *Attachment to Conservative party and intended referendum vote*

	Yes-Yes	Yes-No	No-No	No-Yes	Other	Unweighted N (=100 per cent)
Recalls voting Conservative in 1992	31	10	42	7	11	159
Identifies with Conservatives	25	11	47	7	10	140
Voted Conservative in 1997	15	8	59	10	9	100

Source: *1997 Scottish Election Survey.*

Third, the fall-off in Conservative vote seen here was not found in 1992, the election when the Conservatives believed that this issue bolstered their vote. In the absence of specific referendum proposals in 1992, there is no direct comparison to Table 9, but we can look instead at general attitudes to a Scottish parliament. The election surveys in both 1992 and 1997 asked what is now a standard question about options for governing Scotland. In the 1992 election study, 72 per cent of the whole sample opted for either home rule or independence; in 1997, the proportion was much the same, at 76 per cent. In 1997, as in the specific questions on the referendum, support for some kind of parliament was higher among Conservative identifiers (47 per cent) than among Conservative voters (38 per cent), and for the other parties there was no difference. But in 1992 there was almost no such difference for the Conservatives either (44 per cent for identifiers and 41 per cent for voters). These figures suggest that the Conservatives' stance in 1997 was off-putting in a way that it had not been five years earlier.

The fourth reason to believe that the Conservatives lost support as a result of their opposition to a Scottish parliament comes from a more rigorous analysis of the data in Table 9. One objection to the interpretation that we have made is that the loss of Conservative support could, perhaps, be explained by factors other than the constitutional issue. For example, it is generally agreed that the Conservatives lost votes throughout Britain because they were no longer seen as capable of being a strong government and because some of their MPs had been the subject of political scandal (for example, allegedly taking bribes for asking parliamentary questions). If Conservative identifiers who believed these accusations were also more likely than other Conservatives to believe in a Scottish parliament, then the patterns in Table 9 could be explained by these attitudes to leadership capacity and to politicians' honesty rather than by attitudes to home rule.

The way to test this is to control for various other factors which predict the Conservative vote well, and then to see whether referendum intention continues to be associated with Conservative vote. Consider, for example, all those people who still believed that the Conservatives were capable of running a strong government. Of those in this group who recalled voting Conservative in 1992, 30 per cent intended to vote Yes on the first referendum question; of those who voted Conservative in 1997, 25 per cent intended to do so. Thus, even among those who continued to admire the Conservatives' capacity for firm leadership, intentions for the referendum seemed to influence their decision as to whether to remain with the Conservatives in 1997.

The more thorough way of doing this using many predictors of Conservative vote is, again, logistic regression. Account was taken of 31 factors which predict Conservative vote – attitudes to the record of the Conservative government on keeping their promises, standing up for Britain, and exercising strong government; to their record on crime, education, the health service, prices, standard of living, tax and unemployment; attitudes to John Major; beliefs as to whether Conservative MPs were more open to bribery than other MPs; general views about policies on poverty, private medicine, spending on the health service, education and defence; beliefs about whether workers should have more say in the running of industry and whether there should be redistribution of wealth; attitudes to Britain's membership of the European Union; attitudes to the effectiveness of British state institutions and to British cultural values;[26] general views on the moral standards of British public life; and general demographic variables (age, sex and social class). So this was a very strong set of controls. It was able accurately to predict 94 per cent of the decisions of the whole sample to vote or not vote for the Conservatives in 1997 (including 66 per cent of the decisions to vote Conservative); 76 per cent of those decisions among 1992 Conservative (including 79 per cent of the decisions to vote Conservative); and 84 per cent of those decisions among Conservative identifiers (including 91 per cent of the decisions to vote Conservative). And yet, for each of these predictions, intentions for the first referendum question remained as a further predictor of 1997 Conservative vote. For the analysis involving the whole sample (comparing Conservative voters with all other electors), referendum intention was a stronger predictor of Conservative vote than all others except views on the Conservatives' record in dealing with unemployment. For the analysis involving only 1992 Conservative voters, referendum intention was as strong a predictor of Conservative vote as a tendency to blame the Conservatives for a drop in the average standard of living, and was stronger than all other predictors. Among Conservative identifiers, referendum intention was a stronger predictor of Conservative vote than any other variable. In none of these analyses was the intention for the second referendum question influential on the Conservative vote over and above the effect of the intention on the first question.

So here we have a stringent test of the claim that the Conservatives lost votes because of their stance on the constitution. Even when we take account of all the other reasons why the Conservatives lost votes, we still find evidence that people were influenced in their attitude to the Conservatives by the party's attitudes to a Scottish parliament.

Table 10 *Conservative vote and constitutional preference, 1992 and 1997,among those who identified themselves as 'British more than Scottish' or 'British not Scottish'*

	1992 (per cent)	1997 (per cent)
Voted Conservative	53	19
Home rule	43	61
Independence	7	11
Unweighted N (=100 per cent)	58	67

Source: *1992 and 1997 Scottish Election Surveys.*

One of the reasons the Conservatives lost votes in this way was the point we have already noted about Britishness and attitudes to home rule. Blair and the Labour party seem to have persuaded people that being British was consistent with supporting a parliament. The implications of this for the Conservatives can be seen further if we look at the small group of people who rate their Britishness higher than their Scottishness. This came in response to a question which asked people to place themselves on a scale ranging from 'Scottish, not British' at one end to 'British, not Scottish' at the other. In between were 'Scottish more than British', 'Scottish equal to British' and 'British more than Scottish'. Just eight per cent of the sample chose to rate their Britishness ahead of their Scottishness, a similar proportion to the five per cent who did so in 1992. But, in 1992, this group had been very clearly sympathetic to the Conservatives, as Table 10 shows. They had also been at best sceptical about home rule (as evidenced by the general question about constitutional change). By 1997, the Conservative vote among them had collapsed to just 19 per cent, and the support for home rule had risen to 61 per cent. The continuing low level of support for independence among these people tends to confirm that we are seeing here evidence of a redefinition of Britishness. Asserting Britishness acquired a new political meaning between 1992 and 1997, no longer closely tied to voting Conservative or to being wary of a Scottish parliament.

Table 11 *Attachment to Conservative party and expectations of benefits from Scottish parliament*

	Number of benefits expected						
	0	1	2	3	4	5	Unweighted N (=100 per cent)
Recalls voting Conservative in 1992	44	19	12	10	11	6	159
Identifies with Conservatives	51	20	11	7	8	3	140
Voted Conservative in 1997	58	23	9	7	3	1	100

Source: *1997 Scottish Election Survey.*

Moreover, if the Conservatives lost the argument over the alleged threat which a parliament would pose to Britishness, they also lost the votes of people who did not believe their detailed case on the effects of a parliament. Table 11 shows the number of benefits which people expected from the parliament, separately for 1992 Conservatives, for Conservative identifiers, and for 1997 Conservatives. The Conservative arguments on this seemed to have had only a weak effect, even with their core support. Around one half of Conservative identifiers and previous supporters expected some benefits from the parliament, and just under one half of 1997 Conservative voters expected some benefits. Thus, when the British Conservative leader William Hague reacted on 12 September 1997 to the referendum result by claiming it was a 'sad day for Scotland', he was apparently not in tune with the people whom the Conservatives must win back if they are to recover their electoral position in Scotland.

Conclusion

We have argued three main points in this chapter. The first is that intentions for the referendum were shaped by the expectations which people had of what a parliament would do. The result in the referendum was decisive because most people expected clear welfare benefits, and because they expected higher taxes to be used to pay for these.

The second point is that intentions for the referendum were not shaped by social structure or identity, but by issues of welfare. The referendum vote was fairly uniform across all social classes, all age groups, and both sexes. It was not strongly influenced by national identity, probably because the Labour party and Tony Blair had successfully appealed to a sense of modernising Britishness as one reason for supporting change. Feeling Scottish was certainly one influence on voting in favour, but feeling British was not mainly a reason to vote against.

The third point is that the Conservative party lost votes in the general election because of its stance on the constitution. They lost the argument both with the electorate as a whole, and with people who generally thought of themselves as Conservative supporters. If they are to recover in Scotland, then they will have to find a way of working constructively with and in the new parliament, in order to exorcise the memories of their intransigence through their electoral debacle of the 1997 general election.

Notes

1 This chapter is reprinted from the special issue of *Scottish Affairs, Understanding Constitutional Change*, with kind permission of the authors and the editor.

2 The project was funded by the Economic and Social Research Council, grant number H552255004. The conclusions reported here were the same as when the analysis was repeated using data from the ESRC-funded Scottish Referendum Study, conducted by CREST (an ESRC Research Centre linking SCPR with Nuffield College, Oxford) mostly in September and October 1997. The main difference was that the small proportion (about four per cent) of people in the Election Study who intended to vote 'No-Yes' dropped to less than one per cent in the Referendum Study, to the benefit mainly of the 'No' category.

3 Fieldwork was carried out by Social and Community Planning Research, London. Further details of the study and the questionnaire items can be found on the internet at http://www.strath.ac.uk/Other/CREST. SCPR also carried out the fieldwork for the Scottish Referendum Study.

4 See J Brand, J Mitchell, and P Surridge, 'Identity and the Vote: Class and Nationality in Scotland', in D Denver, *et al.* (eds), *British Elections and Parties Yearbook 1993*, Hemel Hempstead: Harvester Wheatsheaf, 1993; J Brand, J Mitchell, and P Surridge, 'Social Constituency and Ideological Profile: Scottish Nationalism in the 1990s', *Political Studies*, Vol.42, 1994, pp.616-629; and A Brown, D McCrone, and L Paterson, *Politics and Society in Scotland*, London: Macmillan., 1996.

5 B Sarlvik and I Crewe, *Decade of Dealignment*, Cambridge: Cambridge University Press,1983.

6 A Downs, *An Economic Theory of Democracy*, New York: Harper,1957; Sarlvik and Crewe, *op. cit.*

7 Following D Kinder and D Kiewit, 'Sociotropic Politics: The American Case', *British Journal of Political Science*, Vol.11, 1981, pp.129-161.

8 Brand *et al., op. cit.*

9 Logistic regression is a technique which predicts the outcome of a dichotomous dependent variable – for example, voting yes or no – in terms of a collection of potential predictors. For further details, see M Aitkin, D Anderson, B Francis and J Hinde, *Statistical Modelling in Glim*, Oxford University Press, 1989.

10 D Butler and D Stokes, *Political Change in Britain*, London: Macmillan, 1969.

11 Crewe and Sarlvik, *op. cit.*; A Heath, R Jowell and J Curtice, *How Britain Votes*, Oxford: Pergamon, 1985; A Heath, R Jowell and J Curtice, 'Trendless Fluctuation: A Reply to Crewe', *Political Studies*, Vol.35, No.2, 1987 pp.256-277; and A Heath, R Jowell, J Curtice, G Evans, J Field and S Witherspoon, *Understanding Political Change*, Oxford: Pergamon,1991.

12 But see Brown *et al., op. cit.*, for a critique of this theory.

13 Heath *et al., op. cit.*

14 *Ibid.*

15 RJ Finlay, *A Partnership for Good? Scottish Politics and the Union Since 1880*, Edinburgh: John Donald ,1997.

16 P H Scott, *Cultural Independence*, Edinburgh: Scottish Centre for Economic and Social Research, 1989.

17 O D Edwards (ed.), *A Claim of Right for Scotland*, Edinburgh: Polygon, 1989.

18 E Gellner, *Nations and Nationalism*, Oxford: Blackwell, 1983; T Nairn, 'Tartan Power', in S Hall and M Jacques (eds), *New Times*, London: Lawrence and Wish art, 1989, pp.243-253; T Nairn, 'Sovereignty after the Election', *New Left Review*, No.224, July/ August 1997, pp.3-18.

19 A D Smith, *National Identity*, Harmondsworth: Penguin, 1991.

20 B Anderson, *Imagined Communities: Reflections on the Origins and Spread of Nationalism*, London: Verso, 1983.

21 J Kellas, *The Politics of Nationalism and Ethnicity*, London: Macmillan, 1991..

22 M Billig, *Banal Nationalism*, London: Sage, 1995.

23 Lang, I, 'Taking Stock of Taking Stock', speech to Conservative Party Conference, Bournemouth, 12 October 1994, reprinted in L Paterson (ed.), *A Diverse Assembly: The Debate on a Scottish Parliament*, Edinburgh: Edinburgh University Press, 1998.

24 Brown *et al., op. cit.*, ch.6.

25 P Jones, Labour's referendum plan: sell-out or act of faith?', *Scottish Affairs*, No.18, winter 1997, pp.1-17.

26 A Heath and B Taylor, 'British National Sentiment', paper presented at the annual conference of the Political Studies Association, Glasgow, April 1996; A Heath and J Kellas, 'Nationalisms and Constitutional Questions', in *Understanding Constitutional Change*, special issue of *Scottish Affairs*, 1998, pp.110-28.

After the 1997 Elections: A Regional Britain in a Regional Europe[1]

Kenneth O Morgan

I

It was a great privilege not only to attend Freudenstadt VII but also to be invited to offer some keynote thoughts. Throughout the 1990s, Freudenstadt and Chris Harvie in particular have acquired a legendary reputation, a kind of cross between the Köngiswinter conversations and the Elders of Zion. Freudenstadt, in association with the Welsh Studies Centre in the University of Tübingen and with its links with other important cultural and political institutions in the Land of Baden-Württemberg, has become a laboratory of ideas and an intellectual resource of rare potential. Chris himself, an old friend of nearly thirty years' standing (not that he does very much standing in his hyperactive life!), is a Caledonian colossus who bestrides the world from Tübingen to Talybont. He is also both remembrancer and prophet whose sheer intellectual range and idealism point the way ahead to a very different kind of national and world order. It was a pleasure to be in the bracing air of the Friedrich Ebert Stiftung in the mountains of the Black Forest once again, and to enjoy again the stimulation and sheer fun of the world as seen from Freudenstadt. It was also very timely that the seminar met when it did, at the end of June 1997, when Europe, and not merely the Celtic and other nations represented at Freudenstadt, was at the cusp of a new era.

Three circumstances made the timing of the conference especially appropriate. There was the British general election of 1 May with its colossal Labour majority under the leadership of

Eberhard Bort and Neil Evans (eds), *Networking Europe*, Liverpool University Press 2000, 417-28.

Tony Blair. There was the subsequent French general election with its scarcely less stunning victory for the French Socialists, a left government of a very different stamp. And there was the evidence of continuing movement and change within the European community, as there had been since Maastricht and indeed since the end of the Cold War, with the EU assuming a more coherent and purposive new role. Maastricht, after all, spelt out the need for 'an ever-closer union of the peoples of Europe' with EMU as only one step along that road. Perhaps one should add a fourth element of change, namely the very fascinating general election in Ireland. But while it meant a change of government from Fine Gael to Fianna Fáil (eventually – after its PR complexities had been worked out!), it may have done no more than ratify the extraordinary changes within the economy of a fully Europeanised Ireland which have been in train and have led to such immense growth over the past decade.

II

The British general election was an important event. It saw a record Labour majority of 179 over all other parties, and a total of 419 Labour members returned. It was a more massive landslide for the British left even than the Liberals' in 1906 or Labour's in 1945. The swing to Labour was immense all over Britain – up to 20 per cent even in the south-east and the London suburbs, but also resulting in no Tories being returned at all in any of the major cities, while Scotland and Wales also became Tory-free zones. It was the biggest defeat the Tories had suffered since the general election of 1832, when they were led by the Duke of Wellington (who promptly observed 'damn democracy' on hearing of the election returns). It has manifestly produced a great sense of optimism and national renewal in the United Kingdom. Throughout the 1990s, right through the dismal years of John Major, the British people were sunk in introspective gloom or, perhaps, cynicism. For the first time for decades, the many problems which have engulfed Britain since

1945 appear capable of solution. Even the economy, whose troubles brought down every Labour government in history from MacDonald in 1931 to Callaghan in 1979, now appears – at the time of writing – relatively stable. While Tokyo, Bangkok and Kuala Lumpur are 'blown off course', for the SS Great Britain it is steady as she goes.

Over the post-war decades, a number of deep-rooted problems have plagued the history of the British people. First, there has been a rigidity in our constitutional arrangements which is now quite inappropriate for the modern developed state, particularly one within the European Union. Our current constitutional settlement dates from the Glorious Revolution, so-called, of 1688-89, with variations in the reign of Queen Anne. This was all a very long time ago and, as we all know, Queen Anne is well and truly dead. Our constitutional arrangements since then have evolved or, perhaps, lurched along. The problems have been intensified by the fact that our constitution is unwritten, with no entrenchment and no bill of rights. It rests upon convention, and this is underpinned by a culture of concealment. The nature of our constitution emerged starkly during the Scott inquiry over the Arms to Iraq affair three years ago. It emerged that ministers' and civil servants' practices were governed by no rules – only 'guidelines'; and that there were guidelines to those guidelines, to be interpreted as casually as ministers wished. It was amateurism at its most cultivated, a regime of gentlemen not players, the apotheosis of Bertie Wooster.

The outcome of all this casualness and secrecy has been an unusually rigid centralisation. Indeed, Britain is one of the most centrally governed non-despotisms on earth. Victory in the Second World War virtually sealed the fate of ideas of constitutional reform or more open government. It was believed that a Whitehall and Westminster that had defeated Hitler must indeed, as Burke commented back in 1790, be a partnership in all art, all science and every perfection. Mrs Thatcher's alarming Bruges speech in 1988 harked back to the triumphalism of the Second World War. She used it to extol British sovereignty, narrowly defined, by conjuring up the image of Big Ben chiming out for liberty while Europe was under the sway of Fascists and collaborators.

The Labour Party began its history with a strong decentralising thrust – the municipal socialism variously upheld by Keir Hardie and the Webbs. It focused in the main on local government, especially in London and other cities, where Labour was powerful. But the neutering of local government in recent decades, especially with the rate-capping regime of Mrs Thatcher, has removed that safeguard and, in truth, Labour has since 1945 been largely a unionist party looking to a Whitehall whose gentlemen always know best. Local government has been undermined, while there has been no regional government worthy of the name. The Scottish Office and, even more, the Welsh Office have had strictly limited roles, which means that neither Scotland nor Wales has really punched its weight in public discourse in Britain this century. In distant times, a localism in government was thought to mitigate the excesses of a centralised British polity that dated from the Tudors, if not from the Norman Conquest. Alexis de Tocqueville saw this as a major reason why Britain did not have a revolution under the *Ancien Régime*. The landowners took part in local government in the shires whereas French society, from top to bottom, was rigidly governed by the Sun King at Versailles. This has long ceased to resemble reality. Indeed, today we have a situation where traditionally centralist countries like Spain and France have exciting developments in local and urban government, whereas Britain remains rigid and inert.

Second, Britain has long had problems with its role in the world. In 1945 it was part of the Big Three at Potsdam, an obvious member of the UN Security Council, secure in its alliance with the United States, its leadership of the Empire/Commonwealth and its head-ship of the sterling area. With Europe, under Labour and Tory governments alike, its relationship was elusive and erratic. In 1962, Dean Acheson famously observed that Britain had lost an empire and not yet found a role. His remark was uncomfortably true then and it remains true to a degree now. The Second World War made things worse with its images of Britain fighting alone, retreating from Dunkirk, defending its space in the Battle of Britain, bluebirds aloft over the white cliffs of Dover, while Europe collapsed in defeatism. Now, in 1997, let us hope, the Second World War can be put to rest. We have had the fiftieth anniversaries of VE and VJ Day, we have endless recapitulations in films of the Battle of Britain, sinking the Bismarck, launching the Dambusters, marching over the River Kwai. We had innumerable folksy (and often subtly xenophobic) evocations from 'Allo, Allo' to 'Dad's Army'. We have had the merry refrain of the subsequently knighted Sir Cliff Richard (Elton John *avant la lettre*) serenading the aged Queen Mother, herself a heroine of the blitz. The war of 1939-45 had glorious, imperishable features which those who remember it are still proud to recall. But it also did much psychological harm in the long term, in encouraging national isolationism and even xenophobia, especially towards the Germans. We need to say in 1997 loud and clear, 'The War is over'. It is the prophetic future, not a dead past, to which we should be looking.

The misconceptions about Britain's world role were perhaps expressed most clearly in a famous speech by a very gifted and compassionate socialist, Hugh Gaitskell's rebuttal of British entry into the EEC at the Labour Party annual conference of 1962. He evoked sentimental symbols of the Commonwealth – Vimy Ridge and Gallipoli. He declared, astonishing as it seems, that joining Europe would reduce Britain's role to that of Texas or California in the United States. 'A thousand years of history' would be cast asunder.

In fact, there are many signs that at long last the British people are coming to terms with their history. They do seem to recognise that the war is over. To younger people, like my own children born almost thirty years after VE Day and growing up in a multi-cultural European world, anti-European phobia seems old-fashioned and bizarre, as much so as the anti-Semitism and colour prejudice of two generations ago. In the 1997 election, British electors showed a great deal of maturity. They did not respond to crude Tory anti-German prejudice, such as cartoons showing a tiny Tony Blair ensconced on Chancellor Kohl's knee as a ventriloquist's dummy. Nor did they succumb to the anti-Teutonic phobia variously kindled by mad cow disease or penalty shoot-outs. For decades, first Labour and then the Tories had been resistant to the idea of Europe. Change first came under Labour in the period of the leadership of Neil Kinnock, a much underrated party leader who killed off the facile anti-Europeanism of the party in the Bennite heyday. It was a process reinforced by the TUC when they welcomed

Jacques Delors to Brighton in 1988 as 'Frère Jacques'. Under Tony Blair, whatever the timing of Britain's (to my mind inevitable) entry into EMU and a single currency, the United Kingdom is manifestly at the heart of Europe.

These two features of post-war Britain – over-centralisation and fear of Europe – were in many ways connected. They were also to some degree countered by a positive feature – solidarity. The social patriotism and communal partnership of the war were consolidated by a post-war consensus which studiously avoided extremism. Britain became a welfare democracy, created by Attlee's government, sustained by Churchill and a generation of one-nation Tories. Indeed, the role of the Conservative Party down to the 1970s and Heath's period in office should never be underestimated. But this solidarity was challenged by the third great problem of recent British history – Thatcherism. From 1979, the Tories deliberately sought to reverse the post-war consensus which it considered 'debilitating' and undermining national morale by creating a dependency culture. It challenged the solidarity of war-time society, indeed Thatcher herself famously declared that society did not in fact exist. This creed recreated what R H Tawney in the 1920s had called the 'religion of inequality'. It accentuated the centralisation of power by spreading a partisan and unaccountable quango-cracy throughout England and (especially) Wales. In place of collaboration with Europe (after all, mainly the work of Tories like Macmillan and Heath) it sought to invent English nationalism, embodied in the stereotype of *Sun*-reading, lager-toting, flag-waving Essex Man.

All this is now being completely changed, and not only by the advent of a Blair government with a huge majority (with further backing from the Liberal Democrats and the Nationalists of Scotland and Wales). There are signs that British public opinion is to the left of Blair and his colleagues. There were many pointers to this before the polls. There was the remarkable publishing success of Will Hutton's *The State We're In,* a plea for revived Keynesian social welfare and an updated civic republicanism. Another sign was the vivid attack on Thatcherite governmental practices written by the Tory, Simon Jenkins, *Accountable to None.* Together they attacked centralisation, personal and regional inequality and the decline of constructive citizenship. This kind of democratic current may sweep the victorious Labour Party, however cautious it may seek to be, in its wake.

III

The British general election raises the prospect of addressing the first two issues confronting our country – governmental centralisation and our external role. The Blair government is committed to constitutional reform. It is now putting into place fundamental changes to the way our country is run, in terms of accountability and subsidiarity, of a kind we have not experienced for centuries. The changes to date have not been earth-shaking. A Scottish parliament will be limited in its powers, and Wales will be given only an Assembly with no financial or legislative powers. But, in spite of all this, there is immense change under way. Devolution, after all, is a process, not a conclusion. The Scottish people endorsed their own Parliament massively on 11 September, both its existence and its tax powers. The Scottish referendum heralds the greatest constitutional transformation that Britain has known since the Union in 1707. Truly Scotland has been and will be miles better.

The Welsh on 18 September were far more cautious and the division within the Labour Party in south Wales plain for all to see. But even in Wales, the fact of some element of local power being endorsed for the first time in Welsh history is a pointer to a massive change. The swing from No to (just) Yes in Wales marked an immense change in popular opinion compared with 1979, indeed a bigger swing than that in Scotland. Once a Welsh Assembly comes into being in 1999, the new body, as in Scotland, will have a life and a collective personality of its own. It will want to act and to be effective. Indeed, the very closeness of the result in Wales may have advantages in that it may lead to the government making the new Assembly and its powers more intelligible and more attractive than they appeared in the half-hearted presentation in the run-up to the referendum. It may speed on a sense of Welsh citizenship of a kind familiar in Scotland, with the ecclesiastical, financial, legal and educational institutions it has retained over the past 250 years.

More widely, British central-local relations will now be looked at again – notably in Tyneside and Merseyside, as well as with the new civic autonomy for London and its new elective mayoralty. Regional government in varying degrees will surely follow in the different parts of England as well, and a more modern, appropriate form of economic decision-making and social policy-making will evolve as a result.

Britishness will be redefined, and excitingly so. The advent of the Blair government in 1997 makes all this possible, whereas the last devolution venture in 1979 was the product of a dying government offering an uninspiring package to a disillusioned nation at the end of its term of office. This time, constitutional reform is a dynamic first priority, not the last, to be swallowed up in the turmoil of a winter of discontent.

The Blair government is also committed to Europe in a way never previously known. After the pathetic shambles of the Major years, with a phantom premier and policy depending on random raving Europhobes in various forms of captivity, there is a clear commitment at all levels. The Amsterdam summit in May 1997 was incredibly different from all the Tory-attended summits when Europe always meant crisis, coded messages and evasion. There are limits, of course, to the kind of European involvement which a Blair government will embrace. There is still a national view of immigration controls or defence policy for instance. Personally, I agree with the government on this. A European defence policy would only make sense if there were a European foreign policy, and the total shambles of Bosnia – with the Germans, British and French all pursuing their own agendas, and countries like Belgium like candles in the wind – shows how far we are from a European foreign policy that has any substance. Yugoslavia is hardly an argument for any kind of European army. Also, I still believe that NATO has a role in the world, albeit a different one now that it is about to contain significant countries from Eastern Europe as well.

But Britain's relationship with Europe is surely at the dawn of a new age. The semifascist Europhobia of the Referendum Party and other splinter groups was crushed at the polls. The

UK has already signed the Social Chapter. It is dealing with the beef crisis through calm negotiation and scientific inquiry, not nationalistic declamation. It is striking that the first foreign politician that Tony Blair saw after his election was the important (and Anglophile) Dutch socialist leader, Wim Kok. Discussions with the EU henceforth will be governed by demonstrable national needs and growing conformity to the political and juridical framework of Europe. In this context, I do not expect even joining a single currency to be a long-term problem since the will is there, while foreign speculation against sterling appears to be a thing of the past.

IV

The third problem facing Britain, that of solidarity in the face of the Thatcherite challenge, I am not sure that Blair will address. His government has in many ways a conservative social agenda at home. For all his welcome endorsement of the public services, he has declared his support for the low-tax, financially restrictive policies of his predecessors, including limits to the welfare budget and curbs to the rights of the trade unions. Immediately after the election, he chose to see Lady Thatcher in Downing Street, not Jim Callaghan, his Labour predecessor. But there may be hope in another quarter. In its own elections later in May, France returned a Socialist government with a clear left-wing mandate. Its premier, Lionel Jospin, seems to have imposed himself over President Chirac in both domestic and European policy; indeed, Chirac's prestige at the time of writing is scarcely higher than that of the wretched John Major in Britain. European economic and monetary union is now being seen in a wider context, not just one dictated by the markets and by capitalist assumptions about the growth of the money supply and the pressures of inflation, but also by social considerations that include social welfare, fuller employment and the growth of the real economy, much indeed as Robin Cook urged in Britain during our election.

The French Socialists, after all, have emerged in a country which fully absorbs the developmental and social role of the state, not the market version popularised by Thatcher in the era of privatisation and monetarism. Solidarity is above all else a French word. State planning of the economy is of greater antiquity in France than in Britain: after all, public ownership of industry and of banking institutions dates from the Popular Front government of Léon Blum back in 1936, reinforced by the further Popular Front headed by de Gaulle and also including the Communists back in 1945-46. The relation between Jospin and Kohl is distinctly less cosy, with Kohl looking somewhat isolated in the newer configuration of the EU with its majority of centre-left or socialist governments. Kohl also looks less secure at home, too, though the Schröder-Lafontaine party drama to be played out this autumn and the SPD's ageless talent for snatching defeat from the jaws of victory going back to Kurt Schumacher in 1949, remain factors to be considered. Clearly, though, the new kind of social Europeanism in public discourse in France, Italy and elsewhere will impinge on Britain, too. The European Union is moving on beyond the narrow market-led vision that dominated Maastricht. It goes beyond social and political structures, hence the importance of Freudenstadt and the collaborative educational-cultural agenda it has embodied.

V

I conclude with a few words on higher education, which will loom large in our discussions. I do so with much diffidence. I ceased to be a Vice-Chancellor of the University of Wales on 30 September 1995, and there is no dodo so dead as a defunct Vice-Chancellor. But universities can have a major role in promoting the objectives that all of us in Freudenstadt have in mind, through their work in research, in exchanges between students and staff, and their role in regional economic and scientific development.

At Aberystwyth, I was anxious to give our university a distinct profile that would have international impact. We identified at least three areas of distinct specialism – agricultural and rural studies; information technology and computer science; and Celtic studies. As it happened, these three fitted together quite well, bringing together the economic base, the technological mechanism and the cultural heritage. Europe was a valuable resource for all of them. In Baden-Württemberg alone, we had valuable links with Stuttgart-Hohenheim in agricultural science, with Ulm in information science, and with Freiburg in Celtic studies. The Europeanness of our universities has been under-estimated in the past. I found it a great advantage to lead a deputation from a federal University of Wales to Brussels to meet Commissioners and others since, among other things, Wales represented a distinct territory with which people in European nations could identity. Of course, we also have our links with Baden-Württemberg, Catalonia, Lombardy and Rhones-Alpes through the valued 'Four Motors' scheme, which probably works better at the higher education rather than through the industrial level. The regime of John Redwood at the Welsh Office persistently and wilfully underplayed the European role of all the university institutions in Wales – and I include the University of Glamorgan as well here, and also the other important colleges in Welsh higher education.

Lively prospects are now opening up. The existence of elected Scottish and Welsh assemblies will mean a more dynamic role for our universities as energisers and megaphones of our community, and as central mechanisms in the lifelong processes of learning and training. The instructive document *Wales in Europe*, published by the Institute of Welsh Affairs, written by a distinguished diplomat and a respected journalist – Sir John Gray and John Osmond – contains valuable suggestions as to how this might be done within existing inter-European structures. The United Kingdom is no longer in any sense isolated in these key areas of education and training – indeed, the Blair government has given them the highest possible profile as the yardstick of its own success. In this and other ways, we are here in Europe as full partners – and as part of our own lifelong learning process as individuals and institutions, too. Ninety years ago, the University of Wales was hailed as a British paradigm of America's Wisconsin Idea, linking the separate spheres of politics and intellect. Maybe this is an idea whose time has finally come.

So we met at Freudenstadt on the verge of a remarkably exciting era, especially perhaps for those of us from Scotland and Wales. The interface between Europe, regional/nationalism and higher education (including such areas as Chris Harvie's special interest in cultural tourism) has never been more crucial. Events since the Freudenstadt colloquium, especially the referenda in Scotland and Wales in September 1997 and the continued calm competence of both the Blair and the Jospin administrations, have only confirmed these expectations. The future will see the United Kingdom blend, almost imperceptibly, into the framework of an increasingly regionalised Europe, the more so as the United States retreats into its own hemisphere and the tigers of the Pacific Rim face the problems of misdirected investment and half-development in a globalised system. Our civil wars and internal turmoils in western Europe are, or should be, over. As Tony Blair declared on the steps of Downing Street (without the rhetorical aid of St Francis of Assisi this time), we have done our talking. It is now our time to act, all of us.

Note

1 This paper, based on a presentation at the Freudenstadt Symposion of June 1997, was written on 1 October 1997.

The 1998 Belfast Agreement: Peace for a 'Troubled' Region?

Eberhard Bort

The End of a Beginning?

We still do not have, more than one year after the signing of the Good Friday Agreement of April 1998, a functioning government in Northern Ireland, as yet another ultimatum by the Irish and British governments failed to sort out, to the satisfaction of the Unionists, what is euphemistically called the decommissioning of arms by the paramilitary organisations.[1]

Whether this impasse will eventually be solved is far from clear. Obviously, the failure to implement an Executive in July 1999 was a serious set-back. The Unionists blocked the implementation by not signing up to "The Way Forward" document worked out by Tony Blair and Bertie Ahern, which stipulated the forming of a multi-party executive including Sinn Féin, on the promise, or guarantee even, that decommissioning of illegal weapons would commence immediately afterwards. Despite the fact that decommissioning is not a precondition in the Belfast Agreement, and despite the "fail-safe" guarantees (Sinn Féin would be kicked out of the Executive if decommissioning did not happen according to plan), David Trimble's Unionists could not bring themselves to sign up to the deal. The end of a beginning? Or just another set-back on the long road to a lasting peace settlement? The Agreement has been temporarily "parked" over the summer of 1999; it comes "under review" in September 1999.

Still, constructive attitudes are hoped to prevail. What has been achieved in the Peace Process so far is considerable, seen against the history of the 'Troubles'.[2] The parties involved –

Eberhard Bort and Neil Evans (eds), ***Networking Europe,*** **Liverpool University Press 2000, 429-61.**

David Trimble's Ulster Unionists, Sinn Féin, the SDLP, Alliance, as well as the so-called fringe parties and groups like the Women's Coalition – are bound to do the utmost they can do without alienating their followers to make the Agreement work.

Even the arch opponents of the Agreement, like Ian Paisley's Democratic Unionists (DUP) or the UK Unionists, have been seen partaking in the Assembly debates as if there was a possibility of their accepting the structures of the Agreement eventually.[3]

Yet, we must not forget that Northern Ireland, or the North of Ireland (depending on which side you're on; language and names are contested ground), is a deeply divided society:[4]

> "We still absolutely hate each other. We are in spectacular blind hatred. And I do think we have got the potential for another Yugoslavia. Never forget that. We really do have that potential..."[5]

When Irish playwright Frank McGuinness made the above statement in an interview in 1996 about the relationship between Catholics and Protestants, Nationalists and Unionists, Republicans and Loyalists in Northern Ireland (roughly, 40 per cent to 60 per cent, but the gap is narrowing), the first IRA ceasefire had blown up in the Canaray Wharf bomb in London of February and the Manchester bomb of May of that same year. Since then we have seen the reinstitution of the ceasefire in 1997, the inclusive talks which led to the Good Friday Agreement of 1998, the overwhelming endorsement by referenda in the North and South of Ireland of this agreement and the first elections to the Northern Ireland Assembly, changes in the Irish constitution concerning the "national territory",[6] as well as the Nobel Peace Prizes for John Hume and David Trimble in October 1998. But there have also been the frightful scenes of the marching season in Drumcree, the Lower Ormeau Road and elsewhere, punishment beatings, assassinations and the carnage of the Omagh bomb of August 1998.

After more than 3,200 deaths in 25 years, the bloody conflict between militant Irish Unionists and militant Irish Nationalists seemed exhausted, the people of Northern Ireland sick and tired of the sectarian violence. Rooted in the colonial history of Ireland

– the plantation of Protestant, mainly Presbyterian, settlers from Scotland in the north-eastern part of Ireland in the seventeenth century, giving them privileges guaranteed by the Crown over the native Catholic Irish – the dominance of Ulster Unionists in Ulster had led to the partition of Ireland in 1920. For fifty-odd years, a devolved parliament at Stormont – a Protestant state for a Protestant people, as much as De Valera's Ireland was a Catholic state for a Catholic people – had ruled in an openly discriminatory way. In the late 1960s, the Northern Irish Civil Rights Association took to the streets to demand equal (UK) citizenship. Those demands were met with brutality by Loyalist paramilitary forces. The IRA (Irish Republican Army) was revived, the British Army brought in in 1969. The scene was set for a quarter-century of bloodshed.

From Exclusion to Inclusion

There have been plenty of attempts at solving the conflict, after direct rule from London was introduced in 1972 – perhaps the most promising of these was Sunningdale in 1973/74: the establishment of a power-sharing executive involving Unionists and the moderate Nationalist SDLP. But the attempt was brought down by a massive Unionist workers' strike, and a weak British government caving in.[7]

The New Ireland Forum in 1983 devised perspectives which pointed in the direction of the three-stranded approach of the 1998 Belfast Agreement, but as – again – some of the main players (Unionists, Sinn Féin) were not included, and Margaret Thatcher eventually vetoed those perspectives, this approach was seen as yet another failure. A first break-through came with the Anglo-Irish Agreement (Hillsborough Agreement) of November 1985, which – negotiated between London and Dublin over the heads of the Northern Irish political players – gave the South, for the first time, a limited consultative role in the affairs of the minority in Northern Ireland.[8] Still, it was no solution, and did not bring about peace. The Brooke talks of the early 1990s were inconclusive, but can now be seen as having done important groundwork for the negotiations to come.

The crux of all of these approaches had been that major groups of the conflict were either excluded or had excluded themselves from the negotiations seeking a solution. But it is a truism that you have to make peace with your enemies, even if it involves an Irish president or a British prime minister shaking hands with Gerry Adams.

Perhaps the key to inclusive talks was the SDLP leader John Hume's persistence, and eventual success, in convincing Sinn Féin that Irish self-determination would have to be exercised by the peoples of North and South simultaneously but separately, rather than in a single decision by a simple majority of the Irish people.[9]

Sinn Féin's acceptance, *de facto*, of the existence of Northern Ireland as a basis for democratic decision-making opened the way for the Downing Street Declaration of December 1993 and the Framework Document of February 1995. As Niall O'Dowd observed with hindsight:

> ... inclusive dialogue is the only way to resolve our most pressing problem. The failed initiatives of the past quarter-century in Northern Ireland all deliberately excluded the extremes from the negotiations, thereby only exacerbating their sense of isolation.[10]

The Belfast Agreement: "A long Night's Journey into Day"

The inclusive talks process culminated in Easter Week 1998 in all-night negotiations at Stormont, dubbed by the *Independent* as "a long day's journey into day."[11] The result was what Brendan O'Leary has defined as a "consociational agreement",[12] fulfilling all the criteria which the inventor of that term, Arend Ljiphart, postulated:

- cross-community executive power-sharing;
- proportionality rules applied throughout the relevant governmental and public sectors;
- community self-government (or autonomy) and equality in cultural life; and
- veto rights for minorities.[13]

To address the complex question of double minorities[14] (Catholics in the North; Protestants in the island of Ireland), the Agreement employs a three-stranded approach:

(I) Internal Northern Irish Dimension

- A 108-seat Assembly is democratically elected (proportional representation, single transferable vote), with legislative and executive authority, covering the remit of the six departments of the Northern Ireland Office, with power-sharing guarantees, operating where appropriate on a cross-community basis. Key-decisions needing cross-community support are designated in advance, including the election of the Chair of the Assembly, the election of the First and Deputy First Ministers (David Trimble and Seamus Mallon), the standing orders and budget allocations. A committee structure is to link the Assembly to the portfolios of the executive, but also to groups within civil society. Chairs and Deputy Chairs of committees are to be allocated proportionally; and membership in committees is to broadly reflect party strength. The First and Deputy First Ministers are to form an Executive of up to 10 Ministers, again reflecting the strength of those parties which have signed up to the Agreement.

(II) North-South Dimension

- A North-South Ministerial Council for joint policy-making, consultation, co-operation and action is to meet in plenary format twice a year, with representation at top level (Taoiseach, Tanáiste; First and Deputy First Ministers), and at ministerial and administrative levels. Again, these bodies have been agreed since 18 December 1998, but full implementation can only happen when the Northern executive is being formed.

(III) British-Irish Dimension

- A British-Irish Council (or Council of the Isles), consisting of representatives of the devolved governments in Belfast, Edinburgh and Cardiff, as well as the governments of Dublin and London, is to meet twice a year at summit level, and also frequently at ministerial level, with a remit of information, consultation and discussion, particularly in the areas of transport links, agriculture, environmental issues, health, education, and European Union matters. Preliminary meetings have already taken place but, again, the Council can only be properly set up when Scotland and Wales have voted (6 May 1999) and the devolved parliaments and assemblies have established their executives.

In two ways is the Good Friday Agreement an interesting, if not even a revolutionary document. It enshrines the principle of consent and thus gives the people, rather than the 'Crown in Parliament' (i.e. Westminster) ultimate sovereignty. Geraldine Kennedy – slightly incorrect, as she neglects the intricacies of the Scottish situation *vis à vis* England[15] – expressed it thus:

> The principle of consent is revolutionary in British constitutional terms. Northern Ireland will have a unique status within the United Kingdom because, for the first time, the people, rather than the Parliament, will be sovereign and supreme.[16]

Bob Purdie, writing in the *Irish Times* just before the referenda in May 1998, was delighted:

> The old conception of sovereignty, developed by A V Dicey, has now been abandoned, and a good thing too. (...) If the Irish referendums back the Agreement, we will

> enter a new constitutional era in which all of us in these islands can arrange our relations sensibly, and change them when it suits us. Sovereignty will no longer be thought of as a mystical essence, kept in a gilt box under the Speaker's chair at Westminster, or Leinster House, but as the legitimate authority exercised by governments with the consent of the governed. We will exchange Dicey for democracy.[17]

Multiple Identities: "Irish or British or Both"

The other, eminently important passage in the Agreement is that the signatories of the Agreement "recognise the birthright of all the people of Northern Ireland to identify themselves and be accepted as Irish or British or both, as they may so choose..."[18]

This means, as Fintan O'Toole analysed, "that it is people who identify themselves, not governments or tribes who tell them who they are. That nationality is a matter of choice, not an inescapable destiny."[19]

"Even more extraordinarily," he continues:

> saying who you are is not necessarily a matter of either/or but can also be both/and. Has it ever happened before that two sovereign governments and a range of political parties involved in a bloody conflict have stated such radical things so clearly?[20]

Nationality and citizenship are, according to Paul Gillespie, "central issues in the endgame of the Northern Ireland peace process:"

> Contested between nationalists and unionists as to whether they derive from identification with Ireland or Britain, nationality and citizenship are thereby assumed to be not only interchangeable but indivisible as well.[21]

The Agreement opens ways for overcoming this situation so that both nationality and citizenship would no longer be "assumed to be based on exclusivist, zero-sum premises."[22]

Downing Street Declaration, Framework Document, and the Belfast Agreement show in their wording the influence of John Hume, who has always proclaimed that "it is the people of Ireland who are divided and not the territory" and that "they can only be brought together by agreement, not by any form of coercion."[23] Expounding the Framework Document in the Dáil, John Bruton echoed Hume when he hailed the document as "the beginning of work towards a wholly new form of expression of traditional aspirations, focusing on individuals and communities rather than on territory."[24]

Following this line of argument, the Agreement points in the direction of putting "people before territory, by accepting the principle that no human being has a right to rule another against his or her will, and that the nation does not claim to rule over any person in Ireland who does not wish to belong to it."[25]

In this context, it is important to point out that the Agreement is not a singular Irish achievement; it is embedded in changes in international relations and what Gillespie calls "new mental maps", re-examining received assumptions about nationality, citizenship and sovereignty.

Looking at the changing constitutional parameters, particularly the internationalisation of the Northern Ireland question, the political analyst Paul Arthur has argued that

> Wilsonian national self-determination has seen its day. In its place, interdependency offered a new way forward. "People" rather than "territory", "means" rather than "ends" – these were to be the beacons for the way ahead.[26]

The last few centuries have seen nation and state-building proceeding in line, "combining to make these categories, along with cultural essentialism, the hallmarks of national identity."

Allegiance to the territorial nation-state, bound by the ties of nationalism, dominated the agenda,

> whether of the imperial top-down variety we are so familiar with in Britain and the North, or the separatist

> anti-imperialist nationalism driven by the need to escape from that power system but defined nevertheless in relationship with it – Ireland as "not-Britain".[27]

In its classical period, nationalism demanded "exclusive citizenship, border control, linguistic conformity, political obedience and loyalty. Nationality and citizenship became legally and conceptually conflated and inseparably identified with territory."

But, Gillespie argues further,

> these categories, which we take so much for granted in nation-state parlance, are becoming increasingly unbundled in line with greater economic and political interdependence among the most developed states, especially in Europe, and by the effects of economic globalisation in a worldwide setting.[28]

These changes are eroding territorial boundaries and moral imperatives:

> They open up space for multiple allegiances and affiliations outside and beyond the nation-state, giving way to a more contingent set of identities ranging through local, regional, national to supranational and even global dimensions.[29]

This is not an uncontested process: "on the contrary, some of the most profound conflicts in today's world pit defenders of singular identities against proponents of multiple ones." Yet,

> international trends favour the emergence of new forms of thought and behaviour – and therefore new forms of political community. In the European setting, for example, multiple identities can be arranged in a hierarchy or circle, some weaker, some stronger, but complementary, not antagonistic. The same can apply to a new kind of citizenship that is neither national nor cosmopolitan but multiple, expressed through pan-national institutions and protected by international rights

> and courts. Thus it is quite possible to imagine a separation of nationality and citizenship and of both from an exclusively territorial definition. It cannot be assumed any more that the national encompasses total identity and belonging.[30]

Multiple, and not mutually exclusive, identities offer, in the context of Northern Ireland, a possible solution to the zero-sum numbers game of territorial politics. Dual loyalty, nationality, citizenship – even dual sovereignty – might provide a new framework for rights and obligations.

And Kearney, champion of a federal Europe of regions – postmodern, post-nationalist and post-sovereign – contends that "the most likely model of regional democracy to succeeded in Ireland, at the present historical juncture, is one brought about within the context of an integrated Europe of equal regions":[31]

> The emerging Europe has a unique opportunity to be truly democratic by fostering notions of sovereignty that are inclusive rather than absolute, shared rather than insular, disseminated rather than closed in upon some bureaucratic centre. Northern Ireland could be a testing ground.[32]

Furthermore, Unionists have, at long last, begun to understand that the Republic has come to accept the principle of consent "as part and parcel of wider changes in identity that go well beyond classical essentialist Catholic nationalism." Nationalists have reluctantly begun to recognise that Britain's identity is changing fast, both in the ongoing process of devolution and decentralisation (Scottish Parliament, Welsh Assembly, elected mayor and authority for London) and under the challenges of European integration. These learning processes raise hopes for an agreement, which is politically dynamic, interpreted by Unionists as securing and safeguarding the Union, and by Nationalists as a stepping stone on the path to a united Ireland.

The Underpinnings of the Agreement

As Fintan O'Toole has pointed out, the Peace Process and the Belfast Agreement have been the result of long-term "fundamental shifts".[33] He argues that the violent conflict of the past thirty years had the paradoxical effect "to give an illusion of continuity to a period of profound change."[34]

What he calls "the epic language of immemorial and irreconcilable divisions" often employed in the discourse about the North "has hidden the fact that many of the assumptions that held good in 1968 when the killing began simply no longer apply:"

> In 1922, when the last attempt at a comprehensive settlement between Ireland and Britain was being debated in the Commons, Winston Churchill famously contrasted the profound changes in Europe after the first World War with the obstinate constancy of religious divisions in Northern Ireland.
>
> Everything else had undergone "violent and tremendous changes in the deluge of the world. But as the deluge subsides and the waters fall short we see the dreary steeples of Fermanagh and Tyrone emerging once again. The integrity of their quarrel is one of the few institutions that has been unaltered in the cataclysm which has swept the world."
>
> Now, as the flood of violence that has washed over Northern Ireland begins to recede, the dreary steeples of sectarian division between British Protestants and Irish Catholics are still the most prominent features on the landscape.
>
> But beneath them, at ground level, almost everything has changed. Only because the quarrel was conducted with such ferocity was it so hard to notice how pointless it was and how rapidly some of its basic assumptions were being dissolved.[35]

It may have been possible, among other matrixes of explanation, to see the Northern Ireland conflict at its beginning in the 1960s as a "clash of civilisations" between "Irish Catholic nationalism and Protestant British unionism." Yet O'Toole immediately seeks distance from the Huntingtonian term: "The categories were, of course, crude. Ordinary lives and attitudes were much more complex than political or religious labels would allow."[36]

Undoubtedly, the differences between Catholics and Protestants in Ireland were more pronounced in the 1960s. Southern Ireland was still, by and large, a rural and agricultural society, while the Northern Protestants saw themselves as part of an urban and industrial landscape.

> In everyday life, the terms "Irish" and "British" were shorthand for a great deal more than national identity. You could use them to guess with reasonable accuracy what kind of work someone did, whether they used contraceptives (and therefore how many children they had) and what sort of sports they played. Yet, even while the conflict was grinding on, those guesses were becoming, year by year, more inaccurate.[37]

It may well have made some sense, 30 years ago, for Northern Protestants to see themselves as part of a modern, prosperous, "British" economy and the Republic of Ireland, by contrast, as an underdeveloped backwater:

> Even in the early 1970s, gross domestic product per head of population in the Republic was just half what it was in the United Kingdom. And implicit in the contrast was a belief that this was not coincidental. As the Protestants tended to see it, the Irish were poor because they were Catholic. They were, in the Protestant imagination, priest-ridden peasants.[38]

By the mid-1990s, the Republic of Ireland – the "Celtic Tiger" – had overtaken the UK in terms of GDP per capita; it has become a much more urban society; and the political power of the Catholic church has suffered irreparable blows from a series of scandals, from paedophile priests to the Bishop Casey affair of 1992. One clear sign was the success – albeit narrowly – of the referendum on the introduction of divorce in November 1995.

Generally speaking, the differences in social life between Protestants and Catholics has been levelled.

> Irish Catholics, on the whole, take neither their morality nor their politics from their clergy. They use contraceptives and have the same number of children as Protestants. While all of this was going on, the world Irish Protestants knew 30 years ago was disappearing. The North's once mighty heavy industries were becoming obsolete. The shipyards and engineering works that were still the pride of Protestant Belfast in 1968 have long since dwindled.[39]

With the turn-around from an emigrant to an immigrant society, Ireland increasingly sees itself – particularly in the urban areas of Dublin, Cork or Galway, on the threshold of becoming a post-modern, multi-ethnic and multi-cultural society, much more in the Western European mainstream than one or two generations ago. Moreover, the very fundament of Irish nationalism and Irish unionism – in the sense that those words have been used for most of this century – has been eroded:

> Nationalism has been so radically transformed as to be unrecognisable. The Irish nation, in the new Article 2 of the Constitution, is something to which people have a right, but not a duty, to belong. The whole way of thinking that came out of 19th century nationalism, in which the nation had sacred claims on its people, has been reversed.
>
> Now, it is the people who have claims on the nation. Those born on the island have an "entitlement and birthright" to be "part of the Irish nation". But the nation is not entitled to demand their allegiance. The right to belong clearly contains a right not to belong.
>
> By extension, the traditional demand for a united Ireland has been turned into something utterly different from what either Collins or de Valera ever imagined. The new Article 3, by writing in the principle of consent, effectively recognises the legitimacy of Northern Ireland's present place in the United Kingdom.

> At the same time, the eventual united Ireland that it envisages is not what it used to be either. The aspiration now is not towards a monolithic political structure, but to a unity of people "in all the diversity of their identities and traditions".
>
> By definition, a united Ireland that might eventually meet this aspiration would be a complex set of political arrangements, not a centralised nation state in the old sense. Whatever else we want to call that aspiration, nationalism is no longer the right word for it.[40]

The case of traditional Unionism may appear less obvious. Unionists, after all, can say with a great deal of justification that their right to remain within the UK has been accepted and secured. But

> the meaning of that right has been altered forever. From now on it can be exercised only in the context of a much wider set of relationships with Northern Catholics, with the Republic, and with an increasingly decentralised Britain.
>
> Even more profoundly, unionism is clearly no longer the political ideology of a unified Protestant community. It is undoubtedly true that the vast majority of Protestants will continue to regard themselves as British, to oppose a united Ireland, and to vote for parties that do likewise. But the cleavage between David Trimble and Ian Paisley is now so fundamental that it makes little sense to talk of them as belonging to the same broad political movement. And the essence of unionism has long been the idea not just of uniting Northern Ireland to Britain but of uniting Protestants to each other.[41]

The conflict has had a tendency to obscure the internal divisions within Protestantism. After all, there is no monolithic Protestant Church in Northern Ireland, but a plethora of church affiliations – Church of Ireland, Methodist, Presbyterian, Reformed Presbyterian, Free Presbyterian, Evangelical Presbyterian, Independent Evangelical, Baptist, Brethren, Independent Charismatic Fellowship, Independent Pentecostal, Elim, Moravian, Church of

God, Assemblies of God – and, of course, atheists and agnostics who were brought up in one or other of those churches and who might see themselves as part of a broadly defined Protestant culture.

> When people talk about "the religious divide" in Northern Ireland, they are almost never referring to this split within Protestantism. But the divide is there and it relates to other cleavages between city and country, and between rich and poor.
>
> One of the many ironies of the IRA's terror campaign is that it almost certainly pushed Protestants together and helped to conceal the fissures within their culture. With the waning of violence, those cracks are appearing again. The more obvious they become, the clearer it will be that unionism as a monolithic, unifying ideology is dead.[42]

Across the Irish Sea, British identity has been no more stable than Irish identity. In the 1960s, it may have still been possible to imagine Britain as an imperial power. The symbols valued by Northern Irish Protestants – the monarchy, the Empire, the United Kingdom – have, by now, definitely lost their glamour: "After the scandals that culminated in Princess Diana's death, the royal family seems more a source of confusion than a guarantor of eternal stability."[43] Britain's overseas empire has further shrivelled (the latest 'loss' was Hongkong), and the devolution process set in train by the Labour landslide victory in Britain on 1 May 1997 has begun to change the constitutional face of the United Kingdom, and may even lead to an independent Scotland, conjuring up the spectre of the 'break-up of Britain'.[44]

Fundamental changes are under way concerning British identity (or identities). At a conference, "Expanding Nation: towards a multiethnic Ireland" in Trinity College Dublin in September 1998, Prof Tariq Modood of the University of Bristol said a major difference had been found between the attitudes of different minority groups in Britain to religion.[45] It was an important part of the self-definition of South Asians, while for Afro-Caribbeans, skin colour was dominant.

A recent survey of aspects of minority cultures and identities there found that an attachment to an ethnic identity did not necessarily conflict with a sense of Britishness. Nor did a strong attachment to ethnic, cultural, family and religious values mean people felt less British, he said.

The survey showed that ethnicity was coming to mean new things. There was a decline in distinctive cultural practices across the generations. The younger people were less likely to speak a South Asian language, attend a place of worship or have an arranged marriage. Nonetheless, they had a strong association with an ethnic identity, which for some was associated with a Muslim identity, even if they did not practise the religion. "The Muslim religion has become ethnicised."[46]

The general trend in Britain has been away from cultural distinctness and towards cultural mixture and intermarriage. Half of all Caribbean men, one-third of Caribbean women and one-fifth of South Asian men had white partners, while only very few South Asian women had white partners. One parent of 40 per cent of Caribbean children living with two parents was white.

This has changed the whole definition of Britishness:

> While Pakistanis in Bradford have come to see themselves as British, it is the Irish and Scottish who have difficulty with it. There is a desire for hyphenated Britishness among immigrants and their descendants, while there is a growing multi-cultural notion of Britishness from the white majority.[47]

Yet, for a long time, both sides in the conflict in Northern Ireland pretended that all of this change was not happening. Imagining the South as "an impoverished backwater" and Britain as "a mighty imperial power" did, in Fintan O'Toole's acid phrase, "lend an aura of pseudo-epic grandeur to squalid, intimate cruelties:"

> The Protestant policeman murdered in front of his children wasn't just a soft target for sectarian hatred. He was the representative of a mighty empire. The Catholic shop-keeper murdered behind his counter wasn't just a

> victim of venomous bigotry. He was an enemy of Her Britannic Majesty.
>
> Violent division has the strange effect of making people imagine their enemies, unlike themselves, are powerful and unchanging. Catholics and Protestants could each see that their own community was in flux. Neither could see that what was happening to themselves was also happening to the other side.
>
> One of the wry ironies of Northern Ireland, indeed, is that social surveys consistently show both Protestants and Catholics believe (a) their own side is divided and incoherent and (b) the other side is an impressively unified monolith. Both, of course, were right about themselves and wrong about the others.[48]

The Belfast Agreement is the first serious approach accepting that change has happened, on both sides, opening up opportunities to overcome entrenched prejudices:

> It is an attempt to catch up with what we all know in our ordinary lives – that "Irish" and "British" are no longer fixed terms, but open invitations. In the aftermath of empire, on the morning after the long night of ethnic purity, each of us can choose to accept one or the other. Or, preferably, both.[49]

For the first time, the word 'compromise' seems to have lost some of its odious taste. Both sides have given up something by signing the Agreement.: Nationalists their immediate claim to a united Ireland; Unionists their understanding of 'majority rules OK'. Both have gained something in return: "Nationalists have endorsed this Agreement because it gives them equality now with the possibility of Irish unification later."[50] The Unionists get self-government back from London, have a chance of "persuading northern nationalists that the new reconstructed Union offers a secure home for them",[51] and have, by agreeing to the mutual guarantee of minority rights, secured their own potential status as a minority in a future united Ireland, should that become the accepted option of a majority in the North.

Re-building the Northern Economy

But, constitutional and cross-community cultural questions apart, the Peace Process will not succeed, if economic questions are not successfully addressed.

A narrow Marxist analysis of the Northern Ireland conflict was never fully satisfactory, because of the importance of the cultural divide. But any analysis omitting the underlying economic questions of poverty, unemployment an unequal social services also falls short of a valid explanation. Declan Kiberd went so far as to state that:

> the problems of the North are largely to do with the economic exploitation and oppression of a minority which happened to be both Catholic and nationalist.[52]

He sees fifty-odd years of the "denial of economic rights to a minority" having led to a "rebellion by people who feel economically humiliated."[53]

There is enough truth in this analysis to suggest that economic recovery and job-creation play a key-role in the Peace Process. The basis from where to re-build the Northern economy is not promising: "In the 30 years that have ... elapsed the North's economy has atrophied, deprived of the chance to modernise by the appalling violence of the intervening years:"

> Today its degree of dependence on subsidies approaches that of East Germany and the Mezzogiorno in Italy.
>
> As a result, its public sector now accounts for 55 per cent of regional GDP as compared to 40 per cent in the UK, and the proportion at work in that sector is over 50 per cent greater than in the UK.[54]

Former Irish Taoiseach FitzGerald is a strong advocate for assisting economic recovery in the North, in order to give the so-called Peace Dividend a tangible basis:

> Turning around such an economy so that it becomes viable is a huge task, which will need not merely the

> support of the UK but also every assistance we in this State can provide. generous support for a Northern economic recovery should now become a key element in our national strategy.[55]

The European Union's response to the 1994 ceasefires has been the Delors Package or, to give it its proper name, the Fund for Peace and Reconciliation in Northern Ireland, worth £400 million in its first five years; and it is now to be replaced, after Northern Ireland's loss of Objective 1 status (for EU structural funds) by another £400 million package, again over five years, for the six counties of the North and the six border counties of the South.[56]

By December 1997, over 14,000 groups had applied for financial support from the EU coffers; some 7,000 had received grants: a clear sign, in former Regional EU Commissioner Wulf-Mathies's words, of "peace-making from the bottom up", centring on the empowerment of communities and what Inez McCormack has called "the new civic dialogue", and thus complementing the negotiation process on the political level.[57] Most importantly, the money which has gone to cross-community partnerships has meant that people from across the divide had to closely co-operate in the planning of projects for their local communities, which encouraged Monika Wulf-Mathies to sum up: "We must now take risk for peace by trusting communities to take responsibility to make decisions for themselves, and it is working."[58]

The International Fund for Ireland, set up after the Anglo-Irish Agreement in 1986 has, according to a report by the management consultants KPMG,

> made a major contribution to the development of an economic and cross-community dynamic which has had an important role in underpinning the peace process.[59]

In the past twelve years, the fund has supported some 3,600 projects with a total of almost £314 million – 75 per cent of which went to the six counties of the North; and 25 per cent to the six Border counties of the Republic.

The area where a peace dividend has been most clearly seen is tourism. Since 1996, the Northern Ireland Tourist Board and Bord Fáilte (the Southern tourist authority) have been closely co-operating. Interest in Northern Ireland has soared since the ceasefires. In 1995, the year following the first IRA ceasefire, the number of tourists was up by about 60 per cent, compared to the previous year.[60]

This increased influx of tourists is bound to have an effect on the people of Northern Ireland who, for a long time during the 'Troubles', had felt cut off. Intensified contacts, it may assumed, will have, apart from its economic benefits and its impact on job creation, an overall positive effect on the psyche and outlook of the Northern Irish of both communities.

Although it would be naive to advertise it as a model for universal usage – the specific Irish-British circumstances have to be observed – the Belfast Agreement might serve as an example of how ethnic conflicts can be resolved, as suggested by the Irish Taoiseach Bertie Ahern: "The Agreement pushes out the frontiers of democracy, and provides a model of potential interest and inspiration to divided communities in other countries."[61] Paul Gillespie, when travelling through East-Central Europe at the beginning of 1999, noticed keen interest in places like Budapest and Prague in the implications of the British-Irish Good Friday Agreement. Conor O'Clery even noted that

> The fact that a model of conflict resolution had been worked out in Belfast which did not remove Northern Ireland from the United Kingdom meant that it could be presented to the Chinese as an example which did not threaten Chinese unity if applied to Tibet.[62]

And Gerry Adams found himself in the role of a peace envoy to the Basque country, where political groups have appealed to the Madrid government to take the talks process in Northern Ireland as a cue to start negotiations about ending the conflict in the Basque Country.[63]

From "A Protestant State for a Protestant People" to "A Pluralist Assembly for a Pluralist People"

Making peace can be an arduous task. "Peace comes dripping slow," wrote William Butler Yeats; and Tony Kennedy spoke of the "unglamorous business of peace-making".[64] It has been a Peace Process which has largely been top-down, an international, concentrated effort involving the British, Irish and American governments as well as the European Union. The main contribution from "the people" was their exhaustion, and their cautious, often mistrusting welcome of the decline, if not yet end, of the atrocities: "... after nearly 30 years of a dirty war which ended in stalemate, people in the North were ready for peace."[65]

Many an initiative from below has foundered, defeated by internal strife, or simply petered out. Yet one should not underestimate the long-term, undercurrent influence of movements like the Peace People[66] and their legacy of Peace Camps and cross-community groups. The 'All Children Together Movement' of the early 1980s, having founded the first comprehensive all-denominational school in the North in 1981,[67] triggered off a series of such schools, at all levels.[68] Still, the major impulses have come predominantly from the politicians, in Ireland and abroad, not so much from a popular, grassroots movement. That may be regretted. But it is one of the realities this process has to live with. There are others.

Northern Ireland, after 30 years of the 'Troubles', is a more segregated, more polarised, and more embittered society than it was before 1969. The psychological and emotional gaps between the communities have widened over this period. 'Building bridges' – Irish President Mary MacAleese's motto for her presidency – will take time.[69] "These bridges," she said in her inaugural address on 11 November 1997, "require no engineering skills but they will demand patience, imagination and courage."[70]

Courage in the sense that you must make peace with your enemies – it is unpleasant to have to deal with ex-terrorists "who seem to expect gratitude for their generous decision to refrain from killing their neighbours."[71] And, it is tough "to have to guarantee 'parity of esteem' to two traditions that, as Edna Longley once put it, really deserve 'parity of disesteem'".[72] Moreover, it is hard on the victims of terror and their families to see prisoners walk free before their time, often adopting a triumphant mode.[73]

O'Toole sums up the unpleasantness of the whole process: "You wouldn't want to have to create an incredibly complex set of institutional structures just to induce a minimum of trust between the parties. (...) But those are not choices anyone on the island really has.[74]

That these unpleasant challenges are now being met, might well be the central message of the Belfast Agreement: "It's not about what anyone wants, more about what everyone has to live with."[75] And the realistic perspective of its outcome is not heavenly harmony or a sudden outbreak of cross-community happy relations. Seamus Heaney expressed it thus:

> If a North-South Council and an assembly at Stormont acceptable to all can be established, the minority will finally escape from a state where their "Ulsterness" was a "Britishness" forced upon them and become instead a shared attribute. Ulster will remain a site of contention, politically and culturally, but at least the contenders will have assented to play on the same pitch and by agreed rules.[76]

The Assembly Elections

The May 1998 elections to the Northern Irish Assembly did not give the anti-Agreement parties a blocking-minority (30 seats), which meant that the Agreement had passed its first test. The workings of the Assembly have certainly added to an increased sense of political normality in Northern Ireland since. If an Executive were to be formed, the implementation bodies and Council of the Isles could immediately be set up.

Table 1 *Results of the May 1998 Northern Ireland Assembly Elections*

Party	First Preference Vote (%)	Seats	Claim to seats in Executive*
Ulster Unionist Party UUP	21.0	28	4
Democratic Unionist Party (DUP	18.0	20	—
Social Democratic and Labour Party (SDLP)	22.0	24	3
Sinn Féin	17.7	18	2
Alliance	6.4	6	1
Progressive Unionist Party (PUP)	2.5	2	—
Ulster Democratic Party (UDP)	1.2	—	—
United Kingdom Unionist Party (UKUP)	4.5	5	—
Other 'No' Unionists	3.0	3	—
Woman's Coalition	1.7	2	—

*** DUP and UKUP have not signed up to the Good Friday Agreement and are therefore not entitled to seats on the Executive.**

The results of the first Assembly elections are given in Table 1. According to their number of seats, Sinn Féin may lay claim to two ministerial posts in the Executive. Yet, whether this will come to pass, depends – as already pointed out – on whether or not the impasse over decommissioning of paramilitary weapons can be resolved.

Even if the Belfast Agreement is to implemented, the Peace Process will not transform Northern Irish society over night. Fintan O'Toole coated his hopes in the following cautious tones:

> The best that anyone can hope is that sectarianism will become something like it is in Glasgow now, a latent animosity that is mostly expressed in ritual combat between two soccer teams. With political normalcy and relative economic prosperity, Glasgow has not banished the old demons, but it has at least managed to propitiate them with sacrificial offerings that stop them from wreaking too much harm.
>
> What the Agreement does offer, then, is not a chance to transform reality but an opportunity to acknowledge it. People on both sides of the Border will not suddenly wake up in Utopia but in Ireland.
>
> But it will be an Ireland that will have done what it has perhaps never done before — owned up fully to what it is: a complex, contradictory place, a place that doesn't have a history or a people, but histories and peoples, a place that could only be simple or pure after massive bloodletting, and perhaps not even then.[77]

The whole experience leading to the Belfast Agreement showed that things could move once people began to think the unthinkable, Prof Mari Fitzduff of the Institute for Conflict Resolution and Ethnicity in Derry, has argued. The Belfast Agreement, she said, put forward the ideals of equality, diversity and interdependence, which could provide the framework for a multi-ethnic society; the Agreement thus represented a move away from simple definitions of identity.

To measure the distance that has been travelled, one has only to compare James Craig's 'Protestant State for a Protestant people' of the 1920s and 1930s with the statement by the present First Minister, David Trimble, who has stressed that he wanted "a pluralist Assembly for a pluralist people".[78]

And what if this new pluralist Northern Ireland became part of a pluralist Ireland in a pluralist Europe? Conor Gearty paints an optimistic vision:

> There is already a common travel area between Britain and Ireland with no passport control, and this is unlikely to change. Nor is the Republicans' putatively united Ireland likely to leave the EU or to abolish the guarantees of human and cultural rights to be put in place via the agreement. In just a few years, the two countries will have a common currency and constitution (the European treaty), a shared commitment to human rights and a set of assemblies working together in Scotland, Wales, Belfast, Dublin and London which will co-exist with a myriad other co-operative institutions. If Ireland does "choose" to "unite" in this kind of future, how will anybody be able to tell? This agreement renders redundant the concept of a United Ireland, in the traditional and incendiary meaning of the phrase.[79]

Escape from the Nightmare of History?

In spite of devastating and repeated acts of massacre, assassination and extirpation, the huge acts of faith which have marked the new relations between Palestinians and Israelis, Africans and Afrikaners, and the way in which walls have come down in Europe and iron curtains have opened, all this inspires a hope that new possibility can still open up in Ireland as well. The crux of that problem involves an ongoing partition of the island between British and Irish jurisdictions, and an equally persistent partition of the affections in Northern Ireland between the British and the Irish heritages, but surely every dweller in the country must hope that the governments involved in its governance can devise institutions which will allow that partition to become a bit more like the net on a tennis court, a demarcation

> allowing for agile give-and-take, for encounter and contending, pre-figuring a future where the vitality that flowed in the beginning from those bracing words 'enemy' and 'allies' might finally derive from a less binary and altogether less binding vocabulary.[80]

With its blurring of boundaries in its three-stranded approach, attempting to provide the basis for optional and multi-layered identities, the Belfast Agreement, of which it has been said that only poets could have imagined it, has not been the work of litterateurs – but by crossing frontiers in their writing, writers have helped laying the foundations for this break-through towards a settlement based on interactive, integrated, institutionalised discourse. Against the widening gap between the two communities, exacerbated by – dare one say it in the face of Bosnia and Kosovo[81] – 'ethnic cleansing' and enforced segregation, the regionalist political rhetoric of John Hume, the poetry of Seamus Heaney, the academic writings of Richard Kearney, and the journalism of Fintan O'Toole or Paul Gillespie have fostered a discourse of post-nationalism, using linguistic ambiguity for the creation of space for dialogue. In this sense, the Belfast Agreement can be seen as following in the tradition of the 'fifth province' – in its provision of an all-Ireland perspective in Strand II; the 'squaring the circle' exercise of power-sharing in Northern Ireland, with guarantees for both the protection of the minority, and the reassurance of the majority in Strand I; and, finally, its IONA dimension,[82] a Council of the Isles encompassing the totality of relations between the UK and Ireland in a European context in Strand III. Blurring and transcending borders, pooling sovereignty, power-sharing governance – new, and, for UK politics in many respects suspiciously European-looking, ground is broken by this agreement, not without its dangers, but certainly following the openness and inclusiveness of literary and inter-cultural discourse, attempting to translate it into practical politics.

In Seamus Heaney's words, "generations of gifted Northern poets have let the linguistic cat out of the sectarian bag, setting it free in the great street carnival of 'protholics' and 'catestants'."[83] Although he rightly warns that "in Drumcree and on the Lower Ormeau Road, neither the victories of creative spirit nor the dodges of post-modernism are going to have much immediate effect," he also asserts that "it is at the level of creative spirit, in the realm of glimpsed potential rather than intransigent solidarity, that the future takes shape."[84]

Hope and history may rhyme yet in Ireland.[85] The route may be long, and many obstacles will yet have to be overcome in what Mary McAleese has called building "a culture of consensus out of the ruins of a culture of conflict."[86]

History, for James Joyce's Stephen Dedalus, was a nightmare he tried desperately to awake from.[87] It used to be a joke that air pilots advised their passengers before landing in Belfast: "We are now approaching Belfast Airport. Please put your watches back 300 years." The Belfast Agreement is a bold attempt to free the two communities from their entrapment by history and myth. It has not been the threat of war from outside, but the doom and gloom of the continuing bloody conflict which has brought the two sides to the negotiation table – under diplomatic pressure from institutions Northern Ireland is involved in (the UK, Ireland, the US with its 35 million-strong Irish diaspora, and the EU). A lot has been achieved. If nothing else, the peace process since September 1994 has saved hundreds of lives. Conor Gearty calls this "the magnificent achievement of the process and agreement":

> Only its normality blinds us to the enormity of this change. It will not be sacrificed by the British and Irish, come what may. The elements in the agreement crucial to this peace – reform of the police; release of paramilitary prisoners; the rights and equality agenda; and much else – will be carried through, whether or not the assembly is made to work.[88]

But not everyone is as categorically optimistic. There is no lasting settlement yet. Peace is still in the balance. The danger is still there that the process, despite the carefully and intricately constructed Good Friday Agreement, could unravel. If no settlement on the decommissioning issue was reached before the Marching Season (culminating between 12 July and 12 August), it was expected that "the absence of a deal on the new executive could have fatal results for the Belfast agreement."[89] In line with this was an opinion poll of April 1999, showing that a total of 73 per cent of voters in Northern Ireland now supported the agreement (compared with 71.2 per cent support in the Referendum of May 1998), but only 52 per cent believed it would survive another year.[90] Yet, the Marching Season has been relatively peaceful, despite – or because of – the intense negotiations surrounding "The Way Forward" document. And a poll in July, a full week after "The Way Forward" was published, showed 65 % in the North (including 59.5 % of Ulster Unionists!) and 84 % in the South were in favour of forming a multi-party executive including Sinn Féin, as proposed, and decommissioning to happen in its wake.[91]

The Agreement is now, in Mo Mowlam's words, "under review". A new attempt to implement it will be made after this review, expected to commence in September 1999. "It's our duty," John Hume asserted, "to translate the will of the people into reality."[92] And Seamus Mallon, interviewed after he had resigned as Deputy First Minister, added: "The political process will be dead in Northern Ireland for a number of years if the review fails; the opportunity of a lifetime will have been missed."[93]

If the Agreement finally failed, the politicians would have seriously let down the people and their repeated expression of their democratic will. Then, the Agreement's complex structure, its "beauty", allowing both Nationalists and Unionists "good reason for believing that they are right about the long term",[94] would surely be blamed as part of the failure; it would be accused of 'fudging' the hard issues by using 'fuzzy' language, full of ambiguities. Success and failure are often separated by a thin line, indeed.

Reflecting on the present, frail peace in Northern Ireland, Mary Holland reminds us that "the tragic scenes of human suffering from the Balkans, unfolding each night on our television screens, provide a warning of what can happen when we fail to forge an escape from the nightmare of history."[95]

The Belfast Agreement, I would argue, still offers the best escape route. It has been a watershed in modern Irish and Anglo-Irish history. "Whatever follows," Fred Halliday contended after its signing, "the accord has drawn a line under the antagonistic history that preceded it: in all future disputes it is to this agreement that the protagonists will have to return."[96]

Notes

1 Decommissioning is, according to the text of the Agrement, not a precondition for Sinn Féin to enter a Northern Ireland executive, but the governments of the UK and the Republic of Ireland have made it, in the Hillsborough Declaration of Good Friday 1999, a 'voluntary obligation', which Sinn Féin rejected. In the negotiations surrounding 'The Way Forward' document, issued by the two governments at the beginning of July 1999, Sinn Féin indicated that decommissioning soon after the implementation of the cross-party Executive would be possible.

2 For the recent history of events concerning Northern Ireland see Paul Bew and Gordon Gillespie, *The Northern Ireland Peace Process 1993-1996: A Chronology*, London: Serif, 1996; and its predecessor, Bew and Gillespie, *Northern Ireland: A Chronology of the Troubles 1968-1993*, Dublin: Gill and Macmillan, 1993; see also Tim Pat Coogan, *The Troubles: Ireland's Ordeal 1966-1995 and the Search for Peace*, London: Hutchinson, 1995.

3 See Deaglán de Bréadún, 'All sweetness and light in dull day at the office', *The Irish Times*, 15 September 1998; also John Mullin, 'Dull civility marks dawn of assembly', *The Guardian*, 15 September 1998.

4 One of the best introductions is still the late Liam de Paor's seminal *Divided Ulster*, Harmondsworth: Penguin, 1970.

5 Frank McGuinness, 'History is a Malignant Gift: An Interview with Frank McGuinness', *Hard Times*, No.58, Autumn/Winter 1996, p.16.

6 See 'New wording for Articles 2 and 3, *The Irish Times*, 10 April 1998.

7 See Conor O'Clery, 'Why Sunningdale failed', *The Irish Times*, 6 April 1998. The best account of the Ulster Workers' Council strike which brought down the power-sharing executive is Don Anderson, *Fourteen May Days*, Dublin: Gill and Macmillan, 1994.

8 See Mark Brennock, 'Anglo-Irish Agreement put Dublin in the picture', *The Irish Times*, 7 April 1998.

9 See John Hume, *Personal Views: Politics, Peace and Reconciliation in Ireland*, Enfield: Roberts Rinehart Publishers, 1996, particularly the section "Politics Alone', pp.79-90; see also Gerard Murray, *John Hume and the SDLP: Impact and Survival in Northern Ireland*, Dublin: Irish Academic Press, 1998.

10 Niall O'Dowd, 'Heads of state must shore up agreement to prevent failure', *The Irish Times*, 11 April 1998.

11 *The Independent*, 'Ireland's peace is worth the candle' (Editorial), 11 April 1998.

12 Brendan O'Leary, 'The 1998 British-Irish Agreement: Power-Sharing Plus', in *Scottish Affairs*, No.26, Winter 1999, pp.14-35; p.14.

13 See Arend Lijphart, *Democracy in Plural Societies*, New Haven: Yale University Press, 1977.

14 On minority nationalisms, see Rogers Brubaker, *Nationalism Reframed: Nationhood and the National Question in the New Europe*, Cambridge: Cambridge University Press, 1996; of particular value in the context of Northern Ireland is his discussion of external homeland nationalisms.

15 Commentators like Neil MacCormick point out that the Union of Parliaments between England and Scotland of 1707 was a Treaty, a 'marriage of convenience' (David McCrone), leaving intact the Scottish principle of popular sovereignty as expressed in the Declaration of Arbroath (1320) and the Claim of Right (1687), and reinforced in the Scottish Claim of Right of 1987. See Owen Dudley Edwards (ed.), *A Claim of Right for Scotland*, Edinburgh: Polygon, 1989; also Neil MacCormick, 'Decentralisation, Devolution, and Confederal Independence', in Eberhard Bort and Russell Keat (eds), *The Boundaries of Understanding: Essays in Honour of Malcolm Anderson*, Edinburgh: ISSI, 1999, pp.197-208; see also David McCrone, *Understanding Scotland: The Sociology of a Stateless Nation*, London: Routledge, 1992; and Lindsay Paterson, *The Autonomy of Modern Scotland*, Edinburgh: Edinburgh University Press, 1994.

16 Geraldine Kennedy, 'Belfast accord alters North's place in the Union', *The Irish Times*, 8 May 1998.

17 Bob Purdie, letter to *The Irish Times*, 13 May 1998.

18 Belfast (Good Friday, or British-Irish) Agreement, published, *inter alia*, as *Agreement Reached in the Multi-Party Negotiations*, [no date, no place], p.2.

19 Fintan O'Toole, 'Deal that lets you pick who you are', *The Irish Times*, 13 April 1998.

20 *Ibid.*

21 Paul Gillespie, 'Statehood, nationhood need to be unbundled', *The Irish Times*, 4 April 1998.

22 *Ibid.*

23 John Hume, 'Europe can offer Northern Ireland a blueprint for peace', in *The European*, 24 August 1995.

24 Quoted in Bew and Gillespie, p.85.

25 Paul Gillespie, *art. cit.*

26 Paul Arthur, 'Anglo-Irish Relations in the New Dispensation: Towards a Post-Nationalist Framework', in Malcolm Anderson and Eberhard Bort (eds), *The Irish Border: History, Politics, Culture*, Liverpool: Liverpool University Press, 1998, pp.41-55.

27 Paul Gillespie, *art. cit.*

28 *Ibid.*

29 *Ibid.*

30 *Ibid.*

31 Richard Kearney, 'Ireland and the Europe of Regions', in Rüdiger Imhof (ed.), *A&E: Ireland: Literature, Culture, Politics*, Heidelberg: C Winter, 1994, pp.133-145, p140.

32 Richard Kearney and Robin Wilson, 'Northern Ireland's Future as a European Region', *The Irish Review*, No.15, Spring 1994, pp.51-69; p.54.

33 Fintan O'Toole, 'Deal that lets you pick who you are', *art. cit.*

34 See also Eberhard Bort, 'Irland —"Westliches Grenzland der Vereinigten Staaten von Europa"', in Marion Hüchtermann, Michael Jörger, Michael Mötter (eds), *Europa eine Seele geben...*, Munich: Europäische Akademie Bayern, 1998, pp.80-91.

35 *O'Toole, 'Deal* that lets you pick who you are', *art. cit.*

36 *Ibid.*

37 *Ibid.*

38 *Ibid.*

39 *Ibid.*

40 Fintan O'Toole, 'A vote that shattered our age-old ideologies', *The Irish Times*, 29 May 1999.

41 *Ibid.*

42 *Ibid.*

43 Fintan O'Toole, 'Deal that lets you pick who you are', *art. cit.*

44 See Tom Nairn, *The Break-up of Britain*, London: Verso, 1977; and his updating in *Faces of Nationalism: Janus Revisited*, London: Verso, 1997. See also the contributions by John Osmond, Paula Surridge, Alice Brown, David McCrone, Lindsay Paterson, and Kenneth O Morgan in this volume.

45 Carol Coulter, 'North's framework for "multi-ethnic society"', *The Irish Times*, 24 September 1998.

46 *Ibid.*

47 *Ibid.*

48 Fintan O'Toole, 'Deal that lets you pick who you are', *art. cit.*

49 *Ibid.*

50 Brendan O'Leary, *art. cit.*, p.29.

51 *Ibid.*, p.30.

52 Declan Kiberd, 'The Only Thing Keeping Ireland out of the Third World is the Weather: An Interview with Declan Kiberd', *Hard Times*, No.58, Autumn/Winter 1996, p.29.

53 *Ibid.*

54 Garret FitzGerald, 'Chance to reverse North's economic stagnation', *The Irish Times*, 27 March 1999.

55 *Ibid.*

56 Patrick Smyth, '£400m EU plan for North', *The Irish Times*, 23 March 1999.

57 See Patrick Smyth, 'EU's peace programme begins to yield dividends', *The Irish Times*, 5 December 1997.

58 *Ibid.*

59 Quoted in 'Fund praised for peace process role', *The Irish Times*, 5 February 1999.

60 Harvey Elliott, 'Ireland unites on tourism front', *The Times*, 15 February 1996.

61 Bertie Ahern, 'All will gain in new era', *The Irish Times*, 10 March 1999.

62 Conor O'Clery, 'Zhu links Kosovo and Northern Ireland', *The Irish Times*, 8 April 1999.

63 See Stefan Ulrich, 'Europas Separatisten verlieren an Boden', *Süddeutsche Zeiung*, 19 September 1998.

64 Tony Kennedy, 'Waging Peace in the North', *The Irish Times* (Letters), 20 September 1997.

65 Deaglán de Bréadún, 'Making peace is a low-key affair at the cutting edge', *The Irish Times*, 4 April 1998.

66 Peace Nobel Prize in 1978 for Betty Williams and Mairead Corrigan.

67 Lagan College in Belfast, started in 1981 with 26 school-kids and two teachers; has now around 1,000 pupils.

68 There are now, according to my latest count, 25 fully acknowledged integrated primary, and 15 integrated secondary schools all over Northern Ireland, with an enrolment of *c*4,500 and *c*6,000 pupils respectively.

69 An important role is the increasing emphasis on cross-border co-operation. See Eberhard Bort, 'Building Bridges: Cross-Border Co-operation in Ireland', in Gerhard Brunn and Peter Schmitt-Egner (eds), *Grenzüberschreitende Zusammenarbeit in Europa: Theorie — Empirie — Praxis*, Baden-Baden: Nomos, 1998, pp.217-240; see also Etain Tannam, 'EU Regional Policy and the Irish/Northern Irish Cross-Border Administrative Relationship', *Regional & Federal Studies*, Vol.5, No.1, Spring 1995, pp.67-93.

70 Mary McAleese, 'President McAleese's inauguration speech', *The Irish Times*, 12 November 1997.

71 Fintan O'Toole, 'Yes vote means exchanging our illusions for realities', *The Irish Times*, 15 May 1998.

72 *Ibid.*

73 By July 1999, a total of 282 Northern Irish prisoners had been released early under the terms of the Belfast Agreement, 127 loyalists, 144 republicans and nine non-aligned prisoners. Two H-Blocks at the notorious Maze Prison had closed, and the closure of the entire prison was expected by 2001. See Louise McCall, 'Prisoner releases under agreement total 282', *The Irish Times*, 27 July 1999.

74 *Ibid.*

75 *Ibid.*

76 Seamus Heaney, 'Unheard melodies', *The Irish Times* (supplement on *The Northern Ireland Settlement*, containing also the text of the Belfast Agreement), 11 April 1998.

77 O'Toole, 'Yes vote means exchanging our illusions for realities', *art. cit.*

78 Carol Coulter, *art. cit.*

79 Conor Gearty, 'Just a little wobble', *The Guardian*, 19 May 1998.

80 Seamus Heaney, *Crediting Poetry: The Nobel Lecture 1995*, Loughcrew, Oldcastle: Gallery Press, 1995, p.23.

81 "By the standards of Rwanda or the continuing wars in former Yugoslavia, the violence [in Northern Ireland] may have been relatively restrained, but by the standards of anywhere else, it has been pretty terrible." Fintan O'Toole, 'IRA must face up to the grotesque reality', *The Irish Times*, 16 April 1999.

82 IONA — Islands of the North Atlantic, John Hume's favoured term for the Council of the Isles.

83 Seamus Heaney, *art. cit.*

84 *Ibid.*

85 In Heaney's famous phrase from *The Cure at Troy*, London: Faber and Faber, 1990, p.77.

86 Rachel Donnelly, 'President lauds culture of consensus', *The Irish Times*, 21 April 1999.

87 James Joyce, *The Portrait of the Artsist as a Young Man* (1916), Harmondsworth: Penguin, 1992.

88 Conor Gearty, *art. cit.*

89 Ed Maloney, 'Peace process faces delay', *Sunday Herald*, 18 April 1999.

90 Deaglán de Bréadún, 'Poll shows increased support for agreement', *The Irish Times*, 27 April 1999.

91 Deaglán de Bréadún, 'Majority in favour of North executive', *The Irish Times*, 10 July 1999.

92 See Rachel Donnelly, 'Hume stresses principles of agreement', *The Irish Times*, 27 July 1999.

93 See Gerry Moriarty, 'Mallon insists he has nmo regrets about resignation', *The Irish Times*, 29 July 1999.

94 Brendan O'Leary, *art. cit.*, p.30.

95 Mary Holland, 'A reversion to violence is possible', *The Irish Times*, 8 April 1999.

96 Fred Halliday, 'Ireland's Third Way', *Prospect*, May 1998.

A Region is a Region is a Region – is it? Planning in the Stuttgart Region

Helmut Doka

I

The Stuttgart Region is not a region proper – at least not by EU standards. No office in Brussels. So why bother to look at it at all?

Let us take the Stuttgart Region as an example for a Metropolitan Region, this sub-regional political animal that has become pretty popular throughout Germany over the last decades, and in the rest of Europe as well. The Metropolitan Regions are everywhere: Frankfurt, Munich, Kommunalverband Rhein-Ruhr, Berlin-Brandenburg, just to name a few. They differ a lot from each other as to their form, the tasks allotted to them, and their political standing; they have in common that they were established on a level somewhere above the big city and below the "proper" EU region; and in size and economic power many of them will easily rival many EU regions. The Stuttgart Region, for example, is bigger in size and population than the Saarland, Bremen, or Hamburg, which are all considered EU regions. It equals Wales in population and Portugal in GDP (140 billion DM in 1994).

Size and economic power is one thing; but what really gained the Stuttgart Region a special reputation was that in 1994, as the first and so far only region in Germany, it set up a directly elected regional parliament ("Regionalversammlung") for the "Regionalverband", as the successor to the previous regional assembly, which had been made up of delegates from Stuttgart and the surrounding counties. This was a clear signal to

Eberhard Bort and Neil Evans (eds), *Networking Europe*, Liverpool University Press 2000, 463-71.

everybody that here a region claimed to be a political unit and not just an administrative commodity.

The Regionalverband is financed mainly by contributions from its 179 members; it has created an extremely "lean" administration of only about 50 people, who try to enhance their efficiency by a conscious policy of co-operation and "networking" with other authorities and institutions. It may well be argued that this new political approach of "networking" has in itself been one of the most successful and innovative aspects of the Regionalverband's work: playing host to several "round tables", being a catalyst, a mediator, a meeting point for various needs on the regional level – especially in supporting developments towards a sustainable future.

Now what does the Regionalverband actually do? It has been assigned the following tasks by a special State of Baden-Württemberg Act:

- Settlement / Infrastructure: Regional Planning
- Environment: Land Use Planning and Waste Disposal (mineral waste)
- Traffic: Regional traffic planning and responsibility for local train services in the Region
- Commerce and Industry: promotion of the economy and of tourism.

Activities in two further fields my be started if the Regionalversammlung agrees with a 2/3 majority:

- Culture and Sport: funding and organising of conferences, cultural and sporting events;
- Trade Fairs: funding and organising of trade fairs.

There have been activities in all of these fields, but certainly the field of Regional Planning has been the most important one; this sector can serve as an example for the functioning of the Regionalverband as a whole.

The Regional Zoning Plan lays down a framework for the Region's settlement structure and thus for its future. It has a bridging function between the plans made by local authorities, on the one hand, and the more comprehensive objectives of the

The Region Stuttgart in Baden-Württemberg

Verband Region Stuttgart

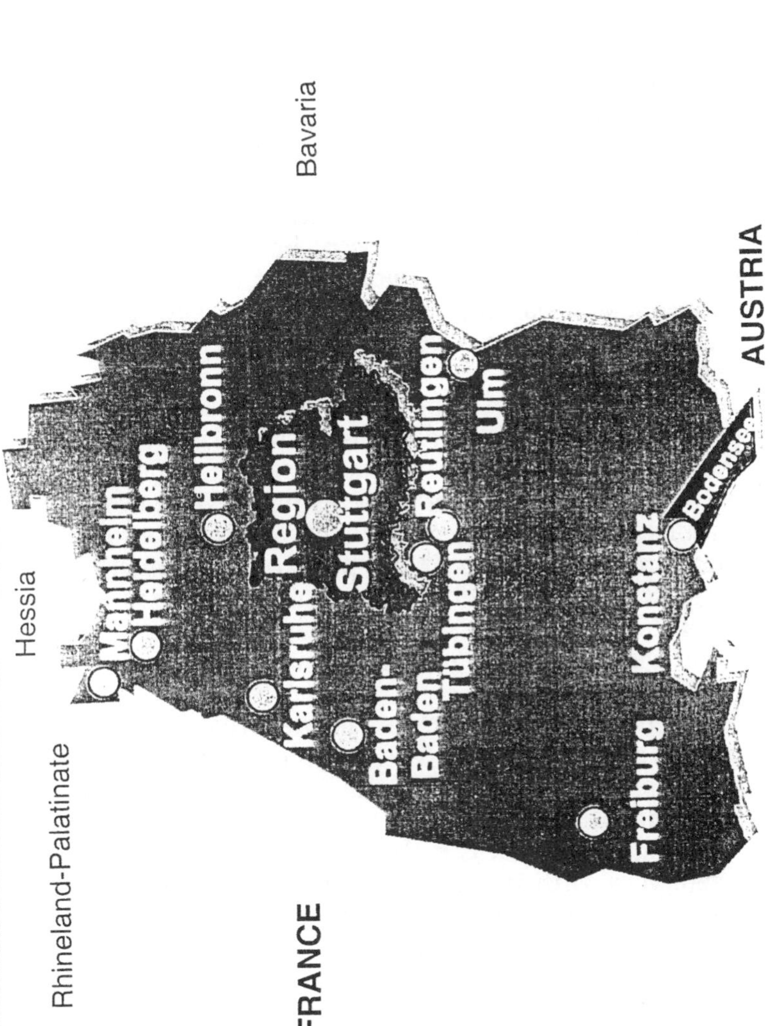

Federal and Land governments, on the other. The current plan was instituted in 1998 after an intense process of discussions with the cities' and the Land authorities; it is to be revised in about 10 to 15 years. Its goals are binding for city planning, e.g. the so-called axes of development, central locations (for certain facilities), green belts, preferred locations for the development of housing and commerce. Two separate plans belong to the Zoning Plan: the Regional Traffic Plan and the Landscape Plan.

Looking at the plans, one will realise the special settlement structure of the Stuttgart Region and the overall goals of the plans: they show a high-density, yet highly decentralised settlement structure, which the plans are trying to preserve and to develop. They are, therefore, trying to prevent development *between* the axes and locate it mainly *along* the lines of the regional rail system, which in itself is being extended and improved.

In the field of public transport, the Verband has a very practical responsibility, too: it is in charge of the S-Bahn-system, the backbone of public regional passenger transport. The spaces between the axes are set aside as natural reserves, for climatic reasons, for recreation and agriculture; and the new attitude of the planners is shown by the principle that open spaces are no longer considered to be just possible sites for future development, but are on equal terms with developed areas, carry the same weight and deserve the same protection in the planning process.

All these planning powers may sound impressive, and to a certain extent they are. The overall results of the work of the Regionalverband have been quite positive, and the planners have succeeded in maintaining good relations with the other levels of planning; their work is highly respected for its quality, and it is often very difficult for communities to argue against them without making their egotism too obvious. Nevertheless, if you compare the political effort and the tasks to deal with, you might well ask questions. Is it necessary to have a parliament of 87 to control an administration of around 50? Does this Regionalverband not constitute another level of administration that makes processes even more cumbersome? Are the limited responsibilities of this body a basis for a positive long-term development?

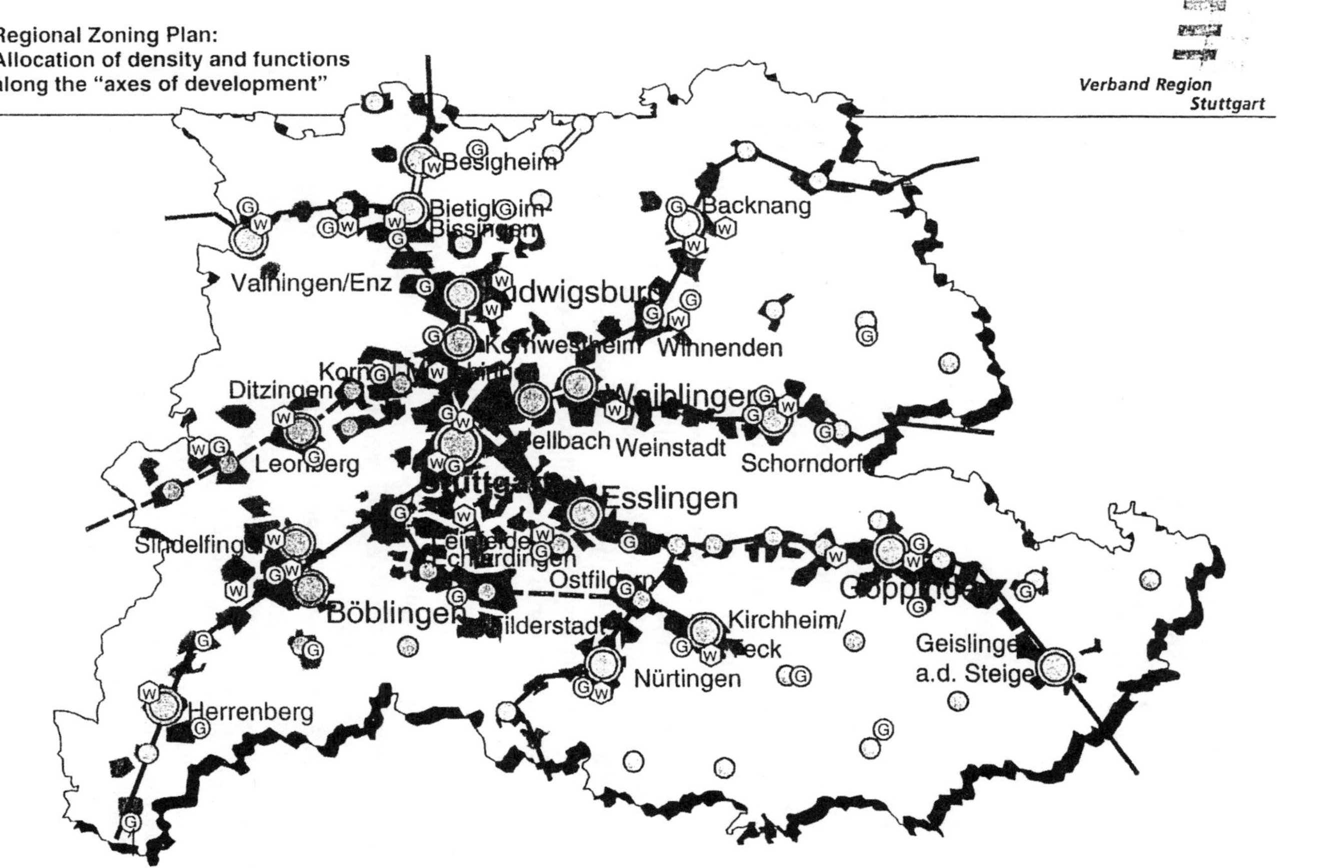
Regional Zoning Plan:
Allocation of density and functions
along the "axes of development"
Verband Region Stuttgart
Besigheim
Backnang
Vaihingen/Enz
Winnenden
Ditzingen
Leonberg
Weinstadt
Schorndorf
Esslingen
Sindelfingen
Ostfildern
Böblingen
Kirchheim/Teck
Nürtingen
Geislingen a.d. Steige
Herrenberg

For me, this is not the point. If it was just for the technicalities of planning, for running public transport lines etc., you could certainly find solutions on a smaller scale than that of a Regionalverband. But I feel that there is more behind these Metropolitan Regions or sub-regions than just technicalities. I feel there is the aspect of regional identity involved and the question of our future European infrastructure as well.

II

We have all experienced the changes the EU has brought to the political, social and economic infrastructures of our countries, and globalisation will bring even more. We have seen a weakening of national governments and parliaments and the rise of regionalism, which in some countries has led to major changes in the tiers of government, as in Britain, France, Spain and Italy – you could probably see it as a strengthening of federal elements in Europe. I feel that this trend will continue, that the national levels will lose even more power to the regions – but that the regions themselves will come under pressure to reorganise according to the changing needs of their people. There is a feeling of regional belonging in the making that in the past the city could claim. The city used to be the area you could cover in a day, the area you used for work or recreation each day. Nowadays, the car and public transport have extended this area, and you travel as easily to a place 30 kms away as you did to one 5 kms away 50 years ago – be it for work or recreation or shopping.

So, in a sense, the citizen nowadays is outgrowing his or her city and needs regional support structures; at the same time cities have to realise that they cannot cope properly with many of their traditional tasks single-handedly any more: traffic, public utilities, cultural events, waste disposal, even city planning and housing are often too much to be handled by the single city, *especially* if it is part of an agglomeration – and there will be more and more agglomerations around.

Businesses today are not so much interested anymore in what a single city can offer, but what a whole region can offer, in terms of business opportunities, workforce, infrastructure, universities, housing, recreation, culture, etc., and so it is, in many cases, the regions which are competing amongst each other to attract businesses. I am pretty sure we will see even more regional bodies below the official EU-regions in the future – and not only Metropolitan Regions, but a mixed lot of territories differing widely in size, shape, colour and structure, but tailored to regional needs.

It should be interesting to watch the developments in the Upper Rhine Valley, for example, where the cities of Freiburg, Basle and Mulhouse are establishing more and more links, so far mainly in the field of public transport and culture; but other fields are to follow; and this is a region that cuts across the borders of three European countries, of which one is not even a member of the EU. EUREGIO – Deutsch-Niederländische Grenzregion, the cross-border region at the German-Dutch border, is cutting across traditional national borders as well, and yet another similar structure may be evolving in the Cologne Area, where the City of Cologne is not looking so much towards the Ruhr Area for its future development but to the west, towards Aachen and Liége.

I admit, much of this is speculation still. We cannot ignore some problems that show up in most regional structures and are clearly visible in our Stuttgart example as well.

III

In order to get the Stuttgart Region established, a lot of compromises had to be made. The idea of a region was strongly supported by the SPD and the City of Stuttgart, half-heartedly by the CDU, and strongly opposed by the vested local interests, represented by the Landräte, the presidents of the counties around Stuttgart. In the long run, I cannot see any justification for the existence of these counties anymore, and neither for having an additional Regierungspräsidium (a state legal supervisor for the communities); all this could well be integrated into a regional administration. However, it would have been too much of a revolution for the traditional Baden-Württemberg structure of administration to achieve so much change in one step.

The members on the Regional Parliament are not all ardently waving the regional flag; many of them are mayors or lord mayors in their home towns, or hold seats on their county or town councils. Some of them ran for a seat on the Regional Parliament only to prevent more regionalism and to save as much of their former powers as possible.

Because the present structure is such a maze of different responsibilities, the public so far has not been over-enthusiastic about the Region; the general attitude is one of friendly indifference, so long as the S-Bahn trains are on schedule. Voter turnout in regional elections is only reasonable because they have been linked to the local elections. Furthermore: on the local or federal levels, citizens could be mobilised over political issues in the past; no such political strategies have been developed for the regional level so far, which may account for some of the indifference.

One can easily see that the Stuttgart Region is still in the making, and although we cannot be absolutely sure what the future development of the Stuttgart Region will be, I am pretty confident that there will be more regional powers (at the moment the Stuttgart Region law is being revised to achieve this) accompanied by more regional networking in our region, and I can see similar trends all over Europe. There is the example of Hannover, which has just established a "Regionalkreis" with a directly elected parliament, too; on the other hand. there is Frankfurt, which is contemplating the destruction of its current regional structures.

Looking at the world outside Europe, however, I feel that regionalism is nowhere as popular, deeply rooted and as well advanced as it is here, that regionalism as a political concept is in fact a kind of a "European idea". If we succeed in making our regions – and sub-regions – a success, Europe will have a valuable infrastructural and political advantage over the rest of the world; it will be able to satisfy the needs of its citizens better, as well as the needs of its economy; and the success of our regions will preserve a colourful cultural diversity and so add to the quality of our lives.

Beyond the Sovereign State: An Afterword to *Networking Europe*

Christopher Harvie

The View from Zollernblick

The Welsh Referendum on 18 September 1997 was a 'damn close-run thing'. If some of what we now know about New Labour had come out, and 3000-odd voters had gone the other way, the tone of this book would have been rather different. The 150 per cent swing to home rule since the debacle of 1 March 1979 – Scotland's swing was only 43 per cent – would have been forgotten. As it is, the Freudenstadt colloquia have played their part, along with many more powerful bodies, in building up the identity of Wales as a European region, in a culture of involvement. This was something which scarcely existed in 1979.

Welsh devolution, in 1997, owed an obvious debt to the Scottish example, and a Scottish solidarity not much evident eighteen years ago. Yet the creation of a culture of autonomy, as a background to the recovery from 1979, ought not to be underestimated, and it was not a one-way traffic in ideas. Wales helped, not least in the desolate period after 1979, when a campaign of extra-parliamentary pressure secured S4C, making the Scots realise that if Wales, flat on the carpet, could get back into the ring, so could we. And culture, in its broadest and most internationalised sense, has been Freudenstadt's stock-in-trade.

In 1987, a few years before Freudenstadt I, I wrote and presented a film for BBC Scotland called *Grasping the Thistle*. After interviewing politicians, bankers, playwrights and trade unionists in Baden-Württemberg and Scotland, I argued that the country would be self-governing within five years. I have been out by nearly ten, but I think I was more on the ball than one

Eberhard Bort and Neil Evans (eds), *Networking Europe*, Liverpool University Press 2000, 473-83.

critic in a post-film discussion: Andrew Neil, then editor of the *Sunday Times*. Neil, whose chief interest was given in *Who's Who* as 'New York', intoned that an autonomous Scotland would be boring and backward-looking compared with the excitement of the global market-place. Much of this pizzazz was, of course, caused by his boss, Rupert Murdoch. Nowadays Neil, grinding his teeth, though not underpaid, is having to live with devolution as Editor-in-Chief of the *Scotsman*. The Scottish Conservative party he once served is a ghost; and his own memoirs, *Full Disclosure*, showed Murdoch as a despot whose political views – he backed Pat Buchanan for the US Presidency – would have shocked us rigid had they been expressed in German. I do not know how long Neil can tolerate the new Scotland, but his global markets and information revolutions plainly have not brought enlightenment or equality to the 'downsized' or the 'Microserf'. Nor have they brought stability to 'Little Tigers', once lauded as perfect apprentice capitalists, now perilously close to extinction.

The phrase that comes to mind is not calm and bureaucratic but a rare vivid line from Scotland's revolutionary pedagogue John MacLean in the 1910s: 'We are in the rapids of revolution.' Since 1989 we have been moving too fast technologically and otherwise to be properly conscious of where we actually are. The value of Freudenstadt has been twofold: firstly the ability to get away from the river, look at the panorama of Europe from this balcony, and take stock; and secondly to facilitate a politics of 'small steps', particularly in the areas of culture, academe and media. These have not just been practical in themselves (like our Welsh Studies Centre at Tübingen) but encouraging in difficult times, when political frustration can too easily fan the embers of old nationalist aggressions.

The Regional and the Global

The rapids of our revolution were echoing behind us in 1991, when Freudenstadt I convened, in the collapse of communist centralism in East Europe. The United States was the patent victor, yet stability in general was challenged by technical innovations generated in the private sector and under way from the 1960s – computers, mass car ownership, air travel, satellite communications, contraception. These, and the reaction to them, have made both Fordism and the defence-and-welfare-based nation-states look groggy. But if the Morlock economies of East Europe are dead, some of the globalising prototypes are not looking much healthier.

Small nations and regions living, as Gwyn Alf Williams once put it, 'in the interstices of others' histories' have, however, weaved and dodged among multinationals and the European Union, so far with success. Joe Lee showed how Ireland's Gross Domestic Product (though not, thanks to profit repatriation, its Gross National Product) per capita increased between 1991 and 1996 from 72 to 98.8 per cent of the European mean (Britain's retreated from 98 to 96.7 per cent) 'by doing all the things economists told us were passé'.[1] This regional confidence is quite new since 1979 and, I think, accounts to a great extent for the swing in favour of Welsh autonomy. But we still have to ask: are we part of a new consciousness, or a process of 'divide and rule'? Is regionalism, in other words, a new, more efficient and more democratic ordering of the modern state, or is it part of the 'post-modern condition': in place of the war–and–welfare state a collection of *micropoli* competing with one another as fortresses for the wealthy, fundamentally non–redistributive defences against insistent and rising poverty?

Something of this could be seen in Britain. The 1997 referenda endorsed a change in political culture, a move – however unfocused – towards a new democracy and a new economy. But not in England, where the metropolitan élite's embrace of the market and its controllers was looking quite sticky. The unexpected continuity of old privilege and New Labour, rather than a generous reconstruction of the welfare state, could have ominous consequences for the relationship between Scotland and Wales and the centre; and will probably have the effect of forcing the quasi–autonomous states further from the metropolitan norm, looking for new versions of civic *virtù*, and new ways of organising international co-operation.

Here are examples of two challenges, one Scots, one Welsh. In *The People Say Yes*, Canon Kenyon Wright, Chair of the

Scottish Constitutional Convention, writes of how self-government fitted into a context of *Kairos*: Hans Küng's ideal of a 'global ethic' aimed at securing universal entitlement to a decent life on a sustainable planet:

> I was convinced that the single great issue of the end of the twentieth century was whether we could find our way to new social, economic and political structures that would allow us to choose life instead of death for our children ... controlling technology for human goals, reversing our ecological decline and giving justice and a minimum standard of human life to all the world's people.[2]

Can one have a global ethic and nations which deal in arms on a huge scale; a crime, drug and sex industry whose impact, when taken together, dwarfs other forms of international trade; and a financial services industry pretty unfastidious about where its finance actually comes from?

In Wales in summer 1997, making a radio documentary, *Whitehall and the Boffins,* I interviewed Sir John Houghton, Chair of the Intergovernmental Panel on Climate Change in his house above Aberdovey. He stressed the need to combat 'greenhouse gases' by pricing and controlling energy use – we get it currently at only about a third of its global cost – and creating community-based alternatives to its exploitation: for instance, combining district heating with power generation and carrying goods by rail and waterway rather than by road and air. The alternative was as grim as Canon Wright's. The impact of global warming is not going to be street cafes and Celtic St Tropezes; it is more likely that the 'threshold effects' of melting ice diverting the Gulf Stream will give Britain, rather soon, the climate of Labrador.[3]

Wright and Houghton are simultaneously conservative and radical, and are thus echoing the 'Wertkonservatismus' of Baden-Württemberg's SPD-*Vordenker* Erhard Eppler. Both envisage the benign use of science to reverse the above threats, in their cases from an essentially religious concern with the natural world and man's purpose in it. They echo R S Thomas' concern at the dislocation of man and nature in 'Cynddylan on a Tractor':

Ah, you should see Cynddylan on a tractor.
Gone the old look that yoked him to the soil;
He's a new man now, part of the machine,
His nerves of metal and his blood of oil.

In thinking global and acting local, Wright and Houghton ask awkward, relevant questions about our prosperity. For over a decade governments have worshipped at the ark of the market, urged on by the World Bank, the International Monetary Fund, and the Nobel Prize Committee. Their instructor-economists have been priests (sometimes remarkably sectarian ones) and rhetoricians rather than analysts. Many are a lot less competent than the old master Adam Smith himself! Neal Ascherson reminded us in 1992 that by itself the market does not redistribute, it does not regulate, and it does not conserve. The incompetent energy exploitation and secrecy of communism was doomed by the Chernobyl crisis of 1986, but capitalism has its own Chernobyls – American big business's disregard of global warming; the hell-for-leather marketising 'structural adjustment programmes' which because they destroy communities and even firms, open avenues for crime, drugs and aggression. These are no longer marginal interruptions to an orderly process; they are part of 'disorganised capitalism' itself.

I want to cite one process: not the immediately topical macho business of Formula One (which fuses two social killers – speed and nicotine) but clothes and fashion. This is worth considering on the 1997 centenary of Nye Bevan – whom Dai Smith managed to commemorate with a superb film starring Brian Cox, all but ignored by the BBC in London. One of Bevan's closest associates was Israel Sieff, who developed Marks and Spencer as the chief retailer of those clothes that J B Priestley saw 'making shopgirls look like film stars'. Bevan saw Marks and Sparks as the social correlate of his health reforms: an industry paying decent wages to British workers to make clothes for their own class – cognate with the 'Fordism' that Gramsci had recognised in the USA.

Now fashion has become internationalised. Air transport and satellite linkage of PCs mean that low–production–cost goods can be sold to a label–conscious public at huge mark–ups. In the case of Nike trainers a wage content of less than $5 a pair in Indonesia becomes an end price of $75 in the USA. This means as much of an 'industrial revolution' as the spinning-machine did in the eighteenth century. But in no way is this benign. The rational consumer is not supplied with cheap goods; instead vulnerable groups like children are targeted and forced by peer-group pressure to pay extortionate prices. The resulting profits do not trickle down but piss off – via the micro-states. The new 'upper-end' of the market provided by the Middle East and New Russia shows the patent complicity between couture and entrenched plutocratic privilege. The sideways linkages of these with pop, the arts, advertising, sports, financial services and journalism are what Tony Blair describes as the 'culture industries of a vibrant New Britain'. Others might see something closer to Thomas Carlyle's division in *Sartor Resartus* (1834) of mankind into dandies and drudges. What we have – as the Formula One episode showed – is a financial complex with little interest in the common wealth, of Britain or anywhere else.[4]

Perhaps we can get a bearing on this quantum change through science fiction. In 1953 Frederik Pohl and Cyril Kornbluth's *The Space Merchants* was a left-wing response to George Orwell's *1984*. It envisaged a world run by multinational companies – General Motors, IG Farben, Indiastries. Their tools were advertising, violence and 'recreational drugs', their executives advertising men. The downside was pollution and limitless inequality, and new forms of slavery. In some ways this shrewdly anticipates the evolution of 'Anglo–Saxon' capitalism, as distinct from the far more 'responsible' and 'mutualised' European variety. Read the Murdoch press and there is not much doubt on whose side such British opinion-formers stand.

We ought not to underestimate this confrontation. I do not think anyone can who has been studying the recent German press and its reiterated criticism of the USA. Behind the battle over the Euro is the increasing tension between European ecological concern and gas-guzzling America. Piggy in the middle is 'New Britain', desperately unsure of where its nationality now is. And unreliable within this scenario are the Celts, who seem to be particularly adept at making variants on the European type actually work.

Rethinking Bevan's Welfare State

The nation is not adequately treated in pro-or-anti-market arguments (I am intrigued about the media dynamism which makes it possible for a pundit like Oxford's Professor John Gray to change horses from neo-liberal to interventionist and still retain credibility). The 'policeman state' mattered to free-market advocates like Adam Smith. It 'contained' the economy, allowing the workers to benefit from the profits of the propertied. But it had to break up cartels and tax evasion, and to secure public health. These 'policemen' – doctors, engineers, sanitary reformers – Nye Bevan called the real statesmen of the nineteenth century. They started to develop the active welfare state associated with Keynes, Beveridge and Bevan himself: not retreating from the Smithian state, but developing it.

The Janus-face of this was the military-industrial complex. This was both a wasteful menace and a prudential control. It produced monsters like the nuclear industry, but the alternative on offer in East Europe also enforced good behaviour on our capitalists. Bevan wanted to diminish it and as Shadow Foreign Secretary, at the end of his life, create alliances against the peacetime foes: hunger, disease, exploitation:

> What we have to seek are new ways of being great, new modes of pioneering, new fashions of thought, new means of inspiring and igniting the minds of mankind.[5]

This agenda still stands, but the nation-state container has been broken. Nowadays multinationals can dwarf states; capital can vanish into the black holes of tax havens. Capitalists can thrive independently of industry while monetary speculation and the exporting of jobs can negate whatever gains ordinary workers can make. Automation was already decimating jobs in the 1980s – North Sea oil yielded about 150,000 jobs for £80 billion investment.[6] Shareholder-oriented capitalism has discovered that the costs of research and development can be recouped faster by using low-wage countries. Just as in the 1920s, what Edward Luttwak calls turbo-charged capitalism has not only destabilised East Europe, but through low wages and redundancies has put increasing burdens on the welfare states.[7] Much has been made of the additional labour-cost burdens of the European welfare states; but these have come about because the tendency has been away from taxes on capital or profits (which firms are skilled in avoiding) and towards taxes on employment.

Bevan's global goal has been met in part, but more by the smaller, rather than by the larger states. Norway gives 0.85 per cent of GDP to overseas aid, Britain 0.27 per cent.[8] We now have to think of ways which harness a Norwegian mode of civic determination to a politics which packs political clout: a moral and ecological internationalism which can take on big business, Brent-Spar style, and win.

Diplomacy for the Regions

The debate in Scotland and Wales in 1997 and 1998 was about the quality of government. But we have not yet thought about what external relations will look like after devolution, if they are to respond to the problems thrown up by disorganised turbo-capitalism. An embryo regional diplomacy is evolving in Brussels – competition for funds and EU offices – which is more like Darwin than Bismarck. In so far as regions are there as tourist/cultural options, bidders to have high-value-added industries, or even toxic waste dumps (if the price is right), then the scene is chillingly close to the post-modern supermarket.

But common interests are growing in areas like education, information technology and ecology, and they will have their effect when defence reductions and realistic charges for energy and transport reconstitute our Europe. If we think of Europe's main goal as sustainability, then this means priorities for education and for the old, Europe will look a different place and its agenda – and that of regional alliances like the Four Motors which are already being built up – will be in the widest sense cultural: the transfer of best practice, the synergy which comes from customarily working together: something which is right up the street of the smaller states. If automated manufacturing technology, as a recent *Spiegel* report has suggested, might result in the retention of only twenty per cent of today's work-force, then only the communities and the planning regions can redistribute the dividends from this into socially-sustaining activities. This politicises such conflicts as the social disadvantaging of women, the inanities of MacWorld visited on regional eating and drinking, not to speak of health.

On the western fringe of Europe, remote from and neglected by the 'core', America had a vivid appeal to the countries of the Celtic fringe – and, for reasons of its own, to Germany. But this was the America of Roosevelt, Raymond Chandler, Woody Guthrie, Louis Armstrong – not of big-business-driven politics, Jesse Helms, the Christian Coalition, Hollywood's toxic mix of infantilism and fanaticism, and the wasting of the environment by the car. A culture change seems imminent: and at its terminus – in America, I hope, as well as in Europe – are communities in which we can, as Louis MacNeice wrote of his loved and hated Ireland, 'see the end of our own actions.'

Drowning in Information?

Why meet here? Why not depend on a 'virtual Freudenstadt'? New communications have been useful in our various projects but, in its hyped-up form, the information 'revolution' is not a help. Information is like water: essential. But too much of the stuff, in the wrong place, and you drown. To type MILLENNIUM into my computer was to be splashed by a tide of global (but mainly American: is this getting obsessive?) daftness. Information has to be selected and tested – and this means civic structures which use it to work out agendas for people, meetings at which we can discuss what we really think of the Emperor's clothes. The alternative is the vacuous marketing of the likes of Cool Britannia, in which culture stops being critical and becomes commodity: something whose dangers become particularly acute when culture becomes manufactured goods as well as the means of information transmission.

It is at the level of culture that regions and small nations must be prepared to co-operate in a new and unorthodox diplomacy. We ought to be re-examining the notion of Europe not as a collection of over-armed ex-military nation-states but as – in the medieval sense – a community of craftspeople, scholars and healers – in Alasdair Gray's words, 'makers, movers and menders'. They – we – ought to be assessing our common problems and their solutions – with higher education institutions as our new embassies. Here, a word of tribute to the British Council – not always expressive of the pluralism of these islands: in Germany its staff have been not just fair but enthusiastic, and this particular Celt would willingly see it continue its work, under whatever name, in a confederal future.

But we can go further than inter-regional co-operation. In a practical sense we need to construct at a European level sources of 'funding for collegiality' which can, in an informal and direct way, make cultural exchange the norm. Individuals could, for instance, get vouchers equivalent to a year's salary in every twenty for such programmes. Networks could make these options linked, known and available. There should be much greater control and taxation of commercial tourism, and indeed of the more mindless forms of human activity; many more options for lifetime education. This is all part of the business of creating conventions of European conviviality which replicate – and remodel – the impact of 'national' education policies in the nineteenth century.

In this a priority is the overthrow of new and unacceptable forms of individual tyranny. New technology has resulted – utterly bizarrely – in neo-feudal forms of control, dominated by individuals of vast power and total incalculability; something which was never the case in the creation of the great transport and communications networks of the nineteenth century. The railways and mails were rapidly subjected to public control, and what Teddy Roosevelt called 'malefactors of great wealth' – the Murdochs and Ecclestones and Gateses – have to be treated similarly, otherwise they will be a cancer on our European democracy.

And here, not in a post-modern but a neo-modern form, what the great Patrick Geddes would have called a 'geotechnic' Europe, there's an essential role for small, elderly nations with fine landscapes, good libraries and nagging consciences. Scotland and Wales and Ireland are repositories for civic *virtù* because they've had to defend it in the past. We have a history as debatable as anyone else's but it has functioned as the grit of a cultural achievement which is weirdly universal – from the hours of Joyce's 1904 Dublin to Shirley Bassey belting out love, sex and survival, to Burns' 'Auld Land Syne', which will see this millennium out.

'It shows us how many ways there are of being alive', E M Forster wrote of Giuseppe di Lampedusa's great novel of Sicily, *The Leopard*. Lampedusa visited Wales in the 1930s, stood on the terraces of Powis Castle at Welshpool and, contrasting the richness of the landscape before him with his own biscuit earth and thin vegetation, envied the Welsh. Looking out at the woods and parishes between Freudenstadt and the Schwäbische Alb – under snow, glittering in the sun, blitzed by these incredible June thunderstorms – we have had the chance to multiply the ways of being alive. Once we have realised this, the possibilities, like Rilke's God, expand a thousandfold. Let us not waste them.

Notes

1 Sources: *Guardian*, 2 November 1994; *Die Zeit*, 7 November 1997.
2 Kenyon Wright, *The People Say Yes*, Dunoon: Argyll Books, 1997, p.112.
3 BBC Radio Four: *Whitehall and the Boffins*, Part II, broadcast on 25 September 1997.
4 See Tom Nairn, 'After Brobdingnag: Micro-states and their Future', in Malcolm Anderson and Eberhard Bort (eds), *The Frontiers of Europe*, London: Pinter, 1998, pp.135-47.
5 Speech of 19 December 1956, in *Hansard*, Vol. 562, cols. 1398–1407.
6 Christopher Harvie, *Fool's Gold: The Story of North Sea Oil*, London: Hamish Hamilton, 1994, p.17.
7 *London Review of Books*, Vol.18, No.9, 9 May 1996, pp.6–8.
8 *Die Zeit*, 7 November 1997.

Contributors

Jane Aaron	Senior Lecturer in English , University of Wales, Aberystwyth.
Keith Armstrong	Poet, playwright and editor, Whitley Bay, Tyne and Wear.
Neal Ascherson	Journalist , and columnist with *The Observer*.
Mathias Beer	Researcher and Lecturer at the Institut für Donauschwäbische Geschichte und Landeskunde, University of Tübingen.
Eberhard Bort	Lecturer in Politics and Associate Director of the International Social Sciences Institute, University of Edinburgh.
Gotlind Braun	Board member of "SPD 60 +" (Federal Council of Senior Social Democrats).
Alice Brown	Professor of Politics, Director of the Scottish Governance Forum, University of Edinburgh; Member of the Steering Committee for the Scottish Parliament.
Muriel Casals	Lecturer in Economics, Autonomous University of Barcelona.
Frank Conlan	European Projects Manager, Údarás na Gaeltachta, Galway.
Patricia Conlan	Lecturer in European Law, University of Limerick.

Phil Cooke	Professor of Urban and Regional Planning, University of Wales, Cardiff.
Helmut Doka	SPD-Member (Regionalrat) of the Stuttgart Regional Assembly.
Neil Evans	Tutor in History and Co-ordinator of the Centre for Welsh Studies, Coleg Harlech.
Alfred Geisel	Former Vice-President of the Stuttgart Landtag, Ex-SPD MP, President of Arbeitsgemeinschaft Sozialdemokratischer Senioren (ASS - working group of senior Social Democrats).
Horst Glück	Deputy Chief-Secretary to the SPD's parliamentary group, Stuttgart.
Christopher Harvie	Professor of British and Irish Studies, Director of Welsh Studies Centre, University of Tübingen.
Friederike Hohloch	Theatre-in-Education Officer, Landestheater Tübingen.
Brian Jones	Lecturer in Management Studies, University of Wales, Bangor.
David McCrone	Professor of Sociology, Convener of the Unit for the Study of Government in Scotland, Director of the Governance of Scotland Forum, University of Edinburgh.
Kenneth O Morgan	Former Vice Chancellor of the University of Wales, Emeritus Professor of History, University of Wales, Aberystwyth.

Kevin Morgan	Professor of Urban and Regional Planning at the University of Wales, Cardiff.
Tom Nairn	Honorary Fellow, Sociology and Graduate School of the Social Sciences, University of Edinburgh.
John Osmond	Director of the Institute of Welsh Affairs, Cardiff.
Lindsay Paterson	Professor of Educational Policy, University of Edinburgh; Editor of *Scottish Affairs*.
Robin Reeves	Editor of *The Welsh Review*, Cardiff.
Dai Smith	Head of Programmes (English Language) at BBC Wales, and Honorary Professor of Adult Continuing Education, University of Wales, Swansea.
Paula Surridge	Lecturer in Sociology, University of Aberdeen.
Beate Weber	Lord Mayor of Heidelberg (SPD); former SPD-MEP.
John Williams	Emeritus Professor of Economic History, University of Wales, Aberystwyth.

List of Maps